Windows Me Annoyances

Windows Me Annoyances

David A. Karp

O'REILLY®

Beijing · Cambridge · Farnham · Köln · Paris · Sebastopol · Taipei · Tokyo

Windows Me Annoyances
by David A. Karp

Printed in the United States of America.

Published by O'Reilly & Associates, Inc., 101 Morris Street, Sebastopol, CA 95472.

Editor: Troy Mott

Production Editor: Jeffrey Holcomb

Cover Designer: Hanna Dyer

Printing History:

March 2001: First Edition.

ISBN: 0-596-00060-X [4/01]
[M]

Table of Contents

Preface

What Is an Annoyance?

I admit it—I'm the guy people call when they need answers. Something doesn't work; my phone rings. Someone can't figure something out; I get an email. More often than not, the problem can be traced to Microsoft Windows, a product with which I've developed a healthy love-hate relationship. Luckily, I've channeled my rage into this book—many of the solutions, tips, workarounds, and warnings you're about to read are my responses to questions I get asked by inexperienced and seasoned Windows users alike.

More than anything else, an annoyance is a way of looking at a problem or an unfamiliar task. It's an attitude that gives you the fortitude and patience to solve any problem, rather than being powerless or frustrated, or feeling like a dummy.

Your computer should *not* be a "black box," something for which you must adjust the way you work and think. It's a hands-on, flexible tool with many capabilities and limitations. Humans design computers and the software that runs on them; so computers by their very nature are imperfect and often troublesome machines.

I've written this book with the philosophy that the more you know about a tool you use—specifically, Microsoft Windows Me—the better your day-to-day experience with it will be. If this contradicts what you've seen in other books or the Windows manual, you're getting the idea.

The Interface

One of the most frequently examined aspects of Windows in this book is the user interface, and this is no accident. The user interface in Windows Me includes everything from the visual components that comprise every window to the way individual dialog boxes are laid out. The interface is how you communicate with your computer and how your computer communicates with you; it directly influences how quickly you learn the various tasks in Windows and how efficiently you carry them out once you've learned them. An interface must be designed carefully and meticulously, intuitive enough to be understood by beginners, yet not too dumbed-down and cumbersome to annoy experienced users.

One of the strengths of Windows Me, and one of the reasons why the Windows PC is the dominant home-computer platform, is that its interface is extremely flexible and configurable. This, of course, is not to say that the default interface is the most effective one possible.

Now, I believe that it's better to light a single candle than to curse the darkness, which is why this book is full of solutions rather than gripes. It should be evident from even a brief look at the vast amount of information here that this book is *not* about "Microsoft-bashing" or complaining of any kind. The focus is on solving problems, and that sometimes means taking a critical view of the Windows interface or the design of a particular Windows component.

The default configuration of Windows Me—the settings that were in use when Windows was first installed—has been designed to showcase the various features of the product, rather than to make the operating system easy to use. One of the problems with this approach is that most users don't take the time to customize the interface and otherwise streamline the operating system. Whether this is caused by the valid fear of screwing something up or simply by a lack of time and patience, it is a common situation that decreases productivity and ease of use. *Windows Me Annoyances* can help change that.

Take the solutions in this book seriously, but don't follow them blindly. Anything that indeed improves the interface can streamline your work and make the overall Windows experience less painful and more enjoyable. However, one person's annoyance is another's feature; what's important is to construct the interface that works best for you.

How This Book Came to Be

Back in early 1995, I was using a pre-release (beta version) of Windows 95 on my machine. Only a few hours after installing it, I became aware of the extent to which the previous version of Windows had *stunted* my machine. A well-designed operating system can unleash the power of the hardware on which it runs, just as a poorly designed operating system can make you want to throw all of your expensive hardware in the thresher. Windows is a little bit of both those extremes.

Now, not being the complacent type, I immediately started compiling a list of questions and complaints about the operating system, some of which had solutions and some of which did not. This was the start of the *Windows 95 Annoyances* web site, which was one of the first web sites devoted to Windows 95. Later, in the summer of 1995, other pre-release users began writing in with their own questions and complaints, and even with occasional solutions to the problems I hadn't yet solved.

As readers' requests for information and additional solutions became more diverse, so did the web site. The site quickly evolved from a simple list of annoyances, to an extensive collection of tips and tricks, and then to a more general support center for Windows 95.

I then wrote the book *Windows Annoyances* in the beginning of 1997, followed by *Windows 98 Annoyances* in 1998. Both, of course, were best-sellers, but that's not important right now. What's important is that, although those books are now used under the short legs of tables, the third book in the series, *Windows Me Annoyances,* is here and has found its way into your capable hands!

Just as Windows Me is more than merely Windows 98 with a face-lift, this book is more than just an update to *Windows 98 Annoyances. Windows Me Annoyances* is a completely new volume, containing many more solutions, more undocumented secrets, and more troubleshooting information than either of the previous two books, yet presented in what I hope you'll find to be the same clear, straightforward format.

Organization of This Book

Chapter 1, *Making the Most of Windows Me,* discusses not only some of the more common annoyances in the operating system, but also many of the improvements in this version over its successor, Windows 98 Second Edition, as well as some of the problems that *weren't* fixed. Also discussed is Me's sister product, Windows 2000.

Chapter 2, *Basic Explorer Coping Skills*, starts by examining the Windows user interface and how to overcome its limitations. That is followed by a discussion of the way you work with Windows and how to take advantage of some of its lesser-known tricks and customization features. This discussion includes advanced tips on Explorer; file-manipulation tricks; undocumented interface tweaks; and, best of all, some workarounds for the awful new Search feature.

Chapter 3, *The Registry*, covers the structure of the Registry and the use of the Registry Editor. This information is important because most of the subsequent solutions make use of this knowledge. In addition to Registry basics, this chapter includes some advanced topics, such as effective searching techniques, finding the right Registry keys, and restoring a corrupted Registry.

Chapter 4, *Tinkering Techniques*, continues with customization and problem-solving topics that take advantage of the Registry techniques discussed earlier. Here are solutions for reducing clutter, protecting your file types, and customizing Windows Me beyond Microsoft's intentions; editing the Start Menu acquires a whole new meaning in this chapter.

Chapter 5, *Maximizing Performance*, presents an often neglected topic. The goal is to get the best possible performance from your system without spending a lot of money or time. If and when you decide to upgrade, you'll also find tips here to help make informed decisions. Special subjects include gaming and virtual memory.

Chapter 6, *Troubleshooting*, starts with general troubleshooting techniques and hardware conflicts and then proceeds to everyone's favorite topic: error messages. Get the inside scoop on System File Protection and System Restore, two highly touted new features in Windows Me. The chapter then winds down with preventive maintenance and data recovery.

Chapter 7, *Networking and Internetworking*, allows you to expand your desktop and your repertoire by setting up a local-area network and connecting to the Internet. More than just the basics, this chapter explores protocols, troubleshooting, and new technologies, such as Internet Connection Sharing and virtual private networking.

Chapter 8, *Taking Control of Web Integration*, is an in-depth examination of the so-called *integration* of Microsoft's web browser, Internet Explorer, with the fundamental interface. This chapter explores the components that constitute Web Integration and how to configure them, including making use of the "Web View."

Chapter 9, *Scripting and Automation*, rounds out the book with a discussion of simple programming using the Windows Script Host (WSH) included with Windows Me. In addition to an introduction to scripting with WSH, you'll find advanced solutions, such as functions for Registry access and filesystem access and how to use scripts and batch files to solve a wide range of problems. The chapter is wrapped up with several cool examples and a look at the seemingly simple Scheduled Tasks feature and how it can be used in conjunction with scripts for a truly automated environment.

The three appendixes are included as references. Appendix A, *Setting Locator*, is a comprehensive list of nearly every setting scattered throughout Windows Me, from folder options to removing tray icons. Appendix B, *DOS Resurrected*, covers DOS commands, which can be surprisingly useful in the Windows world, as well as DOS batch files, which have been around since the beginning of time yet are still undocumented in Windows Me. Finally, Appendix C, *Class IDs of System Objects*, is a listing of common Class IDs (special Registry codes for system objects) used throughout the book.

Getting the Most out of This Book

This book is arranged so that it can be used as a learning tool, as well as a reference. More than just a bag of tricks, it covers a wide range of topics, some informational and some instructional. Although you certainly don't need to read the chapters in order, it is structured so that you can progress easily from one topic to the next, expanding your knowledge and experience as you go. You should be able to jump to any topic as needed; if you find that you don't have the proficiency required by a particular solution, such as knowledge of the Registry, you should be able to learn about it elsewhere in the book (Chapter 3, in the case of the Registry). For additional software and corrections, check out the *Windows Me Annoyances* web site at *http://www.annoyances.org*.

Most topics are presented as problems or annoyances with corresponding solutions. Topics usually begin with a few introductory paragraphs explaining something you don't often find in other references: why you'd want to complete the particular solution. In some cases, you may want to skip ahead to the actual solution procedure, easily identifiable by the bullets or numbered steps.

Software Depository[*]

Throughout this book, various add-on software is mentioned in the solutions to various problems. Now, wherever possible, I try not to make a particular solution absolutely dependent on add-on software—after all, I'd rather you carry around this book than a CD packed with useless shareware.

In some cases, of course, a software solution is either the preferable or the only recourse. Fortunately, nearly all the software necessary to fill the holes in Windows as discussed in this book is freely available on the Internet. However, instead of including a list of web addresses here, all the software mentioned in this book, as well as software yet to be discovered, is listed at *http://www.annoyances.org*.

In addition to links for the downloadable software, you'll also find updates and additional information for the book at that web site, in related web sites and articles, and in recent news.

Also available is *Creative Element Power Tools*, a collection of tools specifically designed to help solve the Annoyances discussed in this book. You can download it from *http://www.creativelement.com*.

Conventions Used in This Book

The following typographical conventions are used in this book:

`Constant width`
: Indicates command-line computer output, code examples, and Registry keys.

`Constant width italic`
: Indicates variables in examples and in Registry keys. It is also used to indicate variables or user-defined elements within italic text (such as path names or filenames). For example, in the path *\Windows*`username`, replace *`username`* with your name.

`Constant width bold`
: Indicates user input in examples.

* After hours, slip software through slot in door.

Bold

Identifies captions, menus, buttons, checkboxes, tabs, keyboard keys, and other interface elements, making the text easier to read.

Italic

Introduces new terms and indicates URLs, variables in text, user-defined files and directories, commands, file extensions, filenames, directory or folder names, and UNC pathnames.

Italic is also used to highlight chapter titles and, in some instances, to visually separate the topic of a list.

"Quotation marks"

Are included only when necessary; if you see quotation marks around something to type, for example, it means that you should type them as well (unless otherwise specified).

This is an example of a note, which signifies valuable and time-saving information.

This is an example of a warning, which alerts to a potential pitfall in the program. Warnings can also refer to a procedure that might be dangerous if not carried out in a specific way.

Path Notation

We use a shorthand path notation to show you how to reach a given Word or Windows user-interface element or option. The path notation is relative to a well-known location. For example, the following path:

Start → Programs → Accessories

means "Open the Start Menu, then choose Programs, then choose Accessories."

Keyboard Shortcuts

When keyboard shortcuts are shown, a hyphen (such as **Ctrl-Alt-Del**) means that the keys must be held down simultaneously, and a plus (such as **Alt+F+O**) means that the keys should be pressed sequentially.

Request for Comments

Please address comments and questions concerning this book to the publisher:

> O'Reilly & Associates, Inc.
> 101 Morris Street
> Sebastopol, CA 95472
> (800) 998-9938 (in the United States or Canada)
> (707) 829-0515 (international/local)
> (707) 829-0104 (fax)

You can also send us messages electronically. To be put on the mailing list or request a catalog, send email to:

> *elists@oreilly.com*

There is a web page for this book, which lists errata, examples, or any additional information. You can access this page at:

> *http://www.oreilly.com/catalog/winmeannoy/*

To comment or ask technical questions about this book, send email to:

> *bookquestions@oreilly.com*

For more information about books, conferences, software, Resource Centers, and the O'Reilly Network, see the O'Reilly web site at:

> *http://www.oreilly.com*

Acknowledgments

I'd like to start by thanking the folks at O'Reilly & Associates. It's a supreme pleasure to work with people who are dedicated to quality and are passionate about their work. In particular, Troy Mott and Bob Herbstman worked especially hard on this book, yet were a breeze to work with. Thanks also to tech reviewers Walter Glenn (author of *Word 2000 in a Nutshell*) and Tom Syroid (author of *Outlook 2000 in a Nutshell*). Special thanks to Tim O'Reilly for his enthusiasm, support, and commitment to quality.

Thanks also to everyone who worked on production of this book, as well as everyone else on the team who worked on this book.

I'd like to thank my family, friends, and well-wishers (in that they didn't wish me any specific harm), all of whom put up with my deadlines and late-night writing binges. Additional thanks to Ruth Kampmann. Finally, my immeasurable gratitude to Torey Bookstein, whose love and support never fail to put a smile on my face.

And, as always, I thank you for your continued support. Without the people who read this book, it's nothing more than a test subject for Newton's first law of motion.

1

Making the Most of Windows Me

Do you get a sinking feeling in your stomach every time you are about to install new software? Does the expectation that the installer will overwrite all your settings and disable other software on your computer make you want to chuck the whole system out the window? Have you calmly accepted the fact that your new operating system will most likely contain more bugs than improvements?

Why fight it? Why not simply join the masses and slip into the mind-numbing abyss of acquiescence, feeling powerless whenever technology isn't as seamless as it is promised by software marketers? Because you know there's a better way. You know there's more to Windows Me than what's mentioned in the documentation, such as it is, and in Microsoft's press clippings.

The purpose of these rants, as well as the goal of the entire book, is not to complain or to criticize. The idea is to acknowledge the problems and shortcomings of the operating system—and the software that runs on it—in an effort to overcome them. If users had a large selection of operating systems from which to choose, the point would be almost moot; each user would simply choose the most appropriate and least annoying software available. However, the real world isn't like that, and most computer users using Microsoft Windows are doing so out of necessity, rather than choice. That puts Microsoft in a position to control what we see and how we work. Realizing you're not alone is the first step to improving your experience with Windows Me and regaining control of your machine before it assumes control of you.

While nobody's particular requirements, preferences, and annoyances will be the same, everyone can benefit when light is shed on the inner workings of an operating system. A little knowledge can be dangerous, but a lot of knowledge can keep your system running smoothly and make your Windows experience relatively aggravation free.

What's Wrong with Windows

There are many reasons that software, and Windows Me in particular, annoys us. One of the most common excuses is that software is designed to be used by a large number of people and to be compatible with a vast array of hardware components, and that no single piece of software can be expected to satisfy everyone. That's true to some extent, but it's too often used as a scapegoat for other problems. One real reason for problems with software is that software designers often don't understand good user-interface design or simply don't understand users and, therefore, create incomplete products that don't work the way we expect or just don't work at all. And another reason is that users don't understand software designers and, therefore, often aren't able to comfortably follow the same lines of logic (or lack thereof) that the designers used.

Another truth, and one that most computer companies will never admit, is that consumer computer technology, in general, is still quite infantile. It's truly amazing what some of these devices are capable of, but the sad fact is that the majority of technology hasn't caught up to most users' expectations or requirements. What's worse is that neither has our understanding of human-computer interaction.

There's also an inherent difficulty with the role of the personal computer that ends up causing all sorts of problems. We expect every computer to flawlessly manage our finances, seamlessly connect us to the Internet and allow us to communicate, run our latest 3D-accelerated games, create magazine-quality documents, and about 50,000 other things. Part of the solution to this has been the proliferation of special-function devices, most notably the Palm OS–based personal digital assistants (PDAs). Instead of trying to do everything (a mistake Microsoft, not surprisingly, has migrated to their Windows CE–based devices), the Palm OS has been kept extremely simple; it does only a few things, and it does them reliably well.

In an interview a few years ago, Bill Gates, head bigwig at Microsoft, bragged that Windows 98 had something like seven times as many lines of code as the software used in air-traffic control systems in the U.S. I was appalled. Think about the millions and millions of lines of code and the countless teams of programmers responsible for all the different elements of Windows Me—each programmer with different levels of skill, experience, and adherence to the theoretical interface standards. Instead of giving us a tighter, simpler product, Microsoft keeps making Windows more complex and cumbersome, adding more pointless wizards and market-driven features.

All of these problems, although valid concerns, are fairly general and not necessarily specific to any particular product. So why is Windows Me, in particular, so annoying? Because it's the underlying technology upon which all of our applications rely and, apart from other flavors of Microsoft Windows, it's our only choice in the matter. (Sure, there's Linux, one of the more popular brands of the Unix OS, but that has its own problems.) Most computer users, for one reason or another, rely on Microsoft Windows, the latest version of which is the focus of this book.

Regardless of the excuses, you should *not* be required to adjust the way you think in order to complete a task on a computer; rather, you should learn how to adjust the computer to work in a way that makes sense to you. This is what this book is about.

Windows Me Annoyances presents solutions that enable you to both customize and troubleshoot Windows. This is an important distinction, because many times solving a problem requires that you know whether something irritating is an inadvertent bug or an intentional feature of the software, and the dividing line isn't always clear. It's important to realize that, if software doesn't act in a way that *you* think it should, it should be regarded as poor design and not necessarily the result of a bug. A bug is an action carried out by a piece of software that wasn't intended by the *designer* of the product.

Now, we can speculate as to the intentions of the various developers of Windows, and sometimes we can even uncover the motivations behind a particular aspect of the software we don't like, but what it really comes down to is *attitude*. By labeling something a bug, we are placing the burden of resolving the problem on Microsoft, and waiting for Microsoft developers to fix a bug that they consider to be a feature can definitely be considered a lost cause.

However, if we lump together the crash-a-day tendency of Windows, the irritating little animations, the clutter on the desktop, the lack of decent documentation, the fact that performance rarely meets expectations, and call them all *annoyances*, we empower ourselves. This is a valuable attitude to adopt; it motivates us to learn more about the operating system so that we can work more efficiently. And, more importantly, it gives us the power to resolve the problems we encounter, so that we can get through the day with some degree of sanity.

So what, in particular, is annoying about Windows? Let me give you a very simple, yet not readily apparent, example. Common file dialog boxes—the little windows that appear that allow you to choose a file to open or specify a filename with which to save—look basically the same in nearly all applications, because they're a function provided by Windows itself. This concept of *common* file dialog boxes was introduced more than a decade ago in Windows 3.1 and has since undergone an evolutionary process as the dialog boxes have been improved in each successive version of Windows.

An annoyance that plagued these boxes since Windows 95 was that they were not resizable and therefore were awkward to use with large displays. This problem, fortunately, has since been fixed, and in Windows Me we enjoy resizable file dialog boxes. Unfortunately, Windows won't remember a file dialog box's size or position, meaning that if you want a larger dialog box, you'll have to enlarge it again and again.

However, a more serious problem (in my opinion), still not remedied in Windows Me, is that of the "Look in" (or "Save in") list. When you go to open or save a file, the only clue to where the currently displayed folder is located in the grand hierarchy is the *name*—not the entire path—of the folder. So, for example, if the current folder shown in a file dialog box is called *images*, there's no way to immediately determine if the folder you're looking at is *c:\projects\images*, or *d:\webpages\personal\images*.

What's worse is that Microsoft *knows* about the problem and has done nothing about it; in fact, they've taken steps to hide it. The smoking gun, if you will, was the online help in Windows 98: if you click on the [?] button and then click on the **Look in** list, you'll see, "To see how the current folder fits in the hierarchy on your computer, click the down arrow." Instead of fixing the problem in Windows Me, Microsoft simply removed the text.*

The simple truth is that this would be very easy for Microsoft to remedy, and it has been for years. In fact, Windows Explorer has an option that allows you to fix a similar problem with folder windows by turning on the "Display the full path in title bar" option in the Folder Options dialog box (under the **Tools** tab). Yet this option has no effect on the file dialog boxes, which ironically are designed to behave just like small folder windows. The full path of the current folder could be displayed just below the **Look in** list. Why has Microsoft neglected to fix this very basic design flaw?

* Some wise guy at Microsoft perhaps saw my criticism in *Windows 98 Annoyances*, and *this* was their solution.

My guess is that it's part of Microsoft's ongoing strategy to hide as much information as possible from the user, in an effort to make the computer easier to use. This is the same type of backward thinking that resulted in folder titles that don't show the full path, the hidden filename extensions, and the Windows installer that overwrites file associations without asking. (See "Protect Your File Types" in Chapter 4, *Tinkering Techniques*, for more information on file associations and how to keep applications from overwriting yours.) What Microsoft fails to realize is that making users ignorant is a cop-out, and not an effective way to make any product easier to use.

Of course, it could also be a question of priority—it's obviously a higher priority to make changes that Microsoft could list on the outside of the Windows Me retail box as marketable "improvements" to Windows (such as System File Protection, discussed in Chapter 6, *Troubleshooting*; and Web browser integration, discussed in Chapter 8, *Taking Control of Web Integration*) than to cater their products to their users' needs. Who knows—perhaps the decision-makers at Microsoft simply prefer "cute" dialog boxes to functional ones.

So, how do they get away with it, year after year?

Microsoft is in a unique position, in that it is powerful and wealthy enough to devote substantial marketing resources to ensure the commercial success of its products, regardless of the quality or intelligence of design. For example, we put up with Windows because the competing products were out-marketed years ago—there simply are no other *practical* choices for the majority of consumers.

Unfortunately, marketing can influence design, rather than just compensate for it. A stellar example of this is the *Web View*. The concept of viewing one's desktop as though it were a web page makes little intuitive sense and does nothing to improve the Windows interface. Yet the irresistible marketing appeal of the Internet combined with Microsoft's undying need to squelch Netscape in the web-browser market has led Microsoft to tie in Internet Explorer to their almost-ubiquitous operating system, leaving the users to suffer with this ridiculous interface.*

The good news, of course, is that this creates jobs for countless thousands—those employed to release patchwork software, provide technical support and training, or, of course, write technical books like this one.

---

* According to U.S. District Judge Thomas Penfield Jackson—the judge who presided over the Microsoft monopoly trial—in his 1999 Findings of Fact, bundling the browser with Windows "unjustifiably jeopardized the stability and security of the operating system." He went on to write, "there is no technical justification for Microsoft's refusal to meet consumer demand for a browserless version of Windows."

Ultimately, the commercial success of any particular product depends on you and me, the consumers. In other words, every purchase is a vote. The problem, of course, is that extensive marketing in the computer industry creates standards to which we must adhere. Purchase decisions are often based upon these standards rather than quality or usability, which helps to explain the success of marginal products like Microsoft Word. It is the goal of this book to help readers live with their purchase decisions.

The Windows Family Tree

As time progresses, the lineage of Windows becomes less linear. Windows 2000, despite its name, is *not* the successor to Windows 98 and Windows 95; Windows Me, of course, has that distinction. Windows 2000 is, instead, the latest installment to the less-consumer-oriented Windows NT line of operating systems, developed in parallel to the Windows 9x line.

Figure 1-1 shows a representative family tree and where Windows Me and Windows 2000 fit in. Note that wider boxes imply a greater installed base, and wider gray arrows imply a greater migration from one product to another. Products appearing farther to the right are perceived to have both greater complexity and more technological sophistication.

There were rumors that what has become Windows 2000 was supposed to be the product that unified the upscale NT line with the consumer-oriented* Windows 9x line. This role has been ostensibly postponed to the Windows XP operating system (code-named "Whistler"), probably Microsoft's most confusing name choice to date.

So why the distinction between DOS-based Windows operating systems and the NT line? We peons were informed at the inception of Windows NT 3.1 that "NT" was an acronym for "New Technology," which is actually quite an accurate description. The NT kernel, or underlying code upon which the interface (Explorer) runs, was completely new and did not rely on DOS.†

* The term "consumer" has almost become a dirty word in the computer industry. Rather than simply meaning "one who acquires goods," it connotes the gadget-hungry, yet technologically unsophisticated, average customer, who uses a three-thousand-dollar computer for little more than playing games, surfing the Internet, and organizing Grandma's recipes. There's certainly nothing wrong with these tasks, but many "consumers" use computers to get their work done, thank you very much.

† DOS, or "Disk Operating System," was the first operating system available for the IBM PC (released in 1981). The first versions of Microsoft Windows (Versions 1.x-3.x) were simply applications that ran on top of DOS. Windows 9x and Me are no different, although Microsoft went to great lengths to hide the dependence on DOS. For more information on DOS and the command line, see Appendix B, *DOS Resurrected*.

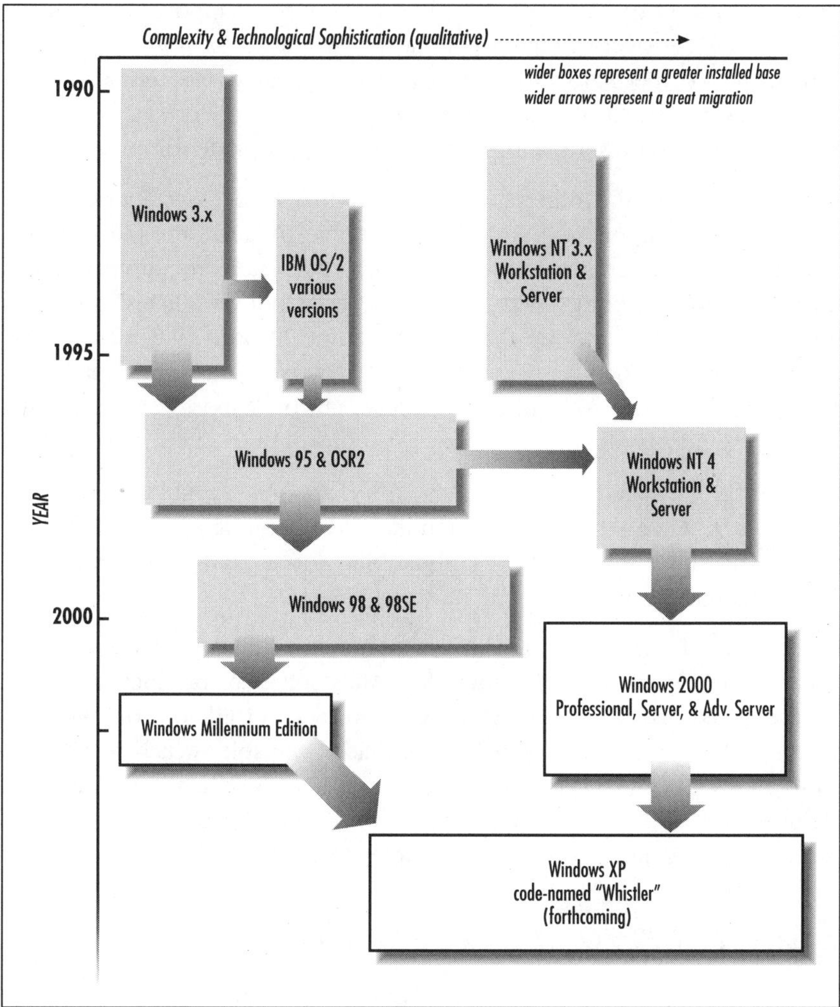

Figure 1-1. The nonlinear Windows Family Tree is hopefully heading toward a future unifying product

This resulted in a (theoretically) more stable environment, much better security, and the ability to be easily ported to work on other processors (such as Compaq's Alpha chip). Over the years, this "portability" has become much less emphasized. More recently, the NT line has been marketed as a web, intranet, and network server; a challenger to Unix; and now, with Windows 2000, a viable home-office operating system.

The problem with earlier releases of Windows 2000 (from NT 3.1, which nobody liked, to NT 4.0, most commonly used as a web server) was that they offered the enhanced features of the NT line without any of the perks prized by the average consumer. What has plagued NT in the past, more than anything else, has been the abysmal industry support for the platform. Given the overwhelming majority of Windows 9x users, a sizeable percentage of the hardware and software available for the PC—even released as recently as the time of this writing—is simply not supported on NT/2000. The result is a platform that is still inappropriate for most users.

Windows Me, on the other hand, is the pinnacle of consumer-oriented technology. It supports, by far, a broader range of hardware and software than any other operating system on Earth. Its system requirements and learning curve are both much lower than for Windows 2000. Games will run better on Windows Me than on Windows 2000, as will most of the more exotic hardware (e.g., cameras, CD writers, game controllers). Just about anything that worked on Windows 95 or Windows 98 will also work on Windows Me.

Of course, if Windows 2000 or its successor eventually replaces Windows 9x/Me as the de facto standard PC operating system, manufacturers will either ensure 2000 compatibility or go out of business. It's only a matter of time.

For the record, the solutions in this edition assume that you have the original shipping version of Windows Me. Microsoft may produce a service release (much like OSR2 for Windows 95 or Second Edition for Windows 98) or make any number of patches publicly available, which may either solve existing annoyances or create new ones. Rest assured that such changes will be documented on the accompanying web site, *http://www.annoyances.org*, along with other news, updates, and relevant information.

Transition to Windows Me

If Windows Me is your foray into Windows, you're lucky to have escaped the early days of changing jumpers, editing the *config.sys* file, running out of "system resources," and suffering with the Windows 3.x Program Manager. However, dealing with the problems of the early days of Windows is a good way to build coping skills and is the only way to appreciate some of the things now taken for granted, such as Plug-and-Play and fast Internet connections. Getting under the hood of Windows is not only a great way to take charge of the operating system and make it conform to the way you work and think, but it's also a very effective method for learning more about Windows and the technology that makes it work.

The basic "shell" interface (Explorer, the Desktop, the Start Menu, and [shiver] the Web View) is relatively unchanged from Windows 98, with the exception of newly painted desktop icons. Those migrating from Windows NT 4.0 will notice slightly more substantial changes, such as menu animation and Internet Explorer integration. Anyone who is accustomed to *any* recent release of Windows, though, will feel immediately comfortable with the Windows Me version, at least on the surface.

What follows are a few highlights and lowlights of Windows Me, most notably for those who have upgraded or who are thinking of upgrading from a previous version. Some may seem insignificant; others may mean the difference between upgrading to Windows Me and waiting for something better to come along. All of these, naturally, add up to the total Windows Me experience.

Drag-and-drop of EXE files finally makes sense

After five years of customer complaints, Microsoft has finally fixed the absurd way Windows handled the drag-and-drop of EXE files. As one visitor to *Annoyances.org* wrote several years ago, "whoever came up with the 'dragging an application creates a shortcut' behavior must be shot immediately." Now, dragging an EXE file works the same as dragging any other type of file. See Chapter 2, *Basic Explorer Coping Skills*, for details, exceptions, and helpful tips.

Enhanced file dialog boxes

As described in "What's Wrong with Windows" earlier in this chapter, most of the file dialog boxes in Windows Me can now be resized. And, although Windows does temporarily remember the dialog box sizes for each application, it doesn't save the settings to disk and forgets them when you shut down. Now, there is no apparent way to set the default size of the file dialog boxes, and some dialog boxes still don't allow resizing (any modified common dialog boxes, as well as the faux common dialog boxes found in Microsoft Office),* so it's an incomplete solution at best.

Also new to file dialog boxes is the "Places Bar," a gray stripe down the left side of most dialog boxes containing icons for prominent file locations. Introduced first in Microsoft Office 2000, it contained links to the Desktop, the *My Documents* folder, and, among other things, *Web Folders*. The default Places Bar in Windows Me is far more useful, doing away with the useless Web Folders shortcut, and including direct links to networked resources, My Computer, the Desktop, and History.

See "Customize the Places Bar" in Chapter 4 for details on making these dialog boxes more useful.

---

* The dialog boxes in Office 2000 aren't modified common dialog boxes, but new dialog boxes written from scratch. This is important because it explains why certain things don't work in Office dialog boxes, such as drag-drop.

Year 2000 (Y2K) compliance

The Y2K bug, for those who have been living in a cave for the past decade, was the result of an industry-wide blunder, wherein apparently nobody saw the year 2000 coming. It affects any hardware or software that stores dates internally with two digits instead of four. Now that Y2K is behind us and the global armageddon the media forecasted never really happened, you can stop worrying. However, if you plan on running any software written before 1998 with Windows 2000, you may want to check with the manufacturer for a newer version, or at least a patch.

Windows Me is the first "consumer-grade" operating system released by Microsoft after January 1, 2000, which should, at least in theory, make it the most Y2K-compliant OS to date. Windows 98 was also supposed to be Y2K-compliant, but at least two Y2K updates were released only a few short months after its inception in 1998. In other words, keep an eye on the Windows update site.

A new look for Find, uh . . . I mean Search

The new Search tool doesn't really add any functionality over the Find tool found in Windows 98 or Windows NT 4.0, but the interface has changed. Instead of a separate window, Search appears as a pane in Explorer. This new interface tends to be confusing, frustrating, and just plain annoying. The good news is that the arbitrary 10,000-file limit has been lifted. See "Fix the Search Tool" in Chapter 2 for details.

Folder Shortcuts

It's finally possible to create a shortcut to a folder that behaves like a folder, instead of like a file. For example, an ordinary shortcut to your *c:\windows\temp* folder cannot be used as part of a path. However, a Folder Shortcut works like a folder: say you have a Folder Shortcut called *Cletus*, located in *c:*, that points to *c:\windows\temp*. You could then reference a file called *c:\Cletus\filename.txt*. The problem is that Folder Shortcuts are difficult to make and have their drawbacks as well. See "Mirror a Folder with Folder Shortcuts" in Chapter 4 for details.

Graphical FTP support

Windows Me and Windows 2000 appear to be the first versions of Windows to offer a File Transfer Protocol (FTP) client that is GUI-based, instead of text (command-line) based. It's actually quite seamless: you can add an FTP address to **My Network Places** and then access it in Explorer as though it were a drive directly connected to your computer. For details, see "Accessing an FTP Site in Explorer" in Chapter 7, *Networking and Internetworking*.

Better hardware support

Each new version of Windows comes with more drivers than any of its predecessors, supporting a larger range of hardware, and Windows Me is no exception. In reality, though, we use new computers with old sound cards and new sound cards with old computers, meaning that upgrading is not always as seamless as Microsoft says on the outside of the box. See Chapter 6 for troubleshooting and maintenance.

Performance, for better or worse

Anyone familiar with software upgrades has come to expect that any new version of an application or operating system will require more disk space and will run slower than its predecessor on the same hardware. This, of course, means lots of dollars spent on lots of megabytes and lots of megahertz. Microsoft is no stranger to what has become known as "bloat-ware," and Windows Me is no exception.

Why don't successive versions of software get leaner and faster? Because for every additional megabyte of hard-disk space an operating system requires, the available storage on the average computer increases by ten megabytes.

At the same time, Windows Me does actually have some functionality that may result in improved performance over previous versions of Windows: "real mode" has apparently been removed, resulting in a quicker boot time and possibly faster application load times. Furthermore, DirectX 8.0 and other refined components promise to make games, videos, and animation run more smoothly than ever.

An operating system being simultaneously slower and faster than its predecessor may seem like bit of a paradox, but that's the reality behind the evolution of personal computers. The key is to make the most of what you've got, and that's what this book is all about.

Suffice it to say, there are actually quite a few goodies that have been added to Windows Me, including lots of little touches here and there that actually work to improve the product.

But I prattle on. If you don't know where to go from here, I suggest turning the page and starting with Chapter 2.

2

Basic Explorer Coping Skills

The face of Windows Me that users see most is Windows Explorer, commonly known simply as Explorer. Explorer (*Explorer.exe*) is the primary shell interface, handling the desktop, the Start Menu, the Recycle Bin, Control Panel, My Computer, the Explorer window, and about a million other things.

Given the amount of time we spend starting programs, finding files, copying folders, and configuring Windows, it makes sense to invest a little time not only to find better ways to accomplish these tasks, but also to learn how to configure Windows to work more like the way we think. In addition, you can make your experience with Windows a lot more pleasurable by giving it a little personality and reducing the various headache-causing annoyances—think of all the money for codeine you'll save.

The ideal user interface should adapt to you, rather than the other way around. One of the primary goals of this book is to show you how to change the way Windows looks, feels, and operates so that it is more closely in tune with the way you think and work. However, there are some fundamental features of the interface that simply can't be changed, such as the way icons and folders are drag-dropped.

There are times, on the other hand, when the design of certain basic Windows functionality is so frustrating that it makes you want to tear your hair out: such as how accessing the Search tool from Explorer disables the folder tree, forcing you either to open a new Explorer window or to turn the folder tree back on (select **View**, **Explorer Bar**, and then **Folders**), which incidentally is the only entry in this menu without a keyboard shortcut. (See "Fix the Search Tool" later in this chapter for several workarounds.)

So, it is the slightly revised goal of all the solutions in this book to arrive at the best compromise between the ideal solution and what is actually possible, while maintaining the lowest practical "annoyance coefficient."

Many of the topics discussed throughout this book require knowledge of the Windows Registry, with the exception of this chapter—I figured you'd want to jump right in. In addition to the Explorer-related tips and tricks, many of the topics of this chapter document the subtle interface differences in Windows Me from previous releases—it's all good stuff. Chapter 3, *The Registry*, covers the Registry thoroughly, and all subsequent material assumes a working knowledge of the Registry.

Lastly, this chapter assumes a basic working knowledge of Windows: files and folders, double-clicking, right-clicking, using menus, and so on.

Coping with Explorer

Explorer is the all-encompassing program that provides the basic working interface to all modern versions of Windows, allowing you to manage the files, folders, and applications on your system. The Windows desktop, the My Computer window, the single-folder windows, the Tree View window, and the Start Menu are all part of the Explorer application. However, in most Windows lore and in most of the solutions in this book, the term Explorer refers specifically to the window that has the Tree View shown in the left pane; it is opened by selecting **Windows Explorer** from the **Start Menu** or by launching *Explorer.exe* from the Start Menu's **Run** command. All other windows used to browse folders—those windows accessible from the My Computer window—are commonly referred to as folder windows or the single-folder view.

In reality, Explorer with the folder view and single-folder windows are exactly the same, except for the folder tree pane, which can be turned on or off by selecting Explorer Bar from the View menu and then selecting Folders. The distinction in this book is purely for semantics and casual conversation.

The good news is that files, folders, and most other system objects are copied, moved, opened, closed, and deleted in virtually the same way in all of these places. Interface consistency is one of the most important aspects of interface design, but, unfortunately, often contradicts other factors, such as intuition and historical consistency. For example, drag-drop in Explorer behaves differently when you're dragging from one drive to another (*d:* to *c:*) than when dragging from one folder to another on the same drive (*c:\docs* to *c:\files*). Why the inconsistency? Because that's the way it has been done in Windows for years, and fixing it would likely confuse too many users. (At least from the perspective of the company that otherwise would have to answer all the technical support calls.)

I've found that Windows Me has the best interface consistency of any Microsoft operating system I've seen. In Windows 98, for example, keystrokes that worked in one situation in Explorer didn't work in other situations, and this has been fixed in Windows Me. Surprisingly, Microsoft has also done away with the "drag an EXE file to create a shortcut" behavior that *nobody* liked; it, too, was inconsistent with the way other files were drag-dropped. Kudos to Microsoft.

One of Explorer's primary annoyances—and, paradoxically, one of its essential features—is the mandatory use of special combinations of keystrokes and mouse clicks to perform simple operations, such as using the **Ctrl** key to copy a file or having to make sure the source and destination folders are both visible before trying to copy or move an object. This behavior, for the most part, can't be changed—but there's enough flexibility in it to accomplish just about anything you want.

Exploring Basic Explorer Settings

Many aspects of the way Windows works can be controlled by changing certain settings, which are scattered throughout several different dialog boxes. The key here is to configure Windows the best you can to make it behave the way you expect it to—which, of course, depends on your level of experience and how you work. The Folder Options dialog box is a good place to start.

Select **Folder Options** from Explorer's **Tools** menu (or double-click **Folder Options** in Control Panel). The first page of the Folder Options dialog box, shown in Figure 2-1, allows you to control four different options—their connection is that they all affect the way Explorer looks.

Tips for various Folder Options settings

- Figure 2-1 shows the choices that most closely approximate the look and feel to which most users will be accustomed.
- The **Active Desktop**, **Web View**, and **Click items as follows** sections are all related to the Internet Explorer Integration, covered in Chapter 8, *Taking Control of Web Integration.*
- The **Browse Folders** option, which is also found in Windows 2000, Windows NT 4.0, and Windows 9x, determines the behavior for single-folder windows only; this setting is ignored in Explorer, where there's never more than one window.

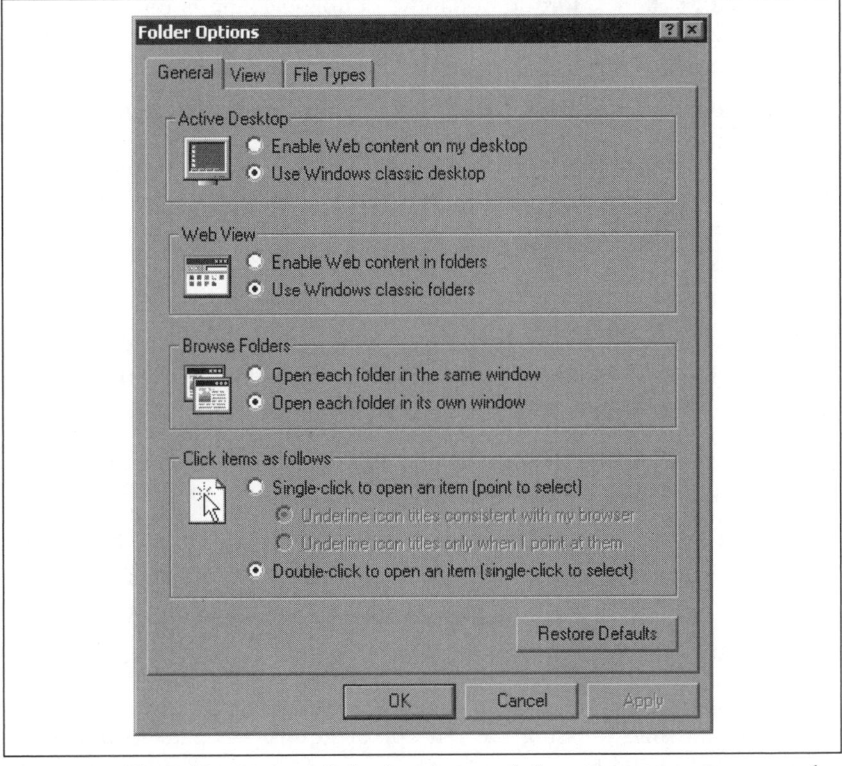

Figure 2-1. The Folder Options dialog box is a good place to start messing around with some basic Explorer settings

- You can hold the **Ctrl** key while double-clicking on a folder to override whatever option you chose for **Browse Folders**. For example, if you've opted to **Open each folder in its own window**, the **Ctrl** key will force a folder to open in a new window.
- The **Single-click to open an item** option is included primarily for conformity with the **Web View**, but it does have the advantage of allowing you to navigate most of Windows without having to double-click (something you can also do with the right mouse button). Note that if you choose the single-click interface, you can no longer click twice slowly on an item to rename it: you must either right-click on it and select **Rename** or carefully move the mouse pointer so that it is hovering over the icon and press the **F2** key.
- The **Double-click to open an item** option can certainly be a pain in the neck for beginners and experienced users alike, but there are significant advantages of requiring double-clicks to open icons. For example, it virtually eliminates the possibility of accidentally opening a program or folder when you try to select, delete, move, copy, or

rename an item.* More importantly, double-clicking is consistent with all other operating systems, such as Macintosh and Unix, as well as with previous versions of Windows. This may not seem like a great argument, but a primary factor of good user-interface design is the use of familiar elements.

What it comes down to, of course, is that you should use what works best for you. Don't blindly accept the defaults just because it came out of the box that way.

Helpful navigation keystrokes

The following tips assume you're using standard double-clicking; if not, just replace "double-click" with "single-click."

- Hold the **Alt** key while double-clicking on a file or folder to view the **Properties** window for that object.
- Hold the **Shift** key while double-clicking on a folder to open **Explorer** at that location. (Be careful when using this, because **Shift** is also used to select multiple files. The best way is to select the file first.)
- Press **Backspace** in an open folder to go to the parent (containing) folder.
- Hold **Alt** while pressing the left cursor key to navigate to the previously viewed folder. Note that this is not necessarily the *parent* folder, but rather the last folder opened in Explorer. You can also hold **Alt** while pressing the right cursor key to move in the opposite direction (i.e., forward); this is similar to the **Back** and **Next** buttons in Internet Explorer, respectively. The Windows Explorer toolbar also has back and next buttons.
- Hold the **Shift** key while clicking on the close button **[X]** to close *all* open folders that were used to get to that folder. (This, of course, makes sense only in the single-folder view and with the **Open each folder in its own window** option turned on.)
- You can right-click on any folder icon to present all of the exploring options, such as **Open** (folder view) and **Explore** (Tree View). This is called the *context menu*—for more information, see "Understanding File Types" in Chapter 3 and "Customize Context Menus" in Chapter 4, *Tinkering Techniques*.

* Most pointing devices (mice, styli, trackballs) with more than two buttons allow the additional buttons to be programmed. I've found that the third mouse button (or the second barrel switch, if you're using a stylus) is ideal for double-clicking.

- Select one icon, then hold the **Shift** key while clicking on another icon in the same folder to select it and all the items in between.
- Drag a *rubber band* around multiple files to select them: start by holding down the left mouse button in a blank portion of a folder window, then drag the mouse to the opposite corner to select everything that appears in the rectangle you just drew.
- Hold the **Ctrl** key to select or de-select multiple files or folders, one by one. Note that you can't select more than one folder in the left pane (Tree View) of Explorer, but you can in the right pane.

  You can also use **Ctrl** key to modify your selection. For example, if you've used the **Shift** key or a rubber band to select the first five objects in a folder, you can hold **Ctrl** while dragging a second rubber band to highlight additional files *without* losing your original selection.
- Press **Ctrl-A** to quickly select all of the contents of a folder: both files and folders.
- In Explorer or any single-folder window, press a letter key to quickly jump to the first file or folder starting with that letter. Continue typing to jump further. For example, pressing the **N** key in your *\Windows* folder will jump to *NetHood*. Press **N** again to jump to the next object that starts with N. Or, press **N** and then quickly press **O** to skip all the Ns and jump to *notepad.exe*. If there's enough of a delay between the **N** and the **O** keys, Explorer will forget about the N, and you'll jump to the first entry that starts with O.

Move or Copy Files at Will

Intuitively, when one drags an object from one place on the screen to another, it would seem reasonable that the object would then appear in the new place and disappear from the old place. In other words, what happens to a file when you drag it from the left side of your desktop to the right side of your desktop should be exactly the same as what happens when you drag a file from one folder to another or from a floppy disk to your hard drive.

The problem is that drag-drop is handled differently in different situations. The decision of what action to take in each situation was made by a committee in Redmond, Washington. Odds are you didn't have a personal representative at that meeting.

So, our aim here is to force Windows to work the way we think, keeping in mind the practical limitations of the operating system. Here's the way it works (note that "object" is a file, folder, shortcut, system object, or anything else with an icon that can be knocked around with your mouse):

- If you drag an object from one place to another on the same physical drive (*c:\docs* to *c:\files*), the object is moved.
- If you drag an object from one physical drive to another physical drive (*c:\docs* to *d:\files*), the object is copied, resulting in two identical files on your system.

  Furthermore, if you drag an object from one physical drive to another physical drive and then back to the first physical drive, but in a different folder (*c:\docs* to *d:\files* to *c:\stuff*), you'll end up with three copies of the object.
- If you drag an application executable (an EXE file), the same rules apply to it that apply to other objects, with the following unfortunate exceptions:*
  - If you drag *any* file named *setup.exe* or *install.exe* from one place to another, Windows will create a shortcut to the file, regardless of the source or destination folder.
  - If you drag any file with the *.exe* filename extension into any portion of your Start Menu or into any subfolder of your *Start Menu* folder, Windows will create a shortcut to the file. Dragging other file types (documents, script files, other shortcuts) to the Start Menu will simply move or copy them there, according to the previous rules.
- If you drag a system object (such as an item in the My Computer window or Control Panel) anywhere, a warning is displayed, and a shortcut to the item is created. This, of course, is a consequence of the fact that these objects aren't actually files and can't be duplicated or removed from their original locations.

  Exceptions are the icons in the Dial-Up Networking window (discussed in Chapter 7, *Networking and Internetworking*); if you drag a Dial-Up Networking connection out of the window, you get neither a copy nor a shortcut, but rather a Dial-Up Networking file.
- If you drag certain icons that appear on the desktop, such as My Documents, Internet Explorer, or the Recycle Bin, any number of different things can happen, each depending on the specific properties of the object.

---

* The behavior in Windows Me is unlike previous versions of Windows, where dragging any EXE file anywhere created a shortcut.

The best way to cope with this confusion is to use a combination of certain keystrokes and the right mouse button to ensure the desired results every time you drag an object. That way, you don't have to try to predict what will happen based on some rules you likely won't remember. All the keystrokes are explained in the previous section, "Helpful navigation keystrokes."

- To *copy* an object under *any* situation, hold the **Ctrl** key while dragging. If you press **Ctrl** *before* you click, Windows assumes you're still selecting files, so make sure to press it only *after* you've started dragging but before you let go of that mouse button. Of course, this won't work for system objects like Control Panel items—a shortcut will be created regardless.

  Using the **Ctrl** key in this way will also work when dragging a file from one part of a folder to another part of the same folder. See "Make a Duplicate of a File or Folder" later in this chapter for more information.

- To *move* an object under any situation, hold the **Shift** key while dragging. Likewise, if you press **Shift** before you click, Windows assumes you're still selecting files, so make sure to press it only after you've started dragging but before you let go of that mouse button. This also won't work for system objects like Control Panel items—a shortcut will be created regardless.

- To create a shortcut to an object under any situation, hold the **Ctrl** and **Shift** keys simultaneously while dragging. If you try to make a shortcut that points to another shortcut, the shortcut will simply be copied (duplicated).

- To choose what happens to dragged files each time *without* having to press any keys, drag your files with the *right mouse button*, and a special menu like the one shown in Figure 2-2 will appear when the files are dropped. This context menu is especially helpful, because it will display only options appropriate to the type of object you're dragging and the place where you've dropped it.*

To aid in learning the keystrokes, notice that the mouse cursor changes depending on the action taken. A small plus sign [+] appears when copying, and a curved arrow appears when creating a shortcut. If you see no symbol, the object will be moved. This visual feedback is very important; it can eliminate a lot of stupid mistakes if you pay attention to it.

---

* If you use ZIP files, you may like the WinZIP utility (see *http://www.winzip.com*), which quite effectively utilizes the right-drag menu described above to zip and unzip files.

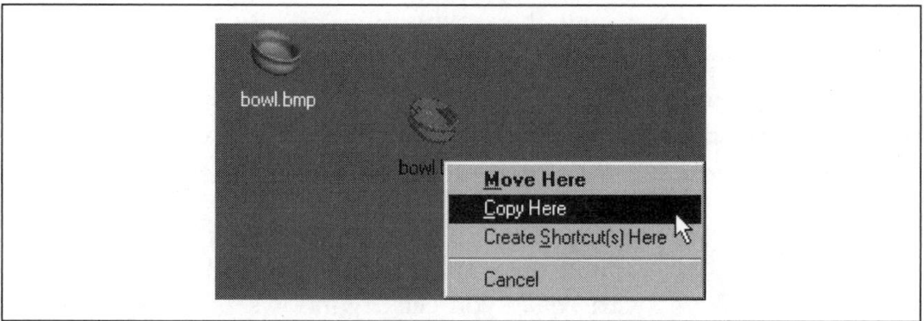

Figure 2-2. Drag files with the right mouse button for more control

There is no way to set the default action when dragging files and therefore no way to avoid using keystrokes or the right mouse button to achieve the desired results. Even if there were a way to change the default behavior, you probably wouldn't want to do it. Imagine if someone else sat down at your computer and started dragging icons: oh, the horror.

Explorer's **Undo** command (in the **Edit** menu, as well as available by right-clicking in an empty area of Explorer or the desktop) allows you to undo the last few file operations.* If you've copied, moved, or renamed one or more objects, the command will read **Undo Copy**, **Undo Move**, or **Undo Rename**, respectively. Additionally, if your Recycle Bin is configured to store files, **Undo Delete** may also appear. However, if you're doing a lot of copying, moving, and deleting of files, it's hard to know to which particular operation the **Undo** command refers at any given time. The easiest way to tell is to click and hold the mouse button over the **Undo** menu item and look in the status bar (select **Status Bar** from the **View** menu if it's not visible), which will tell you exactly with which files the operation dealt. This, of course, is not available on the desktop, but luckily, the **Undo** command works the same regardless of the folder from which you use it.

Copy or Move to a Specified Path

To copy or move a file in Windows by drag-dropping, you must have both the source folder and the destination folder open and visible. There is no provision for specifying a destination folder with the keyboard when copying or moving a file, making these simple tasks that much more difficult for many of us. To get around this limitation, making file management far less awkward, follow the upcoming steps.

* **Ctrl-Z** is a keyboard shortcut for Undo.

Solution 1: Drag patiently

1. Open Explorer (with the Tree View), and navigate to the source folder.
2. Drag one or more items over the tree pane on the left, then hold the mouse cursor over the visible branch of the destination folder. After two or three seconds, Explorer will automatically expand the branch and make the subfolders visible.

   If the destination folder you're looking for is buried several layers deep, you'll have to wait for Explorer to expand each level. This requires a steady hand and a lot of patience. It's an improvement over earlier versions of Windows, but it's usually quicker and easier to open the folders before you start to drag.

   This works on network drives as well, even when the host computer (the machine on which the remote folders are located) is running Windows 95 or NT and doesn't support the "autoexpand" feature natively.

Solution 2: Use copy and paste

This solution isn't exactly intuitive, but it can be convenient if you don't have a mouse or if your screen size limits the number of open windows:

1. Select the file you want to copy, right-click on it, and select **Copy** to copy the file or **Cut** to move the file.*

   If the file is cut, its icon will appear faded (as though it were a hidden file). If the file is copied, there will be no visual distinction.
2. Open the destination folder (or go to the desktop), right-click on an empty area (or open the **Edit** menu), and select **Paste**. Whether the file is copied or moved—or a shortcut is made—depends on the same criteria as if you had dragged and dropped the item. Unfortunately, modification keystrokes (Ctrl, Shift, and Alt) have no effect here, so you'll probably need a little trial-and-error.

   Note that if you cut a file and never get around to pasting it, or cut a second file without pasting the first, the first file that was cut is *not* deleted as you might expect. This is inconsistent with the way that *information* is cut and pasted from application to application, which is what most of us are used to.† If you cut text from one application

* The keyboard shortcuts for **Cut**, **Copy**, and **Paste** are **Ctrl-X**, **Ctrl-C**, and **Ctrl-V**, respectively.

† While you can drag-drop files from Explorer or the desktop into a running application to open the file in that application, the same isn't necessarily true for **Copy** and **Paste**. If you try to copy a file and then paste it into an application such as Word or Word Perfect, the file is inserted as an icon object directly into the document, which is not likely to be of much use for most people.

and don't bother pasting it, the text is lost. Cut, copy, and paste in the context of files work with file *references* rather than the files themselves, so unless you cut a file and then paste it into the Recycle Bin, there isn't much danger of losing anything. Note that you can abort any cut operation by pressing the **Esc** key, which has little visual effect other than returning "faded" file icons to their normal state.

Solution 3: Use a third-party add-on

Creative Element Power Tools (available at *http://www.creativelement.com*) comes with a handy Copy To/Move To utility. Just right-click on any file or folder, select **Move To** or **Copy To**, and then type or point to the destination folder. You can also create new folders on the fly; the software even remembers the last dozen destinations you specified.

Make a Duplicate of a File or Folder

Windows lets you copy and move files from one folder to another by dragging them with different combinations of keystrokes (see "Move or Copy Files at Will" earlier in this chapter). You can also rename a file by clicking on its name or highlighting it and pressing the **F2** key. However, if you want to make a *duplicate* of a file in the *same* directory and assign it a different name, the process might not be as obvious. There are several different ways to do it:

- Hold the **Ctrl** key while dragging a file from one part of the window to another part of the *same* window. This works in folder windows, on the desktop, and in Explorer.
- Use the right mouse button to drag the file from one part of the window to another part of the same window, and then select **Copy Here**, as shown in Figure 2-2.
- For keyboard enthusiasts, press **Ctrl-C** and then **Ctrl-V** to create a duplicate of a file using the clipboard.

Regardless of which solution you use, the duplicate of a file called, say, *Myfile.txt* would be automatically named *Copy of Myfile.txt.* An additional copy of *Myfile.txt* will be called *Copy (2) of Myfile.txt*, while a copy of *Copy of Myfile.txt* will be called *Copy of Copy of Myfile.txt.* Because the filename keeps changing (albeit inconveniently), you can duplicate multiple files simultaneously to fill a directory quickly with dozens of identical files.

If you duplicate a folder, all the contents of the folder will be duplicated, but only the name of the folder will be changed—the names of the files therein will remain intact.

You can also use the Power Rename utility (part of Creative Element Power Tools, available at *http://www.creativelement.com*) to duplicate large numbers of files quickly:

1. Right-click on the file you want to duplicate, then select **Power Rename**. Or open Power Rename, and drag-drop the file into the window.
2. Turn on the **Show what files will look like** option to see a preview of the filename(s).
3. Select the desired renaming criteria so that the duplicate will not be the same as the original.
4. Turn on the **Leave original files (copy)** option, and click **Apply** when you're done. Click **Apply** repeatedly to make lots of duplicates.

You can use Power Rename to make duplicates of a file quickly or simply to avoid the "Copy of" prefix.

Choose How to Delete Files

Deleting files and folders is something we do every day, but under Windows Me's default settings, deleting a single file can incur up to four confirmation messages.

You'll get a nag window when you first drop files into the Recycle Bin or delete them with a keystroke, a second one when you empty the Recycle Bin, a third one if the file that's being deleted is an EXE file (but not for *.dll* files, which are just as necessary as EXE files), and a fourth if the file has a read-only or system attribute set.*

The number and type of confirmation messages you get depends on settings in your Recycle Bin. For example, if your Recycle Bin is configured to store deleted files (the default), but not confirm their deletion, you may not see any warning message at all.

* Not necessarily in that order. If you're deleting certain shortcuts, such as those placed in your Start Menu by some application installers, you'll additionally see a message explaining that, by deleting the shortcut, you're not actually deleting the software to which it links.

Right-click on the Recycle Bin on your desktop, and select **Properties**. The various options here are pretty self-explanatory. However, you should be aware of the following:

- If you highlight an object and press the **Del** key, or right-click an object and select **Delete**, it has the same effect as dropping the object into the Recycle Bin.
- If your Recycle Bin is configured to store deleted objects, you can get back accidental deletions by opening the Recycle Bin and dragging items out of it. If you've configured the Recycle Bin to delete files immediately, you'll need an undelete program (such as the one that comes with Norton Utilities) to get them back.

  You can also right-click any empty area of a folder or the desktop and select **Undo Delete** (assuming the last thing you did was delete an object), but only if you've configured the Recycle Bin to store your deleted objects. See "Move or Copy Files at Will" earlier in this chapter for more information on Explorer's **Undo** command.
- It's possible to permanently delete an object in Windows Me without any confirmation dialog box whatsoever, a feature you should, of course, use with caution. To do this, open the **Recycle Bin Properties**, and turn on the **Do not move files to the Recycle Bin** option. Next, turn off the **Display delete confirmation dialog box**, and click **OK** when you're done.
- Make sure that you specify **Use one setting for all drives** in the **Recycle Bin Properties**. Otherwise, files deleted from drive *C:* may succumb to a different fate than those deleted from drive *D:* or *A:*—inconsistent behavior is the cause of many accidentally deleted files.
- The amount of disk space devoted to the Recycle Bin is specified as a percentage of the amount of free disk space per drive, rather than a fixed number of megabytes. This means that the size of your Recycle Bin will constantly change, and the size of the Recycle Bin on each of your drives will always be different. Now, if you delete a 15-MB file and only 10 MB are available to the Recycle Bin, Windows will delete the file outright instead of storing it (it may warn you first). It follows that you may not be able to predict what will happen when you delete large files, especially when the behavior will be different depending on which drive the file was originally located.
- If you have your Recycle Bin configured to store deleted files, it will hold them until it becomes full and then will permanently erase the oldest contents to prevent "overflow." This means you will never be able to predict how long a deleted file will remain in the Recycle Bin:

a sensitive file may stay in there for weeks, presenting a possible security hazard. Likewise, an accidentally deleted file may disappear after only a few hours, long before it occurs to you to double-check the contents. The lesson: be careful when deleting files, be diligent about checking your Recycle Bin, and give some thought to the Recycle Bin settings.

- Deleting objects from the command prompt (see Appendix B, *DOS Resurrected*), using either the *del* command or the *deltree* command, will always bypass the Recycle Bin. You may want to use *del* to quickly and easily delete one or more files sharing a common trait, such as the filename extension. Just type **`del *.tmp`** to delete all files with the *.tmp* extension in the active folder, for example. Both *del* and *deltree* often complete their tasks quicker than the Recycle Bin, especially for large numbers of objects. Command-prompt commands also have the added benefit of deleting files without forcing you to stare at the flying paper animation.

Why would you want files to be stored in the Recycle Bin? It gives you a way out: if you find that you are careless and delete important files accidentally, you should definitely exploit this feature.

Why would you *not* want files to be stored in the Recycle Bin? First of all, those files don't exist in a vacuum; they take up valuable hard-disk space and can slow system performance. Deleted files are a security risk; it's one of the first places I'd look if I were breaking into someone's system. And, having unwanted files remain on your hard disk can make your system more vulnerable to hard-disk crashes (from corrupted files) and viruses (from email attachments you deleted right away).

There are a few workarounds for whatever Recycle Bin settings you choose, allowing more flexibility and control:

- If you have configured your Recycle Bin to store deleted files, you can still hold the **Shift** key while deleting any given object to permanently erase the object. The files currently stored in the Recycle Bin (if any) will not be affected.
- If you create a shortcut to the **Recycle Bin** in your *Send To* folder, you can right-click any object, and select **Send To** and then **Recycle Bin** to delete it without a prompt.

Force Explorer to Remember Folder Settings

For many of us, it's a chore to get Windows to remember some of the most basic settings. For example, how many times have you turned off the

Web View option in Explorer, only to find that it has been turned back on the next time the folder is opened?

Explorer's inability to remember settings is a long-standing problem with Windows, but it is slightly improved with each successive version of the operating system. Such preferences as the position and size of a window and the sort order, autoarrange, and size of icons can be mysteriously reset to Windows' default values when folders are closed and reopened. The problem is the battle between Explorer's "default" settings, agreed upon by a committee at Microsoft, and the "most recent" settings, repeatedly set by the user and occasionally stored in the Registry. So, which settings should Explorer and your folder windows use next time they're opened?

There are two ways to set a default setting in Explorer:

- Some defaults are set automatically when the corresponding settings are changed: for example, when you adjust the column widths in the Details view, Windows remembers them automatically and uses them for each subsequent Explorer window and single-folder window that is opened. Other settings, such as the visibility and position of the various toolbars and the size and position of the window, are set independently for Explorer and for single-folder windows.

  To disable this functionality, select **Folder Options** from Explorer's **Tools** menu, and choose the **View** tab. Turn off the **Remember each folder's view settings** option, and click **OK** when you're done.

- For some settings, you must take extra steps to ensure that your settings are remembered. For example, whatever icon size (e.g., **Large Icons**, **Small Icons**, **List**, **Details**) you choose will be forgotten as soon as you close the current window. To force Windows to remember your settings for these types of options, follow these steps:

  a. Open Explorer or a single-folder window, and change your settings as desired. See the "Default Set with Folder Options" column in Table 2-1 for the particular settings to which this procedure applies. Make sure that there are no other open Explorer or single-folder windows.

  b. Select **Folder Options** from the **Tools** menu, and choose the **View** tab.

  c. Click **Like Current Folder**, then click **OK** when you're done.

  d. Close the current window, then open a new Explorer or single-folder window to see if your settings have stuck.

In theory, Windows will remember the defaults for all the settings listed as such in Table 2-1. After a time, you may notice that Windows will revert back to its out-of-the-box defaults, and there's really nothing you can do about it, except to make your choices again.

Table 2-1. The Defaults for Different Explorer Settings

Setting	Default Set Automatically	Default Set with Folder Options	Default Never Set
Autoarrange		✓	
Column Widths (Details view)	✓		
Icon size		✓	
Selected Folder (Explorer only)[a]			✓
Sort order		✓	
Toolbar Settings	✓		
Web View		✓	
Window size and Position	✓		

[a] See "Force Explorer to Start with the Folder You Want" later in this chapter for a solution.

Basic Explorer Coping Skills

There are also some exceptions to the previous rules. Some settings, such as icon size, are stored with reference to individual folders when the single-folder view is used. To illustrate, follow these steps:

1. Create a new folder on your desktop, and name it *Lenny*.
2. Open the new folder, and change the icon size by choosing **Large Icons** (or use something else if **Large Icons** is already selected).
3. Now delete the folder, and then create a new folder called *Karl*. When you open *Karl*, you'll notice its icon size is set to your system's default.
4. Without closing *Karl*, rename it (by renaming the icon on your desktop or by right-clicking on the *Karl*'s control box) to *Lenny*. As soon as it is renamed, its icon size will automatically revert to the setting used in the first *Lenny* folder.

This persistence of the icon-size setting (as well as any setting listed as "Default Set with Folder Options" in Table 2-1) is due to the fact that Windows stores these settings for the last two dozen or so folders you access. Your choices are stored in the Registry, rather than in the folders themselves, so there will always be a limit on the number of folders it can remember in this way.

Choose Your Short Filenames

One of the trickiest tasks a software developer faces is the addition of new functionality to an application that needs to be backwards-compatible. In the case of support for long filenames, Microsoft had to implement the functionality without making the new files inaccessible to older 16-bit Windows and DOS programs.

The solution was that every long filename has a short counterpart. That is, a file named *A Big Blob.txt* will appear as *ABIGBL~1.TXT.* Not only does this make it possible to open a file with a long filename in a program that doesn't support long filenames, it makes it clear which filenames have long counterparts.

If you find yourself using the short versions of long filenames often, such as if you rely on what's called a *legacy* application (written before long filename support), you'll want to have more control of how short filenames are chosen:

1. Using any application (either a legacy 16-bit application or a non–long filename–aware 32-bit application), create a document with a short filename, such as *ABIGBLOB.TXT.*
2. Then, in **Explorer**, rename the file to *A Big Blob that ate Manhattan.txt*, or something like that.
3. Go back to the 16-bit application, and instead of *ABIGBL~1.TXT*, you'll see the same, original 8.3 filename. This is due to the fact that the long and the short versions are so similar, and the short version was created *first.* If the long filename is too different, this won't work. Now, this is not the most repeatable or reliable solution, but it's pretty benign, and if you get good at it, can be fairly useful.

Fix the Search Tool

Most of us rely on the Windows Search tool on a daily basis to find and organize files in Explorer. However, a new design in Windows Me (and Windows 2000) merges the Search tool with Explorer in a way that can be very inconvenient.

Instead of the separate Find window found in previous versions of Windows, the new Search tool (more specifically, the Search . . . For Files or Folders tool) is displayed in the left pane of an Explorer window. On the surface, this has little effect, other than that the Search window takes up a little more space on the screen and the search options are arranged in a somewhat different manner.

The problem becomes obvious when the Search tool is invoked from within an open Explorer window: the left pane containing the folder tree simply disappears! The contents of the currently selected folder remain visible, but vanish as soon as a search is performed. The fact that the current window is reused for the Search tool has no apparent benefit, yet it inconveniently and frustratingly invalidates whatever was displayed in the current window.

The only way to return to the previous view at this point is to select **Explorer Bar** and then **Folders** from Explorer's **View** menu—unfortunately, there's no keyboard shortcut, so this procedure is especially cumbersome. When the Tree View is reinstated, a new item, *Search Results*, appears at the bottom. However, if you select another folder and then return to *Search Results*, neither the search criteria nor the search results from your last search are retained. In other words, there's absolutely no point to this design.

The solution is to find a way to activate the Search tool so this doesn't happen. The following two methods will cause the problem described earlier, converting the current Explorer window into a Search window:

- Press **Ctrl-F**, **Ctrl-E**, or **F3** in any single-folder or Explorer window.
- Select **Explorer Bar** and then **Search** from Explorer's **View** menu,* or click the **Search** button on the Explorer toolbar.

On the other hand, there are at least three methods for opening a new Search window, leaving any open Explorer windows intact. Note that each of these methods results in the search being performed in a different default folder:

- Select **Search** and then **For Files or Folders** from the **Start Menu**. **Local Hard Drives** will be automatically selected in the **Look in** list.
- Click on the desktop, and then press **F3**. The Desktop will automatically be selected in the **Look in** list.
- Right-click on any folder icon on the desktop or in an Explorer window, or right-click on any drive icon in My Computer or Explorer, and select **Search**. Said folder or drive will automatically be selected in the **Look in** list.

* If you're looking for the old Find entry in Explorer's Tools menu, it has been removed, making the Search tool that much harder to find for inexperienced users.

There's also another way to open a Search window without disrupting an Explorer window. This solution has the added benefit of allowing you to choose the default search location:

1. Open a Search window using any method, and select whatever search location you want to be the default. The **Local Hard Drives** entry is probably the most useful, but you can choose the *My Documents* folder or any other place you wish.
2. Leave the rest of the search criteria blank, and click **Search Now**.
3. When the search is complete, select **Save Search** from the **File** menu. When prompted, save the *All Files.fnd* file on the Desktop (choose a different name if you like).
4. Double-click on the *All Files.fnd* file at any time to open a new Search window. You can place the shortcut on your desktop, add it to your Start Menu, or put it on a QuickLaunch toolbar for quick access.
5. If you want to assign a keyboard shortcut to this new Search icon, start by moving the *All Files.fnd* file to a safe, out-of-the-way location. Create a shortcut to the file and place it in the same folder, in your Start Menu, or anywhere else that is convenient.

   Right-click on the new shortcut, click **Properties**, click on the **Shortcut key** field, and press the desired keystroke combination. Unfortunately, Windows won't let you choose a shortcut key combination with only the **Ctrl** key, so you can't redefine **Ctrl-F** for this window (believe me—this is the first thing I tried). However, **Ctrl-Shift-F** is almost as convenient, and may serve as a suitable compromise. Click **OK** when you're done, then try it out!

Creative Element Power Tools (available at *http://www.creativelement.com*) comes with a feature that fixes the Search tool, forcing a new Search window to be opened regardless of the method used.

Tweaking the Interface

If you've made it this far, odds are that you already know how to change your desktop wallpaper, create shortcuts on your desktop, and rearrange the items in your Start Menu. The following solutions allow you to customize some of the more subtle aspects of the Windows interface, using methods somewhat less obvious than those found in ordinary dialog boxes.

Probably the most important customizations in this section are illustrated in "Force Explorer to Start with the Folder You Want" and "Customize Drive and Folder Icons." Both of these solutions utilize built-in features of the operating system in ways for which they weren't necessarily intended. The rest of this section should help you tame the Tray, the Control Panel, and the Start Menu—stuff you won't find in the manual.

Force Explorer to Start with the Folder You Want

There are several ways to open an Explorer window, but the most direct method is to use the **Windows Explorer** shortcut in the Start Menu. This has the same effect as selecting **Run** in the **Start Menu** and typing **`explorer.exe`**. That is, the Explorer application is run without any command-line arguments.

When Explorer is run without any arguments, it opens to its default location, the Documents shortcut on your desktop (even if you've deleted the Documents icon from your desktop). You may want to have Explorer open to a custom folder each time, saving the time required to repeatedly navigate through all the folders on your hard disk.

Launch Explorer from a shortcut

The following steps show how to modify your existing Windows Explorer shortcut in your Start Menu. If you want to create a new shortcut instead, right-click on an empty portion of your desktop or the currently open folder, and select **New** and then **Shortcut**. When prompted for an application, point to *explorer.exe* (located in your *Windows* folder):

1. Right-click on the Windows Explorer shortcut, select **Properties**, and click on the **Shortcut** tab.
2. Change the text in the **Target** field so it reads:

   ```
   Explorer.exe /n, /e, d:\myfolder
   ```

   where *`d:\myfolder`* is the folder where you want Explorer to start.
3. Click **OK** when you're done. The next time you use the shortcut, Explorer will open to the specified location.

You may have to use a little trial-and-error to get the desired results. The command-line parameters Explorer accepts are as follows:

```
explorer.exe [/n][,/e][,/root,object][[,/select],subobject]
```

The square brackets (`[...]`) show optional parameters; note the use of commas between each parameter.

The `/n` switch tells Explorer always to open a new window (even if the specified folder is already open somewhere), and the `/e` switch tells Explorer to use the Tree View rather than the default single-folder view. You'll want to use both of these options together in most circumstances.

The `subobject` parameter specifies the folder that is initially highlighted on the tree when Explorer opens (see the example earlier in step 3). If `subobject` is specified, it will also be expanded to show the first level of subfolders (if any).

If you also include the `/select` parameter (not valid without `subobject`), the *parent* of the specified folder is highlighted on the tree and no branches are initially expanded. If `subobject` is a file instead of a folder, it will be highlighted in the right pane as well.

So, for example, if you want Explorer to open to the *My Computer* folder so that no drive branches are initially expanded (handy if you have several drives), type the following:

```
Explorer.exe /n, /e, /select, c:\
```

Finally, the `/root,`*`object`* parameter allows you to choose what appears as the root of all folders in the new window, useful if you want an abbreviated tree. The default, of course, is the desktop. You can specify a folder to be the root by typing **`/root,c:\docs`** or a system object by typing **`/root,{class id}`** (see Appendix C, *Class IDs of System Objects*).

Exploring in context

In addition to launching Explorer with any number of parameters, you can open an Explorer window in the context of an object on the screen, and Windows will choose the parameters accordingly.

For example, you can right-click on any visible folder icon (on your desktop, in an open folder, and even in the tree pane of another Explorer window) and select **Explore** to open a new Explorer window with the folder in question highlighted.

You can also explore from various system objects by right-clicking and selecting **Explore**. This works on the Start button, the My Computer icon, and the My Network Places icon. Figure 2-3 shows the context menu for the Start button; note that **Open** is bold, which is the default action taken when the Start button is clicked.

By default, only the current folder name is shown in Explorer's title bar, which can be rather confusing. You'll find it much more helpful to display the full path (e.g., *c:\Windows\Start Menu\Programs* instead of just

Figure 2-3. Right-click Start for quick Explorer access to the Start Menu folder

Programs). Select **Folder Options** from Explorer's **Tools** menu, choose the **View** tab, and turn on both the **Display the full path in the title bar** and the **Display the full path in the address bar** options.

Taming Mindless Animation

For anyone upgrading to Windows Me from Windows 95, or from Windows NT 4.0, one of the most obvious interface changes is the addition of animated menus, list boxes, and other screen elements. While these affectations may be cute, they can honestly make the fastest, newest computers seem like antiquated 386s. Rather than watch your Start Menu crawl to its open position, you can configure your menus and list boxes to snap to position. You'll be surprised at how much faster and more responsive Windows will feel.

Solution 1: All for one, and one for all

1. Double-click on the Display icon in Control Panel and choose the **Effects** tab.
2. Turn off the **Use transition effects for menus and tooltips** option, and click **OK**.

Solution 2: Individual animation

1. Double-click on the **TweakUI** icon in Control Panel (see Appendix A, *Setting Locator*), and choose the **General** tab.
2. In the **Effects** list, you'll find separate animation settings for individual screen elements:
   — **Window animation** affects maximizing and minimizing windows.
   — **Smooth scrolling** is used for web pages in Internet Explorer and in all Explorer and single-folder windows.
   — **Menu animation** is used in standard menus in all applications and in the Start Menu.
   — **Combo box animation** and **List box animation** add the "smooth scrolling" effect to combo (drop-down) list boxes and all other types of list boxes, respectively.

3. The **Mouse hot tracking effects** option turns off the tooltips everywhere (although not necessarily animation—they're annoying just the same), rather than turning off the way that menus and toolbar buttons follow the mouse around, as you'd expect.
4. Click **OK** when you're finished.

If you have both the **Auto hide** setting in Taskbar Properties and the **Show window contents while dragging** option in Display Properties enabled, turning off the **Window animation** option will also disable the animation for the disappearing taskbar.

Stop Menus from Following the Mouse

In all releases of Microsoft Windows since Windows 95, the Start Menu and the menus in all applications follow the mouse. This allows you to navigate through menus without having to click repeatedly. The problem with this design is that it can be very difficult to navigate menus unless you're able to hold your mouse or other pointing device very steadily. Even the smallest unintentional move in the wrong direction can cause the menu you're using to disappear. This can be even more annoying to those with more sensitive pointing devices, such as touch pads, pens, and other digitizers. Here's how to disable this behavior:

Solution 1

Obtain and install the Old Mouse Mode utility (download it from *http://www.annoyances.org*), which forces the menus in Windows to behave pretty much like Windows 3.x menus.

Solution 2

1. Double-click on the **TweakUI** icon in Control Panel (see Appendix A).
2. In the **Mouse** tab, move the Menu Speed slider all the way to the right (towards **Slow**).

   This will increase the delay when opening menus to it's maximum setting, virtually disabling it. Although this will prevent *submenus* from opening automatically, the top-level menus will still follow the mouse like a starving alley cat.

Get Rid of Shortcut Residue

Shortcuts have three ways of telling you that they're shortcuts. When first created, a shortcut's caption begins with the text, "Shortcut to." The shortcut's icon also has a small curved arrow in the lower-left corner. (See the "before" icon in Figure 2-4.) If you're viewing the folder containing the shortcut in **Details** mode, the **Type** column will read either **Shortcut**, **Shortcut to MS-DOS Program**, or **Internet Shortcut** for *.lnk*, *.pif*, and *.url* shortcut files, respectively. Note that even if you've configured Windows to display your filename extensions, the extensions for shortcuts will always be hidden.

Figure 2-4. Cleaning up shortcuts: before and after

Although one can simply rename the icon so that the "Shortcut to" prefix isn't there, there is no quick way to remove the little arrow for just one shortcut. To turn off these artifacts for good on all shortcuts, follow these instructions:

Solution 1: Remove the "Shortcut to" prefix only

1. Create a shortcut—any shortcut.
2. Manually remove the "Shortcut to" prefix from the name.
3. Delete the shortcut.
4. Repeat the first three steps eight times in succession.

That should do it. Keep in mind that this is a one-way change; there's no way to undo it, without using the TweakUI utility, described later.

Solution 2: Complete control

1. Double-click on the TweakUI icon (see Appendix A) in Control Panel, and choose the **Explorer** tab.
2. The **Prefix "Shortcut to" on new shortcuts** option in the **Settings** section should reflect the state set by Solution 1 (previous). Turn it off or on as desired.
3. To disable or change the curved arrow icon, choose the desired option in the **Shortcut overlay** section. If you choose **Custom**, you can choose any icon, although it should be 16×16 or smaller, or partially transparent, so as not to obscure the original icon.
4. Click **OK** when you're done. The changes should take effect immediately.

If you disable both the "Shortcut to" prefix and the curved arrow icon, the only way to distinguish a shortcut from the actual program or file to which it's linked is either through the shortcut's Properties sheet or by its description in the Type column in Explorer.

Customize the Tray

The tray is the little box (usually in the lower-right corner of your screen, at the end of your taskbar) that, by default, contains the clock and the little yellow speaker. Microsoft calls this space the "Notification Area," because its intended use is to notify you of system status: when you're connected to the Internet, when your battery is low, etc.

Figure 2-5 shows a more-or-less typical tray. Odds are that you have more icons in your tray than you actually want or need. Whether that bothers you or not is anybody's guess.

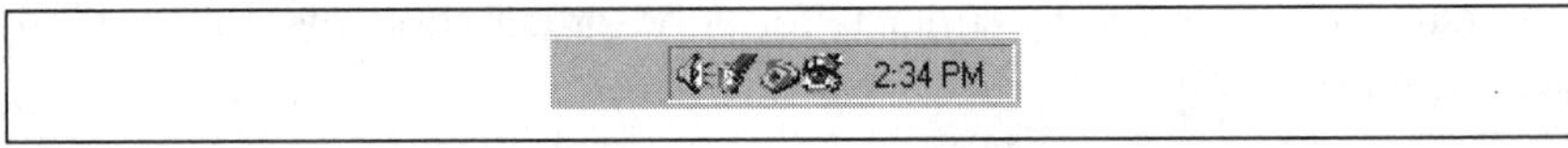

Figure 2-5. The tray contains several (usually too many) icons, as well as the clock

The problem is that there doesn't seem to be any sort of consistency or standards for items in the tray; some icons get double-clicked, some require a single right- or left-click, and some don't get clicked at all. Some items can be removed easily, some can be removed with a setting in some obscure dialog box, and some can't be removed at all. Here are some ways to get a little more control of the tray.

Remove common items from the tray

- To remove the yellow speaker icon (the volume control), right-click on it and select **Audio Properties**, or double-click on the **Sounds and Multimedia** icon in the Control Panel. On the **Sounds** tab, turn off the **Show volume control on the taskbar** option.
- To remove the little modem icon with the blinking lights (for use with Dial-Up Networking), open the *Dial-Up Networking* folder (it's in the Control Panel). Right-click on a connection icon, and select **Properties**. (If you have more than one connection, you'll need to repeat these steps for each one.) In the **Connect using** section, click **Configure**. (This

will display a box similar, but not identical to, the modem settings in Control Panel.) Click on the **Options** tab, turn off **Display modem status** in the **Status control** section, and click **OK** when you're done.

- If you've installed Real Networks' *Real Player* utility (*http://www.real.com*), you'll notice a little blue icon has been placed in your tray (the installer doesn't ask). The program that this icon represents doesn't do anything and can be removed without any adverse effects. (In fact, disabling this program will allow Windows to start a little faster next time.) To disable it, start Real Player and open the configuration dialog box. Disable the **Start Center** option, and click **OK** when you're done. Note that older versions of Real Player may have different procedures for disabling this icon.
- To remove additional tray icons, see Appendix A.

Add your own programs to the tray

1. Obtain and install the Tray utility (download it from *http://www.annoyances.org*).
2. Run *Tray.exe*, right-click on the new icon in the tray, and select **Help** for instructions.

If you remove the yellow speaker, you can still adjust the volume with the Volume Control utility included with Windows, as well with the volume control on your speakers (if applicable). Removing the flashing modem icon will not have any effect on modem performance or Dial-Up Networking functionality.

If you turn off the clock and remove all tray icons, the tray will disappear completely, providing more space for taskbar tasks. It will reappear when any tray icon is added.

Customize Drive and Folder Icons

There may come a time when you may get a little sick of the generic icons used for drives and folders in My Computer and Explorer. Now, you've probably figured out that you can create a shortcut to any drive or folder, choose a pretty icon, and place it on the desktop or in a convenient folder. Unfortunately, the icon isn't reflected anywhere else in Windows, such as in Explorer or My Computer. Here's how to make the change a little more universal as shown in Figure 2-6.

Figure 2-6. Make Explorer and My Computer less drab by customizing drive and folder icons

Solution 1: Customize drive icons

Using the functionality built in to Windows Me's CD-ROM Autoinsert Notification feature (see "Curb CD and DVD Autorun" later in this chapter)—functionality that allows Windows to determine the name and icon of a CD as soon as it's inserted in the reader—there's a simple way to customize the icons of drives other than CD readers:

1. Open a plain-text editor, such as Notepad.
2. Type the following:

```
[autorun]
icon=filename, number
```

   where ***`filename`*** is the name of the file containing the icon, and ***`number`*** is the index of the icon to use (leave ***`number`*** blank or specify `0` [zero] to use the first icon in the file, `1` for the second, and so on).

3. Save the file in the root directory of the hard disk, floppy, or removable drive you wish to customize, naming it *Autorun.inf.*
4. With Explorer or the My Computer window open, press the **F5** key to refresh the display and read the new icons (Figure 2-7).

Solution 2: Customize folder icons

The icon for any individual folder can be customized to suit your taste:

1. Open a plain-text editor, such as Notepad.
2. Type the following:

```
[.ShellClassInfo]
IconFile=filename
IconIndex=number
```

   where ***`filename`*** is the name of the file containing the icon, and ***`number`*** is the index of the icon to use; leave the `IconIndex` line out or specify `0` (zero) to use the first icon in the file, `1` for the second, and so on. Note the dot (`.`) in `[.ShellClassInfo]`.

Figure 2-7. Customized Drive and Folder icons even show up in Explorer

3. Save the file directly in the folder you wish to customize, naming it *desktop.ini*.
4. Open a command-prompt window (*command.com*), and type the following at the prompt:

   ```
   attrib +s foldername
   ```

   where *`foldername`* is the full path of the folder containing the *desktop.ini* file (i.e., *c:\docs*). This command turns on the System attribute for the folder (not the *desktop.ini* file), something you can't do in Explorer. Close the command prompt window when you're done.
5. You'll have to close and reopen the Explorer or single-folder window to see the change (pressing **F5** won't do it).

If you're customizing a drive icon for a removable drive (i.e., Zip, CDR, floppies), you may need to refresh the My Computer or Explorer window every time the media is inserted by pressing the **F5** key, because Windows can only detect the insertion of CDs and DVDs, and then only when the autoinsert notification feature is enabled.

To turn the display of certain drive icons on or off in the My Computer window, use the **My Computer** tab in TweakUI (see Appendix A for more information).

Turning on the System attribute for a folder (as instructed in "Solution 2: Customize folder icons") should have no effect on your system or any other applications.

Make the Control Panel More Accessible

The Control Panel is a virtual folder, which means that it looks and behaves like a normal folder, but it doesn't actually exist as a folder on your hard drive. That's why you can't rename or delete any of the Control Panel's contents, nor can you add items to it.

Using some of the features built into Windows Me to make virtual folders seem more like real folders, you can improve the usability of the Control Panel by making the parts of it you use more accessible.

Solution 1: Easy shortcuts to Control Panel icons

Creating a shortcut to an individual Control Panel icon is an easy way to provide quick access to commonly used settings. Solution 1 is fairly easy to do, but Solution 2, although more complicated, offers more flexibility:

1. Open the *Control Panel* folder in Explorer or the **Cascading Control Panel** menu in the **Start Menu**.
2. Drag any item onto your desktop or a waiting folder.
3. Windows will complain that it can't copy or move the item; confirm that you'll settle for a shortcut.
4. Double-click on the shortcut to access the respective dialog box.

Solution 2: Flexible shortcuts to Control Panel applets

Many Control Panel applets have multiple tabs, each with its own collection of settings and sub-dialog boxes. Anything you can do to decrease the steps in a repetitive task can be helpful. Here's how to make a shortcut to a particular tab of a particular dialog box:

1. Right-click in an empty area of your desktop or an open folder window, select **New**, then select **Shortcut**.
2. In the field labeled **Type the location of the item** (they're really looking for the name of the item, not just the location), type:

   ```
   control.exe sysdm.cpl, System, 1
   ```

   This command has four parts. The first, **`control.exe`**, is the executable that opens the Control Panel. The second, **`sysdm.cpl`**, is the Control Panel module you'd like to open. The third, **`System`**, is the name of the dialog box, used only with modules that have multiple dialog boxes (it's optional otherwise). Finally, **`1`** is the tab you want initially selected (**`0`** is the first, **`1`** is the second, and so on).

   The command in this example opens the second tab of the System dialog box, which happens to be the Device Manager. Table 2-2 shows all the available Control Panel modules and the dialog boxes for which they are responsible. Simply substitute the desired filename and dialog box name in the previous command to customize it.*

3. Click **Next**, type whatever you like for the name of this shortcut, and click **Finish** when you're done.
4. To make any changes or to choose an icon for the shortcut, right-click on the shortcut and select **Properties**.

Table 2-2. Each Control Panel Module Has an Associated Filename (Virtual Folders Not Included)

Description	Filename, Dialog Box Name (If Needed)
Accessibility Options	*access.cpl*
Add/Remove Hardware Wizard	*hdwwiz.cpl*
Add/Remove Programs	*appwiz.cpl*
Date/Time Properties	*timedate.cpl*
Display Properties	*desk.cpl*
Fax Properties	*fax.cpl*
Game Controllers	*joy.cpl*
Internet Properties	*inetcpl.cpl*
Keyboard	*main.cpl*, keyboard
Mouse Properties	*main.cpl*
Network and Dial-up Connections	*ncpa.cpl*
ODBC Data Source Administrator	*odbccp32.cpl*
Phone and Modem Properties	*telephon.cpl*
Power Options Properties	*powercfg.cpl*
Regional Options	*intl.cpl*
Scanners and Cameras Properties	*sticpl.cpl*
Sounds and Multimedia Properties	*mmsys.cpl*
System Properties	*sysdm.cpl*
Users and Passwords	*userpasswords* (no extension)
Wireless Link Properties	*irprops.cpl*

Solution 3: Remove unwanted Control Panel icons

1. Double-click on the **TweakUI** icon (see Appendix A) in Control Panel, and choose the **Control Panel** tab.
2. Uncheck any entries you'd prefer weren't displayed in the Control Panel, and click **OK** when you're done.

* Not all modules respond to the numbered tab, as you might expect; you'll need to employ some trial-and-error to get the desired results.

3. Your changes will take effect immediately in the *Control Panel* folder, but you'll need to log out and log back in to see the change in the Control Panel menu in the Start Menu.

Solution 4: Add a cascading Control Panel menu to the Start Menu

1. Open the **Start Menu**, select **Settings** and then **Taskbar and Start Menu**, and choose the **Advanced** tab.
2. In the list of settings at the bottom of the window, turn on the **Expand Control Panel** option, and click **OK** when you're done.

   Now, instead of a single menu item inside the Start Menu's **Settings** menu, all the Control Panel icons will be listed individually. Unfortunately, Windows ignores the **Scroll Programs** option when displaying this new menu, so if there are too many Control Panel icons, they'll simply go off the screen.

Solution 5: Make a custom Control Panel menu

This last solution produces similar results to Solution 4, but has the following advantages. It's in the top level of the Start Menu, so you don't have to open another menu (e.g., **Settings**) before you see it. Also, you can easily add new items, such as the Volume Control (*sndvol32.exe*), remove unwanted items, and configure the various icons to open more frequently used tabs (as described in Solution 2):

1. Open Explorer and a separate Control Panel window, and place them side by side on your screen.
2. In Explorer, navigate to the *\Windows\Start Menu* folder, and make a new folder inside it called *Control Panel.*
3. Select some or all of the icons in Control Panel, and drag them into this new folder in Explorer. Confirm that you want to make shortcuts to the selected items. Windows will make a shortcut to each icon you drop into the folder, some of which you may want to rename. A new cascading menu will appear in your Start Menu, similar to the existing Control Panel menu under **Settings**, yet placed conveniently above the Programs menu.

Additional Control Panel modules that may have been added by a third-party application or Microsoft add-on are not included in Table 2-2. Furthermore, any subsequent icons added to your Control Panel will not appear in your custom Control Panel (Solution 5) until you create shortcuts for them manually.

Virtual folders are also discussed in "Change the Icons of System Objects" in Chapter 4, as well as in Appendix C.

Customize the Startup Screen

Given that you can spend up to a minute each day staring at the huge Windows Me logo as Windows loads all your drivers and settings, it's probably worth a few minutes to replace it with something at least somewhat attractive. Here's how you do it:

1. The images Windows displays while it's loading and shutting down are simply bitmaps stored on your hard disk. These files are hidden by default, so you'll need to configure Explorer to show hidden files if it doesn't already. Select **Folder Options** from Explorer's **View** menu, choose the **View** tab, select the **Show hidden files and folders** option, and click **OK** when you're done.

2. The startup logo is actually embedded in the file *io.sys*, which is located in the root folder of your boot drive (usually *c:*); Windows uses this standard logo unless it finds the file *Logo.sys* in the same folder. In that case, the *Logo.sys* file (a standard windows bitmap file that has been renamed) is used instead.

   You'll also find the two shutdown logos ("Please wait while . . ." and "It is now safe . . .") in your *Windows* folder, named *Logow.sys* and *Logos.sys*, respectively.

   Make duplicates of your existing logo files in case you want to revert to the default logos at any time. To revert the startup logo to the default, just delete *Logo.sys*.

3. If you want to modify any of the existing files, as opposed to creating new ones from scratch, make copies of them and rename their file extensions to *.bmp*.

4. You can use almost any modern graphics editor to edit bitmap files, such as *MS Paint, Paint Shop Pro* (*http://www.jasc.com*), or my favorite, *Adobe Photoshop* (*http://www.adobe.com*).

   The specifications of the logo files are as follows: **256-color** (8-bit) Windows bitmaps (RGB Windows-encoded, but *not* "RGB mode" for you Photoshop users) and **320×400** pixels in size. Because the aspect ratio (width divided by height) of these files is not the standard 4:3, like most computer screens, the bitmaps will appear vertically elongated in your graphics program, but will be squeezed vertically and will look fine when they're actually used.

To make things a little easier, you'll probably want to work with files that aren't elongated and then squeeze them when you're done. Start by creating new images with these pixel dimensions: **534×400**—if you're modifying the original logos, you can just resize them to these dimensions while you're working on them. Refer to the documentation for the graphics program you're using for details on choosing an image size and resizing an existing image.

You can use scanned photos or images off the Web or make your own logos from scratch. I leave the creative part of this solution in your hands.

5. When you're done making your logos, resize them to **320×400** pixels (you may have to turn off your graphics application's "Maintain Aspect Ratio" feature, or whatever it may be called) and save. If the dimensions are incorrect or if you're not using the correct number of colors, the screens won't work.
6. When you're done, rename the extensions of your new files from *.bmp* back to *.sys* and move them to their proper locations, as described earlier. You may want to back up your work at this point, because subsequent Windows updates may overwrite your logos at any time.

For best results, you might want to convert the images to 24-bit mode (RGB mode in Photoshop) after you open them. That way, when they're resized, the edges will be smoothed. Just before you save, convert the images back to 256-color mode (indexed, 8-bit mode in Photoshop).

You can turn off the display of the startup logo altogether with TweakUI—see Appendix A for details. If your machine reboots instead of shutting down when these logos are replaced, make sure the bitmaps are not corrupted, and use no more than 256 colors.

Curb CD and DVD Autorun

Autorun is a feature intended to make using CDs in Windows easier for inexperienced users, but ends up just irritating many regular Windows users.* Autorun is responsible for starting an audio or data CD the moment it is inserted into your CD drive. If you did not intend to start the CD right away, then you're forced to wait until Windows loads the Autorun application before you can close it and continue with your work.

* Autorun, originally introduced in Windows 95, has the distinction of being the very first Windows Annoyance I wrote about. It took me about five minutes after installing my prerelease version of Windows 95 to get sick of it.

The Autorun feature works by polling the CD drive every few seconds to see if a CD has been inserted. If Windows detects a CD that wasn't there a few seconds ago, it reads the label of the disk and looks for a file called *Autorun.inf* in the CD's root directory. *Autorun.inf* usually contains two pieces of information: a reference to an icon file (for display, along with the CD label, in My Computer and Explorer) and a reference to an Autorun application.* If an Autorun application is specified, Windows proceeds to run the program, which is usually a large, brightly colored window with links to the application's setup program, documentation, and the manufacturer's web site and, hopefully, an Exit button. If, instead, Windows detects an audio CD, the configured CD player is opened and instructed to play the first audio track.

What's worse is that even after all this has happened, the Autorun process starts over again if you double-click on the CD icon in your My Computer window—contrary, of course, to the normal folder window that one would expect to see. You can get around this on a disk-by-disk basis by right-clicking on the disk icon and selecting **Open** or by using Explorer and opening the CD drive from the folder tree.

Naturally, there's no setting provided in the standard Windows interface to make it easy to curb this feature. Here's how you do it:

Disable Autorun

This solution allows you to easily turn off Autorun for CD-ROMs and audio CDs without losing Explorer's ability to automatically identify a disk when it is inserted.

1. Double-click on the **TweakUI** icon (see Appendix A) in Control Panel, and choose the rather ambiguously named **Paranoia** tab.
2. Uncheck the **Play audio CDs automatically** and **Play data CDs automatically** options as desired.

   For those of you with DVD drives, the data CD setting applies to data DVDs (DVD-ROMs) as well. For DVD movies, you'll have to use the "Disable CD and DVD polling" solution.

   The "Disable CD and DVD polling" solution, described later, should also explain the "(Requires AutoInsert Notification enabled)" message on the TweakUI window.
3. Click **OK** when you're done; the change should take effect immediately.

---

* See "Customize Drive and Folder Icons" earlier in this chapter for another solution that uses the *Autorun.inf* file.

If you disable the Autorun feature for data CDs, the Autorun application on any given CD will obviously not run automatically. Fortunately, it's easy to run the setup application or any other application on the CD manually. To do this, right-click on the drive icon in Explorer, and select **AutoPlay**. Alternatively, you can open the root directory of the CD drive in Explorer—on most data CDs that contain software, you'll see something like *Setup.exe* or *Autorun.exe*. Double-click the file to run it. Sometimes, however, the Autorun application file is not obvious, in which case, you can open the *Autorun.inf* file and look at the line that begins with open=. If you don't see an *Autorun.inf* file in the root directory of the CD, it doesn't support the Autorun feature.

You can also hold the **Shift** key while inserting a disk to temporarily prevent the Autorun application from being executed, but this often means holding **Shift** for 10–20 seconds while Windows reads the disk.

Disable CD and DVD polling

The TweakUI solution described earlier disables the Autorun feature, but it doesn't turn off the repetitive polling (reading) of the CD drive, as explained at the beginning of this section. The problem with the polling feature is that inserting a disk can cause Explorer to refresh itself one or more times, which can be frustratingly slow on some systems. Additionally, those using a CD writer will need to turn this off so that the repeated polling doesn't interrupt the CD recording process. This solution will turn off the polling of your CD or DVD drive completely:

1. Double-click on the **System** icon in Control Panel, and choose the **Device Manager** tab.
2. Expand the **CD-ROM** branch, and select the entry corresponding to your CD or DVD drive. If you have more than one CD drive, you'll most likely want to do this for each drive. If you have a CD changer, you'll see a different drive listed here for each disk the changer holds; likewise, you'll want to do this for each one that shows up.
3. Click **Properties**, and then choose the **Settings** tab.
4. Turn off the **Auto insert notification** option.
5. Click **OK**, then click **OK** again. You'll have to restart Windows for this change to take effect.

This solution has the added effect of preventing Windows from automatically updating your CD icon in Explorer with the label and icon of a newly inserted disk. To refresh Explorer manually, press the **F5** key.

Choose the Autorun audio CD player

The Autorun application for a data CD is located on the CD itself. However, because audio CDs don't contain files, the default audio CD player is a sole application, stored on your hard disk, used for all audio CDs. Here's how to configure the default audio CD player:

1. Select **Folder Options** from Explorer's **View** menu (or double-click the **Folder Options** icon in Control Panel), and choose the **File Types** tab.
2. Sort the list of registered file types by clicking on the **File Types** column header. Select **AudioCD** from the list (it will say **N/A** in the Extension column), and click **Advanced**.*
3. Select **Play** from the **Actions** list and click **Edit**.

   If the **Play** action isn't there, there's no default CD player—you'll have to add a new action by clicking **New** and typing **`Play`** for the name.
4. At this point, you can choose a new audio CD player application by typing its executable filename in the **Application used to perform action** field or by clicking **Browse**. The Windows Me default for this action is:

   ```
   "C:\Program Files\Windows Media Player\wmplayer.exe"
     /device:AudioCD "%L"
   ```

   Note that some CD player applications require special command-line parameters, such as `/play`, in order to start playing the disk automatically—refer to the application documentation for details.

   Click **OK** when you're done.
5. Next, highlight the **Play** entry in the **Action** list, and click **Set Default** so the word **Play** now appears in bold.
6. Click **OK** when you're done. The change should take effect immediately.

Naturally, you'll need to enable both Autorun for audio CD drives and **Auto insert notification** (see the two respective solutions, earlier) if you want to have audio CDs played automatically when they're inserted. If you disable Autorun completely, though, the default audio CD player setting still comes into play if you double-click the **CD** icon in My Computer.

* While you're at it, you may also want to perform this procedure for the CD Audio Track file type (CDA extension), which is what's used when you double-click on a single audio track when viewing the contents of an audio CD in Explorer.

See "Understanding File Types" in Chapter 3 and "Customize Context Menus" in Chapter 4 for more information on file types and the default action.

Regaining Control of the Desktop

Microsoft has, in terms of the interface, positioned the desktop as the root of all other objects in the imaginary hierarchy depicted by Explorer's tree. This includes all drives, the Control Panel, the Network Neighborhood, and even all running applications. The following topics cover some fundamental tasks when dealing with the desktop, such as refreshing the desktop and how to make sure your desktop configuration remains intact. For details on the Active Desktop and other Web integration topics, see Chapter 8.

Refresh the Desktop Without Restarting Windows

When Windows starts, it loads the Explorer application, which provides the desktop and the Start Menu. While it's loading, Explorer reads its settings from the Registry (see Chapter 3). If you make a change to the Registry, such as when following some of the procedures in this book, it might not take effect until you reload Explorer, which usually means restarting Windows. However, restarting Windows can take several minutes and will mean shutting down all applications and disconnecting your dial-up connection to the Internet (if applicable). In some cases you can put your changes into effect without restarting Windows, as outlined in the following solutions. Whether any of these solutions work depends on the type of setting you've changed.

Solution 1

Click on any empty area of your desktop or any icon on your desktop with the left mouse button, and press the **F5** key to refresh the desktop.*

Solution 2

In cases where Solution 1 is not sufficient to implement your changes, you can force Explorer to reload without restarting:

1. Press **Ctrl-Alt-Del** to display the **Close Program** dialog box.
2. Select **Explorer** from the list, and click **End Task**.

---

* The **F5** key can also be used to refresh any open folder or Explorer window.

3. You'll immediately see the **Shut Down Windows** dialog box; click **Cancel** at this point.
4. After about five seconds, Windows will inform you that it wasn't able to shut down the Explorer application. Click **End Task** here to finish the job. The taskbar and all desktop icons will disappear temporarily and then reappear as Explorer is reloaded.

This solution can cause your system tray to disappear and not come back. This shouldn't affect any applications with tray icons, but it may make them inaccessible. See "Customize the Tray" earlier in this chapter for details.

Solution 3

In cases where Solution 2 is not sufficient to implement your changes, the following will not only reload Explorer, but reinitialize all your user settings. Unfortunately, it will cause all your running applications to close, but it still doesn't take nearly as long as restarting:

1. Select **Log Off** *username* from the **Start Menu**, and click **OK**.

   If **Log Off** doesn't appear in the Start Menu, select **Settings** and then **Taskbar and Start Menu**. Choose the **Advanced** tab and turn on the **Display Logoff** option.
2. When the Enter Windows Password dialog box appears, enter your password (if any), and click **OK**. (Your username should already be entered in the **User name** field.)

Save Your Desktop Layout

After meticulously arranging all the icons on your desktop, you may find that Windows either rearranges them for no particular reason or simply forgets their latest positions the next time you start Windows. Sometimes a system crash is the cause; other times, it can do it right in front of you while you're staring at it.* Here are some workarounds:

- If you're unable to place the icons where you want on your desktop, autoarrange might be turned on. Right-click on an empty portion of the desktop, select **Arrange Icons**, and turn off the **Auto Arrange** option if it's checked.

* Windows seems to refresh the desktop under certain situations, such as when files are copied to or deleted from the desktop or when settings are changed in Explorer. There's no way to completely predict or control this behavior.

- If you've found that one or more icons are missing from the desktop, it could be that they're hidden under other icons. Right-click on an empty portion of the desktop, and select **Line Up Icons**. This will move all the icons on your desktop so that they are aligned with an invisible grid; by default, the grid spacing is 120×120 pixels.
- If you're also experiencing other settings being lost, such as taskbar settings or display colors, it may be that Windows is having a problem with your user profile. Logging out and then back in again should solve the problem. See "Solution 3" of "Refresh the Desktop Without Restarting Windows" earlier in this chapter for instructions on logging out and then logging back in.
- Obtain and install the EzDesk utility (download it from *http://www.annoyances.org*), which is able to save one or more desktop layouts and restore them at any time.
- Open Explorer, and navigate to the *\Windows\Desktop* folder. Right-click the Desktop folder (not the one at the top of the tree), and select **Properties**. Turn on the **Read-only** option, and click **OK**. This may not prevent Windows from rearranging desktop icons, but it will prevent most applications from cluttering your desktop with new ones. (In the unlikely event that this solution causes a setup program to fail, you may have to turn off the **Read-only** option to proceed.)

Fixing the Start Menu

It's unfortunate that so many of Windows Me's functions and components rely on the Start Menu, because it's such a flawed interface. You're forced to navigate through several levels of menus to get at your applications, the main reason you use a computer; the less useful entries, such as **Settings** and **Run**, are more prominent than any application. Also, any currently open menu can easily disappear if your mouse strays even a few millimeters.*

Now, one thing you can do is to rearrange items in the Start Menu, eliminating all the unnecessary levels and superfluous shortcuts. For example, instead of the Photoshop shortcut appearing in **Start → Programs → Adobe → Photoshop** (four levels deep), you can simply move the shortcut so it appears in the **Programs** menu. This isn't a great solution, but it's a good place to start.

* See "Stop Menus from Following the Mouse" earlier in this chapter for a solution.

Sorting Start Menu items

A consequence of being able to drag-drop Start Menu items in place is that new items are added to the ends of menus, rather than sorted alphabetically with the existing entries. To manually resort any single menu in the Start Menu, right-click on any menu item, and select **Sort by Name**. To sort all your Start Menu folders in one step, you'll need to write a script: see "Wacky Script Ideas" in Chapter 9, *Scripting and Automation*, for details.

Choose scrolling menus or multiple columns

In Windows 98, Microsoft made a change to the way large Start Menu folders were displayed, scrolling them vertically rather than displaying them in multiple columns. Unfortunately, this caused a public outcry among those users who had upgraded from Windows 95 and preferred the old method. In Windows Me, Microsoft has given us the option. Choose **Settings** and then **Taskbar and Start Menu** from the Start Menu, choose the **Advanced** tab, and change the **Scroll Programs** option to your liking. Naturally, another workaround is simply to distribute your Start Menu shortcuts to eliminate menus that are too large.

The curse of personalized menus

One of the biggest flaws in the Start Menu is a new feature called *personalized menus*. This remarkably awful feature made its debut in Microsoft Office 2000 and, unfortunately, has found its way into the operating system.* It's a design by which certain Start Menu entries are indiscriminately and suddenly hidden, flying in the face of one of the most important rules in user-interface design: don't change the interface from one usage to the next. Luckily, it's easy to turn off:

1. Open the **Start Menu**, select **Settings** and then **Taskbar and Start Menu**, and choose the **General** tab.
2. Turn off the **Use personalized menus** option, and click **OK** when you're done.

* In Microsoft Office 2000, the personalized menus feature is also easily disabled. Right-click on the menu or toolbar in any Office application (Word, Excel, etc.), and select **Customize**. Choose the **Options** tab, and turn off the **Menus show recently used commands first** option.

Remove unwanted Start Menu components

Some of the intrinsic items in the Start Menu can be selectively disabled, either to reduce clutter or to implement some level of security on a Windows Me system (for more information on TweakUI or the System Policy Editor, see Appendix A):

Documents
: Double-click on the **TweakUI** icon in Control Panel, choose the **IE4** tab, and turn off the **Show Documents on Start Menu** option.

Favorites
: Double-click on the **TweakUI** icon in Control Panel, choose the **IE4** tab, and turn off the **Show Favorites on Start Menu** option.

Find
: Open the System Policy Editor, and select **Open Registry** from the **File** menu. Double-click on **Local User**, then expand the branches to *\Windows 98 System\Shell\Restrictions*, and turn on the **Remove 'Find' command** option.

Run
: Open the System Policy Editor, and select **Open Registry** from the **File** menu. Double-click on **Local User**, then expand the branches to *\Windows 98 System\Shell\Restrictions*, and turn on the **Remove 'Run' command** option.

  Another option is to right-click on an empty area of the taskbar, select **Properties**, and then choose the **Advanced** tab. Turn off the **Display Run** option, and click **OK** when you're done.

Folder Options (in Settings)
: Open the System Policy Editor, and select **Open Registry** from the **File** menu. Double-click on **Local User**, then expand the branches to *\Windows 98 System\Shell\Restrictions*, and turn on the **Remove folders from 'Settings' on Start Menu** option.

Shut Down (disable only)
: Open the System Policy Editor, and select **Open Registry** from the **File** menu. Double-click on **Local User**, then expand the branches to *\Windows 98 System\Shell\Restrictions*, and turn on the **Disable Shut Down command** option.

Logoff {username}

Right-click on an empty area of the taskbar, select **Properties**, and then choose the **Advanced** tab. Turn off the **Display Run** option, and click **OK** when you're done.

Taskbar & Start Menu (in Settings)

Open the System Policy Editor, and select **Open Registry** from the **File** menu. Double-click on **Local User**, then expand the branches to *\Windows 98 System\Shell\Restrictions*, and turn on the **Remove Taskbar from 'Settings' on Start Menu** option.

Alternatives to the Start Menu

The best thing about the Start Menu is that you don't have to use it. You can start programs by opening associated documents, double-clicking shortcuts on the desktop, or any number of other means:

- Although the desktop is certainly not a great place to store a shortcut to every program on your computer, it's a prime location for the most frequently used programs. If you only use your computer for a handful of applications, you can move all your Start Menu shortcuts directly onto the desktop (hold the **Ctrl** key to copy) and forget about the Start Menu entirely.

  The problem is that Windows will rearrange the items on your desktop frequently and without reason (see "Save Your Desktop Layout" earlier in this chapter). In addition, there can be a clutter problem if you also use your desktop for current documents.

- As a partial fix for the inaccessibility of items in the Start Menu, Windows Me has configurable, dockable toolbars. Like the Start Menu, these toolbars just reflect the contents of one or more folders on your hard disk. By placing icons for your most frequently used applications, folders, and documents in these tiny toolbars, you can make it easier and quicker to open the tasks you need. You can drag toolbars anywhere on the screen, docking them to the taskbar or any other edge of your desktop.

  To display one of the preconfigured toolbars, right-click on an empty area of the taskbar, select **Toolbar**, and choose the one you want (choose **New Toolbar** to make a new one). In addition to the **Address** and **Links** toolbars normally found in Internet Explorer (see Chapter 8 and Appendix B), there's a **Desktop** toolbar that mirrors the contents of your desktop (good for when the desktop is covered by other windows), and the customizable Quick Launch bar.* Select **New Toolbar** to make a new, blank toolbar.

The problem with these toolbars is their inflexibility; they can contain shortcuts and nothing else. See the rest of this section for a better alternative.

- Keyboard shortcuts are a convenient way to supplement whatever scheme you decide to use. Just right-click on any shortcut file, Start Menu entry, or taskbar toolbar icon, and select **Properties**. Click in the **Shortcut key** field, and press the desired keystroke combination. For example, you can set up **Ctrl-Shift-E** to open an Explorer window.
- To shut down windows without having to open the Start Menu, click on an empty area of the desktop, and press **Alt-F4**.
- There's nothing stopping you from using another program to augment or replace the Start Menu. In fact, I urge you to explore alternatives to all of the components Microsoft puts in the box, including Notepad, Outlook Express, and Internet Explorer. See *http://www.annoyances.org* for more third-party software.

  Start with *Route 1 Pro*, which will run on any version of Windows. It implements one or more simple rows of buttons providing quick access to all your programs and files. Its operation is much slicker and more flexible than either the Start Menu or the taskbar toolbars mentioned earlier. If you're looking for a better primary interface for Windows, it may suit your needs. A free download is available at *http://www.creativelement.com/software/route1.html.*

* The folder containing the Quick Launch shortcuts is *c:\Windows\Application Data\Microsoft\Internet Explorer\Quick Launch*. However, when you create a new toolbar, the folder can be located anywhere—odds are you want to put it somewhere more convenient.

3

The Registry

Whenever you change your system colors, install an application, or change a setting in Control Panel, the relevant information is stored in your Registry. The Registry is a database of all the settings for Windows Me, as well as the applications installed on your system. Knowing how to use the Registry effectively is important for improving performance in Windows, troubleshooting all kinds of problems, and, most importantly, customizing Windows Me beyond what is possible with the dialog boxes scattered throughout the interface.

All of your file types (also known as associations; see "Customize Context Menus" in Chapter 4, *Tinkering Techniques*) are stored in the Registry, as well as all of the network, hardware, and software settings for Windows Me and all of the particular configuration options for most of the software you've installed. The particular settings and data stored by each of your applications and by the various Windows components vary substantially, but you can use some special techniques to figure out undocumented settings and uncover hidden functionality. What's especially helpful is that most of the settings stored in the Registry are named in plain English rather than with obscure codes and acronyms. You shouldn't take this fact for granted, but it does help quite a bit in finding settings and troubleshooting problems.

Word to the wise: you can irreversibly disable certain components of Windows Me—or even prevent Windows from running—by changing some settings in the Registry. This is intended to scare you, so that you will use caution when editing the Registry and take appropriate measures to prevent catastrophe. Now, of course, the world will not come to an end if you inadvertently change a zero to a one in some obscure Registry key; most of the Registry settings are benign. The worst that will happen is that you might give yourself an enormous headache when you try to remember which setting you changed that disabled your Internet connection or caused Windows to create a folder called "Bubba" on your desktop every time you start your computer. That said, you can virtually eliminate the possibility of disaster by utilizing the systems in place for safeguarding the Registry, as described in "Backing Up the Registry" later in this chapter. Furthermore, backing up your *entire system* will ensure that none of your valuable data or programs are compromised and will undoubtedly save you hours of hassle in the event of a stupid mistake. Believe me, I've been there.

Getting to Know the Registry Editor

Although the Registry is stored in multiple files on your hard disk, it is represented by a single logical hierarchical structure, similar to the folders on your hard disk. The Registry Editor (*regedit.exe*, located in your *Windows* folder) is included with Windows Me to enable you to view and manually edit the contents of the Registry. Most of the access to the Registry is performed behind the scenes by the applications that you run, as well as by Windows—settings and other information are read from and written to the Registry constantly.

When you open the Registry Editor, you'll see a window divided into two panes (see Figure 3-1). The left side shows a tree with folders, and the right side shows the contents of the currently selected folder. Now, these aren't really folders—it's just a convenient and familiar method of organizing and displaying the information stored in your Registry files.

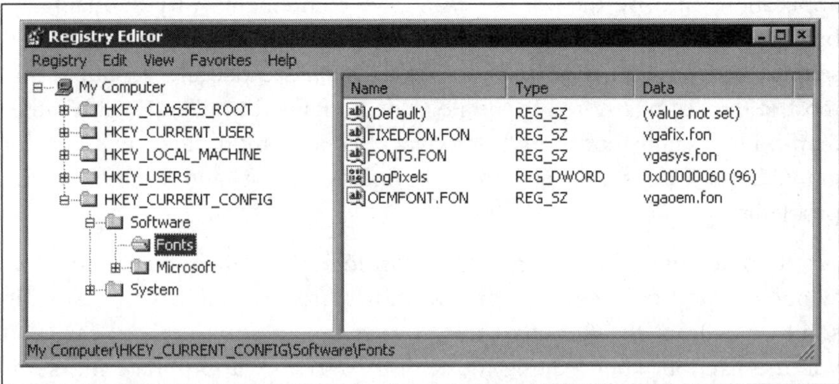

Figure 3-1. The Registry Editor lets you view and change the contents of the Registry

Each branch (denoted by a folder icon in the Registry Editor) is called a *key*. Each key can contain other keys, as well as *values*. Values contain the actual information stored in the Registry, and keys are used only to organize the values. Keys are shown only in the left pane; values are shown only in the right pane (unlike Explorer, where folders are shown in both panes).

To display the contents of a key (folder), just click the desired key name on the left, and the values contained therein will be listed on the right side. To expand a certain branch to show its subkeys, click on the plus sign [+] to the left of any folder or double-click on the folder name.

Editing the Registry generally involves navigating down through branches to a particular key and then modifying an existing value or creating a new key or value. You can modify the contents of any value by double-clicking on it.

To add a new key or value, select **New** from the **Edit** menu, select what you want to add, and then type a name. You can rename any existing value and *almost* any key with the same method used to rename files in Explorer: right-click on an object and click **Rename**, click on it twice (slowly), or just highlight it and press the **F2** key. Lastly, you can delete a key or value by clicking on it and pressing the **Del** key or by right-clicking on it and selecting **Delete**. Note, however, that you can't drag-drop keys or values as you can with files in Explorer.*

You can search for text in key and value names as the contents of values by selecting **Find** from the **Edit** menu. See "Search the Registry Effectively" later in this chapter for tips on using this deceptively simple function. Lastly, select **Refresh** from the **View** menu to refresh the displayed portion of the Registry, in case another running application has changed, added, or removed a key or value since the Registry Editor last read the data.

Similar to Explorer, though, is the notion of a *path*. A Registry path is a location in the Registry described by the series of nested keys in which a setting is located. For example, if a particular value is in the `Microsoft` key under `SOFTWARE`, which is under `HKEY_LOCAL_MACHINE`, the Registry path would be `HKEY_LOCAL_MACHINE\SOFTWARE\Microsoft`. Elsewhere in this book, when a setting is changed in the Registry, this type of Registry path is always given. If you find that you're returning to the same

* There is very little reason to drag a key or value from one place to another in the Registry. The exception is when you want to duplicate a key and all its contents (such as a File Type key). See "Using Registry Patches" and "Understanding File Types," both later in this chapter, for more information.

Registry path often, you can use the **Favorites** menu to bookmark the item, allowing you to return to it easily (similarly to the operation of the Favorites menu in Internet Explorer).

There are five primary, or "root," branches, each containing a specific portion of the information stored in the Registry. These root keys can't be deleted, renamed, or moved, because they are the basis for the organization of the Registry. They are:

`HKEY_CLASSES_ROOT`

This branch contains the information that comprises your Windows file types. See "Understanding File Types" later in this chapter for details on the structure of most of the entries in this branch. A few special keys here, such as `CLSID` (short for *Class ID*; see Appendix C, *Class IDs of System Objects*), contain all registered components of your installed applications. The contents of `HKEY_CLASSES_ROOT` are generally easy to edit, but it's best not to mess with anything in the `CLSID` branch, because almost none of it is in plain English.

This entire branch is a symbolic link,* or "mirror," of `HKEY_LOCAL_MACHINE\SOFTWARE\Classes`, but is displayed separately in this branch for clarity and easy access.

`HKEY_USERS`

This branch contains a sub-branch named for the currently logged-in user; in most cases, it will simply contain one branch called `.default`.

In each user's branch are the settings for that user, such as Control Panel settings and Explorer preferences. Most applications store user-specific information here as well, such as toolbars, high scores for games, and other personal settings.

The `HKEY_CURRENT_USER` branch (see later in this list) is another symbolic link, or "mirror," of the branch belonging to the currently logged-in user. Because only one user can be logged in at any given time and Windows loads only the currently logged-in user, only one branch will ever be shown here. For this reason, you should find very little reason to visit this particular branch.

* A symbolic link is different from a Windows shortcut you'd find on your hard disk. Information in a linked branch appears twice and can be accessed at two different locations, even though it's stored only once. This means that Find may stop in both places if they contain something you're looking for and, as you might expect, changes in one place will be immediately reflected in the mirrored location.

HKEY_CURRENT_USER

This branch simply points to a portion of HKEY_USERS, signifying the currently logged-in user. This way, any application can read and write settings for the current user without having to know which user is currently logged on.

The settings for the current user are divided into several categories; among them are AppEvents, Control Panel, Identities, Printers, Network, RemoteAccess, and Software. The most useful of these branches, Software, contains a branch for almost every application installed on your computer, arranged by manufacturer. Here and in HKEY_LOCAL_MACHINE\SOFTWARE (see later in this list) are all of your application settings. You'll find most Windows settings under, of course, the Microsoft branch.

HKEY_LOCAL_MACHINE

This branch contains information about all of the hardware and software installed on your computer that *isn't* specific to the currently logged-in user.

The sub-branch of interest here is the SOFTWARE branch, which contains all of the information specific to the applications installed on your computer. Both this branch and HKEY_CURRENT_USER\Software (see earlier in this list) are used to store application-specific information. Those settings that are specific to each user (even if your computer has only one user), such as toolbar configurations, are stored in the HKEY_CURRENT_USER branch; those settings that are not user-independent, such as installation folders, are stored in the HKEY_LOCAL_MACHINE branch. You'll want to look in both places if you're trying to find a particular application setting, because most manufacturers (even Microsoft) aren't too careful about which branch is used for any given setting.

HKEY_CURRENT_CONFIG

This branch is a symbolic link, or "mirror," of HKEY_LOCAL_MACHINE\SYSTEM\CurrentControlSet, which, in turn, is a symbolic link of another branch (usually ControlSet001), corresponding to the currently selected hardware profile. There's little reason to mess with this branch.

You'll also see a sixth root branch, called HKEY_DYN_DATA. The DYN stands for dynamic, which means the data represented therein is not statically stored on the hard disk as is most of the rest of the Registry. This particular branch is used by Windows for Plug-and-Play (PnP) administration; it is of very little interest to most users.

The Meat of the Registry: Values

The Registry contains several types of values, each appropriate to the type of data they are intended to hold. There are seven types of values that are displayed in the Registry Editor, each of which is known by two different names (see Table 3-1).* Each type is known by two different names, the common name and the symbolic name (shown in parenthesis).

Table 3-1. Value Types Visible in the Registry Editor

Value Type	Icon Used in RegEdit	Can Be Created in RegEdit?
String (REG_SZ)		Yes
String Array (REG_MULTI_SZ)		No
Expanded String (REG_EXPAND_SZ)		No
Binary (REG_BINARY)		Yes
DWORD (REG_DWORD)		Yes
DWORD (REG_DWORD_BIGENDIAN)		No
Resource List (REG_RESOURCE_LIST, REG_RESOURCE_REQUIREMENTS_LIST, or FULL_RESOURCE_DESCRIPTOR)		No

Although the Registry Editor allows you to view and edit all seven types of values, it only allows you to create three basic types: *String*, *Binary*, and *DWORD*. It's not a coincidence that these three types are not only the most common, but the most useful; you'll find little reason to ever create the other available types:

String values

String values contain *strings* of characters, more commonly known as text. Most values of interest to us are string values; they're the easiest to edit and are usually in plain English. In addition to standard strings, there are two far less common string variants, used for special purposes:

String array value

Contains several strings, concatenated (glued) together and separated by null characters. You can't create these in the Registry Editor, but you can edit them.

* Another type of value, known as REG_LINK, is invisible in the Registry Editor. It facilitates symbolic links; the HKEY_CURRENT_USER branch, discussed earlier in this chapter, is an example.

Expanded string value

Contains special variables, into which Windows substitutes information before delivering to the owning application. For example, an expanded string value intended to point to a sound file may contain `%SystemRoot%\media\doh.wav`. When Windows reads this value from the Registry, it substitutes the full Windows path for the variable, `%SystemRoot%`; the resulting data then becomes (depending on where Windows is installed) `c:\windows\media\doh.wav`. This way, the value data is correct regardless of the location of the Windows folder. You can't create these in the Registry Editor, but you can edit them.

Binary values

Similarly to string values, binary values hold strings of characters. The difference is the way the data is entered. Instead of a standard text box, binary data is entered with hexadecimal codes in an interface commonly known as a *hex editor*. Each individual character is specified by a two-digit number in base-16 (e.g., 6E is 110 in base 10), which allows characters not found on the keyboard to be entered. See Figure 3-2 for an example. Note that you can type hex codes on the left or normal ASCII characters on the right, depending on where you click with the mouse.

Binary values are often not represented by plain English and, therefore, should be left unchanged unless you either understand the contents or are instructed to do so by a solution in this book. Note also the various Resource List value types (see Table 3-1), which are similar to binary values. You'll find very little reason to ever mess with these.

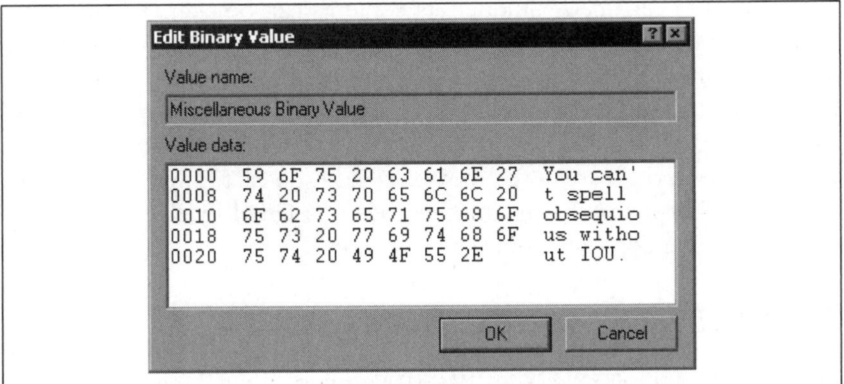

Figure 3-2. Binary values are entered differently from the common string values, but the contents are sometimes nearly as readable

DWORD values

Essentially, a DWORD is a number. Often, the contents of a DWORD value are easily understood, such as `0` for no and `1` for yes, or `60` for the number of seconds in some timeout setting. A DWORD value would be used where only numerical digits are allowed; string and binary types allow anything.

In some circumstances, the particular number entered into a DWORD value is actually made up of several components, called bytes. The REG_DWORD_BIGENDIAN type is a variant of the DWORD type, where the bytes are in a different order. Unless you're a programmer, you'll want to stay away from these types of DWORD values.

You can create a value (or key) anywhere in the Registry and by any name and type that suits your fancy. However, unless Windows or an application is specifically designed to look for it, your addition will have absolutely no effect.

In most cases, editing the Registry involves modifying an existing value, rather than creating a new one. The application that created each value in the Registry solely determines the particular type and purpose of the value. In other words, no strict rules limit which types are used in which circumstances or how values are named. A programmer may choose to store, say, the high scores for some game in a binary value called `High Scores` or in a string value called `Lard Lad Donuts`.

An important thing to notice at this point is the string value at the top of the right pane of every key labeled `(default)`. The default value cannot be removed or renamed, although its contents can be changed; an empty default value is signified by **`value not set`**. In the more simplistic Registry found in Windows 3.1 and Windows NT 3.x, each key had only one value. Starting in Windows 95, a key can contain any number of values; the default value takes the place of the lone value from previous versions. In most cases, the default value doesn't have any special meaning, other than what might have been assigned by the programmer of the particular application that owns the key.

Behind the Scenes: Hives and DAT Files

`HKEY_USERS` and `HKEY_LOCAL_MACHINE` can be thought of as the only *true* root keys, because the Registry's three other root keys are simply symbolic links, or "mirrors," of different portions of the first two (see "Getting to Know the Registry Editor earlier in this chapter). This means that only these two branches actually need to be stored.

Like its predecessors, Windows Me stores the `HKEY_USERS` and `HKEY_LOCAL_MACHINE` branches in two files, *User.dat* and *System.dat*, respectively. On a single-user system, both files are located in your *Windows* folder; on a multiple-user system, the *User.dat* file for each configured user is stored in that user's personal folder. These files are all hidden, meaning that with Explorer's default settings, you won't be able to see or find them. To view hidden files, select **Folder Options** from Explorer's **View** menu, choose the **View** tab, select the **Show all files** option, and click **OK**.

Not all Registry data is stored on your hard disk, however. Some keys are *dynamic*, in that they are held only in memory and are forgotten when you shut down. An example of a dynamic branch is `HKEY_LOCAL_MACHINE\HARDWARE`, which is built up each time Windows is started (an artifact of Plug and Play). Only static (non-dynamic) branches are stored on your hard disk.

Knowing which files comprise the Registry is important only for backup and emergency recovery procedures (see "Backing Up the Registry" later) and for troubleshooting (and so you don't accidentally delete them). The storage mechanism is quite transparent to the Registry Editor and the applications that use the Registry; there's no reason to ever edit the hive files directly. If you want to migrate a key or a collection of keys from one computer to another, you should not try to copy the hive files. Instead, see "Using Registry Patches" later in this chapter for a more convenient procedure.

Backing Up the Registry

The Registry is stored in certain files (see "Behind the Scenes: Hives and DAT Files" earlier in this chapter) on your hard disk, so you can create a backup by simply copying the appropriate files to another location. Although your Registry is not likely to be small enough to fit on a single floppy, it will fit easily on a removable drive (recordable CD, Zip disk, etc.). In addition, most modern backup software, such as the Backup utility that comes with Windows, includes a feature to back up the Registry. It's always a good idea to exploit this functionality.

When you start Windows, the information in the Registry is loaded into memory. While Windows is running, some changes may not be physically written to the Registry files until you shut down your computer; others, such as those made by the Registry Editor, are usually written immediately. For this reason, if you've made any substantial changes to the contents of the Registry, you may want to restart Windows *before* backing up the Registry to ensure that the files on the disk reflect the most recent changes.

Remember, if you have more than one user configured, you'll want to include the *User.dat* file for *each* user in your backup.

Windows Me comes with the Registry Checker (a.k.a. ScanReg), a simple utility (introduced in Windows 98) that handles several Registry maintenance tasks, such as checking for errors, optimizing the files, and backing up the entire Registry every time Windows is started. This is especially useful, because a single application crash can crash Windows, which, in turn, can corrupt a Registry file, making it impossible to start Windows! See "Using the Windows Registry Checker" later in this chapter for details.

Quite simply, you can manually make duplicates of the appropriate Registry files at any time to effect a pretty good Registry backup; see "Make a Duplicate of a File or Folder" in Chapter 2, *Basic Explorer Coping Skills*, for details.

Although it's very useful and quite easy to make backups of the Registry in another location on your hard disk (which is what the Windows Registry Checker does), it certainly can't prepare your computer for an actual disaster. If your hard disk crashes or gets infected with a virus or if your computer is stolen or is dropped out of a seven-story building,* those Registry backups on your hard disk won't do you much good. The most effective Registry backup is simply a matter of making a copy of all hives on your hard disk and keeping that copy somewhere other than inside your computer. If you back up your entire system regularly, such as to a tape drive or other backup device, you should ensure that the backup software you use specifically supports safeguarding the Registry. See Chapter 6, *Troubleshooting*, for more information on backing up and using backup devices.

One useful shortcut is a *local backup*, similar (conceptually) to a local anesthetic. If you plan on modifying a specific value or key, it's wise to back up just that key, because restoring it in the event of a problem is much less of a hassle than restoring the entire Registry. See "Using Registry Patches" later in this chapter for details.

If you don't already back up your entire system regularly, you should make a habit of backing up your Registry at least once a week, because it can save you hours of work if your system should fail.

* Any number of stories will do.

Using the Windows Registry Checker

The Registry Checker (a.k.a. ScanReg) is a simple utility that handles several Registry maintenance tasks. Windows automatically runs ScanReg at startup, at which time it makes a backup of the Registry files, checks them for errors, and, if needed, optimizes them.

Although ScanReg runs automatically and transparently, you can also manually check and back up the Registry at any time. Although this "interactive" mode isn't strictly necessary, it does let you perform a Registry backup or check for errors without having to restart Windows and test new configuration options (see later in this section).

You won't find the Registry Checker on the Start Menu; to run ScanReg manually, select **Run** from the Start Menu and type **`scanregw.exe`**. There's also a DOS version (*Scanreg.exe*), but if you try to run it from within Windows, it'll switch you to its Windows sibling automatically.

ScanReg maintains, by default, five separate backups of your Registry files, as well as some other important system files, including *Win.ini* and *System.ini*. It compresses the backups into, by default, five separate *.cab* files,* named *rb000.cab*, *rb001.cab*, and so on. Any Registry backups in which ScanReg has detected corruption will, however, be stored in *Rbbad.cab*.

You'll have to check the file dates for the most recent backup (view the files in Explorer's Details view, or type **`DIR`** if you're in DOS), because their numbers aren't a reliable indicator of their age. The *.cab* backup files are located in the hidden *\Windows\sysbckup* folder; you'll see this folder if you've configured Windows to display hidden files (see earlier in this section).

You can configure how many simultaneous backups are kept by editing the *Scanreg.ini* file (located in the *\Windows* folder) and setting the `MaxBackupCopies=5` line to any value you want. A higher setting (more backup files) will increase the likelihood of finding a good copy in the event of a serious problem, but will also consume more disk space. The size of your Registry backup files depends upon the combined sizes of your Registry files, as well as how effectively they can be compressed.

---

* Cabinet files (**.cab*) are the files in which Microsoft compresses and distributes their applications. They're similar to *.zip* files in their use, but you'll find far less support for them in the computer industry. To view the contents of a *.cab* file, just double-click on it in Explorer. You can extract files embedded in *.cab* files by drag-dropping them out of the *.cab* window and into a folder or the desktop. This is especially handy for retrieving individual files from the Windows distribution CD. To create *.cab* files, you'll need the Cab Maker utility, available for download from *http://www.annoyances.org*.

Assuming that your two Registry files add up to about 2MB (this varies significantly depending on how many applications you've installed, as well as other factors) and that Windows will be able to compress them about 50%, the default setting of 5 backups would therefore consume about 5MB of disk space (5×2MB×50%). The default setting is a good compromise and should suit most configurations. You can reduce the number if you need the extra space or increase it if you do a lot of tinkering and feel you'll be more likely to need them. If you rely on and trust another backup procedure and you need the space, you can disable the automatic backup altogether by changing the line `Backup=1` to `Backup=0` in the *Scanreg.ini* file.

See "Restoring a Corrupted Registry" later in this chapter for more information on getting at the Registry Checker's backups. ScanReg also optimizes your Registry when needed; see "Compacting the Registry" later in this chapter, for more information.

Extra Registry Checker Duties

You can configure ScanReg to back up additional files along with the Registry, although it should by no means be considered a substitute for a full system backup. This is helpful for saving prior versions of important system files, allowing their easy retrieval if something happens. Of course, if your hard disk crashes or your computer is stolen, these automated backups are lost along with everything else. It is therefore a good policy to make solid backups of your Registry and other important configuration files to tape or removable disk.

In addition to your two Registry files, *System.ini* and *Win.ini*, ScanReg will include in its backup any additional files you specify in the *Scanreg.ini* file, as follows:

```
Files = c:\msdos.sys, c:\logo.sys
Files = c:\autoexec.bat, c:\config.sys
Files = c:\windows\bob.pwl
```

Multiple filenames can be combined on a single line or separated so each has its own line, as shown. You can ignore the `dir code` setting that's explained in the INI file—its only purpose is to allow you to specify files in key directories without having to spell out the directory names, which is useful only if you're writing one file for use on several computers.

Of the files included in the previous example, the only one you should definitely include in your own backups is *Msdos.sys.* The others can be included or left out at your discretion. For example, *Logo.sys* is simply the startup screen (see Chapter 2), although you may want to back it up if you've spent a long time on it and fear that installing a future Microsoft upgrade will cause it to be overwritten. Feel free to include any other INI or other configuration files you deem important, keeping in mind that the more files you back up, the longer it will take (which could slow system boots marginally).

Automate Off-Disk Backups

The Registry Checker provides automated backups of your Registry every time you start your computer, right out of the box. However, if you're diligent enough to make manual backups, you'll benefit from a more automated procedure for that, as well. If you use a backup program to back up your entire system (highly recommended), then you probably also have the option of using the built-in scheduler that comes with most backup software.

Example 3-1 uses a DOS batch file (see Appendix B, *DOS Resurrected*) in conjunction with the *PKZip* utility (download it from *http://www.annoyances.org*) to compress the latest versions of your Registry files into a single archive and then copy that archive to a floppy disk. Open a plain-text editor, such as Notepad, and type the contents of Example 3-1.

Example 3-1. A Simple Batch File Used to Automate Manual Backups of the Registry

```
@echo off
format a: /u/q
pkzip -& -whs a:\regback.zip c:\windows\system.dat c:\windows\user.dat
```

Replace `c:\windows` if your copy of Windows is installed in a different location. If you'd rather back up to a different location, replace `a:` with the drive of your choice.

The first line turns off the display of the commands that follow. The second line takes care of two things: it prompts for a floppy and then erases it. The final line also does two things: it compresses the two Registry files and copies them to the floppy. The `&` parameter tells PKZip to use more than one floppy diskette, if necessary, and the `whs` parameter (which is required and case-sensitive—don't use uppercase) tells PKZip to include hidden and system files.

To include additional files in the backup, just list them at the end of the *pkzip* line; see the discussion of the Registry Checker earlier in this section for suggestions of other important system files.

Restoring a Corrupted Registry

There are several ways to restore a corrupted Registry. The appropriate method depends on how serious the problem is and how diligent you've been about keeping backups. Naturally, you'll want to consider the restoration process when deciding on a backup procedure.*

Details aside, restoring a corrupted Registry essentially involves copying your backup over the Registry files in use, replacing the damaged hives with good ones. However, the more backups you restore, the more recent settings will be overwritten with old information; how old the backups are depends solely on how often you back up. Duplicating a dozen files every Thursday suddenly doesn't seem like such a waste of time.

If you can't start Windows, or if you see a warning message about a corrupted Registry every time you start Windows, you'll need to follow these steps, in order, until the problem is solved:

1. Try shutting down and starting again. Surprisingly, this often works.
2. Boot off your startup disk (see "Make a Startup Disk" in Chapter 6), which will take you to the command prompt. If you don't have a Windows Me startup disk, there's no way to get to the command prompt without loading Windows.

   Check your hard disk for errors by typing **`scandisk`** at the command prompt. If it finds any errors, confirm that you want to fix them, and restart.
3. Delete your swap file, *Win386.swp*, located in your root directory, by typing **`DEL \WIN386.SWP`** at the prompt. Then, delete all the files in your Temp folder by typing **`DEL \windows\temp\*.*`** (assuming your Temp folder is *\Windows\Temp*—see "Clean Up and Customize System Folders" in Chapter 4 for more information). You may not believe me, but this often works. Try restarting after this, too.
4. Copy your *most recently* backed-up Registry files to their original locations, replacing the files that are there. Type **`scanreg`** at the command prompt to restore the most recent automated backup.† Restart when you're done. If that doesn't work, try restoring the *next-most-recent* backup (if available).

---

* It reminds me of a compression utility that was released a number of years ago, intended to replace the popular ZIP format. While the compression statistics were impressive (archives were reported to be 1/100th the size of the original data files), less impressive was the complete inability to retrieve any of the original files after they had been compressed.

† Because automated Registry backups are created every time you restart Windows, all of the available backups may be *too* recent to do any good.

5. If all else fails, you'll probably have to reinstall Windows. Sorry to be the bearer of bad news. See Chapter 6 for other troubleshooting information.

If, on the other hand, the problem is not fatal, and you simply want to recover from a mistake you made when editing the Registry or to repair damage done to your settings by a thoughtless application installer, you can selectively restore any previously backed-up copy of the Registry (see "Backing Up the Registry" earlier in this chapter for details).

When you install Windows Me, copies of your Registry files are made and remain unmodified until the next time Windows is installed. The backup, *System.1st*, is located in your root directory. If all else fails, you can, at least to some extent, restore your system to its installed state by copying these files over those in use. Although it won't have any of your most recent settings, it should, at the very least, allow you to start Windows without reinstalling.

Using Registry Patches

In addition to editing the Registry with the Registry Editor (see earlier in this chapter), you can make changes by using Registry patches. A Registry patch is simply a text file with the *.reg* extension that contains one or more Registry keys or values. If you double-click on a *.reg* file, the patch is applied to the Registry, meaning that the contents of the patch are *merged* with the contents of the Registry. This tool is especially handy for backing up small portions of the Registry or copying Registry data to someone else's computer.

Create a Registry Patch

1. Open the Registry Editor, and select a branch you wish to use. The branch can be anywhere from one of the top level branches to a branch a dozen layers deep. Registry patches include not only the branch you select, but all of the values and subkeys in the branch. Don't select anything more than what you absolutely need.

2. Select **Export Registry File** from the **Registry** menu, type a filename, and press **OK**. All of the values and subkeys in the selected branch will then be duplicated in the patch. Make sure the filename of the new Registry patch has the *.reg* extension.

Creating a Registry patch is the easy part; the hard part is determining the Registry keys from which you should make patches. See "Finding the Right Registry Key" later in this chapter for details.

Edit a Registry Patch

Since Registry patches are just plain text files, you can edit them with any plain-text editor, such as Notepad (*notepad.exe*). The contents of the Registry patch will look something like the text shown in Example 3-2.

Example 3-2. Contents of a Registry Patch Created from HKEY_CLASSES_ROOT\.txt

```
REGEDIT4

[HKEY_CLASSES_ROOT\.txt]
@="txtfile"
"Content Type"="text/plain"

[HKEY_CLASSES_ROOT\.txt\ShellNew]
"FileName"="template.txt"
```

The first line, `REGEDIT4`, tells Windows that this file is a valid Registry patch; don't remove this line. The rest of the Registry patch is a series of key names and values. The key names appear in brackets (`[...]`) and specify the full path of the key. The values contained within each key follow. The name of the value is given first, followed by an equals sign, and then the data stored in each value. The value names and value data are always enclosed in quotation marks. A value name of `@` tells the Registry editor to place the value data in the `(default)` value (as shown in the fourth line of the example).

If you are familiar with the particular information contained within the Registry patch you've just created, you can edit anything you wish and save the changes when you're done. Note that only making changes to a Registry patch doesn't mean anything; your changes won't take effect in the Registry until the Registry patch is applied.

You can apply a Registry patch at any time and to any computer. For example, if a particular application stores its custom toolbar in the Registry, you can use a Registry patch to copy the toolbar to another computer, saving time that would otherwise be spent painstakingly configuring the 431 toolbar items on the new machine.

Apply a Registry Patch

1. Double-click on a Registry patch file (with the *.reg* extension) in Explorer or on your desktop. It doesn't matter if the Registry Editor is running or not.
2. Answer **Yes** to the warning message that asks, "Are you sure you want to add the information in *c:\windows\desktop\MyPatch.reg* to the Registry?" Immediately thereafter, you'll see the message, "Information in *MyPatch.reg* has been successfully entered into the Registry."
3. You can also open the Registry Editor and select **Import Registry File** from the **Registry** menu, select the patch, and click **OK** to merge the file. There is no difference between this way and double-clicking the file; do whatever is convenient.
4. If the Registry Editor utility is currently running and you are viewing a key that was modified by the patch that was just applied, Registry Editor should refresh the display automatically to reflect the changes. If it doesn't, press **F5** or select **Refresh** from the **View** menu.

When you apply a Registry patch, you are *merging* the keys and values stored in a patch file with the Registry. Any keys in the applied patch *that didn't already exist* will be added to the Registry. Pre-existing keys in the patch will be left alone. If a specific value already exists, the value will be changed to whatever is in the patch. However, any values already in an existing key that *aren't* in the Registry patch will remain. This means that if you create a patch, rename a key or value (different from changing its data), and then apply it, the original key or value will remain intact, and you'll have a duplicate.

Although the Registry Editor has a search feature, it doesn't allow you to search and replace. If you have a branch of settings you wish to change—for example, if you've moved an application from one drive to another—you can use a Registry patch. Just create a patch of the branch in question and use your favorite text editor's search-and-replace feature to change the values in the patch (for example, replace all occurrences of *c:\big_program* with *e:\big_program*). When you apply the patch, all the settings will be changed for you. Note that you should use this with caution (examine the patch carefully before and after the search and replace), because you can screw up many settings unwittingly. See "Search the Registry Effectively" later in this chapter for more information.

"Backing Up the Registry" (earlier in this chapter) is a good safeguard against any mistakes made when applying Registry patches. Likewise, creating Registry patches is a good way to back up portions of the Registry to safeguard against other modifications.

If you're creating a Registry patch on your computer for use on another, make sure any folder names or drive letters are corrected for the new computer. If, for example, a Registry patch created on one computer references *c:\my_folder\my_program.exe*, you'll need to make sure to change all occurrences of the text to *d:\her_folder\my_program.exe* to reflect any applicable differences.

To apply a Registry patch without displaying the two annoying confirmation messages (which can be useful when applying patches from DOS batch files or Scripts), launch them with *regedit.exe* and the `/s` parameter (for "silent" operation), as follows:

```
regedit /s c:\path\regfile.reg
```

See Chapter 9, *Scripting and Automation*, for a discussion on the Windows Script Host, which documents how to automate changes to the Registry.

Finding the Right Registry Key

The two main obstacles you'll encounter when trying to make a change to the Registry are (1) where a setting is located in the Registry and (2) what modifications are necessary to effect the desired changes. Sometimes it's obvious, such as a value called `ShowSplashScreen`, with its contents set to `1`; changing the `1` to a `0` would most likely result in turning the option off. Other times you'll see a long, seemingly meaningless series of numbers and letters. Although there are no strict rules as to how values and keys are named or how the data therein is arranged, a little common sense and intuition will get you through most situations.

Here's a solution that will help you find the corresponding Registry key for a particular setting in Windows. For this example, we'll find the Registry setting associated with showing or hiding hidden files in Explorer, and then we'll create the appropriate Registry patch.

A Registry patch is a convenient way of automating changes to the Registry, and therefore to Windows and your applications, and is useful if you frequently change a setting or a group of settings. It's also a convenient way to propagate a group of settings to one or more other computers. This solution provides a way to come up with a Registry patch that corresponds to one or more options in the interface.

The idea is to take *snapshots* (make Registry patches) of your entire Registry *before* and *after* a change is made in Explorer (or another program). By comparing the two snapshots, we can easily see which Registry keys and values were affected:

1. Make sure no applications are running, because they could write to the Registry at any time, adding unexpected changes.
2. Open the Registry Editor, and highlight the `HKEY_CURRENT_USER` branch. Select **Export Registry File** from the **Registry** menu, and export the entire branch to a file called *User1.reg* (or something like that), stored somewhere convenient, such as your desktop. Then, select the `HKEY_LOCAL_MACHINE` branch and repeat the steps, exporting it instead to *Machine1.reg.**
3. Next, we will make our desired change. In this case, select **Folder Options** from Explorer's **Tools** menu, and choose the **View** tab. In the **Advanced Settings** list, change the **Hidden Files and Folders** option, and click `OK` when you're done.
4. Immediately switch back to the Registry Editor, and re-export the `HKEY_CURRENT_USER` and `HKEY_LOCAL_MACHINE` branches into new files, such as *User2.reg* and *Machine2.reg*, respectively, as described earlier in step 2.
5. What we now have is a *snapshot* of the entire Registry taken before and after the change (or changes) was made. It's important that the snapshots be taken immediately before and after the change, so that other trivial settings, such as changes in Explorer window positions, aren't included with the changes we care about.
6. All that needs to be done now is to distill the *changed* information into a useful format. Windows comes with the command-line utility, File Compare (*fc.exe*), which can be used to find the differences between our *before* and *after* files.† At the command prompt, first use the *CD* command to change to the directory containing the Registry patches (such as *\Windows\Desktop*, if they're on your desktop—see Appendix B for more information on the *CD* command), and then type the following:

```
fc /u user1.reg user2.reg > user.txt
fc /u machine1.reg machine2.reg > machine.txt
```

* Although the Registry has five main branches, the others are simply symbolic links (mirrors) of portions of these two. See "Getting to Know the Registry Editor" earlier in this chapter for details.

† There are several superior, Windows-based third-party alternatives, such as UltraEdit-32 (available at *http://www.ultraedit.com*) and Norton File Compare (part of Norton utilities, available at *http://www.symantec.com*).

The Registry

7. These commands will scan both pairs of files and write *only* the differences between the files into new text files: *user.txt* for the changes in HKEY_CURRENT_USER and *machine.txt* for the changes in HKEY_LOCAL_MACHINE. The *user.txt* file should look something like this:

```
Comparing files user1.reg and USER2.REG

***** user1.reg
[HKEY_CURRENT_USER\Software\Microsoft\Windows\CurrentVersion\
     Explorer\Advanced]
"Hidden"=dword:00000001
"ShowCompColor"=dword:00000000
***** USER2.REG
[HKEY_CURRENT_USER\Software\Microsoft\Windows\CurrentVersion\
     Explorer\Advanced]
"Hidden"=dword:00000002
"ShowCompColor"=dword:00000000
*****
```

8. From the previous listing, it's evident that the only applicable change was the `Hidden` value, located deep in the HKEY_CURRENT_USER branch. (There may be some other entries, but if you inspect them, you'll find that they relate only to MRU lists from RegEdit and can be ignored.)* Note that for this particular setting no changes were recorded in the HKEY_LOCAL_MACHINE branch, so *machine.txt* ends up with only the message, `"FC: No differences encountered."` This means our changes were only reflected in the HKEY_CURRENT_USER branch.

9. You'll also notice that the lines immediately preceding and following the line we care about are also shown; they're included by FC as an aid in locating the lines in the source files. We're lucky in that one of the surrounding lines in this example happens to be the section header (in brackets), which specifies the Registry key in which this value is located.†

   In most cases, you'll have to search the Registry snapshots (easier than searching the Registry) for the changed line; for this example, you'd search *USER2.REG* for `"Hidden"=dword:00000002` and then make note of the line enclosed in square brackets `([...])` most immediately *above* the changed line. This represents the key containing the `Hidden` value.

* MRU stands for Most Recently Used. Windows stores the most recent filenames typed into file dialog boxes; from this example, you'll notice several references to the filenames you used to save the Registry snapshots. See Chapter 4 for more information on MRU lists.

† For more information on section headers, see "Using INI Files" later in this chapter (*.ini* files have a similar format to Registry patches).

In *user2.txt*, the **Hidden** line is located in the section:

```
[HKEY_CURRENT_USER\Software\Microsoft\Windows\CurrentVersion\
     Explorer\Advanced]
```

10. The next step is to convert the output from File Compare into a valid Registry patch. Because the FC output is originally derived from Registry patches, it's already close to the correct format. Start by removing all of the lines from *user.txt*, except the *second* version of the *changed* line—this would be the value in its after setting, which presumably is our goal. You'll end up with this:

```
"Hidden"=dword:00000002
```

11. Next, paste in the key (in brackets) above the value. (In the case of our example, it was part of the FC output and can simply be left in.) You should end up with this:

```
[HKEY_CURRENT_USER\Software\Microsoft\Windows\CurrentVersion\
     Explorer\Advanced]
"Hidden"=dword:00000002
```

12. Lastly, add the text **REGEDIT4** followed by a blank line at the beginning of the file. The final result should look something like this:

```
REGEDIT4

[HKEY_CURRENT_USER\Software\Microsoft\Windows\CurrentVersion\
     Explorer\Advanced]
"Hidden"=dword:00000002
```

13. Save this file into a new file called *User-final.reg* (or something like that). If the settings you've changed have resulted in changes in the **HKEY_LOCAL_MACHINE** branch, simply repeat steps 9–12 for the *machine.txt* file as well.

14. If your setting resulted in changes in both **HKEY_CURRENT_USER** and **HKEY_LOCAL_MACHINE**, you can consolidate the two patches into one file. Likewise, you can consolidate the Registry patches from several settings into a single file for one-step operation. If consolidating, make sure you have only one instance of the **REGEDIT4** line.

For some settings (such as the one in this example), you may want to make two patches: one to turn it on, and one to turn it off. Simply double-click the patch corresponding to the setting you desire.

You may notice that some changes involve the removal of a key or value. The problem is that values and keys cannot be deleted with Registry patches; see "Automating the Deletion of Registry Items" later in this chapter for details.

This solution will help you find the appropriate keys and values associated with a particular Windows or application setting, and it can also help locate *hidden* settings (those with that don't appear dialog boxes). The setting in the previous example is located in a key that contains other settings, some of which aren't included in the Folder Options dialog box. Experiment with some of the more interesting sounding values, such as `CascadePrinters` and `ShowSuperHidden`.

There are some caveats to this approach, mostly in that the File Compare utility will often pull out more differences than are relevant to the change you wish to make. It's important to look closely at each key in the resulting Registry patch to see if it's really necessary.

See Chapter 9 for a discussion on the Windows Script Host, which documents automating changes to the Registry that don't involve Registry patches.

It's always smart to create a corresponding *undo* Registry patch while you're using a solution like this. For example, because our Registry patch contains the differences in the *after* file, *user2.reg*, the corresponding *undo* patch would contain the corresponding lines in the *before* file, *user1.reg*. Applying the *undo* patch effectively returns the keys and values stored within to their state before the setting was changed. Obviously, an important caveat is that an undo patch for one computer won't necessarily be an effective undo for another computer.

Automating the Deletion of Registry Items

An important drawback to using Registry patches is that they can be used only to replace or augment information in the Registry. No provision for removing keys or values is included in Registry patches, yet some important changes can only be made by removing keys or values. For example, to remove the Bitmap Image entry from Explorer's **New** menu, you need to delete the key `HKEY_CLASSES_ROOT\.bmp\ShellNew` entirely, and no Registry patch can do that.

Here, we enlist the services of the Windows Script Host, which includes a functionality for manipulating Registry information. Chapter 9 documents writing scripts for the Windows Script Host and, in particular, Registry functions like the one used in this solution:

1. Open a plain-text editor, such as Notepad, and type the following:

   ```
   Call RegistryDelete("HKEY_CURRENT_USER\.bmp\ShellNew", "")

   Sub RegistryDelete(KeyName, ValueName)
     Set WshShell = WScript.CreateObject("WScript.Shell")
     WshShell.RegWrite KeyName & "\" & ValueName, ""
     WshShell.RegDelete KeyName & "\" & ValueName
   End Sub
   ```

   The first line invokes the `RegistryDelete` subroutine, listed immediately after. Simply put the full path of the Registry key you wish to delete between the quotation marks, making sure *not* to include a trailing slash (a "\" at the end).

   To delete a single value rather than an entire key, specify the value name between the second pair of quotes, like this:

   ```
   Call RegistryDelete("HKEY_CURRENT_USER\.bmp", "Content Type")
   ```

   To remove the `(default)` value of a key (which can't be deleted), just use a standard Registry patch, and simply set the default value to an empty string (`@=""`).

2. Save the file, calling it something like *Delete.vbs*. Double-click on the script file to execute it.

Another instance where it might be useful to delete a Registry key is removing special icons from the desktop. In this case, use the same script, but replace the Registry path with:

```
HKEY_LOCAL_MACHINE\Software\Microsoft\Windows\CurrentVersion\
     explorer\Desktop\NameSpace\{class ID of object to be deleted}
```

See Appendix C for a list of handy class IDs (the stuff between the curly braces). See "Clear the Desktop of Unwanted Icons" in Chapter 4 for more information on getting stubborn icons off the desktop.

If you wish to use VBScript files on NT 4.0 or Windows 95 systems, you'll need to download and install the Windows Script Host (WSH)—see "Further Study" in Chapter 9 for more information. The WSH, of course, comes with Windows 2000, Windows Me, and Windows 98, so no external application is required.

Currently, there is no provision for *renaming* a Registry branch using either Registry patches or WSH scripts. However, there are a few more involved ways to do it. For example, you can export the branch to a Registry patch and, using your text editor's search-and-replace feature, rename the keys as desired (see "Using Registry Patches" earlier in this chapter for details). Then you can apply the revised patch normally and use a script as described earlier to remove the old branch. From a programmatic standpoint, you can recursively read an entire branch and write it to its new location, deleting the original when you're done.

See "Clear Unwanted Entries from Explorer's New Menu" in Chapter 4 for more information on the **New** menu.

Search the Registry Effectively

The Registry Editor has a simple search feature, allowing you to search through all the keys and values for text. Just select **Find** from the Registry Editor's **Edit** menu, type the desired text, and click **Find Next**. Because the Registry can become quite large and have a wide variety of settings and information, it is important to learn to search effectively, so you don't miss anything or waste a lot of time wading through irrelevant results. Additionally, the Registry Editor doesn't have a search-and-replace feature, so doing something as simple as changing every occurrence of *c:\program files* to *d:\program files* can be a monumental chore. Here are some tips that may help:

- Make sure that all three options in the **Find** window's **Look at** section are checked, unless you know specifically that what you're looking for is solely a Key, Value (value name), or Data (value contents). You'll also usually want the **Match whole string only** option turned off.
- Many folder names in the Registry are stored in both long and short versions. For example, say you want to move your *Program Files* folder from one drive to another (see "Clean Up and Customize System Folders" in Chapter 4 for more information). When you install Windows, any settings pertaining to this folder may be stored in the Registry as *c:\Program Files* or *c:\Progra~1*. Make sure you search for both.
- If you're searching the Registry for both `Program Files` and `Progra~1`, you may want to just search for `progra`, which will trigger both variations. Because this will trip upon other uses of the word `program`, try placing a backslash (\) in front of it, like this: `\progra`, to limit the search to only directory names beginning with those letters. A minute of mental preparation can save you an hour of searching.
- You may want to search the Registry for an interface element, such as a new item added to a context menu or text in a list in a dialog box. If the text contains an underlined character, you'll need to add an

ampersand (&) to the search string. For example, say you've installed a program that creates *.zip* files (such as WinZip; *http://www.winzip.com*), and the program has added the command **Add to Zip** to the context menu of all files that you wish to remove. You'll need to search for `add to &zip` to match the text properly; a search for `add to zip` will probably turn up nothing. Note also that text searches are *not* case-sensitive, so you don't have to worry about capitalization.

- Searching begins at the currently selected key. If you want to be sure to search the entire Registry, make sure the `My Computer` entry at the top of the Registry tree is highlighted before you begin. However, if you know the setting you want to change is in, for example, `HKEY_LOCAL_MACHINE`, you should highlight that key beforehand to reduce search time and eliminate irrelevant results.
- Although the Registry Editor has a search feature, it doesn't allow you to search and replace (which is probably a good thing). If you have a branch of settings you wish to change (for example, if you've moved an application from one drive to another or want to, say, replace every occurrence of *notepad.exe* with another application), you can use a Registry patch—see "Using Registry Patches" earlier in this chapter. Just create a patch of the branch in question and use your favorite text editor's search-and-replace feature to change the values in the patch. When you apply the patch, all the settings will be changed for you. Note that you should use this with caution, because you can screw up many settings unwittingly by searching and replacing common pieces of text.
- If you find yourself wanting to use search and replace more often, and the previous Registry patch tip isn't sufficient, you may want to try the Registry Search and Replace utility. It's a bit safer and more flexible, too. See "Registry Tools" at the end of this chapter for more information.

Compacting the Registry

As you may have noticed, your Registry can become quite large. This is due, in part, to the empty space inside your Registry files. If you're familiar with the way data is stored in the Registry, you know that the Registry is a database. As with all databases, when information is removed or added, the database file is *not* rewritten entirely (in order to improve performance). Instead, new information is simply appended to the end of the file, and gaps are left in the file where information has been removed. After a lot of use, this can cause the files that make up the Registry to become enormous. See Figure 3-3 for a diagram of this process.

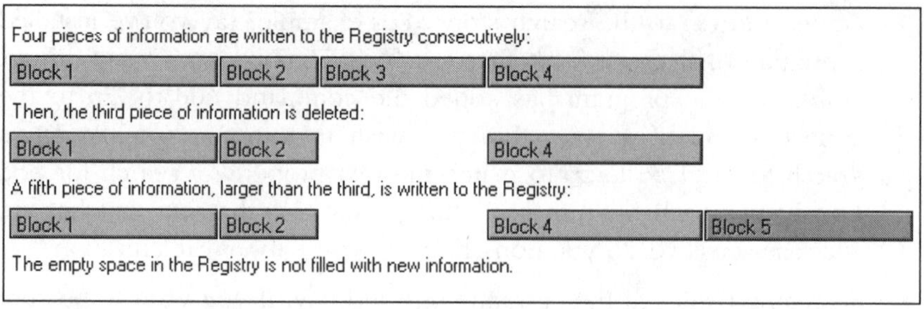

Four pieces of information are written to the Registry consecutively:

Block 1	Block 2	Block 3	Block 4	

Then, the third piece of information is deleted:

Block 1	Block 2		Block 4	

A fifth piece of information, larger than the third, is written to the Registry:

Block 1	Block 2		Block 4	Block 5

The empty space in the Registry is not filled with new information.

Figure 3-3. The process by which the Registry accumulates empty space

Compacting any database file like the Registry involves reading all of the settings and then writing them, in order, into a new file. This way, the empty space is eliminated and the entries are stored consecutively, resulting in less wasted space and better performance.

If you wanted to compact your Registry in Windows 95, you had to go through a long, convoluted process that involved making a Registry patch of the entire Registry and then rebuilding it from within DOS. In Windows 98, not only is there an included utility that can compact the Registry, it is done for you automatically whenever the amount of wasted space goes above 500 KB.

To optimize the Registry manually, you must first restart your computer and boot with the Windows Startup Disk to enter DOS without loading Windows. Type **`SCANREG /OPT`** at the DOS prompt. If you try to do this from within Windows, it won't work.

If you find that the automatic Registry optimization noticeably slows your boot process, you can disable it by changing the line `Optimize=1` to `Optimize=0` in the *Scanreg.ini* file. For more information on the *Scanreg.ini* file and the Registry Checker utility, see "Backing Up the Registry" earlier in this chapter.

Using INI Files

If you've been using a Windows PC for any length of time, you've probably come across files with the *.ini* filename extension. Initialization files (or *Configuration Settings*, as they're known in any recent release of Windows) were used in the old days to store settings for applications, as well as Windows itself, before the Registry was implemented. INI files are simply text files (editable with any plain-text editor, such as Notepad) that are specially formatted to store such settings. Because INI files are limited in their maximum file size (64 KB) and are not as efficient as the Registry, application developers have been encouraged to abandon INI files and instead store settings in the Registry. Since some applications still use INI files to store certain settings, it may become necessary to look for and change settings in INI files as well.

An example of an application that may still use an INI file today is an application installer. An INI file would allow a program to read and store settings without having to rely on the Registry; that way, the settings would be accessible regardless of the computer on which the program was run. INI files are also handy (for the same reason) for programs that run over a network. Windows also includes a few INI files, although they're generally used only to maintain compatibility with older applications.

To edit an INI file, just double-click it, and it will open in Notepad. To configure another text editor to be used with INI files, see "Creating File Types" earlier in this chapter and "Customize Context Menus" in Chapter 4.

A typical INI file looks like this:

```
[Names]
name1=Benjamin
name2=Doug
name3=Gary

[Cities I've visited]
name1=Brockway
name2=Ogdenville
name3=North Haverbrook
```

Section names are always enclosed in square brackets (`[...]`); the lines that follow are the settings contained in that section. A section continues until the next section begins or until the end of the file. Settings include a setting name, followed by an equals sign, and then the data assigned to that setting.

You'll notice that the structure of INI files is similar (but not identical) to that of Registry patches, discussed earlier in this chapter

In addition to searching the Registry, you may want to search all INI files for a particular setting:

1. Select **Search** and then **For Files or Folders** from the **Start Menu**.
2. Type **`*.ini`** in the **Search for files or folders named** field, and type the text for which you want to search in the **Containing Text** field.
3. Double-click on any file in the search results to view it, and use your text editor's search feature to find the specific text in the file.

System.ini and Win.ini

Some settings for Windows 3.x, Windows 9x, and Windows Me are stored in the files *System.ini* and *Win.ini.* These files are primarily still included in the *Windows* folder to maintain compatibility with older applications that expect to find or store certain settings in them. There's little interest anymore in either of these files pertaining to Windows. If you're familiar, for example, with the now-obsolete `Load=` and `Run=` in the `[Windows]` section of *Win.ini*, that functionality is taken care of by the *Startup* folder in the Start Menu, as well as several locations in the Registry. See "Error Messages" in Chapter 6 for details.

Understanding File Types

The term *File Types* describes the collection of associations between documents and the applications that use them. The most apparent use of this feature is that, for example, Windows knows to run Notepad when you double-click on a file with the *.txt* extension. The traditional method for configuring these associations to suit your needs is discussed in "Customize Context Menus" in Chapter 4, but it goes quite a bit deeper than that.

It all starts with file extensions, the letters (usually three) that follow the period in most filenames. For example, the extension of the file *Readme.txt* is *.txt,* signifying a plain text file; the extension of *Resume.wpd* is *.wpd,* signifying a document created in WordPerfect. By default, Windows hides the extensions of registered file types in Explorer and on the desktop, but it's best to have them displayed.

File extensions not only allow you to easily determine what kind of file a certain file is (because icons are almost never descriptive enough), but also allow you to change Windows' perception of the type of a file by simply renaming the extension. Note that changing a file's extension doesn't actually change the contents or the format of the file, only how Windows interacts with it.

To display your file extensions, select **Folder Options** in Explorer's **Tools** menu, choose the **View** tab, and turn off the **Hide file extensions for known file-types** option. Click **OK** when you're done.

By hiding file extensions, Microsoft hoped to make Windows easier to use—a plan that backfired for several reasons. Because only the extensions of registered files are hidden, the extensions of files that aren't yet in the File Types database are still shown. What's even more confusing is that, when an application finally claims a certain file type, it can appear to the inexperienced user as though all of the old files of that type have been renamed. It also creates a "knowledge gap" between those who understand file types and those who don't; try telling someone whose computer still has hidden extensions to find *Readme.txt* in a directory full of files. Other problems have arisen, such as trying to differentiate *Excel.exe* and *Excel.xls* in Explorer when the extensions are hidden; one file is an application and the other is a document, but they may have the same icon.

The `HKEY_CLASSES_ROOT` branch of the Registry stores information on all your file types. File extensions (preceded by periods) are listed first on the tree, followed by the actual file types.

The Registry keys named for file extensions contain information that points to the other keys, which describe the file types. For example, if you navigate to the key `HKEY_CLASSES_ROOT\.txt` (note that the period *is* included here), you'll notice that there's not a lot of information there. The important (and often sole) piece of information is the `(default)` value, which is set to the name of another key, located lower down the tree. In the case of *.txt*, the `(default)` value contains the text `txtfile` (see Figure 3-4). This, in effect, is a reference to `HKEY_CLASSES_ROOT\txtfile`, which is the key that contains the actual information for file type, as shown in Figure 3-5).

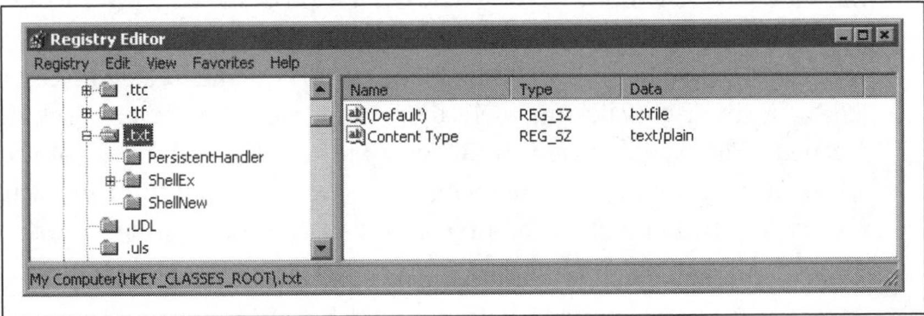

Figure 3-4. The Registry key named for the filename extension contains a pointer to another Registry key (see Figure 3-5)

All of the details of this file type are stored in the `txtfile` branch, such as the formal name shown in the **Type** column in Explorer (in this case, "Text File"), the icon used for all files of this type, and the applications used to open the file. Many different extension keys can point to this branch, so a file type like `txtfile` can have many filename extensions associated with it. This architecture can make it a little trickier to understand the way file types are stored in the Registry, but it does provide a more flexible system of file associations.

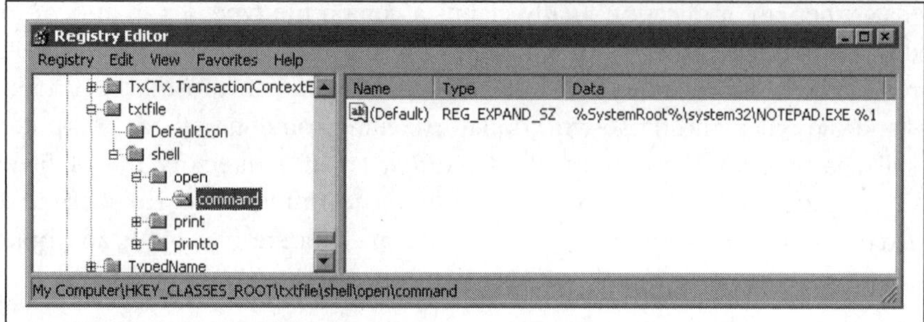

Figure 3-5. The second Registry key contains the file-type information; several keys named for file extensions can point to this key

Creating File Types

There are several ways that file types are created:

- The structure shown in Figures 3-4 and 3-5 is what you'll usually get when an application claims a file type.* In this case, the Text File file type was created when Windows was first installed. If you use the File Types dialog box in Explorer (see "Customize Context Menus" in Chapter 4) to create a new file type, you'll get something similar.
- If you've ever double-clicked on a file with an extension with which Windows is unfamiliar (called an *unregistered* file type), you've seen the **Open With** window asking you which program you want to use with that type of file. (You can also get to this dialog box by right-clicking on any file while holding the **Shift** key and selecting **Open With** or by right-clicking, selecting **Properties**, and then clicking **Change**.) File types created in this way are recognized by the `_auto_file` suffix; for example, choosing a program this way for a file with the *.dat* extension will create a file-type key called `dat_auto_file`.
- Finally, you can create a file type manually, either by editing the Registry directly or by applying a Registry patch.

Regardless of the method by which a file type has been created, the structure in the Registry is virtually the same. All of the major components of a file type are shown in Figures 3-4 and 3-5. First, a key is created that is named for each extension associated with the file type (usually only one,

* During the installation process for most applications, including Windows itself, the installer adds or modifies information in the Registry to associate itself with any number of file extensions. This can cause a serious problem when an installer grabs an association from another program without asking. See Chapter 4 for details.

for starters).[*] The `(default)` value of this key contains the name of the file-type Registry key; it does not contain the full Registry path, however, nor does it contain the formal name of the file type (shown in Explorer). For example, put `txtfile` here and not `Text File`. The `Content Type` value shown in Figure 3-4 may appear for some file types, but is not necessary for normal operation.

A key called `ShellNew` may also appear underneath the file extension key. The existence of this key tells Windows to include the extension in the **New** menu (found in Explorer's **File** menu), allowing the user to create a new, empty file of that type, and without having to open any application. The reason that the `ShellNew` key is located underneath the extension key and not the file-type key (discussed later in this section) is that a file type may have more than one extension, and Windows needs to know which extension to use when creating a new file. The `ShellNew` key is usually empty, although there may be a value called `FileName` that points to a template file (a file on your hard disk that Windows will use to create a new, blank document). In most cases, the `FileName` value is omitted, and Windows will create a zero-byte (empty) file with the appropriate extension.

Most of a file type's definition is located in the main file-type key, the name of which is specified in each of the extension keys listed earlier. In Figure 3-5, the `txtfile` key is the main key containing all of the settings for the Text File file type. First of all, the `(default)` value in this key specifies the formal, aesthetic name of the file type—the text that appears in the **File Types** dialog box in Explorer and in the **Type** column in Explorer's **Details** view.

If the value named `AlwaysShowExt` is present (always empty) in this key, the extension for this file type will be displayed in Explorer, even if the user has elected to hide extensions for file types that are registered (see earlier). You may also see a binary value entitled `EditFlags`. If this value is omitted or set to `00 00 00 00`, you will be allowed to edit this file type in the **File Types** dialog box in Explorer. If `EditFlags` is set to `01 00 00 00`, the file type won't be visible in Explorer's **File Types** dialog box. Other possibilities for this value exist, each signifying what is and is not allowed in the **File Types** dialog box.

---

* An example of a file type with two or more extensions is the HTML file type (used by web browsers), which is associated with *.html*, *.htm*, *.shtml*, and *.shtm* files.

Beneath the file-type key are three or four independent subkeys. `DefaultIcon` contains only the `(default)` value, set to the filename of the file containing the icon used for the file-type. Icons are specified by filename and icon index, separated by a comma; for example, `c:\windows\system32\shell32.dll, 152` specifies the 153rd icon in the *shell32.dll* file. The specified file can be any *.ico* or *.bmp* file, as well as an *.exe* or *.dll* file containing one or more icons. To use the first icon in the file, specify `0` (zero); the second icon is `1` (one), and so on. The easiest way to choose an icon is with the **File Types** dialog box in Explorer, which will allow you to browse and choose icons without typing or guesswork.

Internet Shortcuts don't launch applications directly; instead, they redirect the URL contained therein to Windows, which then delegates the task to an application suitable to the type of URL. As part of Windows' rigidity, it also won't allow you to change the icon for Internet Shortcuts. To do this, delete the `EditFlags` value (explained earlier in this chapter), as well as the `IconHandler` key, located in the `shellex` branch.

Most of the meat is stored in the `shell` key. Its subkeys define what happens when a file of this type is double-clicked and which commands appear in the file type's context menu (accessed by right-clicking). Underneath `shell` is a separate key for each command shown in the context menu; that is, when you right-click on a file of this type, these are the commands that will appear at the top of the list. Most file types have an *Open* command (with a key by the same name). You may also see *Edit*, *Print*, *PrintTo*, *Play*, and *View* here. You can add, remove, or change any of these commands you wish. Underneath each one of *these* keys is a key called `command`. Each `command` key's `(default)` value is set to the application filename used to carry out the respective command. Figure 3-4 and Figure 3-5 show this structure.

For example, if Notepad is associated with the *Open* command for text files, the contents of `HKEY_CLASSES_ROOT\txtfile\shell\open\command` will be `Notepad.exe "%1"`. Now, the `"%1"` (including the quotation marks) is very important—`%1` is where Windows substitutes the application's command line, and the quotation marks are necessary in case there are any spaces in the filename of the clicked file. So, if you were to right-click on any file with the *.txt* extension (say, *c:\documents\my file.txt*) and select **Open** from the context menu that appears (see Figure 3-6), Windows would carry out the command `Notepad "c:\documents\my file.txt"`, which will launch Notepad and instruct it to open the document.

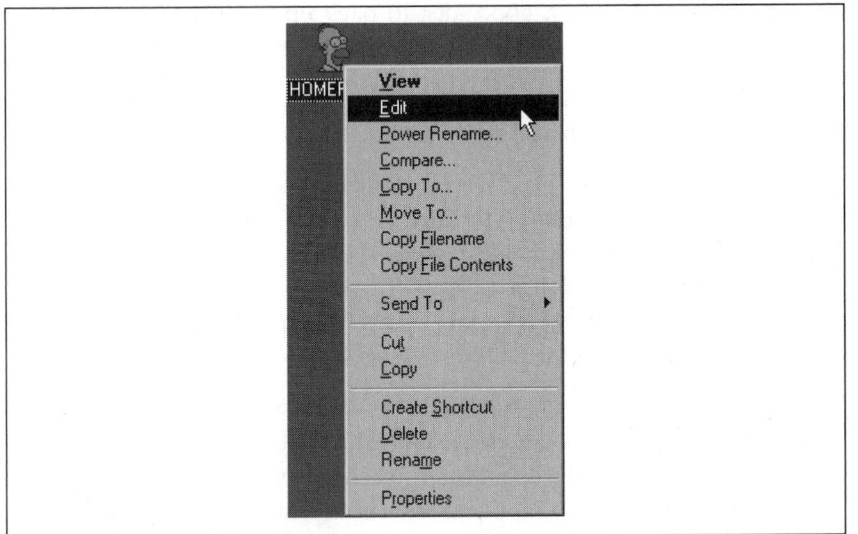

Figure 3-6. A context menu for the bitmap file type shows the default View option, as well as the extra Edit and Power Rename options

While there can be several available commands for any given file type, only one of the commands will ever appear in bold. This command is called the *default* and is the one that Windows uses when you double-click on a file instead of right-clicking. Usually, *Open* is the default, but any existing command can be set as the default.* To make a different command the default, specify the name of the command in the `(default)` value of the `shell` key. For example, if a file type contains *Open*, *Edit*, and *Print*, and you type `edit` in the `(default)` value, the *Edit* command will appear bold in the file type's context menu, then *Edit* will be the command carried out when you double-click. If the `(default)` value is empty, the *Open* command is assumed to be the default. If there's no *Open* command, Windows uses the first key it finds.

The `shellex` key contains references to *shell extensions*, programs designed to work especially with context menus. For example, the *Add to Zip* command shown in Figure 3-6 is a shell extension added by WinZip. Unless you're a programmer, these Registry entries will be of little use to you, with the following exception: you can remove some unwanted context menu commands and extra tabs in property sheets of certain file types by removing the corresponding keys to shell extensions here. I don't

* Note that although the word *open* is often spelled with all lower-case letters in the Registry, it still appears capitalized in the context menu. Windows will preserve the case of all other commands as you've typed them, but will automatically capitalize *Open*.

have to tell you that it's a good idea to back up any file-type key with a Registry patch before you make any changes.

You might also see `CLSID` and `ddeexec` keys in various places in file-type keys. These also have special uses, but are of little interest to most users.

Since there are so many parts to a standard file type, the best way to duplicate or safeguard a file type is to create a Registry patch (see "Using Registry Patches" earlier in this chapter). If you're creating an entirely new file type, it might be easiest to start by exporting an existing file type, changing the particular components, and then reimporting. Save that carpal tunnel syndrome for Chapter 5, *Maximizing Performance.*

Having a good grasp of file types can be very useful for resolving annoyances. For example, you can create individual Registry patches for any file types that get commonly overwritten, such as *.jpg*, *.gif*, *.bmp*, *.txt*, *.doc*, and *.html*. If an unwanted application claims a file type you have backed up, simply apply the Registry patch to restore your preferences. See "Protect Your File Types" in Chapter 4 for more information.

For more information on the **File Types** dialog box in Explorer, see "Customize Context Menus" in Chapter 4. See "Change the Icons of System Objects" in Chapter 4 for another use of the `DefaultIcon` key.

Registry Tools

The Registry Editor is included with Windows for viewing and changing the contents of the Registry. Unfortunately, this utility is quite limited, especially when compared with some of the other tools available. The following is a list of a few software utilities intended for use with the Registry, available at the time of this writing. Naturally, you'll want to back up your Registry before playing with an unfamiliar tool. See *http://www.annoyances.org* for more information on downloadable software:

Registry Search and Replace
: This is a full-featured tool used to make a global search and replace in the Registry much easier and quicker. Its interface could use a little streamlining, but otherwise it's fine.

Norton Utilities
: This commercial package comes with an enhanced Registry Editor, as well as many other tools. It's commercial software, so no freebees here. The Norton Registry Editor is similar to the Windows Registry Editor, but comes with several perks, such as a utility that tracks changes in the Registry, a search-and-replace utility, and other stuff.

TweakUI

The options in this little Control-Panel add-on make certain Windows settings more accessible, settings that would otherwise require editing the Registry. TweakUI is available from *http://www.annoyances.org*. See Appendix A, *Setting Locator*, for details.

Creative Element Power Tools

This collection of tools for Windows Me and Windows 2000 includes a bunch of context-menu add-ons that aren't otherwise possible with simple changes to the Registry. Creative Element Power Tools can be downloaded from *http://www.creativelement.com*.

4

Tinkering Techniques

Why would we want to tinker with the operating system? Well, if you were perfectly happy with Windows Me right out of the box, odds are you wouldn't be reading this book. We tinker with Windows to make it better: to improve the interface, to reduce the amount of work required to complete a task, to make it run more smoothly and efficiently, and most of all, to make it less annoying (you saw that one coming).

The most important part of software design is the interface. The interface is the only link we humans have with the machines we use—the better the interface, the better the link, and the more useful the machine will be. Because the Windows Me software has already been designed and written, the most we can hope to do is to tinker with it so that it works more like we think it should.

The unfortunate methodology behind the design of the Windows interface is that it's supposed to be usable by the lowest common denominator: the person who has never seen Windows before. Don't get me wrong, one of the most important interface design considerations is its ability to be used by the uninitiated. But there are three main problems with this approach if not done correctly. One, such an interface can be inherently condescending. Two, no user is a beginner forever. Three, users are not all the same.

What many people don't realize is that it is possible to have an elegant, simple interface that is easy and comfortable to use by beginners, yet is not limited in its usefulness as users gain experience. A dumbed-down interface is not the answer.

One of Windows' strong points is its flexibility. For example, the fact that you can reprogram almost any system object on the desktop to serve a different function, is one of the main reasons that Windows enjoys such a large market share (see also "What's Wrong with Windows" in Chapter 1, *Making the Most of Windows Me*). Although the variety of solutions presented here are a testimony to the power and flexibility of Windows Me, I'd also like to note the need for such solutions in the first place.

This chapter takes advantage of the basic topics covered in Chapter 2, *Basic Explorer Coping Skills*—such as shortcuts, system objects, and some of Windows' more obscure settings—as well as usage of Registry, discussed in Chapter 3, *The Registry*, to customize Windows beyond Microsoft's intentions. We'll start by clearing some of the clutter caused by the installation of Windows and move on to customizing whatever is left over to suit your needs. Although most of these solutions target specific annoyances in the operating system, each one can be used to illustrate a broader concept.

Now, we certainly don't expect every user to feel compelled to take all the advice in this book; not everyone is going to want to turn off the Documents menu in the Start Menu or remove certain system objects from the desktop, for example. However, by excavating the Registry and many of the more obscure dialog boxes, you should see other things along the way that will assist you in resolving your own annoyances.

If you haven't reviewed Chapter 3, I suggest you do so at this point. It covers the Windows Registry and the Registry Editor, which are used extensively in many of the solutions in this chapter and later in the book. Many solutions require that you change a setting in the Registry and then restart Windows for the change to take effect. You'll learn from these examples how this whole system works and, hopefully, how to solve problems that aren't covered by the material here.

Registry patches, discussed in Chapter 3, are great for backing up portions of the Registry and can be used to undo any changes you may decide to make here. Once you've made a change you like, you may want to back it up in a Registry patch of its own, so you can easily restore it if it's overwritten by an application installer or Windows Update.

Cleaning Up the Desktop

The default configuration of Windows Me—including the way the desktop and Start Menu are configured and which Windows components are included—was decided upon by a committee at Microsoft. The motivation was not so much ease of use as it was how to best showcase the features included in the new operating system. This criterion may be great for the marketing department at Microsoft, but it doesn't make for a very pleasant experience for the user.

The best place to start when customizing an interface is to throw out all the stuff you don't want, which will make much more room for the stuff you do want. By not being forced to wade through dozens of icons to find the one you want, you can complete your work more easily and with less aggravation.

Clear the Desktop of Unwanted Icons

When you first install Windows Me, the desktop is littered with icons, some of which can be removed easily and some of which cannot. Although the Recycle Bin is intended as a means by which objects throughout Windows can be deleted by dragging and dropping them into it, many items cannot be deleted this way. This inconsistency is partly due to Microsoft's concern that users will irreparably damage the operating system and partly due to the Microsoft support department's expectation of having to repeatedly answer the question, "How do I get my MSN icon back?"

There are two types of objects that reside on the desktop (not including the taskbar or Start Menu). Those objects that are physical files or shortcuts to files are simply stored in your desktop folder (usually *\Windows\Desktop*); these items can be deleted or moved as easily as any other file on your hard disk. All other objects are *virtual objects*, in that they don't represent physical files on the hard disk. Virtual objects include My Computer, the Recycle Bin, and My Network Places. What follows should help you remove any unwanted icons from your desktop that can't be removed using traditional means.

Following the solutions for the common desktop icons, see "Hide All Icons on the Desktop" for a more global solution.

My Network Places

The My Network Places icon appears on your desktop if you have any networking components installed, including those for your Internet connection.* See Chapter 7, *Networking and Internetworking*, for more information on networking:

1. Double-click on the **TweakUI** icon (see Appendix A, *Setting Locator*) in Control Panel, and choose the **Desktop** tab.
2. Remove the check mark from the **My Network Places** item, and click **OK**. (If you've renamed the icon, it will be listed under the new name.)

The obvious consequence of hiding My Network Places is that all of the resources it provides will then be unavailable. If you're not on a network, this is not likely to pose a problem. For those on a local network, any resources previously available through the My Network Places will be unavailable unless mapped to a drive letter (see "Setting Up a Workgroup" in Chapter 7 for more information).

Soultion 1: Recycle Bin

Having the Recycle Bin icon on your desktop can be convenient, but because there are other ways to delete an object (such as right-clicking on it and selecting **Delete** or selecting an item and pressing the **Del** key), it really isn't necessary. Furthermore, there's a *Recycled* folder on every drive (it's hidden, so you'll have to configure Explorer to show all files), which works just like the Recycle Bin desktop icon. Solution 1 shows one way to hide the Recycle Bin:

1. Double-click on the **TweakUI** icon (see Appendix A) in Control Panel, and choose the **Desktop** tab.
2. Remove the check mark from the **Recycle Bin** item, and click **OK**.

Solution 2: Recycle Bin

There's a more interesting solution, one that may provide a little insight into the Registry and Windows system objects. We can add a **Delete** option to the Recycle Bin's context menu, which may be useful, for example, if you're setting up one or more computers for someone else and want to give them the option of removing the Recycle Bin easily. (See Chapter 3 for information on making Registry patches to automate changes like this.) Figure 4-1 shows the altered context menu.

---

* Although Windows 2000's *My Network Places* folder contains local network resources as well as Internet connections, the Windows Me equivalent only contains local network resources and is of little or no use on a computer not connected to a local network.

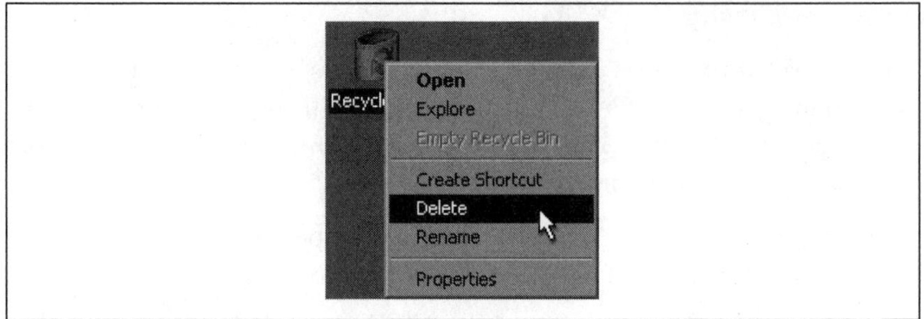

Figure 4-1. Adding the Delete option to the Recycle Bin's context menu

Follow these steps to add the **Delete** option:

1. Open the Registry Editor (if you're not familiar with the Registry Editor, see Chapter 3).
2. Expand the branches to `HKEY_CLASSES_ROOT\CLSID\{645FF040-5081-101B-9F08-00AA002F954E}\ShellFolder\`. You know you have the right Class ID key if its `(Default)` is set to `Recycle Bin`. It may be easier to locate this key by searching for the first few characters of the Class ID or for the text `Recycle Bin`.
3. Double-click on the `Attributes` value, and replace the contents with `70 01 00 20`. Note that this is a binary value, and the input box may not behave like a normal text box; if you mess up, just choose **Cancel** and try again.
4. Close the Registry Editor—the change should take effect immediately.
5. You now have the option of deleting the Recycle Bin at any time by right-clicking on it and selecting **Delete**.

Solution 2 will also add the **Rename** option to the Recycle Bin's context menu. See "Customize the Recycle Bin Icon" later in this chapter for more information. To restore your Recycle Bin to its default, removing the **Rename** and **Delete** options from its context menu, start by following the previous instructions for the Registry. Instead of the value specified in step 3, however, change it to `40 01 00 20`. Note that this won't restore the Recycle Bin's original name—you'll have to do that manually. If you've deleted it with Solution 2, use TweakUI (Solution 1) to get it back.

My Computer

The My Computer icon provides access to the Control Panel and all of your drives. Because these resources are also accessible through Explorer and the Start Menu, the My Computer icon on the desktop isn't strictly required. You may want to remove it to avoid clutter or as part of some security measure.

The following process doesn't actually remove the icon from the desktop, although it does render it invisible while still allowing access if you know where to look. Although there isn't a perfect solution for getting rid of this icon without clearing all the icons from the desktop, the following solution should satisfy many of you:

1. Double-click on the **Display** icon in Control Panel, and choose the **Effects** tab. See Figure 4-2.
2. Select the **My Computer** icon in the **Desktop Icons** box, and click **Change Icon**.
3. Choose a blank, transparent icon to replace the one that's there. Don't look for one included with Windows; you'll probably have to create it using your favorite icon editor (one that supports transparent pixels; see *http://www.annoyances.org* for third-party software). Press **OK**.
4. Right-click on the **My Computer** icon, select **Rename**, and replace the title with a single space.

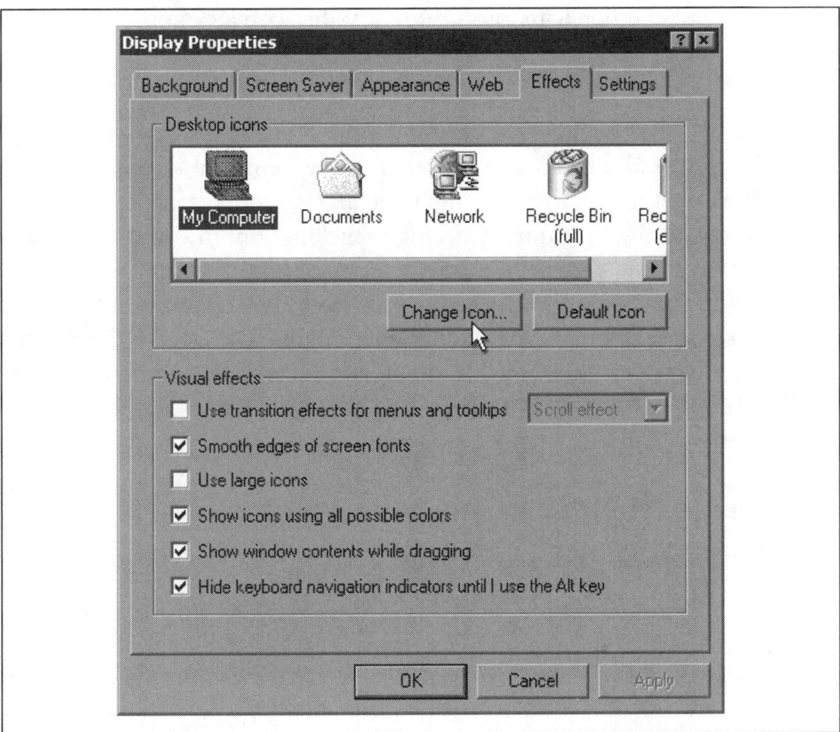

Figure 4-2. Use Display Properties to change the icon of My Computer

Really stubborn icons

Once in a while, you'll encounter an icon on your desktop that you just can't get rid of. Whether it's from another Microsoft upgrade or some other application, the information is usually stored in the same place.

TweakUI, as described in some of the previous solutions, should be the first place you look to remove a desktop icon, because it's the easiest method. In some situations, though, TweakUI won't list the icon or simply won't be capable of removing it. Here's a last resort for getting rid of stubborn icons:

1. Open the Registry Editor. (If you're not familiar with the Registry Editor, see Chapter 3.)
2. Expand the branches to: `HKEY_LOCAL_MACHINE\SOFTWARE\Microsoft\Windows\CurrentVersion\explorer\Desktop\NameSpace\`.
3. The key itself will most likely be devoid of values, but it should have a few subkeys, which will be named something like `{645FF040-5081-101B-9F08-00AA002F954E}`. These codes are called Class IDs and point to other parts of the Registry that contain more information about them. Class IDs are stored in the `HKEY_CLASSES_ROOT\CLSID` branch and are discussed in Appendix C, *Class IDs of System Objects*.
4. Start by clicking on a key and looking at the `(Default)` value to the right. It *should* contain a description of the item. If it doesn't, you can still find out to what it is by right-clicking on the key name in the left pane, selecting **Rename**, then right-clicking on the text itself, and selecting **Copy**. This will copy the key name to the Clipboard. Then move to the top of the Registry tree (select **My Computer** at the root), and select **Find** from the **Edit** menu. Right-click on the **Find What** field, and select **Paste**. Click **Find Next** to search through the Registry for that key. When you find it, do a little digging in that key and its subkeys to find out what it's really for.
5. If one of the keys under the `...Namespace` branch turns out to match the item you're trying to get rid of, you can go ahead and delete the key.*

   Now, deleting an item here is a little like deleting a shortcut in Explorer: it doesn't actually delete functionality from your system, it only removes the pointer to the information from the desktop namespace key. If you're worried that you might want it back some day, highlight the key, select **Export Registry File** from the **Registry** menu, and save it to a file. See Chapter 3 for more information on Registry patches.

---

* See "Automating the Deletion of Registry Items" in Chapter 3 for a way to write a script that makes it easy to remove icons repetitively from the desktop.

6. When you're done making changes, close the Registry Editor and refresh the desktop. See "Refresh the Desktop Without Restarting Windows" in Chapter 2 for more information.

Hide All Icons on the Desktop

The following solution will disable the display of all icons on the desktop, including any files in your *Desktop* folder, as well as the virtual icons discussed in the previous sections. It doesn't involve the actual deletion of any data, it merely instructs Windows to leave the desktop blank.

This solution won't affect your taskbar or Start Menu. A benefit of this solution is that, unlike the previous solutions in this section, it has no effect on the desktop contents when viewed in Explorer. So, for example, your My Network Places icon will still be accessible there, even if it's no longer displayed on the desktop.

If you hide all icons on your desktop, it will no longer respond to right-clicks. To open Display Properties, use the Control Panel:

1. Open the Registry Editor (if you're not familiar with the Registry Editor, see Chapter 3).
2. Expand the branches to: `HKEY_CURRENT_USER\Software\Microsoft\Windows\CurrentVersion\Policies\Explorer`.
3. Double-click on the `NoDesktop` value. If it's not there, select **New** from the **Edit** menu, and then select **Binary Value**; type **`NoDesktop`** for the name of the new value.
4. Replace the contents with `01 00 00 00`. Note that this is a binary value, and the input box may not behave like a normal text box; if you mess up, just choose **Cancel** and try again. If at any time you wish to restore the desktop icons, type `00 00 00 00` into the `NoDesktop` value or just delete the value altogether.
5. Click **OK** and close the Registry Editor. You'll have to log out and then log back in for the change to take effect.

Customize My Computer

Aside from the Start Menu, the My Computer window is the gateway to all the resources on your computer, including all your drives, folders, files, printers, and the Control Panel. There are many ways to customize My Computer, including adding and removing items from the window and changing the look and behavior of the icon itself.

To customize the icons of the drives in the My Computer window, see "Customize Drive and Folder Icons" in Chapter 2.

Rename My Computer

This one's easy, and it takes effect immediately. The name you choose will appear as the caption of the My Computer icon, both on the desktop and in Explorer, as well as the title of the My Computer window and anywhere else the My Computer object is referenced.

To rename the My Computer icon, right-click on it and select **Rename**. Type whatever name suits your fancy, and press **Enter**.

Change the My Computer icon

1. Double-click on the **Display** icon in Control Panel, and choose the **Effects** tab. (See Figure 4-2.)
2. Select the **My Computer** icon in the **Desktop Icons** box, and click **Change Icon**. Click **Browse** to choose another file; the default is *Explorer.exe.*
3. Once you've chosen an icon, click **OK**. Your changes will take effect immediately.

Redirect the Desktop icon

All of My Computer's default resources are also available in Explorer and the Start Menu, so you may prefer to connect another program to the My Computer desktop icon. For example, if you prefer Explorer's hierarchical Tree View to My Computer's Macintosh-style navigation, you can configure My Computer to launch Explorer:

1. Open the Registry Editor (if you're not familiar with the Registry Editor, see Chapter 3).
2. Expand the branches to: `HKEY_CLASSES_ROOT\CLSID\ {20D04FE0-3AEA-1069-A2D8-08002B30309D}\shell`. You know you have the right Class ID key if its `(Default)` value is set to `My Computer`.
3. You'll see an existing key already in this branch named `find` representing the **Search** command in the My Computer icon's context menu. Select **New** from the **Edit** menu, and then select **Key**. Type **`Open`** for the name of the new key, and press Enter.
4. Right-click on the new `Open` key, select **New** again and then **Key**. Type **`Command`** for the name of this new key, and press **Enter**.
5. Click once on the new `Command` key, double-click on the `(Default)` value in the right pane, type **`explorer.exe`** in the box, and press **Enter**. Your Registry Editor window should resemble Figure 4-3, except that I've also included some optional command-line parame-

ters (discussed in "Force Explorer to Remember Folder Settings" in Chapter 2). You can, of course, replace `explorer.exe` with the full path and filename of any other program you'd rather use.

6. Close the Registry Editor when you're finished. Click on an empty area of the desktop, and press **F5** to refresh the desktop so that this change will take effect. Double-click the **My Computer** icon at any time to start the specified application.

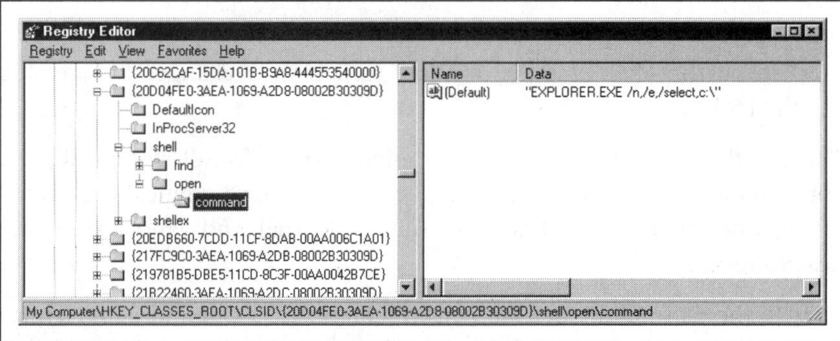

Figure 4-3. Use the Registry Editor to customize the My Computer icon

Now, right-clicking on the My Computer icon will display a context menu with two separate Open commands: one bold and one normal. The bold item will launch the customized action, and the normal one will open the traditional My Computer window. Using this method, you can also add entries to My Computer's context menu; see "Customize Context Menus" later in this chapter for details.

Add entries to the My Computer window

The My Computer window, by default, contains links to all your drives, as well as to the Control Panel.* To add more system objects to the My Computer window and, consequently, to Explorer, follow these steps:

1. Open the Registry Editor (if you're not familiar with the Registry Editor, see Chapter 3).

2. Expand the branches to:

```
HKEY_LOCAL_MACHINE\Software\Microsoft\Windows\CurrentVersion\
     explorer\MyComputer\NameSpace
```

   You might want to create a Registry patch of this branch before continuing, in case you want to restore the default.

* In previous versions of Windows, the Scheduled Tasks, Printers, and Dial-Up Networking icons also appeared in the My Computer window, but they've been moved into the Control Panel in Windows Me (and Windows 2000).

3. Under this branch, you should see one or more keys—each named for a different Class ID. For help in identifying unlabeled keys, see "Really stubborn icons" in the section "Clear the Desktop of Unwanted Icons" earlier in this chapter.
4. To add a new key, select **New** from the **Edit** menu, and then select **Key**. You can then enter any Class ID for the name of the key, and the corresponding system object will be added to the My Computer folder. See Appendix C for a table of Class IDs, or copy and paste a Class ID from elsewhere in the Registry.
5. Refresh the My Computer window to see your changes by pressing the **F5** key.

This solution does not work as you might expect for all system objects. For example, the My Network Places icon will behave erratically if placed in My Computer. You'll have to use a little trial and error to get the desired results.

As with the Start Menu and the Send To menu, you can add items (shortcuts, folders, etc.) to the My Network Places window by adding shortcuts to the *\Windows\Nethood* folder, should that appeal to you.

Remove unwanted entries from the My Computer window

There are two ways to remove icons from the My Computer Window. The first is to follow steps 1–3 in the previous "Add entries to the My Computer window" and simply delete any keys for unwanted objects. Not only is that time consuming, it affects *only* namespace objects—not drives. The following solution is simpler for this particular task and allows removal of drives as well:

1. Double-click on the **TweakUI** icon in Control Panel, and choose the **My Computer** tab.
2. Uncheck any drives you wish to be hidden from My Computer, and click **OK**. Note that removed items should also be removed from Explorer.

Customize the Recycle Bin Icon

Although you can rename any file or folder on your hard disk, as well as almost any system object (including My Computer and My Network Places), Windows won't allow you to rename the Recycle Bin—at least, not without a little fuss. To rename the Recycle Bin to something more compelling, such as "Garbage," "Trash," or "Inanimate Carbon Rod," follow any of the following procedures.

Add the Rename option to the Recycle Bin's context menu[*]

1. Open the Registry Editor (if you're not familiar with the Registry Editor, see Chapter 3).
2. Expand the branches to: `HKEY_CLASSES_ROOT\CLSID\{645FF040-5081-101B-9F08-00AA002F954E}\ShellFolder\`. You know you have the right Class ID key if its `(Default)` is set to `Recycle Bin`.

   It may be easier to locate this key by searching for the first few characters of the Class ID or for the text "Recycle Bin."
3. Double click on the `Attributes` value, and replace the contents with `50 01 00 20`.[†] Note that this is a binary value, and the input box may not behave like a normal text box. If you mess up, just choose **Cancel** and try again.
4. Close the Registry Editor. The change should take effect immediately.
5. You now have the option of renaming the Recycle Bin at any time by right-clicking on it and selecting **Rename**. See Figure 4-1 for a preview.

Manually rename the Recycle Bin

1. Open the Registry Editor (if you're not familiar with the Registry Editor, see Chapter 3).
2. Expand the branches to: `HKEY_CLASSES_ROOT\CLSID\{645FF040-5081-101B-9F08-00AA002F954E}`. You know you have the right Class ID key if its `(Default)` is set to `Recycle Bin`.
3. Double-click on the `(Default)` value in the right pane, and replace the text `Recycle Bin` with any new name you wish. Click **OK**, and then close the Registry Editor.
4. Click on an empty area of the desktop, and press **F5** to refresh the desktop so that this change will take effect.

---

* This is similar to "Solution 2: Recycle Bin" in "Clear the Desktop of Unwanted Icons" earlier in this chapter.

† Use the value `40 01 00 20` to revert the Recycle Bin back to its default configuration. Note that this won't restore the name to its default, which you'll have to do manually. If you've deleted it with Solution 2, use TweakUI (Solution 1) to get it back.

Change the Recycle Bin icon

1. Double-click on the **Display** icon in Control Panel, and choose the **Effects** tab. (See Figure 4-2.)
2. Select the **Recycle Bin** icon (either full or empty) in the **Desktop Icons** box, and click **Change Icon**. Click Browse to choose another file; the default is *Explorer.exe.*
3. Once you've chosen an icon, click **OK**. Your changes will take effect immediately.

If you have Norton Utilities installed, you can right-click on the **Recycle Bin**, select **Properties**, and choose the **Desktop Item** tab to rename the Recycle Bin.

Change the Icons of System Objects

Although direct support isn't built into Windows for changing the icons used for the various system objects, such as the Control Panel, Dial-Up Networking, and the generic folder, it can be done. The icons discussed here are referred to as *shell icons* and are standard Windows icons used for Windows' *virtual objects*; that is, objects other than individual drives, folders, files, and shortcuts. Following are the three ways to change the icons of system objects.

Solution 1: Basic system objects

1. Double-click on the **Display** icon in Control Panel, and choose the **Effects** tab.
2. The **Desktop icons** section lists, by default, five icons: **My Computer**, **My Documents**, **My Network Places**, **Recycle Bin (full)**, and **Recycle Bin (empty)**. Select any icon here, and click **Change Icon** to choose a new one. Click **Browse** to choose another file.
3. Once you've chosen an icon, click **OK**—your changes will take effect immediately.

Solution 2: Default folder and drive icons

This solution allows you to choose the default icon for all drives and folders. To change the icon for a particular drive or folder, see "Customize Drive and Folder Icons" in Chapter 2. Despite the fact that **Drive** and **Folder** are listed in the File Types window, the default icons can not be changed without editing the Registry:

1. Open the Registry Editor. (If you're not familiar with the Registry Editor, see Chapter 3.)
2. For the icon used for drives, expand the branches to: `HKEY_CLASSES_ROOT\Drive\DefaultIcon`. Likewise, for the icon used for folders, expand the branches to: `HKEY_CLASSES_ROOT\Folder\DefaultIcon`.
3. Double-click on the `(Default)` value in the right pane. This value contains the file containing the icon and a number specifying the index of the icon to use (0 being the first icon, 1 being the second, and so on).

   You can specify any valid icon file here. If the file is not in your system path (see Chapter 6, *Troubleshooting*), you'll need to specify the full pathname (e.g., *c:\icons\ugly.ico*). If the file only contains one icon, or if you want to use the first icon in the file, you can omit the trailing comma and number.

   The default icon used for drives is `C:\Windows\System\shell32.dll,3`, and the default icon used for folders is `C:\Windows\System\shell32.dll,8` (assuming Windows is installed in *C:\Windows.*).
4. When you're done, close the Registry Editor. You may have to log out and then log back in for this change to take effect.

Solution 3: All other system objects

1. Open the Registry Editor. (If you're not familiar with the Registry Editor, see Chapter 3.)
2. Expand the branches to: `HKEY_CLASSES_ROOT\CLSID\{`*`class id`*`}\DefaultIcon`, where {*`class id`*} is one of the Class IDs listed in Appendix C. If the Class ID for the object you want to change is not listed there, do a search in the `HKEY_CLASSES_ROOT\CLSID\` branch for the formal name of the object (e.g., `Recycle Bin`). You can back up this entry before you change it by creating a Registry patch at this point (see Chapter 3).
3. Double-click on the `(Default)` value in the right pane.
4. By default, most system objects will have the `(Default)` value set to something like `shell32.dll,17`, which means that Windows will use the eighteenth icon in the file *Shell32.dll* (0 being the first icon, 1 being the second, and so on).
5. You can specify any valid icon file here. If the file is not in your system path (see Chapter 6), you'll need to specify the full pathname (e.g., *c:\icons\ugly.ico*). If the file only contains one icon or if you want to use the first icon in the file, you can omit the trailing comma and number.

6. If a file contains more than one icon, the easiest way to find out which number corresponds to the icon you want is to browse the file in Windows. To browse an icon file, take any existing Windows shortcut (or create a new one), right-click on it, and select **Properties**. Choose the **Shortcut** tab, click **Change Icon**, type the desired filename, and count from the left—zero (0) is the first, one (1) is the second, and so on.
7. This change should take effect the next time you refresh the folder containing the object you've just customized. For example, press the **F5** key while the desktop is active to refresh any desktop icons.

Although you can't change the icons for applications, you can change the icons for shortcuts to those applications, such as those used in the **Start Menu** and on the desktop. Just right-click on the desired shortcut, click **Properties**, choose the **Shortcut** tab, and click **Change Icon**. You can also change the default icon used for application documents (e.g., the icon used for all files with the *.txt* extension). See "Customize Context Menus" later in this chapter for more information.

Files and Folders

Probably the most important customization of files and folders is discussed in the section "Customize Context Menus," where you'll learn about one of the best features of the pseudo-object-oriented interface design in Windows Me.* Examine the topics in this section to learn more and to improve your working experience with Windows.

Love it or hate it, the Web View is part of Windows Me. While the Web View primarily allows you to customize the superficial look of your folders, there are ways to put it to good use. See Chapter 8, *Taking Control of Web Integration*, for more information.

Clean Up and Customize System Folders

The default Windows Me installation occupies tons of hard-disk space and has a myriad of files scattered in more than 230 different folders. Although the sheer number and size of these files aren't necessarily problems with

* True object-oriented design dictates that objects (in this case, files and folders) be aware of their own traits. This design is only mimicked in Windows Me. Instead of each file's knowing which application is used to edit it, Windows determines how to handle a file based solely on the filename extension. This design has advantages and disadvantages, but Microsoft's decision to hide filename extensions, the basis for file associations, only makes the whole system more difficult to understand and master.

today's large, cheap hard drives, the amount of clutter that results can make finding documents, resolving conflicts, and performing other housekeeping very difficult.

One of my personal pet peeves about Windows is the dozen or so folders that accomplish the same thing. For example, *Program Files*, *Common Files*, *Microsoft Shared*, and *MSApps* all contain installed applications and their components. The *My Documents*, *Favorites*, *Personal*, *Received Files*, *My Pictures*, and *My Files* folders all are designated places to store documents and other personal files. Most users have enough trouble keeping track of documents without having to worry about all these extraneous folders. So, why do we have a dozen places to put things when we only need two or three?

As Windows has evolved, the various committees at Microsoft have repeatedly changed their minds about what the various "system" folders have been called and what they should contain. Had Microsoft's designers been more careful, the entire Windows system would be much simpler and more stable, and there would be far less confusion and irritation among developers and users alike. The good news is that there is something you can do to help clean up the mess.

The following solutions allow you to reassign most of Windows' system folders; of course, which folders you wish to customize and where you wish to move them is entirely up to you. Solutions 1 and 2 show how to move or rename some folders only. To effectively delete a folder, you must consolidate it with another, as described in Solution 3.

Solution 1: Relocate some system folders

1. Double-click on the **TweakUI** icon (see Appendix A) in Control Panel, and choose the **General** tab.
2. Choose the folder you wish to change from the **Special Folders** section, and click **Change Location**. Note that you'll have to open up Explorer first and create any folders you wish to use that don't already exist; otherwise TweakUI won't let you do it.

   The drawback to this solution is that TweakUI only lets you configure a few folders. If the one you want to change is not listed, you'll have to use one of the other solutions, listed later in this section.
3. When you're done, you'll have to manually copy the contents of the old folder to the new location.

Solution 2: Drag a system folder

1. Open Explorer, and navigate to the folder you wish to rename or move.
2. Simply rename the folder or drag it to a new location, just as you would any other folder. Most of the time, if you rename or move a system folder, Windows will keep track of it, changing Registry settings on the fly. It is usually obvious that a folder change is being tracked because of the slight delay in increased disk access immediately following the change.

The drawback to this solution is that it doesn't work for all system folders, and in the cases where it does work, it can cause problems. After you make a change, it is best to search the Registry for the old folder name or location and manually change any references to the neglected entries. See Solution 3 for more information.

Solution 3: Relocate all system folders

This solution should let you relocate any folder that is relocatable. Obviously, it's best to back up not only your data, but your Registry settings as well. I also don't need to tell you to proceed with caution and to investigate the contents of any folder you wish to change *before* you actually make the change:

1. Open the Registry Editor (if you're not familiar with the Registry Editor, see Chapter 3).
2. Most of the system folders that can be reassigned are stored in one or more of the following Registry paths. Each key is intended to store certain folders—although, in practice, you may see some folders scattered from place to place. You'll have to look through each of these to find the particular folder you want to change:
   - The shell folders for the currently logged-in user are specified in:

     ```
     HKEY_CURRENT_USER\Software\Microsoft\Windows\CurrentVersion\
         Explorer\Shell Folders
     ```

   - Additional shell folders for the currently logged-in user are specified in:

     ```
     HKEY_CURRENT_USER\Software\Microsoft\Windows\CurrentVersion\
         Explorer\User Shell Folders
     ```

   - The common shell folders, used by all users, are specified in:

     ```
     HKEY_LOCAL_MACHINE\Software\Microsoft\Windows\CurrentVersion\
         Explorer\Shell Folders
     ```

— Additional common shell folders, used by all users, are specified in:

```
HKEY_LOCAL_MACHINE\Software\Microsoft\Windows\CurrentVersion\
    Explorer\User Shell Folders
```

— The *Program Files* and *Common Files* folders (shared by all users) are both defined in:

```
HKEY_LOCAL_MACHINE\SOFTWARE\Microsoft\Windows\CurrentVersion
```

For *Program Files*, you'll need to change both the `ProgramFilesDir` and `ProgramFilesPath` values; for *Common Files*, just change the `CommonFilesDir` value.*

— The *Application Data* folder for the current user is defined by the `DefaultDir` value in:

```
HKEY_CURRENT_USER\Software\Microsoft\Windows\CurrentVersion\
    ProfileReconciliation\AppData.
```

3. To change a folder location, you must first find the corresponding entry in any of the Registry keys listed in step 2. Just double-click the appropriate value (or values) and edit the entry as you please. If there is more than one occurrence of the item you wish to change, you must change them all.

4. Ideally, you should only have to specify the location of the Desktop folder once, and every application should simply look it up there before accessing it. In practice, you may find that some folders will be referenced in other places in the Registry as well, so to fully implement the desired change, you must change every reference accordingly.

   There can be hundreds of references to some of these folders, especially *Program Files* and *Common Files*, so you'll probably need to use a program like Registry Search and Replace (download it from *http://www.annoyances.org*). Another killer is that some references may contain the short filename version of a folder, while others may contain the long filename version (i.e., *C:\PROGRA~1* for *c:\Program Files*). Make sure to get them all.

5. Close the Registry Editor when finished. You'll most likely have to restart Windows for the desired change to take effect.

---

* *Common Files* is a subfolder under *Program Files*, which contains more application-specific folders. In fact, you may see some duplication in the contents of *Program Files* and *Common Files*; consolidating these folders may reclaim more free disk space and reduce the possibility of version conflicts.

6. If you redirect the location of a folder like *Program Files* or *Common Files*, make sure you move the actual files located in these folders to the new locations as well. Otherwise, several programs that rely on these folders won't be able to find their files.

   Also, in some cases, if you've relocated a folder in the Registry without creating it in Explorer, Windows will do it for you. However, it's good practice to make sure that any folders specified in the Registry also exist on your hard disk.

To effectively *remove* a system folder, the best thing to do is simply to consolidate it with another system folder. The benefits of doing this are substantial.

For example, Windows Me comes with the *My Documents* folder, which helps to enforce a valuable strategy for keeping track of personal documents by providing a single root for all documents, regardless of the application that created them. This allows you, for example, to sort your documents by project rather than by program. The problem is that this design is seriously undermined by the existence of other system folders with similar uses, such as *My Pictures*, *Favorites*, *Personal*, *Received Files*, and *My Files*.* Consolidating all of these system folders so that they all point to the same place, such as *c:\Documents* or *c:\Projects*, causes several positive things to happen. Not only does it provide a common root for all personal documents, making your stuff much easier to find and keep track of, it also allows you to open any document quickly by using the **Favorites** menu in the **Start Menu**.

Here's how to consolidate two folders into one, using *My Pictures* as an example:

1. Using the previous solution, relocate the *My Pictures* folder (specified in:

   ```
   HKEY_CURRENT_USER\Software\Microsoft\Windows\CurrentVersion\Explorer\
       Shell Folders)
   ```

   so that it is using the same folder as your *My Documents* folder.

2. Restart Windows for the change to take effect.

3. Copy all the files and folders contained in *My Pictures* into *My Documents*.

4. Delete the *My Pictures* folder.

---

* *My Files* is the counterpart to *My Documents*, which is used by some versions of WordPerfect and other non-Microsoft application suites. The *Personal* folder was used by Office 95, but not enforced in subsequent releases. Depending on which programs you've installed or have used in the past, these folders may or may not appear on your system.

Note that this should also stop Windows from automatically creating the *My Pictures* folder when you try to delete it.

Special Case—The Temp folder

Nearly all applications in Windows use the *Temp* folder to store working files, which are created temporarily while an application is running and are deleted when the application closes. By default, the location of this folder is *\Windows\Temp*, but it can be easily and safely moved to a different location.

There are several reasons why you might want to do this. As any experienced Windows user knows, crashing is, unfortunately, a daily experience. When an application crashes, it doesn't get a chance to delete any temporary files it had created, which means that the *Temp* folder can quickly fill up with hundreds of files that look something like *~DF13F4.TMP*. Not only can this consume lots of disk space, but if any files were open when the application that created them crashes, they become corrupted, which can degrade system performance and cause other problems. If you have more than one hard disk or hard-disk partition, it can be beneficial to relocate the *Temp* folder to a drive other than the one on which Windows is installed.

The *Temp* folder isn't specified in the Registry like the others. Instead, it's an *environment variable* (actually it's two). Environment variables are settings that, like Registry settings, are available to all running applications and are kept in memory from Windows startup until you shut down. Environment variables also have the advantage of being accessible from the command prompt (DOS). The *system path*, another environment variable, is discussed in "The Path Less Traveled" in Chapter 6.

1. Start the System Configuration Utility (*Msconfig.exe*),* and choose the **Environment** tab.
2. There are two variables we care about here: `TEMP` and `TMP`. Both are used (as opposed to just one), in order to support an inconsistency in older applications. Double-click on each entry to change its value. Chose any existing folder on your system (create it in Explorer if you haven't yet), and then specify the full path here (e.g., *c:\temp*).

---

* In previous versions of Windows, environment variables were set with one or more lines in the *Autoexec.bat* file, which is now obsolete.

In some cases, each of these variables may point to different folders; even if you don't necessarily want to relocate this folder, I recommend changing both entries so that they all point to the same place. The check marks to the left of the variable names allow you to disable variables without deleting them.

3. Click **OK** to close the System Configuration Utility.

Although the files in your *Temp* folder (or folders) are intended to be used only while some applications are running, these files are often left behind even after the applications that created the files are closed. Subsequently, this folder can become quite large, full of files that aren't being used. And any files left over from a crash may be corrupted, even causing problems when Windows starts. I recommend writing a startup script, as described in Chapter 9, *Scripting and Automation*, that automatically clears the *Temp* folder every time Windows starts.

Occasionally, an older installation program may write one or more files to the Windows Temp folder to be processed when the system is rebooted. If you were to write a startup script (see Chapter 9) that cleared the temp folder automatically and specified it to load from the *StartUp* folder in the Start Menu, then this script would be run after said files are processed. In other words, you should be safe.

Customize Context Menus

A *Context menu* is the short menu* that appears when you use the right mouse button to click on a file, folder, application titlebar, or nearly any other object on the screen. Most of the time, this menu includes a list of *actions* appropriate to the object on which you've clicked. In other words, the options available depend on the *context.*

The context menu for files, the most commonly used and customized context menu, depends upon the type of file selected, which is determined by the filename extension. For example, all text files (with the *.txt* extension) will have the same context menu, regardless of what they contain or which application was used to create them.†

In addition to the standard context menu items, such as **Copy**, **Paste**, **Delete**, **Rename**, and **Properties**, you'll usually see **Open**, **Print**, and **Print To** (at the top of the list), which represent customizable *actions* that can be performed with the selected file. Each of these actions is linked to an

* Microsoft sometimes calls this a "Shortcut Menu," which is somewhat misleading.

† This is why Windows gives you a stern warning when you try to change a file's extension.

application: if you right-click on a *.txt* file and select **Open**, Windows will launch Notepad (by default) and instruct it to open the selected file. This *association* is what this topic is about.

The *default* action—the action that is carried out when a file of a given type is double-clicked—will appear in **bold** text. If a file type is not registered with Windows, double-clicking on a file of that type will open the **Open With** dialog box, allowing you to choose an associated application on the spot. The exception to this occurs when a file type *has* been registered, yet has no actions associated with it (useful if you want to identify a file type, but not necessarily open it).* In this case, nothing will happen when the file is double-clicked.

The default action is also what can cause the most controversy. Say you have grown accustomed to double-clicking on *.html* files on your hard disk and having them opened in Netscape Navigator (in other words, Netscape is the default application for that file type). One day, out of necessity or obligation or whatever, you install one of Microsoft's updates to Windows, which happens to contain a new version of Internet Explorer. Unless you're careful to choose the correct advanced options, suddenly, and without warning, all of your *.html* associations are changed, making Internet Explorer the default application.

Although the most obvious reason to customize a file's context menu is to control the default action, what makes context menus so powerful is that you can assign as many different actions as you like to any given file type. In the case of *.html* files, for example, you could add an **Edit** action to open your favorite text editor, a **View with Netscape** action, and a **View with Internet Explorer** action—all in addition to the default action.

It's possible to add, remove, or modify context menu items for nearly any file type. The File Types window, shown in Figure 4-4, is the only dedicated tool provided by Microsoft to manage file associations in Windows; it has been somewhat improved in Windows Me from previous versions. Some thought has been given to both experienced and novice users, although it still lacks the streamlining such an important feature deserves.

For the most flexibility in customizing context menus, you'll want to see how file associations are actually stored in the Registry, as described in "Understanding File Types" in Chapter 3.

* An example is the way DLL files are registered with Windows by default.

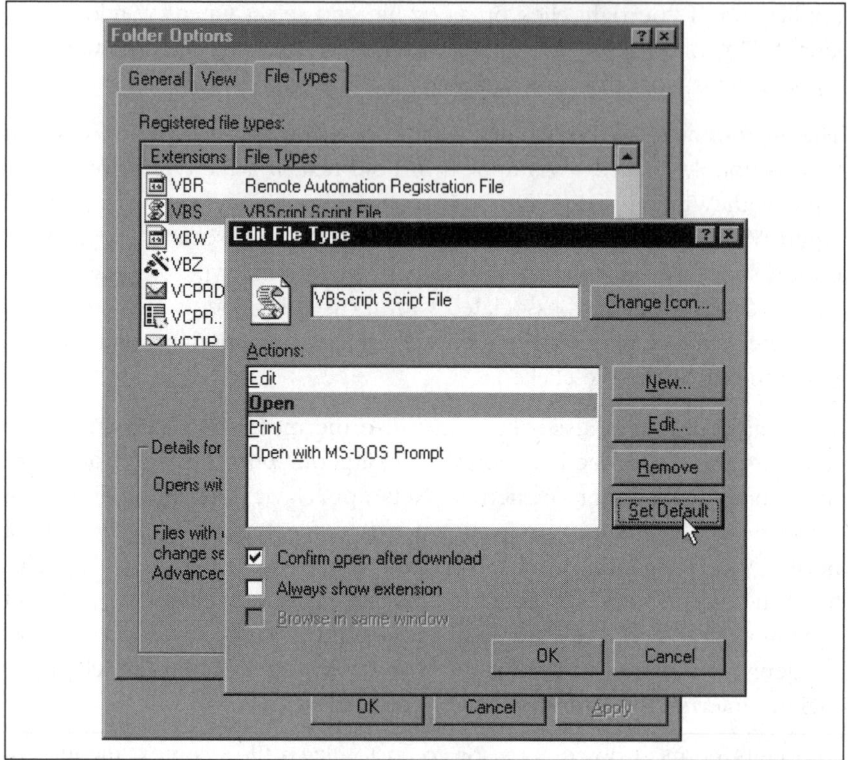

Figure 4-4. The File Types tool has been significantly improved in Windows Me from previous versions, although it could benefit from some additional streamlining and automation

Use file types to add, remove, or edit context menus

1. Select **Folder Options** from Explorer's **View** menu (or double-click the Folder Options icon in Control Panel), and choose the **File Types** tab.
2. Select the desired file type from the list, and click **Advanced**. You can sort the entries by filename extension or file-type description to make any given file type easier to find.* (The **Change** button only displays the limited **Open With** dialog box.)

   Keep in mind that some file types may be claiming more than one extension. For example, the *.htm* and *.html* extensions are most likely associated with the same file type. If you are editing such a file type, it won't matter which extension you select. See "Link a filename extension to an existing file type" later in this chapter for more information.

* The ability to sort the entries is a new and sorely needed feature in Windows Me. Previously, finding file types in this window has been difficult: for example, the entry for the *.xls* extension was listed under "Microsoft Excel Spreadsheet," putting it alphabetically under "M" instead of "E" for Excel or "X" for XLS.

3. The **Actions** list box contains a list of the customizable context menu items. Each one has a name and a command line (the application filename followed by command-line parameters, if applicable). Some actions have DDE commands, which are used only by certain applications—you probably won't have to bother with this setting.*

   The bold item is the default action, also shown in bold at the top of the context menu. If there's no bold item, and therefore no default, double-clicking a file of that type will do nothing. To make *no action* the default, you'll have to delete the current default (bold) action. If you don't want to remove any actions, just add a new, temporary action, make it the default, and then delete it.

4. Press **OK**. The changes should take effect immediately; your desktop and any open Explorer or single-folder windows will automatically refresh within a few seconds.

Link a filename extension to an existing file type

Sometimes two filename extensions share the same file type—that way, you don't have to go to the trouble of creating and modifying a separate set of actions for each extension. In cases where two file formats are similar enough to warrant file-type sharing, such as *.jpg* and *.gif* files, follow the upcoming steps.

To see a list of all the extensions owned by a given file type, sort the **Registered file types** list by file-type description. Note that two *different* file types can have the same description and would therefore be different yet indistinguishable in this view:

1. In the File Types window (see earlier in this section), configure a single file type as desired.
2. Click **New**, and type the filename extension without the dot (e.g., **`txt`**) in the **File Extension** field. If the extension is currently associated with another file type, that link will be broken, then replaced with the one you choose here.
3. Click **Advanced >>** to show a second list of existing file types, and choose any desired file type to claim ownership of the new extension.

---

* DDEs are poorly documented commands used by Windows to communicate with applications that are already open; for example, when using the **Print** context menu command for *.doc* (Microsoft Word) files, Windows simply communicates with Word and instructs it to open the file.

If, instead, you want to create a new file type, either choose **<New>** or make no choice at all. A new file type will be created and named for the extension; if you type **`xyz`**, the new file type will be named "XYZ File."

4. You can then proceed to edit the new entry. If you've linked the new extension with a new file type, all of that file type's properties (e.g., actions, icon, description) will appear in the new entry as well.

Choose a file-type association on the fly

If you have double-clicked on a file with an extension that has not yet been registered, you might've seen the **Open With** dialog box and been presented with a list of applications currently associated with other file types. From that point, you can select an application, type a name for the new type, and continue.

This is the same box that appears if you open the File Types window, select a file type from the list, and click **Change**. To get this window for an already registered file type without going through this hassle, follow these steps:

1. Hold the **Shift** key while right-clicking on any file of the given type.
2. Select **Open With** from the menu. This menu item won't be visible unless you press the **Shift** key.
3. The **Always use this program to open these files** option will be turned off by default, allowing you to choose an application without affecting your current associations. Unfortunately, there's no way to add a nondefault context-menu item with this method.

To configure your file types so that you don't have to hold the **Shift** key, follow these steps:

1. Open the Registry Editor (if you're not familiar with the Registry Editor, see Chapter 3).
2. Expand the branches to `HKEY_CLASSES_ROOT/*/`. On this branch, you can place context menu actions that will appear on files of all types, even those that have not yet been registered.
3. Select **New** from the **Edit** menu, select **Key**, then type **`shell`**. Select the new `shell` key, and repeat the process to create an `openas` key, and again to create a `command` key.

4. You should then be able to navigate to `HKEY_CLASSES_ROOT/*/shell/openas/command`. Double-click on the `(Default)` value, and type the following:

```
rundll32.exe shell32.dll,OpenAs_RunDLL %1
```

5. Press **OK**, and close the Registry Editor when you're finished. Right-click on any file and select **Open With** to use this feature.

Another way to get to the **Open With** dialog box is to right-click on any file, select **Properties**, and then click **Change**.

Customize context menus for drives, folders, and desktop icons

Folders, drives, and desktop icons also have customizable context menus, but the File Types window (described earlier) has limitations on what can actually be changed. Refer to "Understanding File Types" in Chapter 3 for more information on the Registry structure involved in this solution:

1. Open the Registry Editor (if you're not familiar with the Registry Editor, see Chapter 3).
2. For folder context menus, expand the branches to `HKEY_CLASSES_ROOT\Directory\shell\`. For drive context menus (visible in Explorer and the My Computer window), expand the branches to `HKEY_CLASSES_ROOT\Drive\shell\`. For the context menus of any system objects, such as My Network Places, expand the branches to `HKEY_CLASSES_ROOT\CLSID\{`*`class id`*`}\shell\`, where `{`*`class id`*`}` matches one of the codes listed in Appendix C, including the braces.
3. Select **New** from the **Edit** menu, select **Key**, type the name of the new item you want added to the list, such as **`Open`** or **`Edit`**, and press **Enter**.
4. Highlight the new key, select **New** from the **Edit** menu, and then select **Key** again.
5. Type **`command`** for the name of this new key, and press **Enter**.
6. Double-click on the `(Default)` value in the right pane, and type the full command line (path and filename of the application executable, followed by any applicable command-line parameters) you want associated with this entry.
7. Close the Registry Editor when you're finished. These changes should take effect immediately.

Once you've set up your file types the way you want them, see the next solution, "Protect Your File Types," to prevent other applications from changing your file types without asking.

Protect Your File Types

One of the most irritating aspects of using Windows is when the settings you've spent time customizing are overwritten or forgotten. A common practice employed by some software developers is to jerryrig an application so that it overwrites your file associations, either when it's installed or, even worse, every time the program is run. That way, their program becomes the default.

For some proprietary file types, such as Excel Files (*.xls*), this isn't much of a problem, because there aren't any other programs that use these files. The impact is greater on more general file types, such as the large quantity of graphics formats (*.gif*, *.jpg*, *.tif*, *.bmp*, and *.png*), where there are literally hundreds of applications that use these files. It's not unusual for several of these applications to be installed simultaneously on a single system, all competing for the dubious distinction of being the default. Probably the most high-profile example of this competition is that between competing web browsers. Not only are file associations in play, but URL associations as well—every time you click a link in any application, the URL association is what's used to decide which web browser application to use. See Chapter 8 for details on URL associations.

Ideally, only you should be in the position to decide which program you use for each task. Unfortunately, it's essentially impossible to write-protect (prevent the overwriting of) any Registry settings—including file types—in Windows Me. Although Windows NT and Windows 2000 have the ability to set user permissions in the Registry, Windows Me simply does not have that functionality.

Probably the most effective protection against overwritting file types is to back up the portions of the Registry that are at risk, allowing you to easily restore them should the need arise. This is accomplished with Registry patches; see "Using Registry Patches" and "Understanding File Types," both in Chapter 3, before continuing.

The procedure outlined later would be a good one to follow, for example, before installing an application you believe might overwrite an existing file type. Repeat these steps for each file type you wish to protect:

1. Open the Registry Editor (if you're not familiar with the Registry Editor or Registry patches, see Chapter 3).
2. Expand the `HKEY_CLASSES_ROOT\` branch, and locate the keys that you wish to protect.

Any given file type is stored as one or more extension keys and a file-type key. For example, the extensions *.txt* and *.log* may both be linked with the `txtfile` file type. So, to save the entire file type, you'll need to save each of the following Registry branches:

```
HKEY_CLASSES_ROOT\.txt
HKEY_CLASSES_ROOT\.log
HKEY_CLASSES_ROOT\txtfile
```

If you only save the extension keys or the file-type key, the Registry patch will be incomplete. You can only select one key at a time, so start with one and repeat step 3 for each remaining key.

To see a list of all the extensions owned by a given file type, open the File Types window (see "Customize Context Menus" earlier in this chapter), and sort the **Registered file types** list by file-type description. Note that two *different* file types can have the same description and, therefore, would be indistinguishable in this view.*

3. When you've highlighted a Registry key you want to export, select **Export Registry File** from the **Registry** menu, and specify a filename for the patch. Because you'll be exporting at least two patches, don't worry too much about the names just yet. Make sure not to export two branches to the same file, however; one will simply overwrite the other.

   Also, don't try to export the entire `HKEY_CLASSES_ROOT` branch, because it contains much more information than we need for this purpose, and restoration of a patch will have unpredictable effects.

4. Once you've exported all the keys you're interested in, close the Registry Editor.

   You should have at least two Registry patches from this exercise, perhaps more. Because they're just plain text files, we can easily merge them together into a single file with Notepad. Choose one file to be the *main* patch, and then cut and paste the contents of the other patches into it. The only editing you'll have to do is to remove the `REGEDIT4` line from all but the main patch, so that it only appears once—at the top of the file.

   If you're exporting multiple complete file types, you might want to merge the individual patches into *several* separate Registry patches—one for each file type.

* Keep in mind that file-type descriptions will not necessarily be the same as the key names that contain the file types. See "Understanding File Types" in Chapter 3 for details.

5. Save your changes to the main patch, and then delete all the other patches.

   Whenever a particular file type that you've backed up becomes overwritten by an errant application, just double-click on the patch you made to restore it.

   In most cases, when you apply a Registry patch, it will simply overwrite the information that's there with whatever is in the patch. However, in some circumstances, there may be leftover context-menu items from any newly installed applications.

6. To apply the patch automatically whenever you start Windows, place a shortcut to the patch in your Startup folder (usually *\Windows\Start Menu\Programs\Startup*). Type the following into the shortcut's command line:

   ```
   regedit /s c:\filetypes\text.reg
   ```

   where `c:\filetypes\text.reg` is the full path and filename of the Registry patch you wish to apply. Note the `/s` switch, which runs the Registry Editor in *silent* mode, skipping the two prompts that normally appear when Registry patches are applied.

Although there's only so much you can do to prevent your file types from being overwritten, other work commands do exist. Try adding a context menu item for each program installed on your system, such as "Open with Notepad" and "Open with WordPerfect" for text files. That way, whatever the default is, you'll always have your preferred applications handy.

One sticking point you may encounter when trying to reconfigure file types is that some actions use Dynamic Data Exchange (DDE). DDE is a method of communication between applications, sometimes used by Windows to communicate with the applications it launches.* If a particular file type for an application stops working for some reason, it could be that the DDE information has changed or been erased altogether. If this is the case, you'll usually have to reinstall the application to restore the DDE-enabled file types, because there's little standardization with DDE.

* For example, when you right-click on a *.doc* file and select **Print**, Windows opens the file in Wordpad (or Word, if installed) and then sends a DDE message to the application to print the document. This is opposed to opening separate copies of the associated application for each selected document to be printed.

Clear Unwanted Entries from Explorer's New Menu

If you right-click on the desktop or an open folder (or open Explorer's **File** menu) and choose **New**, you will be presented with a special list of registered file types that can be created on the spot. Choose one, and Explorer will create a new, empty file with the appropriate extension in that location.*

This list is maintained by certain Registry entries, and since most of us will not need to create new Ami Pro documents on the fly, there is a way to remove these unwanted entries. Having an extra entry here and there is not necessarily a big deal, but it can be quite frustrating if you're forced to wade through a long list of file types every time you want to create a new file. The following solutions should allow you to overcome this annoyance.

Solution 1

1. Double-click on the **TweakUI** icon (see Appendix A) in Control Panel, and choose the **New** tab.
2. Uncheck any unwanted items, or click **Remove** for those items you know you'll never want again.

Note that this doesn't prevent applications from adding subsequent items, either when they're installed or the next time they're run.

Solution 2

1. Open the Registry Editor (if you're not familiar with the Registry Editor, see Chapter 3).
2. Select **Find** from the **Edit** menu, type **`ShellNew`**, and press **OK**.
3. Every `ShellNew` key that is found will be a branch of a particular key named for a file extension (see "Understanding File Types" in Chapter 3). If you don't want that file type in your New menu, delete the entire `ShellNew` branch.
4. Repeat this for every unwanted file type, and close the Registry Editor when finished. The changes will take effect immediately.

---

* In some cases, Windows duplicates a special template to make the file, rather than creating a new, empty file.

Solution 3 (advanced users only)

If either of the previous solutions is ineffective for removing a particularly stubborn entry, you have a last resort. For example, some applications actually replace this entry every time they're started, completely ignoring your preferences. Two popular programs known for this annoying behavior are Adobe Photoshop v4.0 or later (*http://www.adobe.com*) and JASC's Paint Shop Pro v4.0 or later (*http://www.jasc.com*). The following solution works on both of those applications and should work on any other program that does this as well.

You'll need a good hex editor, such as UltraEdit-32 (*http://www.ultraedit.com*), which we'll use to actually change the program executable.

If this is done incorrectly, it can damage an application. But if you back up any files before altering them, you eliminate this possibility.

The following example assumes you're using UltraEdit-32 v5.0 or later to fix this problem in Paint Shop Pro v4.0. Although the specifics may change for later versions of these programs or for a different editor and "patient," the technique is the same:

1. First, follow the instructions in the previous Solution 1 or Solution 2 to get rid of any existing entries.
2. Because Paint Shop Pro automatically adds the `ShellNew` branch (explained earlier in Solution 2) every time it starts, we'll start by assuming that this happens in the main executable. Make sure that Paint Shop Pro is not running before you start messing around with the files.
3. Make a backup of the *Psp.exe* file in the Paint Shop Pro installation directory. See "Make a Duplicate of a File or Folder" in Chapter 2 for more information.
4. In UltraEdit-32, select **File** and then **Open**, and select *Psp.exe* from the Paint Shop Pro installation directory.
5. Because this editor is used to edit ASCII (plain text) files as well as binary (hex mode) files, make sure it's in hex mode (make sure the **Hex Edit** option is checked in the **Edit** menu).

6. Select **Find** from the **Search** menu, type **`shellnew`** in the **Find What** field, check the **Find ASCII** option, and click **Find Next**. When UltraEdit-32 finds the first occurrence of ShellNew, close the **Find** box, and change the text so it reads **`ShellNix`**—a change that small (like the "ix") isn't likely to disrupt anything in the program, but it's enough for Explorer not to include it in the **New** menu.
7. Repeat the process for all additional occurrences of ShellNew. When you're finished, select **Save** from the **File** menu and close UltraEdit-32. The change should take effect the next time you start Paint Shop Pro.
8. If you can't find the ShellNew text in the application you're editing or if replacing it as described earlier doesn't do the trick, there are other places to look. For example, many programs have several *.DLL* files in the same directory. Use Explorer's **Find** feature to look through all the files in the application's directory for the text ShellNew. Repeat the previous steps in any file in which it's found.

If you use Solution 1 and then look in the Registry, you'll see that TweakUI has simply renamed the `ShellNew` branch as `ShellNew-` for those branches you've chosen to disable. Only if you click **Remove** in TweakUI are the branches actually removed.

Admittedly, Solution 3 is extreme, but sometimes the programmers have been so stubborn that it's your last resort. Also, if you get a hankering for some tinkering, learning this type of customization can come in very handy.

Photoshop and Paint Shop Pro are both mentioned in Solution 3 for example only. Although they both exhibit this design flaw, they are otherwise good programs. In fact, the figures in this book were created with both programs.

Clear Unwanted Entries from the Search Menu

If you select **Search** from the **Start Menu**, you'll see several different search options. The two built-in entries, **For Files or Folders** and **On the Internet**, are pretty self-explanatory, and neither can be removed. However, the additional entries are specified in the Registry and can be easily removed:

1. Open the Registry Editor (if you're not familiar with the Registry Editor, see Chapter 3).
2. Expand the branches to: `HKEY_LOCAL_MACHINE\Software\Microsoft\Windows\CurrentVersion\explorer\FindExtensions`.

3. In this branch, you'll find several keys and subkeys, most of which represent entries in the **Search** menu. You should be able to ascertain which keys correspond to which menu items. If you run into a key without an intuitive name or descriptive value contained therein, at the very least, you'll find a class ID (described in Appendix C). A quick search through the Registry will locate another instance of said class ID, which should provide a clue as to its purpose.
4. It's generally safe to delete any keys from this branch, although it's advisable to first back up the entire `FindExtensions` branch by creating a Registry patch (see "Using Registry Patches" in Chapter 3).

   If, for example, you wanted to get rid of the **On the Internet** entry, you'd delete the `WebSearch` key, located in the `static` branch.

Although it's easy to delete unwanted Search menu entries, you can't add a new entry simply by creating links here—that's something that must be done programmatically.

Mirror a Folder with Folder Shortcuts

Windows Shortcuts are tiny files that link to applications, documents, drives, folders, and some system objects. They're convenient in that they behave the same as the objects to which they're linked when you double-click them or drag-drop other objects on them. If you drag a file into a folder's shortcut, for example, it's the same as dragging the file into the folder.

The inherent problem with Window Shortcuts is that they are files, and as such, have the same limitations as files. They are sorted in Explorer with the rest of the files; shortcuts to folders are not grouped with folders as you might expect. Furthermore, shortcuts to folders cannot be specified in a path. For example, if you create a shortcut to the folder *d:\Cletus* and place that shortcut in *c:\Brandine*, then you can't reference objects stored in *d:\Cletus* by typing *c:\Brandine\Cletus*.

Enter **Folder Shortcuts**, a new undocumented feature in Windows Me (and Windows 2000). Folder shortcuts behave exactly like folders because they *are* folders. With a little tweaking, any empty folder can be turned into a Folder Shortcut, a mirror of any other drive or folder on your system, on your network, or even on the Internet!

If you create a Folder Shortcut and then try to delete it, you *will* be deleting the target folder and all of its contents. Folder Shortcuts must be dismantled before they can be removed. See later in this chapter for details.

Folder Shortcuts, once in place, are indistinguishable from the folders to which they link. If you create a Folder Shortcut to *d:\Cletus* and place it in *c:\Brandine*, then it will appear as though there's a folder called *Cletus* located in *c:\Brandine*; in other words, *c:\Brandine\Cletus* will be a valid path.*

Create a Folder Shortcut

Here's how to make a Folder Shortcut to an existing folder on your hard disk or on your local network (see later in this chapter for details on creating a Folder Shortcut to an FTP folder):

1. Choose an existing folder in Explorer—it can be located on any drive, including your network. Create a standard Windows Shortcut to that folder on your desktop, and name the new shortcut `target`. (The shortcut filename will actually be *target.lnk*, although the *.lnk* filename extension will be hidden in Explorer.)

   The easiest way is to drag-drop the folder icon using your right mouse button, and then select **Create Shortcut(s) Here** from the menu that appears. See "Move or Copy Files at Will" and Figure 2-2 in Chapter 2 for more information on this process.

2. Next, make a new folder on your desktop, and call it *Dingus*.† To help protect a Folder Shortcut from accidental deletion, make the folder read-only. Right-click on the folder icon, and select **Properties**. Turn on the **Read-only** option, and click **OK**.
3. Drag-drop the `target` shortcut you made into the new folder.
4. Open a plain-text editor, such as Notepad, and type the following four lines:

   ```
   [.ShellClassInfo]
   CLSID2={0AFACED1-E828-11D1-9187-B532F1E9575D}
   Flags=2
   ConfirmFileOp=0
   ```

5. Save this into the new folder, and call it *desktop.ini*.
6. Open an MS-DOS command prompt (*Command.com*), and change the active directory to the new folder by typing **`CD c:\windows\desktop\dingus`**, replacing `c:\windows\desktop\dingus` with the actual path of the new folder.‡

---

* For those of you familiar with Unix, Folder Shortcuts are very similar to symbolic links.

† The name actually doesn't matter, but to make things easy on us, use fewer than eight letters right now. You can always rename it later.

‡ A handy shortcut is to simply type **`CD`**, followed by a space, and then drag-drop the icon for the new folder onto the MS-DOS Prompt window.

Tinkering Techniques

If you're successful, the DOS prompt will look like `C:\Windows\Desktop\dingus>`.

7. Next, type **`ATTRIB +h +s desktop.ini`**—this will turn on the Hidden and System attributes for the *desktop.ini* file, which you can't do from within Windows. Type **`exit`** when you're done.

   See Appendix B, *DOS Resurrected*, for more details on the `CD` and `ATTRIB` commands.

8. If the new folder is open, close it now. The next time you open the folder, you'll see the contents of the target folder, rather than the two files, *desktop.ini* and *target*.

The new Folder Shortcut can now be copied or moved anywhere you like. For the sake of safety, you should take certain steps to mark this new folder as a Folder Shortcut. Although it will be described as a "Folder Shortcut" in Explorer's Type column, as well as in the folder's Properties dialog box, it will be otherwise indistinguishable. In addition to naming it something like *Shortcut to Dingus*, you can also change the icon of the Folder Shortcut—see "Change the Icons of System Objects" earlier in this chapter for details. If you don't choose an icon, the Folder Shortcut will assume the icon of the folder to which it's linked.

I strongly recommend using an empty folder to transform into a Folder Shortcut. If there are any objects stored in said folder, they will become inaccessible in Windows; they will be visible only in DOS or after you dismantle the Folder Shortcut, as explained later. There should be no effect on the contents of the target folder, however.

If you find the need to create Folder Shortcuts more easily, see "Mirror a Folder with Folder Shortcuts" in Chapter 9 for a Windows Script Host (WSH) script that automates this process.

A Folder Shortcut can also be used to mirror an FTP site, effectively allowing you to transfer files across the Internet using Explorer. See "Accessing an FTP Site in Explorer" in Chapter 7 for details.

Dismantle a Folder Shortcut

It's important to realize that once you create a Folder Shortcut, you can't remove it using traditional methods. If you try to delete a Folder Shortcut by dragging it into the Recycle Bin, for example, Windows will simply delete all the contents of the *target folder*. To remove a Folder Shortcut, you must first dismantle it. Because DOS doesn't recognize Folder Shortcuts, we can use DOS to delete the two files we created earlier:

1. Open an MS-DOS command prompt (*Command.com*), and change the active directory to the new folder by typing **`CD c:\windows\desktop\dingus`**, replacing `c:\windows\desktop\dingus` with the actual path of the new folder.*

   If you're successful, the DOS prompt will look like `C:\Windows\Desktop\dingus>`.

2. Next, type **`ATTRIB -h -s desktop.ini`**—this will turn *off* the Hidden and System attributes for the *desktop.ini* file, which you can't do from within Windows.

3. Type **`DEL *.*`** to remove the files *desktop.ini* and *target.lnk*. Type **`EXIT`** when you're done.

   See Appendix B for more details on the `CD`, `ATTRIB`, and `DEL` commands.

4. If the new folder is open, close it now. The next time you open the folder, you'll see the contents of the target folder, rather than the two files *desktop.ini* and *target*. The folder can now be safely deleted.

Tinkering Techniques

Print Out a Directory Listing

What would seem to be a simple function, the ability to print out a list of files in any given directory, does not exist in Windows Me. However, there are a few ways, using folders' context menus, to add this functionality to Windows.

One of the nice things about context menus (and also one of their limitations) is that they are implemented in a way that is compatible with the way DOS programs have worked for nearly 20 years. For example, if you right-click on a *.txt* file and select **Open**, and the Open action is associated with Notepad, Windows simply launches Notepad with the text file specified in the command line, like this:

```
C:\windows\notepad.exe somefile.txt
```

Using this simple syntax, we can add an action associated with a simple DOS batch file to the context menus for folders:

1. Open a text editor, such as Notepad, and type the following two lines into a new document:

   ```
   CD %1
   DIR >LPT1
   ```

* A handy shortcut is to simply type **`CD`**, followed by a space, and then drag-drop the icon for the new folder onto the MS-DOS Prompt window.

The *DIR* command is what actually generates the directory listing, and the > character instructs Windows to redirect the output from the command to the printer port (`LPT1`; use `LPT2` instead, if applicable).

You can use any of the *DIR* command's options to further customize this feature. To specify the desired sort order, change the pervious line to the following:

```
DIR /O:xxx >LPT1
```

where *xxx* can be any or all of the following letters, in order by preference: `N` to sort by name, `E` for extension, `S` for size, `D` for date, `G` to group directories first, `A` by last access date (earliest first). See Appendix B for more information on the *DIR* command.

2. Save the two-line file into your *Windows\Command* folder, and call it *Printdir.bat.*
3. Right-click on the file in Explorer, select **Properties**, and choose the **Program** tab. Turn on the **Close on Exit** option, choose **Minimized** from the **Run** list box, and click **OK**.
4. Next, Open the Registry Editor (if you're not familiar with the Registry Editor, see Chapter 3).
5. Expand the branches to `HKEY_CLASSES_ROOT\Directory\shell`.
6. Select **New** from the **Edit** menu, and then select **Key**.
7. Type **`Print Contents`** for the name of this new key, and press **Enter**.
8. Highlight the new `Print Contents` key, select **New** from the **Edit** menu, and then select **Key** again.
9. Type **`command`** for the name of this new key, and press **Enter**.
10. Double-click on the `(Default)` value in the right pane, and type the following:

    ```
    C:\Windows\Command\PRINTDIR.BAT
    ```

    assuming that `C:\Windows\` is your Windows folder.
11. To use the new feature, just right-click on any folder icon, and select the **Print Contents** option to print its contents.

Creative Element Power Tools (*http://www.creativelement.com*) comes with a context-menu add-on, allowing you to print or copy a folder's contents to the clipboard, among other things.

Turn File Icons into Thumbnail Previews

Windows tries hard to be as graphical as possible, which can sometimes be its downfall. Case in point: when was the last time you found the icon for an application or associated document to be the least bit helpful in determining what was inside?

In Explorer, when you view a folder containing icons (*.ico* files), cursors (*.cur* files), or animated cursors (*.ani* files), their file icons are *previews* of their contents instead of simply generic icons for the application with which they're associated. Now, Windows has the capability to generate these types of thumbnail previews for other kinds of files as well, and a new feature in Windows Me takes it even further.

Before using either of these solutions, double-click on the **Display** icon in Control Panel, choose the **Effects** tab, and turn on the **Show icons using all possible colors** option.

Solution 1: Icon previews for bitmap files

The advantage to this solution is that once the change has been made, it will be enabled automatically for all folders on your system. The disadvantages are that this solution works only for *.bmp* files, and the thumbnail previews will never be larger than the rest of your system icons (usually 32 × 32 pixels):

1. Open the Registry Editor. (If you're not familiar with the Registry Editor, see Chapter 3.)
2. Expand the branches to `HKEY_CLASSES_ROOT\Paint.Picture\DefaultIcon`, and change the `(Default)` value to `%1`. If the *.bmp* file type is no longer associated with MS Paint, the correct Registry location will be somewhere other than in `Paint.Picture`. Try looking in the `(Default)` value of `HKEY_CLASSES_ROOT\.BMP` for the current file type (see "Understanding File Types" in Chapter 3 for more information).
3. Close the Registry Editor and press **F5** to refresh any open windows to reread the icons for bitmap files. You might have to log out and then log back in for the change to take effect.

To increase the size of icons, double-click on the **Display** icon in Control Panel, choose the **Appearance** tab. Select **Icon** from the **Item** menu, and type in a larger value for the size, such as **48** or **64**. Note that this will make all icons on your system (those on the desktop, and in the **Large Icons** display in Explorer) larger.

Solution 2: Use built-in icon previews for all graphic files

The advantages of this solution are that it works for more file types, including *.bmp*, *.jpg*, and *.gif* files, and that the previews can be larger than normal icons. The disadvantages include that the option needs to be enabled for each folder you view (you wouldn't want to set it as the default). Also, it's fairly limited: there's no way to change the size of the previews, and any image files that it doesn't understand are shown simply with their standard file icons rather than being hidden. If you are viewing a folder with more than just a few images in it, the display is less than ideal.

Open Explorer, and locate any folder that contains at least one graphic image file (*.jpg*, *.gif*, or *.bmp*). Select **Thumbnails** from the **View** menu (this option may not be available if you have Internet Explorer integration disabled—see Chapter 8). Select one of the other view modes (such as **Details** or **Large Icons**) to restore the display to normal.

If you've configured Explorer to display hidden files, you'll notice a new hidden file, *thumbs.db* (which contains the thumbnail data), in any folder you view. This file can be deleted safely.

If you need a better thumbnail preview, try a third-party application, such as Acdsee-32 (*http://www.acdsee.com*). It not only has a superior thumbnail viewer, but is a much better and faster image viewer than Internet Explorer (the only thing Microsoft provides for viewing *.jpg* and *.gif* files).

Customize the Places Bar

The Places Bar is the gray bar along the left edge of the File → Open and File-Save dialog boxes in Windows Me. The Places Bar made its debut in Microsoft Office 2000 and is now standard in Windows Me and Windows 2000. If you don't see the Places Bar on your system, it may not be enabled—see the following Solution 1 for details.

This bar has a maximum of five buttons, each of which points to a different folder on your system. By default, these places are History, Documents, Desktop, Favorites, and Web Folders. (How many of us really use Web Folders?) It's best to close all running applications, especially Office 2000 applications, to prevent them from interfering with your selections.

There are two solutions that allow you to customize the Places Bar. TweakUI (Solution 1) is the easier solution, but it doesn't apply to all file dialog boxes (such as those in older applications or Microsoft Office). Solution 2 is only for Microsoft Office 2000 dialog boxes but involves editing the Registry. Perhaps a subsequent Windows or Office update will resolve the discrepancies.

Solution 1: Use TweakUI

1. Double-click on the **TweakUI** icon (see Appendix A) in Control Panel, and choose the **Open** tab.
2. Select **Custom places bar**, and then choose the desired system folders from each of the lists. Your selections will appear in the Places Bar in the same order as you choose them here. You can also type the full path of any existing local or network folder here; the folder's actual name and icon will appear on the corresponding button.

   You can also choose either **Show default places** or **Hide places bar** at this point, both of which should be self-explanatory.
3. Click **OK**.

Solution 2: Use the Registry (affects Microsoft Office 2000 only)

1. Open the Registry Editor. (If you're not familiar with the Registry Editor, see Chapter 3.)
2. Expand the branches to `HKEY_CURRENT_USER\Software\Microsoft\Office\9.0\Common\Open Find\Places`. You should see two subkeys here: `StandardPlaces` and `UserDefinedPlaces`.
3. First, you'll have to disable the existing items; otherwise, your custom items won't be shown. One by one, highlight each key under `StandardPlaces` (e.g., `Desktop`, `Recent`), and select **New** and then **DWORD Value** from the **Edit** menu.

   Name the new value *Show*, and leave the value of `0` unchanged. Don't worry if you want to keep one or more of the defaults; it's easier in the long run to disable them all here and then recreate the five you want to keep. Also, make sure the values you add are `DWORD` values; otherwise, this won't work.
4. Next, highlight the `UserDefinedPlaces` key, and add five new keys. Name them `Place1`, `Place2`, `Place3`, `Place4`, and `Place5`.

5. In each of these new keys, you'll want to create the following values, filling in the appropriate information in each value:

   A String value called Name

   This contains the caption that will appear under this place (example: Desktop).

   A String value called Path

   This contains the full folder path for the place (example: *c:\windows\desktop*).

   A DWORD *value called* Index

   This allows you to choose how your places are sorted. Enter 0 for the first place, 1 for the second, 2 for the third, and so on. The key names typed in the previous step (Place1, Place2, etc.) do not determine the sort order.

6. After you've entered all the new places, open any Office 2000 application to try it out. This may require some trial and error to get it right.

   One of the things that make this difficult is that Office tends to indiscriminately add new keys and values, which can clutter up what you're working on. If you've done it right, however, the seemingly random keys and values that appear will have no effect on what actually appears in the dialog boxes.

7. To allow more than five buttons on the Places Bar, expand the Registry branches to HKEY_CURRENT_USER\Software\Microsoft\Office\9.0\Common\Open Find\Places. Select **New** and then **DWORD Value** from the **Edit** menu. Name the new value ItemSize, and leave the value of 0 unchanged.

8. When you're done, you'll want to make a Registry patch to back up your settings, just in case a subsequent Office update overwrites them. See "Using Registry Patches" in Chapter 3 for more information.

9. You can also get the Office PlaceBar Customizer from Microsoft's Office Update web site (*http://www.officeupdate.com*), which will enable you to make these changes more easily from within Office.

Making Windows Your Own

The toolbars in applications, the icons on the Windows desktop, the various splash screens that appear, and the entries in the Start Menu are all designed to appear a certain way when first installed. Unfortunately, the criteria used to make those decisions are often based more on showcasing various aspects of the software than on actually making the application easier to use. So, why settle for the defaults?

Much of the rest of this chapter falls loosely under the category of customizing, but the following topics specifically deal with changing the defaults to make Windows easier to live with.

Tweaking the Start Menu Button

As is Microsoft's intention, the Start Menu is the starting point for most tasks in Windows Me. It would seem reasonable, then, that one not only should be able to customize this menu with the most commonly used features, but also should be able to rid the **Start Menu** of the items that aren't used.

Now, if you didn't already know it, you can add, remove, and rearrange most of the items in your Start Menu by dragging and dropping (see "Fixing the Start Menu" in Chapter 2 for more information). You can also sort any single menu alphabetically by right-clicking on any entry in the menu and selecting **Sort by Name**. However, there are certain intrinsic, unmovable entries, such as the **Documents** and **Favorites** menus, that not only get in the way if they're not used, but can make it easier for "prying eyes" to do their prying.

A new feature in Windows Me is "personalized menus," a process by which some Start Menu items are indiscriminately hidden from time to time, but the lack of any control (other than to disable the feature altogether) makes it virtually useless. See "Fixing the Start Menu" in Chapter 2 for details on dealing with this feature, as well as several ways to selectively hide or disable unwanted Start Menu items.

The button on the Taskbar used to open the **Start Menu** consists of a small Windows logo and the word "Start." Although there's no built-in way to customize this button, advanced users with the correct tools and a little sense of geeky adventure will be able to accomplish this in only a few minutes. Figure 4-5 shows a **Start Menu** button that's been customized.

Figure 4-5. The Start Menu button after some slight alterations

Here's how to edit the various aspects of the **Start Menu** button. You'll need a good hex editor to complete either of the following solutions. The example assumes you're using UltraEdit-32 (available at *http://www.ultraedit.com*), a very good text editor that can also be used to edit binary files, thereby making it a suitable hex editor.

If this is done incorrectly, it can damage the application. Anyone who is not somewhat familiar with a hex editor should not attempt this procedure. But if you back up any files before altering them, you eliminate the possibility of permanent damage.

Change the word "Start" (requires a hex editor)

1. Make two duplicates of the file *Explorer.exe* (it's in your *\Windows* folder). Put one in a safe place, and put the other somewhere convenient, such as on your desktop. The one in the safe place is your backup in case the operation is not successful.
2. Open the conveniently placed copy of *Explorer.exe* in your hex editor. (Not only would it be foolish to try to edit the original *Explorer.exe*, but Windows won't allow it, because it's currently in use.) UltraEdit-32 should automatically switch to hex mode once the file is opened.
3. Select **Find** from the **Search** menu, and type **53 00 74 00 61 00 72 00 74** in the **Find What** field. These numbers are Unicode values in hex and represent the word "Start," where each letter is separated by a null character (#00). You should find several occurrences of this, but if you look at the "translation" on the right, you'll notice that each one of them is just part of the phrase "Start Menu"—except for one. In the original release of Windows Me, it's the last occurrence of **Start**, located towards the end of the file. Your screen should look something like Figure 4-6.

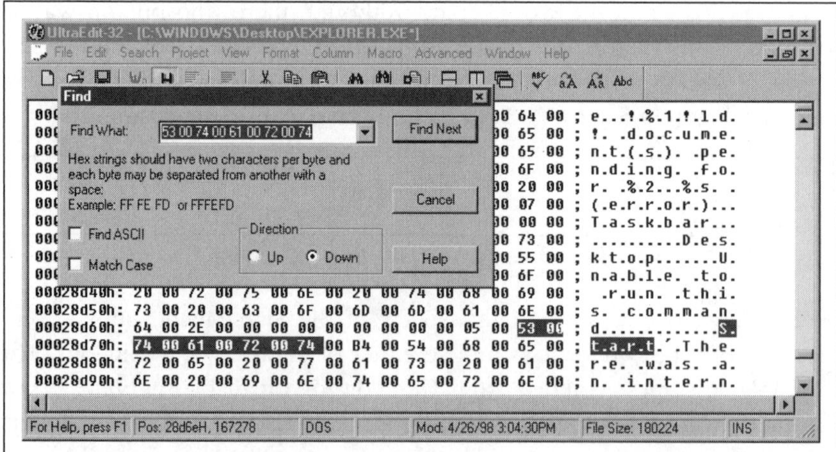

Figure 4-6. Use a hex editor like the one shown to search for the word "Start" in Explorer.exe

4. Close the **Find** window when you've found the correct occurrence of this value.
5. You can replace any of the five characters here, *but do not change the null characters* (represented by dots). You can replace a character either by clicking on it on the right side and typing directly or by clicking on its corresponding hex code on the left side and typing a new code (see Table 4-1 for a listing of hex codes).

   Although you can't specify a word longer than five characters, you can have a shorter word by including spaces (#20) for the remaining characters.

   If you make a mistake, it is usually easier and safer to simply close the file and reopen rather than trying to repair the damage.
6. When you're done, select **Save** from the **File** menu, and close the hex editor.
7. The next step is to put the altered file in place of the existing one. Assuming you've made *two* duplicates of *Explorer.exe* as recommended earlier, this will be no problem, although you won't be able to do it while Windows is running. Select **Shut Down** from the **Start Menu**, choose **Restart in MS-DOS mode**, and click **OK**.
8. Assuming the *altered* file was saved on your desktop, you would type the following:

   ```
   copy c:\windows\desktop\explorer.exe c:\windows
   ```

   Replace `c:\windows` with the actual location of your copy of Windows, if different.
9. Type **`exit`** to return to Windows. The Start Menu button should now reflect your changes.

Change the icon (requires an icon editor)

1. Make two duplicates of the file *User.exe* (it's in your *Windows\System* folder). Put one in a safe place, and put the other somewhere convenient, such as on your desktop.
2. Open the conveniently placed copy of *User.exe* with an icon editor that can read *.dll* and *.exe* files.*
3. Explorer uses the flag logo, the very first icon in *User.exe*, for the **Start Menu** button. What you need to be aware of is that there are several versions of this icon in the file, each a different size. Depending on the screen fonts you've chosen (in particular, the **Active Title Bar**

Tinkering Techniques

* Go to *http://www.annoyances.org* for downloadable software, such as icon editors.

setting in the **Appearance** tab in **Display Properties**), Windows may be using the 10×10, 12×12, 14×14, 16×16, 22×22, or 32×32 variations. Your best bet is to update them all.

4. When you're done, save your changes and close the icon editor.
5. The next step is to put the altered file in place of the existing one. Assuming you've made *two* duplicates of *User.exe* as recommended earlier, this will be no problem, although you won't be able to do it while Windows is running. Select **Shut Down** from the **Start Menu**, choose **Restart in MS-DOS mode**, and click **OK**.
6. Assuming the *altered* file was saved on your desktop, you would type the following:

   ```
   copy c:\windows\desktop\user.exe c:\windows\system
   ```

   Replace `c:\windows` with the actual location of your copy of Windows, if different.
7. Type **`exit`** to return to Windows. The Start Menu button should now reflect your changes.

The hex codes for the characters you can use to change the word "Start" in the Start Menu are shown in Table 4-1.

Table 4-1. Abbreviated ASCII Character Set with Hexadecimal Values

A = 41	N = 4E	a = 61	n = 6E	0 = 30	$ = 24	\ = 5C
B = 42	O = 4F	b = 62	o = 6F	1 = 31	% = 25	] = 5D
C = 43	P = 50	c = 63	p = 70	2 = 32	& = 26	^ = 5E
D = 44	Q = 51	d = 64	q = 71	3 = 33	= 27	_ = 5F
E = 45	R = 52	e = 65	r = 72	4 = 34	(= 28	` = 60
F = 46	S = 53	f = 66	s = 73	5 = 35	) = 29	{ = 7B
G = 47	T = 54	g = 67	t = 74	6 = 36	* = 2A	| = 7C
H = 48	U = 55	h = 68	u = 75	7 = 37	+ = 2B	} = 7D
I = 49	V = 56	i = 69	v = 76	8 = 38	, = 2C	~ = 7E
J = 4A	W = 57	j = 6A	w = 77	9 = 39	- = 2D	
K = 4B	X = 58	k = 6B	x = 78	! = 21	. = 2E	
L = 4C	Y = 59	l = 6C	y = 79	" = 22	/ = 2F	
M = 4D	Z = 5A	m = 6D	z = 7A	# = 23	[= 5B	

Change Installation Defaults

During the installation of Windows, you (or one of your cronies) were asked to enter your name and company name, as well as the CD key on the back of your CD jacket. Those and other settings that result from the installation are all written to the Registry at the end of the installation process. Fortunately, it's easy to change these values when they pose problems, even long after the installation has been completed. All of these values are stored in the Registry, so go ahead and fire up the Registry Editor (see Chapter 3 for details), and try the following solutions.

Registered user

Your registered name and company name are not only displayed in Windows' various About boxes, but are inserted as the default name and company name for installation of many third-party applications. Although there's the possibility that you may have misspelled your own name during installation, it's more likely that your computer came with Windows preinstalled, so the registered user is something like "Dell Customer." Whether you've bought your computer from someone else, switched employers, or simply decided to drop your middle initial, you shouldn't be stuck with those old defaults:

1. Expand the branches to `HKEY_LOCAL_MACHINE\Software\Microsoft\Windows\CurrentVersion`.
2. To the right, among a myriad of settings, are the three settings in which we're interested. You can change **RegisteredOwner** (your name) and **RegisteredOrganization** (your company) to anything you want simply by double-clicking on them and typing.
3. Your changes will take effect immediately.

Changing the registered-user values will only change the registered-user information for Windows, not for the applications already installed on your system, most of which store registered-user information separately from Windows.

CD key

Why would you want to change the CD key? Well, subsequent installations of Windows (but not *newer* versions) will require that you enter the CD key again. However, setup checks the current installation, and if what you enter doesn't match the Registry value, Windows setup won't let you continue. Perhaps you purchased your system with Windows preinstalled, but didn't get a Windows CD:

1. Expand the branches to `HKEY_LOCAL_MACHINE\Software\Microsoft\Windows\CurrentVersion`.
2. The `ProductKey` value contains the CD key used during the last installation of Windows. Make sure to replace it with the full 25 digits, since the Setup dialog box will allow no fewer and no more than 25 digits.

Installation path

The drive letter for your CD drive was recorded during installation, theoretically making it easier to find the CD whenever you add a driver or optional Windows component later on. For example, if your CD drive is drive *D:*, then the original installation path would be *d:\win9x*. All it takes is a simple hardware upgrade to change your drive letters, thereby invalidating this setting.

If you find yourself accessing the CD frequently to add or remove drivers or optional Windows components, you might want to abandon the CD altogether, instead storing the Windows Me distribution files on your hard disk. That way, whenever you add or remove a Windows component or add any new drivers, the files will be read right off the hard disk, quickly and without any prompts. If you have the space (it requires a little over 100 MB, which many of you probably won't be able to spare), you can just copy the contents of the *\win9x* folder on your CD into any out-of-the-way folder on your hard disk (*\windows\install* is a good place). Don't bother copying any of the other folders, including the *\win9x\ols* folder, which is just used for the bothersome "Online Services" files.

Regardless, follow these steps to change the default installation path:

1. Expand the branches to `HKEY_LOCAL_MACHINE\Software\Microsoft\Windows\CurrentVersion\Setup`.
2. In this key, you'll see most installation directories used for things like the temporary install directory,* the location of the *\Windows\System* folder (don't change this), and, of course, the location of the setup files.

   Double-click on the `SourcePath` value to change it. If you're specifying a new location of your CD drive, type **`d:\win98\`**, where **`d:`** is the drive letter of your CD drive. Otherwise, just include the full path of the location of the distribution files, wherever they may be.

If you've changed the location for Windows setup files, Windows will simply prompt you for the correct location when it needs them. So there's no danger of not being able to install drivers if you specify an incorrect or obsolete folder for the `SourcePath` value.

* The temporary install path (specified in the `SetupTempDir` value) is the directory that Windows setup will use to store about 80 MB of data when you install. If you're running low on disk space and have another drive or partition with more space, you can redirect this folder so that subsequent installations of Windows will have the room they need to complete.

Add New Folder Options

At first glance, the **Advanced settings** list in Explorer's Folder Options window is presented in a somewhat awkward list format, apparently to accommodate the large number of options. (This window is accessible by selecting **Folder Options** from Explorer's **Tools** menu or by double-clicking the **Folder Options** icon in Control Panel and choosing the **View** tab.) However, the less-than-ideal presentation is actually designed to allow customization, permitting you to add or remove items from the list. See Figure 4-7 for an example of a customized version of this window.

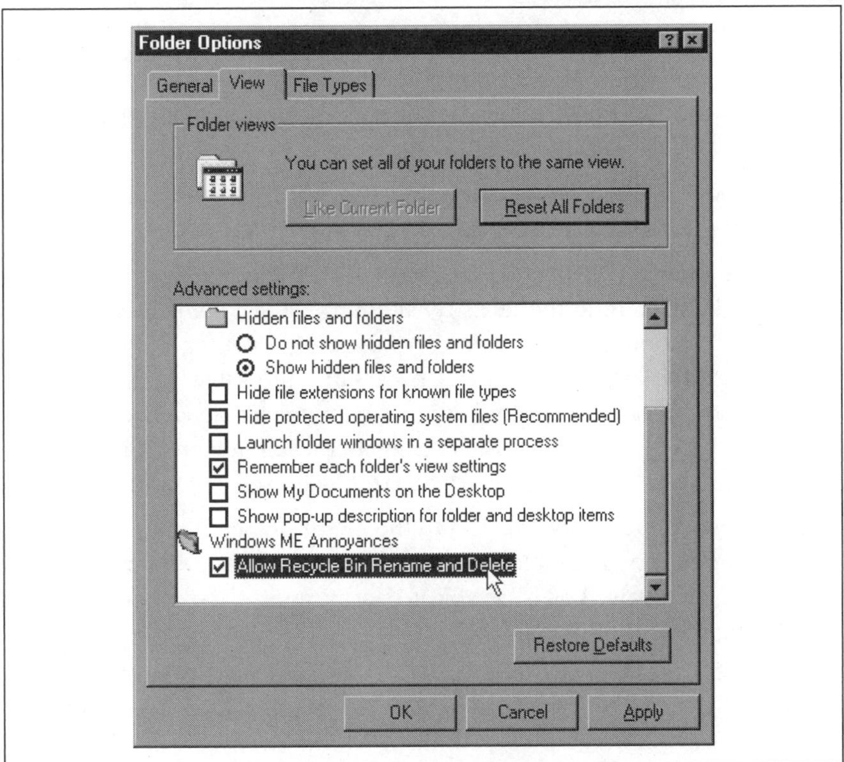

Figure 4-7. The Advanced Folder Options dialog box is a flexible, customizable list of Registry settings

Although this process isn't necessarily intended for you to extend or change any particular features of Explorer, it does allow you to provide a fairly clean interface for virtually any Registry setting (including any that might affect Explorer). The idea is that you link up a checkbox or radio button to a value—any value you choose—in your Registry. This would, for example, allow you to make certain Registry changes accessible to yourself or others (such as users in a workgroup that you administer), reducing the need for them to mess around in the Registry. You can also remove unwanted options that you don't want easily changed.

The format is actually quite remarkable, because you don't have to be a programmer to utilize this feature. You can add new options to a certain portion of the Registry and then tie those options to other Registry settings. The downside is that the syntax requires that numerous parameters be typed, which can be cumbersome. The following procedure should allow you to make changes to existing settings, as well as add your own settings fairly easily:

1. Open the Registry Editor (if you're not familiar with the Registry Editor, see Chapter 3).
2. Expand the branches to: `HKEY_LOCAL_MACHINE\Software\Microsoft\Windows\CurrentVersion\explorer\Advanced`.

   Notice that the actual hierarchy in the Folder Options window is reproduced here in the Registry, although the list items may appear in a different order than their corresponding Registry entries. This is because the list captions aren't necessarily the same as the names of the corresponding Registry keys, yet both collections are sorted alphabetically. For example, the **Remember each folder's view settings** option is represented by the `ClassicViewState` key in the Registry.
3. Take this opportunity to back up the entire branch by highlighting the `Advanced` key and selecting **Export Registry File** from the **Registry** menu. This way, you'll be able to easily restore the defaults without having to reinstall Windows.
4. At this point, you can remove any unwanted keys from this branch; the `Text` value in each key should be enough to explain what each key is for.
5. To add a new item, start by simply creating a new key, keeping the hierarchy in mind—for example, are you adding an option to an existing group or are you creating a new group for additional options? Name the key anything you want, although the more descriptive, the better.

6. The values inside each key determine the key's properties. To add a property to the key, create a new value named for one of the properties. Then, double-click on it, and type the contents for the value, as described in the following tables. Table 4-2 lists the properties that affect the visual appearance of a specific item, and Table 4-3 lists the properties that affect what happens when a specific item is turned on or off in the Folder Options window.

Table 4-2. Visual Properties of Folder Options Items

Value Name	Datatype	Description of Value Contents
Type	String	This can be set to either `group`, `checkbox`, or `radio`, representing a folder, checkbox, or radio button, respectively. Checkboxes are square options and can each be either on or off. Radio buttons are round options that are linked to other radio buttons in the same folder, in that only one at a time can be selected (you can have multiple groups of radio buttons). And folders, of course, are used to organize the various other options. This parameter is required by all items.
Text	String	This is the actual caption of the option as it will appear in the dialog box. This can be as long as you want (better too descriptive than too vague), but the paradigm dictates that only the first word be capitalized and that there be no period. This parameter is required by all items.
Bitmap	String	This is the icon used for folder items. By default, it's a rather ugly bent arrow. The syntax `filename,index` is the same as for the *DefaultIcon* property for file types, as documented in "Understanding File Types" in Chapter 3. You can omit `filename` and instead specify only a number (the comma is still required) to use the default selection of rather ugly icons. For example, you can use `,207` for the default folder icon, but it'll be black-and-white instead of yellow. This parameter is required for all folders; it does not affect checkboxes and radio buttons.
HelpID	String	This is the filename and optionally the help context ID of the help documentation for this item. If the user selects the item and presses the F1 key, this specifies the help note that will appear. The syntax is *`filename#id`*, where *`filename`* is the name of a *.hlp* or *.chm* file, and *`id`* is the help context id of the topic you want to display. This parameter is optional.

Tinkering Techniques

Table 4-3. Registry Properties of Folder Options Items

Value Name	Datatype	Description of Value Contents
HKeyRoot	DWORD	This is an eight-digit number representing the root of the Registry path containing the target Registry setting. Use the *hexadecimal* number 80000000 for HKEY_CLASSES_ROOT, 80000001 for HKEY_CURRENT_USER, 80000002 for HKEY_LOCAL_MACHINE, 80000003 for HKEY_USERS, 80000004 for HKEY_PERFORMANCE_DATA, 80000005 for HKEY_CURRENT_CONFIG, and 80000006 for HKEY_DYN_DATA. For some reason, it must be separated from the rest of the Registry path, specified in RegPath, later. This parameter is required for all checkbox and radio items.
RegPath	String	This is the path of the Registry location of the target Registry setting, not including the root (see HKeyRoot, earlier). For example, for HKEY_CURRENT_USER\Software\Microsoft\Windows\CurrentVersion, you would only enter Software\Microsoft\Windows\CurrentVersion here. This parameter is required for all checkbox and radio items.
ValueName	String	This is the name of the target Registry value in which the setting data is stored when the option is turned on or off in the Folder Options window. The target key is specified in the RegPath and HKeyRoot parameters, listed earlier. This parameter is required by all checkbox and radio items.
Checked-Value	Should match target value datatype	This holds the data to be stored in the target Registry value specified by the RegPath and ValueName parameters earlier, when said option is turned *on*. If you're configuring an option to be used on both Windows 9x/Me and Windows NT/2000 systems, use both the CheckedValueW95 and CheckedValueNT parameters instead. This parameter is required by all checkbox and radio items.
UnChecked-Value	Should match target value datatype	This holds the data to be stored in the target Registry value specified by the RegPath and ValueName parameters above, when said option is turned *off*. This value is optional; if omitted, it is assumed to be 0.
Default-Value	Should match target value datatype	This is the default value, used only if the target Registry value (specified by the RegPath and ValueName parameters listed earlier) does not exist. As soon as the option in the Folder Options window is turned on or off at least once, this parameter is ignored, and Windows instead reads the state of the target value, comparing it to CheckedValue and UnCheckedValue to determine if the option should appear checked or unchecked. This value is optional; if omitted, it is assumed to be 0.

The value type (String, Binary, DWORD) of the `CheckedValue`, `UnCheckedValue`, and `DefaultValue` parameters all depend on what the target value requires. For example, if the option you're setting is a `DWORD` value, then all three of these parameters must also be `DWORD` values.

7. After you've created keys and entered the appropriate property values, your Registry should look something like Figure 4-8, and the resulting Folder Options window should look like Figure 4-7.

   If you try to add a setting using the previous procedure and it doesn't show up in Folder Options, maybe something's missing. Make sure you include all the required property values for the item in question.

8. Close the Registry Editor when you're finished.

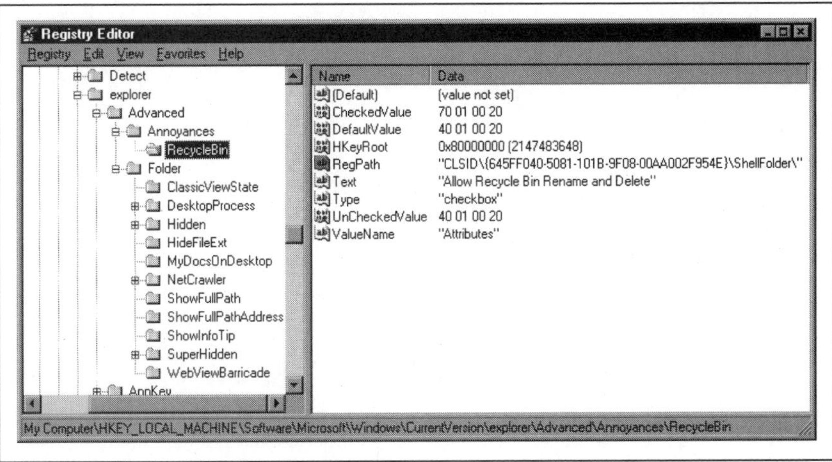

Figure 4-8. Settings that appear in the Advanced Folder Options list are configured in the Registry

The examples shown in Figure 4-7 and Figure 4-8 shows how another solution in this book ("Solution 2: Recycle Bin" of "Clear the Desktop of Unwanted Icons" earlier in this chapter) can be turned into an advanced Folder Options setting. Here, a single checkbox allows you to easily turn on and off the *Rename* and *Delete* commands in the Recycle Bin's context menu.

When the Folder Options dialog box is displayed, each option is set according to the value of the setting specified by `ValueName`; the value is simply compared with `CheckedValue` and `UnCheckedValue` and then set accordingly. When the **OK** button is pressed in Folder Options, the settings in the Registry are then written using the same criteria.

To reproduce a setting elsewhere in the Windows interface or the interface of a third-party application, you'll first need to find the respective Registry setting—see "Finding the Right Registry Key" in Chapter 3 for more information.

See Chapter 3 for more information on Registry patches, a good way to reproduce your customization on any number of computers. Note, however, that because Registry patches can't be used to remove Registry keys, you'll have to use WSH scripts if you want to automate the removal of items from advanced Folder Options settings (see "Automating the Deletion of Registry Items" in Chapter 3 for more information).

5

Maximizing Performance

Although your computer spends 99.9% of the time waiting for you to do something, what concerns us is that other 0.1% of the time when 12 seconds can seem like an eternity.

A common misconception is that a computer with a faster processor, say 1.1 GHz, will automatically be faster than, say, a 600-MHz system. While the increased processor speed is an obvious benefit in some specific circumstances, such as when performing intensive statistical calculations, using 3D modeling software, or playing some high-end games,* the real-world performance of a computer is really measured differently.

In most cases, our qualitative assessment of a computer's speed is based on its ability to respond immediately to mouse clicks and keystrokes, start applications quickly, open menus and dialog boxes without a delay, start up and shut down Windows quickly, and display graphics and animation smoothly. For the most part, all of these things depend more upon correctly optimized software, the amount of installed memory, and the amount of free disk space than on raw processor power.

Because financial limitations prevent most of us from simply buying new hardware every three months, most of this chapter is devoted to solutions that will help improve the performance of your existing system without requiring any additional monetary investment. For example, the way Windows uses the swap file (virtual memory) can be inefficient, and dealing with this bottleneck can result in performance increases all across

* See "Get the Most Out of Your Games, Speed-Wise" later in this chapter.

the system. In your approach to these problems, consider that your computer has a given theoretical top speed, and all you need to do is fix whatever is slowing it down so that you can approach that speed.

Upgrading, discussed at the end of the chapter, is a somewhat different story—there, your aim is to raise the theoretical top speed. Start by asking yourself where your money is best spent, which isn't always obvious. For example, there are always faster processors available, but often something as simple as adding more memory can have a much bigger impact on performance.

Now, I'm the last one to condone throwing money at a problem. Even if money were no object and we could simply buy a new computer or component whenever the proverbial ashtray gets full, we'd still have to take the time to install and troubleshoot the new hardware and to reconfigure all the software.* So, upgrading is not necessarily the best choice either to resolve a problem or to improve performance. Spending a little time fine-tuning your hardware and software and perhaps spending a little money replacing certain components *can* make a difference.

Naturally, there is a certain point past which your computer is going to turn into a money and time pit. The older your system is, the less you should want to keep it alive. It's easy to calculate the point of diminishing returns: just compare the estimated cost of an upgrade (both the monetary cost and the amount of time you'll have to commit) with the cost of a new system (minus what you might get for selling or donating your old system). I stress this point a great deal, because I've seen it happen time and time again: people end up spending too much and getting too little in return. A simple hardware upgrade ends up taking days of troubleshooting and configuring, only to result in the discovery that yet something *else* needs to be replaced. Taking into account that whatever you end up with will still eventually need to be further upgraded to remain current, it is often more cost effective to replace the entire system and either sell or donate the old parts.

Removing Software Bottlenecks

In some ways, Windows Me takes good advantage of your hardware, a liberating change from the stifling experience of Windows 3.x from years past. In other ways, however, Windows itself can be a bottleneck, causing frustration and wasted time. Because all the software you run is

* Thinking of upgrading your entire system? See "Transfer Windows onto Another Hard Disk" later in this chapter for a great way to avoid having to reinstall all your applications.

dependent upon the operating system, tweaking Windows for better performance can result in performance gains across the board.

First, there's one easy thing you can do to make Windows substantially more responsive than when you first install it. Windows Me adds animation to almost every visual component in the operating system, something that can make your new Pentium 4 seem like a 386. Fortunately, it's easy to turn off some or all of the animation, which will make Windows more responsive and easier to work with. See "Taming Mindless Animation" in Chapter 2, *Basic Explorer Coping Skills*, for more information.

Another easy thing you can do is to speed up the display of menus. Rather than waiting for the standard half-second or so delay before menus are opened, you can reduce this value so that menus are opened more quickly. Double-click on the **TweakUI** icon in Control Panel (see Appendix A, *Setting Locator*), and choose the **Mouse** tab. Move the slider for **Menu speed** all the way to the left, and click **OK**. See also "Stop Menus from Following the Mouse" in Chapter 2 for yet another tweak for menus.

The third solution I consider essential is to clean out all the junk in Windows. Remove all the applications you don't use anymore; not only are they taking up disk space, but many applications install extensions in Windows that will slow down everything. A single program may not make much of a difference either way, but they do add up. Double-click the **Add/Remove Programs** icon in Control Panel and remove anything you don't need. Next, click the **Windows Setup** tab, and likewise remove any Windows components you don't need. Click **OK** when you're done. The last part is to disable any unwanted programs that start automatically when Windows starts, such as your Antivirus autoprotect feature (see "Taming Antivirus Software" in Chapter 6, *Troubleshooting*) and anything else that takes up memory or has an appetite for processor cycles (see "The Places Windows Looks for Startup Programs," also in Chapter 6, for details.)

The following solutions should help alleviate some of the most bothersome Windows bottlenecks. These tips, combined with those in the subsequent section, "Fine-Tuning and Upgrading Hardware Components," should help you get the most out of the Windows platform.

Speed Up System Startup

Several factors can impact the amount of time it takes for your computer to load Windows. As you install software and add devices, Windows gets more and more bogged down. There's not a whole lot you can do about that, short of removing programs or formatting your drive and reinstalling from scratch. However, you should systematically check out all of the following factors, trimming and cleaning up where you can:

- You should have a minimum of 64 MB of RAM, but 128 MB or even 256 MB is better. Memory prices continue to drop, making it remarkably inexpensive to add more RAM to your system, and doing so will *significantly* improve performance all across the board.
- A slow hard disk can slow down the bootup process. Make sure you defragment often (see "Fine-Tuning and Upgrading Hardware Components" later in this chapter). If you're using an older hard disk, you might consider upgrading, which will not only get you more disk space, but will also improve disk performance.
- You may not have sufficient free disk space for your swap file. Windows uses part of your hard disk to store portions of memory; the more disk space you devote to your swap file, the easier it will be for Windows to store data there. See "Optimize Virtual Memory (or, Stop Windows from Wildly Accessing Your Hard Disk)" later in this chapter for more information.
- Sometimes having too many files in your *\Windows\Temp* folder can not only slow Windows startup, but prevent Windows from loading at all. Windows and your applications use this folder to temporarily store data while you're working with documents. When those applications and documents are closed (or when the applications just crash), they often leave the temporary files behind, and they accumulate fast. See "Clean Up and Customize System Folders" in Chapter 4, *Tinkering Techniques*, for more information on the *Temp* folder, including a hint on automatically clearing out the *Temp* folder when Windows starts.

Some applications, such as older versions of Microsoft Office, can be configured to use the *Temp* directory to store *autorecovery* files—files that are used to recover data that wasn't saved and otherwise would be lost in the event of a system crash or power outage. You should make sure your programs are *not* configured to store these files here, but rather in another location, such as a "backup" folder, independent of the *Temp* folder.

- If you have more than 600 fonts installed on your system, it may be negatively impacting on the time it takes to load Windows. If you can survive without 400 different decorative fonts (especially if all you ever use is Times Roman), try removing several hundred of them. If you periodically need a lot of fonts, you might want to invest in font management software, such as Adobe Type Manager, which can remove and reinstall fonts in groups at the click of a button.

- Network drivers for your network card and Dial-Up Networking (see Chapter 7, *Networking and Internetworking*) will always take a little while to load, initialize the hardware, and log on to the network. You can usually tell when the network is being initialized, because Windows will stop using the hard disk for a period of 5–20 seconds. Try disabling any drivers and networking options (such as drive letter mapping) that you don't need. See Chapter 7 for details.
- For the more diligent readers, there's an essentially unnecessary timed delay at the beginning of the Windows boot process. Using a plain-text editor, such as Notepad, edit your *Msdos.sys* file, located in the root directory of your boot drive (usually *C:*). Add the line `BootDelay=0` to the `[Options]` section of the file (or just modify the line if it's already there), and save the file.*

Msdos.sys is a read-only and hidden file. To show hidden files, select **Folder Options** from Explorer's **Tools** menu, choose the **View** tab, and select the **Show hidden files and folders** option. To make the file editable, right-click on the file icon, select **Properties**, and turn off the **Read-only** option.

- You may have noticed that Scandisk is sometimes run when Windows is starting; this usually happens if the system was not shut down properly last time. This is generally a good idea; however, it's easy to disable if you find that it's happening more often than is reasonable. Open the System Configuration Utility (*Msconfig.exe*), and click the **Advanced** button under the **General** tab. Turn on the **Disable Scandisk after bad shutdown** option, and click **OK** when you're done.
- Antivirus programs are commonly configured to be run whenever you turn on your computer. These programs are always in memory, scanning programs as you open them and files as you download them. In most cases, this is overkill. For most users—especially those who take the proper precautions—getting a computer virus is about as likely as getting struck by lightning. I wouldn't necessarily recommend getting rid of all Antivirus programs; just restrict their use to manually scanning your system when you want, and disable the automatic feature. You'll notice a faster startup for Windows and for applications as well. See "Taming Antivirus Software" in Chapter 6 for details.

* See "Using INI Files" in Chapter 3, *The Registry*, for more information on editing this type of file.

- If you have the Active Desktop enabled (see Chapter 8, *Taking Control of Web Integration*), it could substantially delay the Windows boot process.
- Some system vendors (Compaq and NEC, to name a couple) install their own proprietary shell interfaces on top of Explorer (the default shell). These interfaces are usually designed to hide the default Windows desktop and show a "friendlier" startup screen. Not only does this just make it more confusing for those who may have previously used Windows, it also usually increases Windows' startup time considerably. Open the *System.ini* file (located in your *Windows* folder) in a text editor, such as Notepad, and look for the line that begins with `shell=`.[*] If the line is there and `Explorer.exe` is not specified on the right side of the equals sign, remove the line entirely, and save the file. If you know your system is using such a shell, but you can't find it specified here, see the next paragraph.
- Probably the most common thing that slows down the loading of Windows is all of the programs that are configured to load at boot time. There are several places these programs are specified. Look carefully in each location, and feel free to remove anything you don't want running. See "The Places Windows Looks for Startup Programs" in Chapter 6 for details.
- Run the Microsoft System Information utility (*Msinfo32.exe*), and expand the tree branches to *\Software Environment\Running Tasks*.[†] Look at each entry to the right for any programs that may be running. Each program that runs is taking up memory, taking time to load, and possibly causing conflicts.

  This window merely lists programs that are running at any particular time—it doesn't provide a means to control them. If it's not obvious how to stop a running process (for example, if it doesn't have a visible window that you can close), press the **Ctrl-Alt-Del** to display the **Close Program** box, highlight the task in question, and click on **End Task**. To permanently disable a program, thereby preventing it from loading automatically again, see "The Places Windows Looks for Startup Programs" in Chapter 6.

---

* See "Using INI Files" in Chapter 3 for more information on editing this type of file.

† There's a bug in Office 97 setup that may overwrite the system-information utility included with Windows Me. This is caused by the fact that the two versions are installed to different directories, a Microsoft oversight. If you're using the Office 97 version of System Information, look in the Applications Running branch of the tree.

Note that this list may be intimidating, and most of the entries are simply necessary Windows processes. Naturally, it's best not to delete something simply because you see it here, but rather to use the list to gain more understanding of the system.

- Lastly, much of speeding up your computer involves cleaning out files you don't need anymore. It's best to back up your system before deleting anything, or at least to rename (or move) files to see if they're being used before you get rid of them permanently. See "What to Throw Away" later in this chapter for more information.

Have Windows Power Down Your Computer Automatically

You may have noticed that some computers—especially laptops—are able to shut themselves off when you choose **Shut Down** from the **Start Menu**, rather than displaying the "It's now safe to turn off your computer" screen. This is convenient and makes for faster shutdowns.

In order to configure your computer to behave this way, you'll need the following: if you're using a desktop (as opposed to a portable) computer, you must have an ATX-compliant case and motherboard. You can tell an ATX system from the power button; if it's a momentary pushbutton (that doesn't stay in when you press it), you've likely got an ATX case. The difference is that power switches in ATX systems send a "shut down" command to the motherboard, rather than simply cutting power.

Secondly, you must have Advanced Power Management (APM) enabled in your system BIOS. Enter your system BIOS setup screen when first starting your computer (usually by pressing the **Del** key), and make sure any options labeled "Advanced Power Management," "APM," or "APM-aware OS" are enabled. Refer to your motherboard documentation or system manual for details. If APM is correctly enabled, you should see an icon labeled **Power** or **Power Management** in the Control Panel. If you don't, either your system doesn't fully support APM or Windows hasn't recognized it.* To force Windows to recognize APM, run the Add New Hardware Wizard in Control Panel and have it automatically detect any new hardware.

If these two conditions are met, Windows should automatically power down your system the next time you shut down.

* Contact your motherboard manufacturer to see if there's a BIOS update available that will fix this problem.

Optimize Virtual Memory (or, Stop Windows from Wildly Accessing Your Hard Disk)

One of the most frustrating and irritating things about Windows is the way that it can seize up for several seconds—sometimes up to a minute—with random, pointless disk activity. This is caused by the way that Windows handles disk virtual memory by default.

Normally, Windows loads drivers and applications into memory until it's full and then starts to use part of your hard disk to "swap" out information, freeing up more memory for higher-priority tasks. The file that Windows uses for this type of "virtual memory" is the swap file, usually (but not always) called *Win386.swp* and located in your Windows folder. Because your hard disk is so much slower than your physical memory, the more Windows does this swapping, the slower your computer will be. Naturally, adding more memory will reduce Windows' appetite for virtual memory.

Although the default configuration is to "let Windows handle disk cache settings," this obviously does not yield the best results. Here's how to eliminate random disk activity and improve overall system performance.

Part 1: Virtual memory

One of the reasons the default settings yield such poor performance is that the swap file grows and shrinks with use, quickly becoming very fragmented (as illustrated by Figure 5-2 later in this chapter). The first step is to eliminate this problem by setting a constant swap-file size.

Note that making the swap file constant will also result in a more constant amount of free disk space. If your hard disk is getting full, consider this solution to restrict Windows from using up every bit of free space:

1. Double-click on the **System** icon in the Control Panel, and choose the **Performance** tab.
2. Click **Virtual Memory**, and then select the **Let me specify my own virtual memory settings** option. Figure 5-1 shows the **Virtual Memory** window.
3. The location and size of your swap file are displayed here. If you want to choose a different drive (assuming you have more than one) to store your swap file, run **Disk Defragmenter** (*Defrag.exe*) on that drive *first*, and then choose that drive from the **Hard Disk** list.

4. Now, choose a permanent size for your swap file, in megabytes. A good size is roughly three times the amount of installed RAM: if you have 64 MB of physical memory, try a 200 MB swap file. If you consistently use many applications at once, try increasing this value. If you're low on disk space and have a lot of physical memory, you can try a lower amount.

   To see how much memory you have installed, go back to the **System Properties** window (you'll have to click **Cancel** here), choose the **General** tab, and look at the last line of the summary.

   Type the desired swap-file size in both the **Minimum** and **Maximum** fields (as shown in Figure 5-1).

5. Press **OK**, and then **OK** again, and confirm that you want to restart your computer. When you restart, you may notice that you have less free disk space, due to the increased swap-file size.

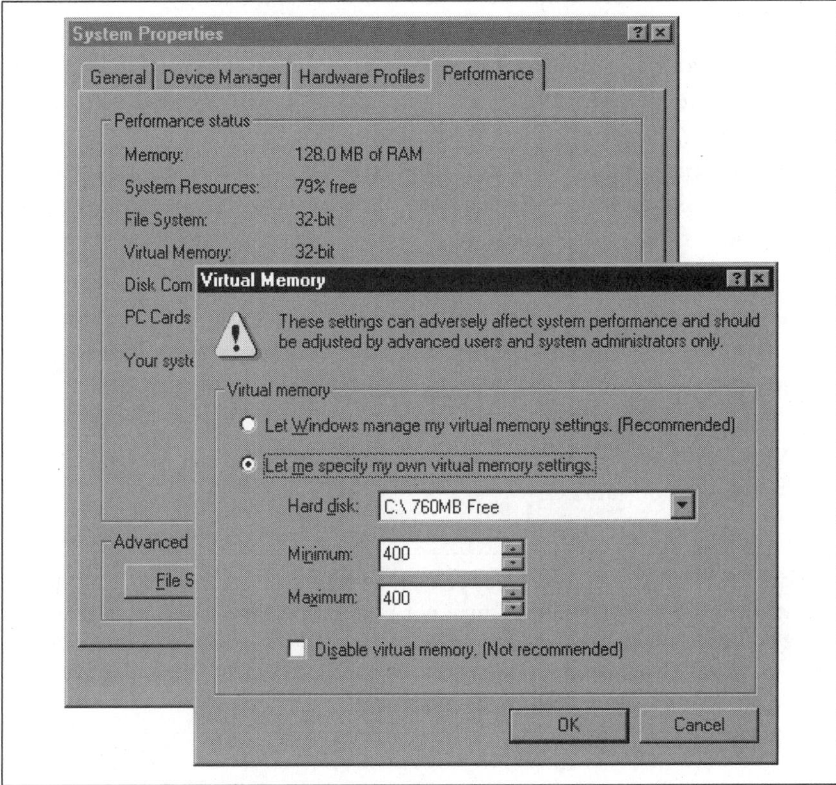

Figure 5-1. Change the way Windows handles virtual memory to improve overall system performance

Part 2: Defragmenting the swap file

Part 1 will eliminate the possibility of your swap file's becoming fragmented, but it won't defragment an already fragmented swap file. You'll need to defragment it at least once for it to remain that way in the future. See Figure 5-2 later in this chapter for details on file fragmentation. Note that this is not an easy task if you don't have the right tools. Here are several ways to accomplish this:

- If you have Norton Utilities 3.0 or later (*http://www.symantec.com*), you'll be able to optimize the swap file easily using the *Speedisk* utility. Speedisk is also able to move your swap file to the physical beginning of your partition, which can also improve performance. The Disk Defragmenter utility that comes with Windows Me is actually a scaled-down version of Norton Speedisk, but it is not capable of defragmenting the swap file.
- If you don't have software capable of defragmenting your swap file, there are two alternatives. If you have more than one partition or hard disk in your system, start by moving your swap file to a different drive letter (see the previous section for details). Then, run Disk Defragmenter (*Defrag.exe*) on the partition you wish to hold the swap file permanently, which will set aside a large chunk of contiguous free space. Lastly, move the swap file back to the original partition, making sure its size is set constant.
- If you don't have a second partition, your other choice is to disable your swap file temporarily by turning on the **Disable Virtual Memory** option in the **Virtual Memory** window (see Figure 5-1). After restarting Windows, run Disk Defragmenter (*Defrag.exe*) to set aside a large chunk of contiguous free space. When you're done, go back to the **Virtual Memory** window, and re-enable the swap file, making sure its size is set constant.

Note that if you have fewer than 64 MB of physical memory, there is a risk that Windows may not boot properly without a swap file. If this happens, you should be able to load Windows in Safe Mode and re-enable your swap file. See "What to Do When Windows Won't Start" in Chapter 6 for details.

Part 3: Physical memory

The more physical memory you have installed, the less frequently Windows will use your hard disk, and the better your system performance will be. Adding memory is a cost-effective way to improve Windows' performance across the board. See the discussion of memory in "Fine-Tuning and Upgrading Hardware Components" later in this chapter for details.

Get the Most Out of Your Games, Speed-Wise

Dude, don't tell me only kids play games. I know you play Freecell more often than you check your email. The difference, of course, is that Freecell spends much more time waiting for you to move a card than it spends on any calculations. Speed is primarily a concern with the more processor-intensive games, such as 3D action games or anything with animation.

Improving game performance, as with improving performance in any other application, involves removing software bottlenecks and occasionally upgrading hardware. However, games are unique in that they can benefit greatly from certain types of hardware, such as 3D accelerators and sound cards with digital signal processors. Games also suffer the most from background applications and out-of-date drivers. Here are some ways to improve performance in the more processor-intensive games:

- Most high-end games rely on DirectX, essentially a set of optimized video, sound, and game input drivers supported by Microsoft. Make sure you have the latest DirectX drivers by using the Windows Update feature or going to *http://www.microsoft.com/directx/*.
- Many games are also optimized to work with specific types of video and sound hardware. For example, a particular game's setup screen might allow you to choose between Direct3D and OpenGL for the video output; sometimes you even need to choose a particular card (e.g., 3DLabs). Your 3D accelerator might support several standards, but a given game might run better using the DirectX drivers, and another game might prefer the OpenGL setting.
- The speed at which a video card can draw to your screen is somewhat dependent on the current color mode and resolution (see the discussion of video cards in "Fine-Tuning and Upgrading Hardware Components" later in this chapter). If your games are running slowly, try reducing the color depth and resolution—either globally in Windows or in a particular game's setup screen (if it supports it)—to

increase the speed. It's funny, though—I've seen some games run smoother in 24-bit mode than 16-bit mode, even though in theory the extra colors should cause a performance hit.

- Games are highly optimized for speed, which often makes them finicky—a game might run beautifully with one video card but horribly with another. Check the documentation (manual, readme file, online FAQs) released by the game manufacturer for details that may affect you. Also look for updates to the game software that can fix performance issues, as well as add features and even new levels.
- Most 3D accelerators and even some games allow you to modify or disable certain 3D features, such as 8-bit palletized textures, gamma adjustment, zbuffer, and bilinear filter. In most cases, you'll probably just end up leaving these alone. However, some games might have conflicts with some hardware, and fiddling with these settings may make one or more of your games run smoother.
- Check out some of the hundred or so game-related web sites. In addition to game reviews, hints, and walkthroughs, many of these sites contain loads of information about special hardware and software settings that will enable a given game to run better on your system.
- Any unnecessary background applications should be disabled, either temporarily or permanently. Each program that runs invisibly or in your system tray takes precious CPU cycles away from the processor-intensive games and can make the difference between 20 frames per second and 30 frames per second. See "Speed Up System Startup" earlier in this chapter, as well as "Taming Antivirus Software" in Chapter 6, for details.
- If a game runs off a CD or DVD, the Windows Autorun feature, which continually polls the CD drive, may be interrupting data transfer. Symptoms include hiccups in video clips and music and slow loading of levels. See "Curb CD and DVD Autorun" in Chapter 2 for details. Note that old CD drives can also cause problems like this; for more information on improving CD drive performance, as well as upgrading tips, see "Fine-Tuning and Upgrading Hardware Components" later in this chapter.
- If you're playing a network game, either on a local network or over the Internet, you can improve performance by optimizing your network settings. See Chapter 7 for details.
- Lastly, high-end games are very dependent on game hardware, such as 3D accelerators and sound cards. High-end video and sound cards not only will add features, but also will handle many of the calculations

themselves, freeing up your processor significantly. A good 3D accelerator will literally blow you away with 3D effects and performance that are simply not possible otherwise. Your gaming system will actually benefit much more from a fast 3D card than from a doubling of processor power. Likewise, a good sound card with a digital signal processor (DSP) can add background sounds that will bring any game alive. I'm not trying to sell you any hardware, but don't overlook the value of dedicated hardware if you're serious about gaming.

What to Throw Away

By erasing unneeded files and folders from your hard disk, you'll not only get more disk space, but make your drive more responsive and reliable. Additionally, removing drivers and applications that are no longer used clears more memory for your other applications, which can substantially improve overall system performance.

Even before you install your first application, your hard disk is littered with files from the Windows installation that you most likely don't need. The standard installation of Windows Me puts about 3,000 files in more than 160 folders, consuming more than 300 MB of disk space.

Whether you need a particular file can be subjective; the 3MB of WAV files that one person might consider excessive might be valued by another. Naturally, it makes sense to be cautious when removing any files from your system. The removal of certain files can cause some applications, or even Windows itself, to stop functioning. It's always good practice to move any questionable files to a metaphorical purgatory folder before committing to their disposal. And I don't have to tell you that routinely backing up your entire hard disk (see Chapter 6) is very important. What follows are some tips to help you identify the more common files and folders that can be safely removed, as well as those that should be left alone.

Windows Me files that can be deleted

The following tips apply to files located in your Windows folder or a subfolder thereof. Select **Search** and then **For Files or Folders** from the **Start Menu**, type **`c:\windows`** in the **Look in** field (assuming Windows is installed on drive *c:*), and type the filename as described later in the **Search for files or folders named** field. For example, to search for all files with the "TMP" filename extension, you would use the asterisk wildcard character, like this: **`*.tmp`**.

Note that this is only a guideline; I'm not instructing you to delete all of these files (okay, maybe I am a little). If you're in doubt about a specific file, see the "If in doubt" section that follows for details on finding out what's inside of most types of files. The following files are safe to delete:

- Any file with the filename extension: **.log*, **.old*, **.- - -*, **.bak*, and **.000*, **.001*, **.002* (and so on).
- Any files with the extensions **.bmp* (bitmap files), **.wav* (sound clips), and **.avi* (video clips). These can take up a great deal of space and usually are superfluous.
- In the Windows folder only, there are a ton of text files (**.txt*), which are essentially "Readme" and log files, and can be safely deleted. Double-click on any text file to view its contents.
- The Online Services folder and most of the shortcuts found on the Windows Desktop (i.e., *\Windows\Desktop*).
- Any files or folders found in your *\Windows\Temp* folder. You won't be able to delete some files in this folder, because they will be in use by whatever applications you may have open. But applications in previous Windows sessions may not have deleted files there, and those types of files tend to accumulate very rapidly. It's not uncommon to find dozens of megabytes of useless files here. If you find files in your *Temp* folder that have a date and time *earlier* than the last time you started your computer, you can safely delete them. See "Clean Up and Customize System Folders" in Chapter 4 for more information on the *Temp* folder, and even a hint on automatically clearing out the *Temp* folder when Windows starts.
- The following file dates are common to older versions of Windows (releases other than the American English editions may have different dates); some files with these dates may still be around if you've upgraded to Windows Me:

  March 10, 1992, 3:10 AM—Windows 3.1
  November 1, 1993, 3:11 AM—Windows for Workgroups 3.11
  July 11, 1995, 9:50 AM—Windows 95
  August 2, 1996, 1:30 AM—Windows NT Workstation 4.0
  August 12, 1996, 3:50 PM—Windows 95 OSR2
  May 11, 1998, 8:01 PM—Windows 98
  April 23, 1999, 10:22 PM—Windows 98 Second Edition

- If there's a folder named *WIN32S* in your *Windows\System* folder, it can be safely removed. It was used only in Windows 3.x to allow certain 32-bit applications to run, but some older applications inadvertently create it in even new versions Windows; it also may be around if you upgraded from an earlier version of Windows. If you remove this directory, make sure to remove any references to it in your *System.ini* file, and restart Windows.
- See "Clean Up and Customize System Folders" in Chapter 4 for more information on all the extra empty folders that Windows won't let you delete.

Files found elsewhere on your system

In addition to those files in your Windows folder, there are plenty of files elsewhere that you can consider deleting:

- There are some unnecessary files in the root directory of your boot drive (usually *c:*); these include files with the extensions **.txt*, **.prv*, **.log*, **.old*, and **.- - -*. Most files with the **.dos* extension (except for *Bootsect.dos*—see "Files NOT to delete" later in this chapter) are also safe to delete.
- Other files that can be deleted include *Mscreate.dir*, an absolutely useless, empty, hidden file created by older Microsoft application installers. There may be hundreds of these empty files on your hard disk (see the discussion of FAT32 and slack space in the "Hard Disks" section in "Fine-Tuning and Upgrading Hardware Components" later in this chapter).
- Folders named *~Mssetup.t*, *msdownld.tmp*, or something similar are temporary folders created when some applications or Windows updates are installed. They can all be removed, as long as you've restarted your computer since said installation took place.
- If you're trying to create more disk space, you can also delete application help files (**.hlp* and **.chm*) you may never need. Also, many applications include bitmaps (**.bmp*), sound clips (**.wav*), and video clips (**.avi*), which take up enormous amounts of disk space for virtually no reason.
- For some reason, some programs (including the tutorial that comes with Windows) insist on installing video clips (**.avi*, **.mov*, and **.mpg*) to your hard drive. These files can be quite large, each eating up as much as several megabytes of disk space. To view a video clip before deleting it, just double-click the file icon.

Specific Windows components you can remove

Most optional Windows components can be removed by double-clicking on the **Add/Remove Programs** icon in Control Panel, choosing the **Windows Setup** tab, and unchecking any unwanted components. The following components are particularly wasteful:

- Everything in the *Accessibility* category
- In *Accessories*: Desktop Wallpaper, Document Templates, and Imaging
- In *Communications*: MSN Messenger Service
- Everything in the *Desktop Themes* category
- In *Multimedia*: Multimedia Sound Schemes and Sample Sounds
- Everything in the *Online Services* category
- The *Address Book* and *Outlook Express* options, only if you don't use Outlook Express
- The *WebTV for Windows* option (may be required for some hardware)

Files NOT to delete

In your travels, you may encounter some of the following files, all of which should be left alone:

- Any files in your root directory, as well as in the *\Windows* and *\Windows\System* folders, that are not mentioned earlier should be left alone. This includes *Bootsect.dos*, *Boot.ini*, *Ntldr*, and *Ntdetect.com*, which are used if you've set up a dual-boot system with Windows NT. And this especially includes *Io.sys*, *Msdos.sys*, and *Command.com*, which are the files that allow you to boot your computer.
- Your Registry files, *System.dat* and *User.dat* (as well as *System.1st*, in the root directory of your boot drive), should always be left alone.
- Any files and folders in your *\Program Files* or *\Windows\MSAPPS* directories that have names like *Microsoft Shared* and *Common Files*. These files can be used by several applications simultaneously, which is why they haven't been placed in the folders of the applications that put them there.

If in doubt

Before you delete any questionable file, there are several things you can do to get a better idea of what the file contains:

- Start by double-clicking a suspicious file to open it in its default application. If you then see the **Open With** dialog box, it means the specific filename extension has not yet been registered. In that case, your best bet is to drag-drop the file into an open Notepad window.
- Right-click on the file, and select **Properties**. If the file has a **Version** tab, it's likely an application, driver, DLL, or other support file. Choose it to view the manufacturer, copyright date, and possibly the application it accompanies.
- If you're not sure if something should be deleted but want to try anyway, move it to another directory first to see if everything works without it for a day or so. If all is clear, toss it.
- Check the file's **Last Accessed** date (right-click on it, and select **Properties**). If it's recent, most likely it's still being used. For information on removing a particular application, contact the manufacturer of that application or refer to the application's documentation.

Special consideration: Hidden files

Some files on your hard disk are hidden files—files that, by default, can't be seen in Explorer. To configure Explorer to show hidden files, select **Folder Options** from Explorer's **Tools** menu, and choose the **View** tab. Turn on the **Show hidden files and folders** option, and click **OK**. Any hidden files will be visible, but their icons will be somewhat transparent.

Most hidden files have been hidden to protect them from deletion. If you see a hidden file, think twice before deleting it for this reason. On the other hand, some hidden files are truly unnecessary and are hidden only to reduce the clutter they would otherwise generate. An example is the temporary hidden file Microsoft Word creates alongside every open document.

To hide or unhide a file, right-click on it, and select **Properties**. Check or uncheck the **Hidden** option as desired, and click **OK**.*

* The *ATTRIB DOS* command is used to list the attributes of files (e.g., Hidden, Read-only), as well as to turn those attributes on or off. It's also the only way to turn on or off a file's system attribute. See Appendix B, *DOS Resurrected*, for details.

Special consideration: System file protection and system restore

When I first installed Windows Me, I proceeded to delete the superfluous *Internet Connection Wizard* folder,* as I do whenever I install a new version of Windows. This time, I was in for a surprise—seconds after I deleted it, I saw it reappear as though Windows was telling me, "Just kidding!"

It turned out to be the System File Protection feature, which continually scans your system, replacing system files as it sees fit. Unfortunately, this approach creates several problems, not the least of which is the 12% of your hard drive's total capacity it consumes. See "Disabling System File Protection" in Chapter 6 for more information on this feature, as well as on the related feature, System Restore.

If you do decide to disable System File Protection, you can then safely delete the Internet Connection Wizard.

Fine-Tuning and Upgrading Hardware Components

It's frustrating how our computers never seem to be as fast as they were when we first bought them. It's even more frustrating that documentation (both the Windows manual and the docs that come with your hardware) never makes mention of improving performance. And certainly, no manual will tell you how—and when—to upgrade.

A computer is ultimately the sum of its parts, so any discussion of improving performance starts with each component. You're not likely to see any such discussion in Windows' documentation, and the documentation that comes with most components is pretty pathetic, to say the least.

Some parts, such as hard disks, can be optimized to your heart's content, potentially with substantial performance gains. On the other hand, when it comes to such components as your processor or motherboard, there's not much you can do to them short of replacing them entirely. In the rather special case of memory, an upgrade usually consists of simply adding more memory modules.

When I am asked which of the components mentioned here is the most important in a system, the answer is both easy and impossible. On one hand, all of the components work together to form a complete system and

* Windows runs the Internet Connection Wizard once: the first time you try to access the Internet after installing Windows Me, regardless of whether you already have a Dial-Up Networking connection configured. In some cases, you'll see this useless wizard appear again and again.

therefore are equally important to a well-tuned computer. On the other hand, the quality and speed of certain components can affect overall system performance and efficiency more than others. Additionally, certain parts that are important to some users are insignificant or even unnecessary to others. One thing for sure is that a single component *can* be a significant bottleneck, hindering the performance of the rest of the system.

What follows is a collection of tips, hints, and tweaks—specific to each component in your system—that can really make a difference in the hardware you already have. Also included are some upgrading tips, such as what to look for in a new monitor.*

As stated at the beginning of this chapter, sometimes it's more cost-effective to replace an entire system rather than laboring over software settings or simply swapping components, especially if most of said components are more than a few years old.

For example, knowing where to spend your money and where to hold back is important; if you buy something you know is going to be obsolete in six months, such as the CPU, don't buy the top of the line, because the extra money will likely be worth very little down the road. However, spending a lot on a good monitor that will last for years is smart and will pay off in the long run.

When purchasing a new, prebuilt system, you should be aware that the quality of some of the components is often less than what you'd get if you bought the components separately. Computer system vendors make more money by including substandard, generic parts in their systems rather than name-brand, top-of-the-line components, although some mail-order firms often allow you to customize your system with various higher quality components. The moral when buying a new system is to look at more than just the CPU speed and the sticker price, so shop around. This goes for laptops as well as desktop computers.

Name-brand components are important in that they're more likely to be supported by their manufacturers in the years to come. When I first upgraded my laptop to Windows Me, I was disappointed to find that updated drivers for my DVD decoder were simply not available, and there were no plans to ever make them available. And, since it was a laptop, the DVD decoder was not a modular, replaceable part. Had the vendor simply included a name-brand decoder, their loyal customers would still have fully functional decoders, capable of playing *Repo Man* in all its glory.

* See also *PC Hardware in a Nutshell* by Robert Bruce Thompson and Barbara Fritchman Thompson (O'Reilly).

A good test for any hardware manufacturer is to see if they still support products they stopped making years ago. Check the technical support area of a company's web site to see if they have drivers and troubleshooting information for their old products. If they support yesterday's products today, they're likely to support today's products tomorrow. If a company doesn't have some kind of support on the Internet, it's time to choose a different company. In short, do your research now before you spend a dime.

See "Fixing Device-Specific Problems" in Chapter 6 for troubleshooting information regarding each of the following components.

Monitors

Good use of your monitor is important, especially if you use your computer for long periods of time. First of all, you shouldn't be looking up or down at a monitor; it shouldn't be tilted at all, but rather placed directly at eye level. If you're too high or low for this, you can adjust the monitor height with a stand or adjustable desk, or use an adjustable chair. Using a monitor at eye level is not only more comfortable, but also decreases the risk of back and neck injury.

If you keep the glass clean, your images will be sharper as well; spray some window cleaner on a paper towel (not on the monitor directly) to clean it. Also, if you wear glasses, you should consult your optometrist for eyewear made especially for computer screens. Reading or driving glasses simply don't have the proper focal length for this purpose. Lastly, the contrast and brightness should be set so that black appears dark black and not washed-out gray (try adjusting these with an MS-DOS Command Prompt window open), and text is bright and high-contrast. Try turning the contrast control all the way up and the brightness control slightly above its minimum setting.

Another monitor adjustment that most people overlook is color-correction. If you work with digital images and you have a high-end monitor, consider using a *colorimeter* to measure the way your monitor displays colors, allowing your graphics software to compensate and display your images more accurately.

Lastly, monitors use a lot of power, so if you routinely leave your computer on for long periods of time, you can safely turn your monitor off to conserve electricity and lower those power bills.

What to look for in a new monitor

The monitor is arguably the most important single component in a computer system and, next to the printer, usually the most expensive. Your monitor is what you spend the most time looking at; your eyes will thank you for choosing wisely, especially if you wear corrective lenses or are prone to headaches. The monitor is the component least likely to become obsolete; a good monitor will probably outlast every other component in your system, so it's the best place to put your money. My advice to those looking for a new computer is that it's best to take some money out of the computer budget and spend it on the monitor. *Don't skimp here!*

A large, crisp screen makes your computer more pleasing to use. Don't settle for anything less than a 17-inch display (14-inch for laptops), although even larger displays are becoming more affordable. If you can afford it, invest in a bigger, better-quality monitor, and postpone that CPU upgrade for a while.

If buying a CRT (as opposed to a flat-panel screen), look for a flat, square screen surface—bulging, round screens, although cheaper, distort images and are obsolete. You'll want lots of controls to adjust not only brightness and contrast, but image size and position, color temperature (the saturation, or "warmth," of brighter colors), rotation, and the "pincushion" effect. *Insist* on digital controls (push buttons); analog controls (dials) don't have memory, so you'll need to adjust the controls every time you change the video mode (which happens more frequently than you may think). Don't waste your money on built-in speakers unless you have limited desk space or can afford the novelty; separate speakers will provide better sound and save you some money.

Flat-panel screens (also called LCD, TFT, or plasma displays), usually only about an inch thick, are getting cheaper and in most cases are superior to conventional CRT monitors. In addition to weighing much less and taking up much less desk space, flat-panel screens don't flicker, don't distort images, use much less power, and are much more reliable. Digital flat-panel displays are superior in almost every way to analog flat-panel displays, although they're more expensive and only work with specific video adapters.

Combined with Windows Me's ability to support multiple monitors, the potential of a couple of flat monitors hanging on the wall side by side, with the Windows desktop spanned between them, is intriguing, to say the least.

Note that everything that appears on the monitor is put there by the video card; see the next topic for more information on improving the display.

Video Cards (Display Adapters)

The first thing you should do with your display adapter is to configure it to show the highest color depth it will support. Your current settings may be configured to display a measly 256 colors. That may seem like a lot, but it's not; the real problem is the difference between the way that Windows handles colors in 8-bit (256-color) mode and 16-bit (65,536-color) and higher modes.

Have you ever noticed that all the colors on your screen become distorted for a split second whenever you view certain web pages? Do the photographic images you view appear spotty or excessively grainy? Do you notice ugly bands or streaks where a smooth sky or gradient should appear in a picture? Do you find that Windows won't display 256-color icons or animated cursors?

All these problems are symptoms of an *adaptive palette*. When your display is set to 256 colors, it means that there can never be more than 256 individual colors in use at any given time. Because 256 isn't nearly enough to represent all the colors in the spectrum, Windows simply chooses the best 256 colors each time you display something on your screen, such as a digital image, a video, or a web page with graphics. If you have multiple images showing at the same time, they all must share the same group of colors (the palette); Windows must choose colors most common to all the images—a greater number of images means poorer matches in each image. Furthermore, if you have multiple application windows open, each trying to use 256 colors, Windows will calculate the palette based on the needs of the active window and then display all the other inactive windows based on the active window's palette. This can look absolutely horrendous in some circumstances.

However, since as 65,536 colors (16-bit mode, or 216 colors; sometimes called *High Color*) is sufficient to display photographic images, the palette is fixed and does not have to *adapt* to what is on the screen. This gives a richer, faster display; web pages, games, and photos look better; and you don't have to put up with the bother of a constantly changing palette. 24-bit and 30-bit color modes (sometimes called *True Color*) work similarly to 16-bit mode, except that they provide more color depth for even better image quality.

To set the color depth, double-click on the **Display** icon in Control Panel, and choose the **Settings** tab. To the left is a drop-down list labeled **Colors**, with all of the color depth settings your video card supports. Select **High Color (16-bit)** or **True Color (24-bit)** from the list.

There are two limitations of your video card that may affect the settings here. First, the amount of memory on your video card dictates the maximum color depth and resolution you can use. The memory required by a particular setting is calculated by multiplying the *horizontal size* times the *vertical size* times the *bytes per pixel.* If you're in 16-bit color mode, then each pixel will require 16 bits, or 2 bytes (there are 8 bits/byte). At a resolution of 1024 × 768, that's 1024 × 768 × 2 bytes/pixel, or about 1.57 MB. Therefore, a video card with 2MB of memory will be able to handle the display setting, but a card with only 1MB will not.

As you adjust your color depth, Windows may automatically adjust other settings depending on your card's capabilities. If you increase your color depth, your resolution might automatically decrease; likewise, if you raise the resolution, your color depth might go down. See "What to look for in a new video card," immediately after this section, for information on upgrading the memory on your video card, as well as upgrading your video card.

The other limitation that may affect your available settings is the refresh rate that your card will be able to generate (this does not apply to flat-panel or laptop displays).* Although the maximum refresh rate is not dependent on the amount of your card's memory, you may have to lower your resolution to achieve the desired rate. Windows should automatically adjust your refresh rate to the highest setting your card supports, but this is not always the case. If you notice that your display appears to be flickering, especially under florescent lights, you'll need to raise your refresh rate, either by adjusting the refresh rate setting directly or by lowering your resolution or color depth. Consequently, if you hear a slight *whine* from your monitor, it means your refresh rate is too *high*. The minimum refresh rate you should tolerate is 72 Hz. People with corrective lenses seem to be more sensitive and might require a higher setting to be comfortable. Most cards available today support refresh rates of 75 Hz and higher, so this is usually not a problem. Double-click on the **Display** icon in Control Panel, and choose the **Settings** tab. Click **Advanced**, and then choose the **Adapter** tab. If your display driver supports it, you can adjust your refresh rate with the **Refresh Rate** setting. If the setting is not there, you'll either need to obtain a more recent video driver, reduce your resolution or color depth, or get yourself a better video card.

* The refresh rate is *not* the speed at which your video card can draw things on the screen, but rather how many times per second the image on the screen is *redrawn.*

In many circumstances, you can *significantly* improve your video card's performance by getting newer drivers from the manufacturer (see Chapter 6), which may be superior to the ones that come with Windows. Optimized drivers can increase speed, offer higher resolutions with more colors, give you more control over the refresh rate, and offer better stability than the plain-vanilla drivers that come with Windows.

What to look for in a new video card

The video card is what puts the image on your monitor, so a faster video card almost always translates to a faster display. Most video cards available today will be more than fast enough to satisfy most users; the exception is in the area of 3D accelerators.

Although most manufacturers claim their video cards offer "stellar 3D performance," most of them will sorely disappoint you. 3D acceleration primarily benefits 3D games, so if you don't play 3D games (Freecell doesn't count), you'll probably want to save your money. A 3D game will play terribly on even the fastest computer if you don't have a decent 3D accelerator, so do your research before investing in any particular card. The technology advances so rapidly, your best bet is to visit one of the hundreds of game-related web sites out there—most of them will have up-to-date hardware reviews and recommendations. At minimum, you'll want a 3D card that supports OpenGL and DirectX 8.0 or later.

In addition to speed, the other major consideration is memory. The amount of memory on your video card (not to be confused with the memory on your motherboard) is responsible for the maximum resolution and color depth your card will support; for 3D accelerators, video memory is also used to store 3D textures. In short, more memory is better—it's always a good idea to get more video memory than you think you need. See earlier for details on the relationship between video memory, resolution, and color depth.

Resist the temptation to allow an advertised benchmark to influence your purchase decisions. Bar graphs and charts that compare the performance of various cards are just devices used by magazine editors to sell more magazines. Benchmarks generally measure rather arbitrary quantities, such as data throughput and characters-per-second, rather than more important things like adherence to industry standards, driver reliability, and application and game support.

Most video cards come in different flavors, mostly specific to the connector type on your motherboard and the connector type on your monitor. All modern Windows systems accept PCI and AGP cards. AGP is an enhanced form of PCI, intended to improve 3D performance by widening the data bus between the motherboard and video card. If your motherboard has an AGP slot, you'll want an AGP card. And although all analog monitors use the same 15-pin connector, some manufacturers are now including OpenLDI connectors on their video cards for use with digital flat-panel displays (see "What to look for in a new monitor" earlier in this chapter).

Lastly, it's important to have a brand-name video card, because no-name or clone video cards aren't widely supported and may be difficult to get to work down the road.

Motherboards

With the exception of jumpers, all of a motherboard's settings are located in the BIOS (sometimes called *CMOS*) setup screen. The settings available in a computer's BIOS setup screen will vary significantly from one system to another, but there are some settings that are common throughout them all. The BIOS setup is usually accessed by pressing a key—such as **Del** or **Esc**—immediately after powering on your system and before the initial beep.

Make sure all of the settings you understand are correct: the configuration of your hard disk, floppy drives, keyboard, and ports should all match your system. Make sure your BIOS correctly reports the amount of memory in your system; it's possible that it's not using all that's installed.

Nearly all modern motherboards have built-in serial, parallel, and USB ports, as well as the disk controller; this means that these devices can be configured in BIOS setup as well. You should disable any ports or other devices that aren't being used, which will reduce the likelihood of conflicts and reduce the number of drivers Windows has to load, improving overall system reliability and performance, respectively.

If your BIOS has built-in antivirus support, disable it immediately. This feature causes compatibility problems with Windows and can slow down your system. Additionally, antivirus software (see Chapter 6) does a much better job, mostly because it can be updated to detect the newest viruses.

Many systems have advanced BIOS settings that can improve performance as well. A little investigation can yield some good results, but be very careful not to change any settings you don't understand. Your motherboard or system manual should explain each setting. It's a good idea to write down any settings there before you change them.

See "Processors" and "Memory," both later in this chapter, for additional tips.

What to look for in a new motherboard

The motherboard is what holds the processor, memory, and internal expansion cards. Even laptops have motherboards, but it's not nearly as distinct a component as it is in desktop computers.

The most important thing to look for in a motherboard is support for the processor you intend to use—both today and tomorrow. Motherboards and processors are usually purchased in pairs, but because most motherboards support a wide range of CPU speeds, it's best to choose a motherboard that can accommodate faster chips later on.

The more PCI slots and memory slots, the better. Don't bother with ISA slots unless you have old expansion cards you still need to use. All new motherboards will have a built-in hard-disk controller and built-in serial, parallel, and USB ports. Many new boards also have the option of a built-in ultra-wide SCSI controller for much less than a standalone controller would cost, a worthwhile investment if you're serious about hardware. Some motherboards have built-in sound cards, although you'll almost always be better off getting a third-party sound card.

A motherboard with lots of jumpers and switches can be difficult to configure, so look for boards with only a few, well-labeled jumpers. In fact, make sure *all* of the connectors are clearly labeled in English *on the board*, and not simply numbered.

Processors

In most cases, there's little or nothing you can do to improve the performance of an existing processor, save replacing it. The exceptions are with regard to cooling and "overclocking."

A cooler processor will run faster; a processor that is allowed to overheat will cause system crashes. A decent fan is the solution—you should have one mounted on top of your processor as well as in the front of your computer and in your power supply. Cheap fans won't do as good of a job cooling your CPU and may even wear out quickly, resulting in excessive noise.

Overclocking is the process of instructing your processor to run at a higher clock speed (MHz) than its rated speed. For example, you may be able to overclock a 500 MHz chip to run at 550 MHz, or even faster. Supposedly, Intel and other chip makers have taken steps to eliminate overclocking (theoretically prompting more purchases), but it may still be possible with some chips. You should be able to find an article on the Web that will work with your specific processor and motherboard.

What to look for in a new processor

The processor is the highest profile component, and a fast processor often translates to a fast overall computer, especially with respect to games. But processors also become obsolete the fastest; given how expensive they can be, it's often most cost-effective to *not* get the fastest processor available.

Note that a processor's clock speed is just one of several factors upon which overall system speed is dependent; jumping from 500 MHz to 1.0 GHz will *not* double the speed of the computer. However, a 1.0 GHz Pentium-4 will outpace a 1.0 GHz Pentium III.

Do some math before deciding on a CPU. Divide the processor speed by the price to get the megahertz-per-dollar value of each chip.* You'll find that the fastest chips are rarely the best deal. True, a faster chip will last slightly longer before it needs to be upgraded, but the extra money (which can be substantial) to get the top of the line today won't matter so much when it's time to upgrade later on. Besides, several years from now, you're not likely to care about the miniscule speed difference between an 800 MHz chip and a 900 MHz chip.

Your best bet is one or two steps below the top of the line, if you can afford it. If money is tight, go for a slower processor. You can always upgrade later if you have a motherboard that supports faster chips. In fact, the *combined* price of buying the slower CPU now and the faster CPU later will often be *lower* than buying the faster CPU now.

That said, consider the combined price of a brand new motherboard and processor with the price of the fastest processor your current motherboard will accept. Sometimes it pays to replace both units, especially if your existing motherboard is more than a few years old.

Memory

Like processors, there's little you can do to improve memory performance aside from simply adding more of it. The exception is how efficiently your memory is being used. By removing software loaded automatically by Windows that you don't use, you'll be leaving more memory available for other applications—see "What to Throw Away" earlier in this chapter for details. Also, your system memory is supplemented by virtual memory: see "Optimize Virtual Memory (or, Stop Windows from Wildly Accessing Your Hard Disk)," also earlier in this chapter, for a useful solution.

* If you're deciding between different types of processors, you'll want to compare their benchmarks rather than their clock speeds. Use a third-party benchmark, such as Norton System Information.

What to look for in new memory

There are no two ways about it: the more memory, the better (at least up to a point). Adding more memory to a computer will almost always result in better performance. Windows loads drivers, applications, and documents into memory until it's full; once there's no more memory available, Windows starts storing chunks of memory on the hard disk (in the form of your swap file) to make room in memory for more information. Because your hard disk is substantially slower than memory, this "swapping" noticeably slows down your system. The more memory you have, the less often Windows will use your hard disk in this way and the faster your system will be.

Like everything else, though, there is a point of diminishing returns; depending on how you use your computer, 128 MB or 256 MB might be enough for more uses.

The nice thing about memory is that it is a cheap and easy way to improve performance. When Windows 3.x was first released, 32 MB of RAM cost around a thousand dollars. The same quantity of memory (a faster variety) at the release of Windows Me cost the same as two tickets to the movies.

The type of memory you should get depends solely on what your motherboard demands—refer to the documentation that came with your motherboard or computer system for details. That simply leaves one thing to think about: quantity. In short, get as much memory as you can afford.

Memory comes in memory modules, which are inserted into slots on your motherboard. The higher the capacity of each module, the fewer you'll need—the fewer modules you use, the more slots you'll leave open for a future upgrade.

Hard Disks

As far as your physical hard drive is concerned, the best thing you can do is to make sure your drive is securely fastened to your computer case and is adequately cooled. More important, however, is how you take care of the *inside* of your hard drive; namely, the data stored on it. There are several things that you can do maximize the performance, capacity, and reliability of your drive, and all involve manipulating your files.

The best way to ensure maximum performance from your drive is to regularly (weekly) defragment it. Figure 5-2 shows how frequent use can cause files to become fragmented (broken up), which can slow access and retrieval of data on the drive, as well as increase the likelihood of lost data.

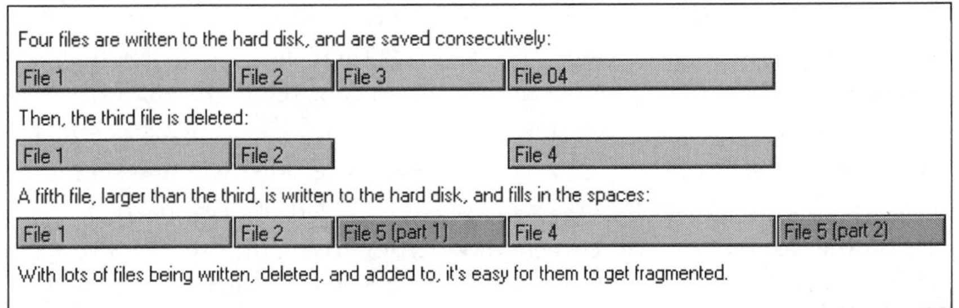

Figure 5-2. File fragmentation on your hard disk can slow performance and decrease reliability

To defragment your drive, run the Disk Defragmenter (*Defrag.exe*), which rearranges the files on your hard disk so that they are no longer fragmented. It also defragments the free space, and optionally places the files you access more frequently (such as programs and recently modified documents) at the start of the drive and less frequently accessed files at the back of the drive.

In addition to defragmenting your drive, you can adjust a few Windows settings to optimize your hard-disk performance to your needs. Double-click on the **System** icon in Control Panel, and choose the **Performance** tab. Click **File System**, and choose the **Hard Disk** tab to display the hard-disk performance settings for your machine. The disk cache is configured by selecting one of three options for the **Typical role of this machine** setting. Experiment with each of these to achieve the best results, although most users will benefit most by keeping it at **Desktop computer** here. If you choose **Network Server**, Windows will devote more memory to the disk cache; although this should result in better disk performance, it will reduce the memory available for other applications. If you have plenty of memory to spare (64 MB or more), you should try it. Make sure **Read-ahead optimization** is all the way to the right, and click **OK** when you're finished.

The next thing you can do is to verify you're using the most efficient filesystem Windows Me will support. If you've upgraded from an older version of Windows, it's possible that you're still using a 16-bit FAT (file allocation table) filesystem, and Windows Me comes with something better: FAT32.

Clusters are the smallest units into which a hard disk's space can be divided. A hard disk formatted with the traditional FAT system, found in Windows 95 and all previous versions of Windows and DOS, can have no more than 65,536 clusters on each drive or partition. This means that, the larger the hard disk, the larger the size of each cluster. The problem with large clusters is that they result in a lot of wasted disk space. Each cluster can store no more than a single file (or a part of a single file); if a file does not consume an entire cluster, the remaining space is wasted. For example, a 1.2-GB drive would have a cluster size of 32 KB; a 1-KB file on a disk with a 32 KB cluster size will consume 32 KB of disk space; a 33-KB file on the same drive will consume 64 KB of space, and so on. The extra 31 KB left over from the 33-KB file is called *slack space*, and it can't be used by any other files. With thousands of files (especially those tiny shortcuts littered throughout a Windows installation), the amount of wasted slack space on a standard 2-GB drive can add up to hundreds of megabytes of wasted space.

The FAT32 filesystem included in Windows Me can handle over 4 billion clusters, resulting in much smaller cluster sizes. The same 1-GB drive formatted with FAT32 will have only a 4-KB cluster size. Figure 5-3 illustrates the slack space created by files stored on a traditional FAT system versus the same files stored on a FAT32 system.

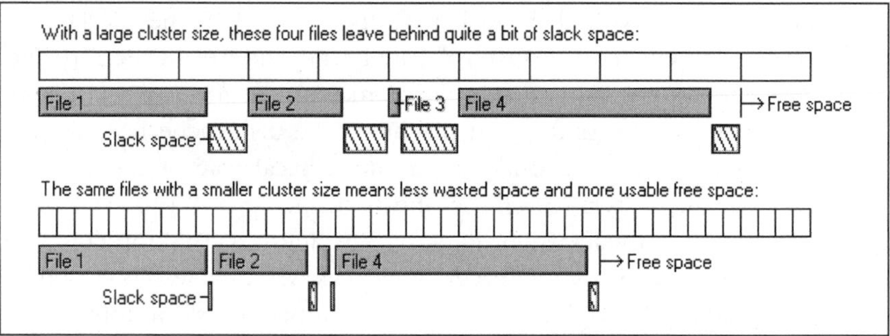

Figure 5-3. FAT 32 stores files more efficiently by allowing smaller cluster sizes

You can see how much space is wasted by any given file by right-clicking on the file icon, selecting **Properties**, and comparing the **Size** value with the **Size on disk** value.* The same works for multiple selected files and folders; highlight all the objects in your root directory to see the total amount of wasted space on your drive.

The other advantage of FAT32 is that it supports larger partitions. Traditional FAT wouldn't allow you to have a partition larger than 2GB (larger drives would have to be divided up), but FAT32 supports partitions up to 2 terabytes (2,048 GB, or more than 2 trillion bytes).

* You can also see the space wasted by all the files in a given folder by typing **`dir /v`** at the command prompt (see Appendix B).

To find out if a hard disk is formatted as FAT32, right-click the drive icon in **Explorer** or **My Computer**, and click **Properties**. To convert any hard drive to FAT32, open a command-prompt window, and type **`CVT d:`**, where **`d:`** is the drive letter of the drive you wish to convert.*

There are some minor drawbacks to FAT32 that warrant attention: Once you convert a drive to FAT32, you can't convert it back to traditional FAT without special software, such as PartitionMagic. FAT32 is not compatible with Windows NT 4.0 and earlier, a problem if you have a dual-boot system (Windows 2000 doesn't have this limitation). FAT32 has a bug that can cause the amount of free space on your drive to be occasionally calculated incorrectly; run Scandisk (*Scandskw.exe*) at any time to temporarily correct the problem.

There are two additional steps you can take to maximize the capacity and performance of your hard drive: see "Optimize Virtual Memory (or, Stop Windows from Wildly Accessing Your Hard Disk)" and "What to Throw Away," both earlier in this chapter.

What to look for in a new hard disk

A hard disk should be fast, capacious, and reliable. Look for a solid brand rather than a closeout deal. Get the largest capacity you can afford, because you'll use it. Besides, hard drive costs are plummeting, and it's not unusual for one drive to cost only a few dollars more than another of half the capacity.

Probably the most important feature, however, is the speed. The speed of a hard disk is measured in two quantities, access time and transfer rate. The access time, measured in milliseconds, is the average length of time required to find information. The transfer rate, measured in megabytes per second, is the speed that the drive can transfer data to your system. Although the access time is almost always quoted alongside the capacity of a drive (look for 9 ms or faster), the transfer rate isn't always publicized. However, if you're looking for maximum performance, it's a good thing to look for. Lower access times and higher transfer rates are better.

Access time and transfer rate are influenced primarily by two properties of any hard drive: the RPM (the speed at which the disk spins in revolutions per minute) and the type of connection that it uses. Typical drives spin at 5,400 RPM; better ones spin at 7,200 RPM; the fastest drives spin at 10,000

* PartitionMagic 3.0 or later (*http://www.powerquest.com*) will also convert a drive to the FAT32 filesystem. Furthermore, it allows you to resize and even combine partitions, so you can make better use of that old disk you had to split up in an earlier version of Windows.

RPM. The type of connection, on the other hand, must match the type of hard-disk controller you have (e.g., EIDE, SCSI, Ultra2-Wide SCSI, etc.). See the subsequent topics on hard-disk controllers and SCSI controllers for details.

Whether you end up upgrading your hard disk or buying a new computer, check out "Transfer Windows onto Another Hard Disk" later in this chapter for a handy solution.

Hard-Disk Controllers

Most hard-disk controllers typically don't have any settings (small computer system interface (SCSI), described later in this chapter, being the major exception). If you're still using an older hard-disk controller, you're almost always better off eliminating it and using the one built into your motherboard (if applicable).

What to look for in a new hard-disk controller

The hard-disk controller is what your hard disk and (usually) floppy drives plug into. With the exception of SCSI controllers, the discussion of hard-disk controllers is limited to the IDE variety, the one almost exclusively built into your computer's motherboard. The only time when you might consider upgrading your controller is to accommodate a new hard disk your current controller doesn't support. In this case, you should compare the price of said controller with the price of a brand new motherboard with the controller built in: surprisingly, the prices are often very close.

The only other time you're likely to be shopping for a new controller is when the one you're using is full. A single IDE controller can support a maximum of two drives; most motherboards come with two controllers, supporting a maximum of four drives. These drives can be hard disks, CD drives, tape drives, CD writers, and so forth. To support more than four devices, you'll need another controller. In most cases (with the exception of SCSI controllers), get the cheapest Plug-and-Play card you can find.

SCSI Controllers

The art of SCSI is in the cabling. You may experience slow performance with your SCSI devices if your SCSI termination is incorrect or if your SCSI chain (the length of all your SCSI cables added up) is more than the recommended maximum for your adapter type. For standard SCSI (10–20 MB/sec), the chain should be no longer than 3.0 meters (9.8 feet); for Ultra SCSI (20–40 MB/sec), the maximum chain length is 1.5 meters (4.9 feet).

And for Low Voltage Differential (LVD) Ultra2 and Ultra160 (80–160 MB/sec) SCSI chains, the chain should be no more than 12 meters (39.2 feet).

Many SCSI controllers also have a built-in BIOS, along with a few pages of settings. Each SCSI device attached to your SCSI controller may have different requirements, so check the documentation that came with your devices and make sure the SCSI controller's settings (max data rate, sync-negotiation, termination power, etc.) match the requirements of *each* specific device.

What to look for in a new SCSI controller

For many of us, the choice is not which one to buy, but whether to buy one at all. The only reason to get a SCSI adapter is to support one or more SCSI devices, such as hard disks, CD/DVD drives, scanners, tape drives, removable cartridge drives, optical drives, and CD recorders. Because most, if not all, of these are available in IDE form (requiring no additional purchase, because IDE controllers are built into most computers), most users won't need a SCSI controller at all.

Personally, I love SCSI (don't worry; it's just platonic). A single modern SCSI adapter can support up to 14 SCSI devices; you'd need seven IDE controllers to do that. SCSI also offers better performance and more flexibility than IDE; SCSI devices can be internal or external, for example. Keep in mind that USB is invading some of SCSI's territory, such as support for scanners and external drives, so that may be your best bet.

There are several varieties of SCSI, including Fast SCSI, Ultra SCSI, and LVD Ultra2/Ultra160 SCSI—whatever you get should be capable of supporting the specific SCSI devices you own or intend to use.

A good SCSI controller will be Plug-and-Play and will have its own BIOS, so you can boot off of a SCSI hard disk. Getting a brand-name SCSI controller (such as Adaptec) is important because without adequate software support, a SCSI controller is worthless.

If you want to squeeze every bit of performance out of your system and are willing to pay a little more, a 10,000 RPM LVD Ultra160 SCSI hard disk with a matching controller is hard to beat.

CD and DVD Drives

A CD or DVD drive may run slower than it is designed to if there's a problem with the controller; see "Hard-Disk Controllers" and "SCSI Controllers," both earlier in this chapter, for details.

The next thing to check is Windows' CD-ROM settings. Double-click on the **System** icon in Control Panel, and choose the **Performance** tab. Click **File System**, and choose the **CD-ROM** tab to display the CD drive performance settings for your machine. Adjust the **Supplemental cache size** to your liking; the resulting memory required is displayed later in this section. The more memory you use here, the better; if you have 32 MB or more of RAM, move the slider all the way to the right. If you have less than 32 MB of RAM, make it smaller by moving to around 30% of the maximum; the memory you save will be better spent elsewhere. If you don't use your CD-ROM much, move this slider more to the left to leave more memory available for other applications.

Lastly, match the setting of **Optimize access pattern for** to the speed of your drive. Click **OK** when you're finished.

If none of that helps, your best bet is to simply replace the drive.

What to look for in a new CD or DVD drive

A CD drive should do two things well. It should be fast, and it should recognize all of the different types of CDs you want to use: CD-ROMs, multisession CDs, recordable CDs, audio CDs, photo CDs, and multimode CDs (containing both data and music). A good DVD drive will be able to do anything a CD drive can, as well as read DVD disks (some older DVD drives can't read recordable CDs, for example).

The speed of a CD drive is measured by how much faster it spins the disk than an ordinary audio CD player; a 16x CD drive is obviously 16 times faster. DVD drives are also rated in this way, but separately for their ability to read CDs and DVDs, respectively.

The two numbers to look for in a CD drive's performance ratings are access time and transfer rate. The access time, measured in milliseconds, is the average length of time required to find information, and the transfer rate, measured in kilobytes per second, is the speed that the drive can transfer data to your system. CD-ROM drives are much slower than hard disks, so access times will be in the range of 80 ms to 120 ms, as opposed to 6 ms to 12 ms for hard disks—look for an access time of 200 ms or less. The transfer rate is usually 150 kilobytes per second *times* the speed of the drive; an 8x CD drive should have a transfer rate of about 1.2 MB per second. Lower access times and higher transfer rates are better.

The brand of CD drive you purchase isn't that important; Windows should support nearly anything you throw at it. In fact, CD drives are getting to be as common as floppy drives, so as long as it's fast and supports all of the different types of CDs, it should be alright; the more expensive drives aren't necessarily any better than the cheap ones. (They may, however, be sturdier or better looking.) The only choices worth mentioning are the loading mechanism and whether the drive is IDE or SCSI.

Most CD and DVD drives use a motorized tray to load and eject CDs, but there are also caddy and slot drives. The caddy is a plastic cartridge that holds the disk and helps keep dust out of the drive and away from the disk—any drive that supports caddy loading is going to be obsolete, so don't even bother. Drives with motorized trays are the cheapest and most common, but I find trays ugly and often very flimsy. By far the best loading mechanism is a slot drive; the disk is simply inserted into a slot, similar to most CD players found in automobile dashboards. Slot drives may be a little more expensive and a little harder to find, but they're worth it.

Lastly, if you already have a SCSI controller, you'll be happier with a SCSI drive: they're often faster, in that there's less of a burden on the processor to access a SCSI drive than an IDE drive. Also, SCSI drives are better at extracting CD audio data, useful for making MP3 files or CD copies. If you don't have a SCSI controller, though, you'll be fine with any IDE drive.

Tape Drives, Removable Cartridge Drives, and CD Recorders

The best thing you can do to improve performance with any of these drives is to keep them clean. Dust and dirt, especially in tape drives, mean poor performance or even an early death.

What to look for in a new tape drive, removable cartridge drive, or CD recorder

These types of drives allow you to store a lot of data on special media. However, each system has its own set of advantages and disadvantages and its own intended purpose.

For backing up your system in the case of an emergency, you'll be hard-pressed to beat a tape drive. Its reliability, speed, low media cost, and backup software make it the ideal backup device.

For archiving data (storing important documents for long-term storage), as well as sharing data with others, CD recorders are terrific solutions. Blank CDs are extremely cheap, often costing less than a buck per 650 MB disc, and are compact and extremely reliable. The best part is that almost anyone will be able to read the disks, which means you won't have to spend the money on a second drive if you use it to share data. Many CD writers also support rewritable CDs (CD-RW), which can be erased and rerecorded repeatedly. Although these disks are convenient in some situations, they have their drawbacks. They're quite effective when used in conjunction with packet-writing software (such as Adaptec's DirectCD), which allows you to write to a CD as though it were just another drive in Explorer (no "mastering" software required). The fact that they're rewritable means that you can turn a CD-RW drive into a 600 MB removable cartridge drive. The downside is that the disks can't be read in most normal CD readers, and they cost much more than normal blank CDs.

For repeatedly transferring large quantities of data from one place to another, though, removable hard disks (such as the Iomega Jaz) are the answer. The cartridges are much more expensive than either blank CDs or tapes, but they're very fast, fairly reliable, and don't require special backup software to use: they just show up as another drive letter in Explorer. In many cases, it's much faster to transfer extremely large files with a removable cartridge drive than with an Ethernet (network) connection.

See "Back Up Your Entire System" in Chapter 6 for a comparison of different types of backup devices. It's a good idea to research the cost of the *cartridges* before investing in a particular technology. A drive that seems like a good deal in the store may turn out to be a money pit when you take into account the expensive media. Try comparing your cost to store, say, 1GB (which isn't as much as it sounds) using each type of drive, including both the cost of the drive and the cost of the media. Other things to consider include speed, reliability, and availability of the media. Don't forget portability—how likely are others to be able to read these media you use?

Modems

I have to preface this by saying that modems are indeed obsolete, like it or not. Both DSL and cable modem connections,* which can be 20–30 times as fast as a 56 K modem connection, often cost no more than a standard dial-up Internet connection plus the cost of a dedicated phone line. Think about that before you read another word . . .

Now, the most common cause for slow connection speeds is a noisy phone line. Noise can corrupt the data being transferred; if your modem gets corrupted data, it must request that the data be sent again. If 15% of the data needs to be resent, your modem will be 15% slower than it should be. Start by connecting a telephone handset to the phone line or to

* See Chapter 7 for more information on Internet connections and high-speed solutions.

the jack labeled "phone" on the back of your modem, and make a normal call. If you hear any crackling or interference, it means the line is very noisy (you may not be able to hear low-to-moderate noise, however). If you suspect line noise, try replacing the phone cord or even the entire wall jack. Note that the phone cord shouldn't be any longer than is absolutely necessary.

Also, make sure there isn't anything else connected to the phone cord between the computer and the wall. That is, any answering machines, fax machines, and telephones should be plugged into the back of your modem (the jack labeled "phone"), and your modem should be plugged *directly* into the wall. These devices can interfere with transmission since the signal must pass through them in order to reach your computer.

On the software side, make sure you have a driver made especially for your modem. A generic modem driver may work with your modem, but a new driver supplied by the manufacturer of your modem might enable higher connect speeds (such as 33.6k and 56k), as well as compression and better error correction.

If you have an external modem, make sure it's connected to a USB port or high-speed serial port, equipped with a 16550A chip or better. Otherwise, your serial port may be the bandwidth bottleneck.

What to look for in a new modem

I'll make this short and sweet—unless you have some very specific and unusual requirements for a modem, get the cheapest Plug-and-Play 56 K modem (preferably PCI) you can find. Also, internal modems are better—and cheaper—than external ones, but their installation does require that you crack open your computer.

Network Cards

Network cards and their drivers usually come with lots of settings, which usually come preconfigured out of the box for compatibility rather than performance. For example, the default setting for the bidirectional feature (allowing data to be transmitted in both directions simultaneously) on most network cards is disabled, because some types of configurations don't support it. As long as all network cards in your workgroup support it and you're using 10-baseT cabling instead of the older 10-base2 (most cards support both connectors), you should enable bidirectional communication. Refer to the documentation that comes with your network card for details on specific settings.

Obviously, for the best performance you should be using the most recent drivers for all of your network adapters. Furthermore, Windows has a tendency to install more drivers than are truly necessary for the type of connection you're using. Extra drivers not only waste memory, but slow network communications as well. In some cases, extraneous or incorrectly configured drives on a single machine will bring an entire local network to its knees. See Chapter 7 for more information on the drivers required for your connection, and try removing all unnecessary ones.

What to look for in a new network card

The most important feature of a network card is compatibility. Make sure the card you choose is able to communicate with the rest of your network and comes with drivers for Windows 9x/Me. Buying a name brand will help ensure that you'll always be able to find drivers. Look for a Plug-and-Play, PCI Ethernet adapter. If you have a laptop, get a Cardbus Ethernet adapter *without* a dongle—the pop-out connectors are superior, and more reliable than they look.

You'll need a network card for each computer you wish to connect to your network. You'll also need a hub—get one with *more* than enough ports to handle the number of computers and network printers (if any) you want to use. Lastly, connect everything with category-5 patch cables. If you're connecting only two computers, you can omit the hub and use a single category-5 *crossover* cable instead.

If you plan on using Internet Connection Sharing, you'll need *two* network cards in the host computer and one in each of the client computers. See "Sharing an Internet Connection on a Workgroup" in Chapter 7 for details.

Sound Cards

It doesn't make much sense to talk about the performance of a sound card, but rather the performance of the rest of the system when the sound card is heard. A DMA or other hardware conflict (see Chapter 6), as well as an out-of-date or poorly configured driver, can cause your system to slow down or even hang when you try to listen to music or sound effects. Consult the web site of your sound-card manufacturer for updated drivers and any performance tips.

Many sound cards come with drivers that offer support of older DOS games. These drivers may be necessary for DOS games, but they are almost never needed in Windows. Furthermore, Windows Me goes to certain lengths to disable DOS, so those old DOS games might not even be playable anymore. These drivers not only take up valuable memory and slow system startup, but may cause slowdowns when you try to use sound in Windows.

See "Get the Most Out of Your Games, Speed-Wise" earlier in this chapter for more information on games and your sound card.

What to look for in a new sound card

It used to be that a good sound card had to be fully Soundblaster-compatible, but that's true mostly for DOS games. Modern sound cards should be fully compatible with Microsoft's DirectX 8.0 drivers or later.

A cheap sound card will suffice for the simplest tasks, such as playing audio CDs or listening to lame sound effects in web pages. Better sound cards will have environmental 3D sound, digital surround-sound outputs, and a digital signal processor to offload the burden on the sound card. Digital outputs are especially important if you plan on playing DVD movies on your PC, but are only useful if you have a digital audio receiver to connect them to.

All of these things translate to better sound, but only if you have a decent pair of speakers. Cheap PC speakers tend to sound tinny, so splurge a little bit. Try your local musician supply store rather than your local computer store when speaker shopping. Naturally, keep in mind that connecting a $600 surround-sound speaker system to a 10-year old off-brand sound card will get you nowhere, so be reasonable.

Printers

The most common printing bottlenecks are bad drivers and bad cables. Try replacing both to spruce up your printer.

Your printer cable should be new and securely fastened at both ends. A long printer cable can be convenient, but a shorter one is more reliable and may provide faster printing—don't use a longer cable than is necessary. Longer cables may even simply not work with some printers, yielding only gibberish or even nothing at all. Make sure you have a bidirectional cable, which allows communication in both directions. Many newer printers also require the more expensive IEEE-1284 cables for best performance and reliability. Also, remove any switching boxes, printer-sharing devices, and extraneous connectors unless they're absolutely necessary.

If your parallel port is built into your motherboard (as most are), you should go to your system BIOS setup screen (see "Motherboards" topic earlier in this chapter) to make sure your parallel port is configured for its optimal setting. Refer to your motherboard or system manual for details.

If your printer is shared by two or more computers over a workgroup, the printer should be connected to the computer that uses the printer the most. If you are experiencing slow printing over a network, you should look into a print-server solution; this is often just an expansion card installed in your printer, allowing you to connect it *directly* to your network instead of just to one of the computers on your network. This usually results in faster, more reliable, and more convenient printing. See Chapter 7 for more information.

As far as the software goes, most of the drivers included with Windows should work fine. In fact, many new printers come with special software that allows you to control the printer on-screen, but which usually requires lots of memory and disk space; some even seem to slow down the printing process. If Windows supports your printer *without* this special software, use the Windows driver instead for the fastest printing.

What to look for in a new printer

There's such a wide range of printers available, it's impossible to cover all of the choices. The decision is usually based upon your budget and your needs. Get a solid brand-name printer; a good printer should be a workhorse, lasting for years. The choice most people make is usually between inkjet and laser printers. Simply put, laser printers are more expensive, faster, and have better print quality than inkjet printers. Inkjet printers are less expensive, take up less space, yet print in color.

A laser printer should have a resolution of at least 600 dpi (dots per inch; higher numbers are better) and should print at least 8 pages per minute—some printers go up to 16 pages per minute and support resolutions of up to 1200 dpi or more. Check the price of a new toner cartridge for each printer you're considering; this can be an expensive maintenance consideration.

Inkjet printers also print at 600 dpi and higher and commonly print 3–5 pages per minute (1–2 ppm for color). Some printers advertise higher resolutions than 600 dpi, but those figures aren't very realistic.

If you're getting a second printer only to print photos and other color output, consider a dye-sublimation printer. Dye-sub printers are about the same price as better inkjets, but the output is superior—no dots! Dye-sub printers tend to be slow, however, and aren't suitable for pages and pages of black text.

If you plan to share a printer over a network (wise if you have two or more computers but don't feel like investing in two or more printers), make sure the one you get is networkable. This doesn't necessarily mean that it can connect directly to your network hub (although some can with an optional print-server expansion card), but rather that its drivers support being shared on a network. Some cheaper printers don't support this, so do your research. See Chapter 7 for details on setting up a local-area network and sharing printers.

Mice and Other Pointing Devices

If you have any software that came with your mouse,* it's probably unnecessary and just taking up memory and disk space. Unless you need it for some advanced features, such as programming a third mouse button, you should remove the software, because Windows supports nearly all mice out of the box.

Other than that, dust and dirt will kill any mouse, so keep it clean for best performance.

Double-click on the **Mouse** icon in Control Panel to adjust the sensitivity of your mouse. You can also adjust the double-click speed and turn on "pointer-trails" to increase visibility on laptop displays. The mouse is a primary method of input, and fine-tuning these settings can go a long way to improving your relationship with your mouse. (Speak to your mouse occasionally; make it feel loved and appreciated.)

What to look for in a new pointing device

Cheap mice are usually all right, but aren't as responsive or long-lived as better mice. Try lots of different kinds in your local computer mega-store, and choose one that's sturdy, comfortable, and not dreadful to look at. It should have a long cord and a plug with thumb screws so you don't need a screwdriver.

Most mice have two buttons, and some have three. Windows uses only two, but additional buttons can be programmed to take over other common operations, such as double-clicking or pasting text. The downside is that superfluous buttons can get in the way and can be confusing for new users.

* Examples include "Intellipoint" for Microsoft mice and "Mouseware" for Logitech mice.

Personally, I hate mice. I find a stylus (pen) to be much more comfortable, natural, and precise. You can get a pressure sensitive, cordless, battery-less stylus and a tablet for under a hundred bucks—more than a mouse, but worth it if you use Photoshop or other graphics software. My advice: try a tablet before you invest in another rodent.

Other alternatives to consider include trackballs, touchpads, and trackpoints, like the ones that come with newer portable (laptop) computers. These often take up less desk space, require less movement of your hands (which can reduce hand fatigue), and don't require cleaning.

Before subscribing to the mouse mantra, do a little footwork and see if you can find something you like better.

Regardless of the specific type of pointing device, make sure the connector is supported by your computer. If you have a USB port, a USB device is absolutely your best bet. Get one that uses a serial port or PC/2 mouse port only if you don't have USB.

Keyboards

Double-click on the **Keyboard** icon in Control Panel to adjust the various settings of your keyboard. Moving the **Repeat Rate** slider all the way to the right will do wonders to make your computer seem faster, especially when scrolling through a long document or moving the cursor through a lot of text. The **Repeat Delay** is different, though—just adjust this to your liking, and test the setting in the box below.

Sticky or dirty keys can slow things down when you're typing; you can pull your keys off one by one and remove whatever is caught underneath. Some people have actually been successful cleaning the entire keyboard by immersing it in plain water (unplugged, of course) and then waiting for it to dry. Most keyboards are cheap, so consider replacing yours if it's not in top condition.

Keep in mind that most keyboards haven't been effectively designed for use with the human hand (no matter what Microsoft tells you in trying to market their "Natural" keyboard). Your best defense in reducing hand and back strain is to position your keyboard (and yourself, if you have an adjustable chair) so that your elbows are at the same level as your hands, and that your arms are well supported. And if your chair tilts forward, it may induce a more comfortable sitting and typing position.

A wrist rest may be comfortable, but it may be putting too much pressure on the median nerves in your wrists. If you're experiencing wrist pain or numbness, try eliminating the wrist rest and consulting a physician.

Another way to increase typing performance is to just not use your keyboard as much. Try one of the latest natural-speech dictation programs available. Some of Chapter 7 in this book was dictated (just for fun).

Regardless, most keyboards are of low quality, so it's likely there's a better one out there than the one you're using.

What to look for in a new keyboard

Get yourself a solid keyboard; the brand doesn't matter (although, in my opinion, the keyboards IBM made in the late eighties and early nineties are still the best conventional keyboards out there). Just make sure it has a nice long cord and is well made.

Most keyboards are very flimsy and cheap. Shop around to find one with a solid feel and good quality keys; your fingers will thank you. Some people like soft-touch (mushy) keyboards, while others like tactile (clicky) keyboards; get one to suit your taste and that won't hinder your work.

Compact keyboards not only take up less desk space but require less movement of your hands, which can reduce hand fatigue. Larger keyboards usually feel more solid, though, and may be more comfortable for those with larger hands.

True ergonomic keyboards are now getting more affordable and more popular. Some of the more radical designs have split, adjustable keyboards, curved to fit the motion and shape of your hands. Try one before buying: they aren't for everyone.

Carefully scrutinize the so-called "Natural" keyboards from Microsoft and other manufacturers, which mimic the more carefully designed, higher-quality ergonomic keyboards. These devices usually aren't any better for your hands than standard flat keyboards and can actually do more damage than good. The most important thing in an ergonomic keyboard is not the shape or the marketing lingo, but its ability to be *adjusted*. If you're experiencing any pain or numbness in your hands, wrists, arms, back, or neck, drop this book immediately and talk with a physician. In short, take repetitive stress injuries seriously.

Lastly, question hand entry altogether. Companies like Dragon Systems and IBM have released what they call "natural-speech" dictation systems, which allow you to speak comfortably into a microphone and dictate as you would to a human assistant or inhuman tape recorder. These can be quite effective but, like everything else, aren't for everyone.

The Box and Power Supply

The computer case and power supply don't directly affect performance, but there are differences in design and features that warrant attention. Look for a case with several fans for better cooling, plenty of drive bays for future expansion, and easy access. A well-designed case won't have sharp edges inside (I learned this the hard way) and won't require you to dismantle the entire computer to accomplish something as simple as adding more memory. Some cases can be opened without the need for a screwdriver, making that task just a little easier.

It's remarkably difficult to find a well-made computer case these days; most manufacturers want them cheap and small. Bigger cases do have room for more drives and usually have better power supplies, but anything larger than a midsize case is usually unnecessary. Make sure you get at least a 300-watt power supply, although your needs may demand more power. See the discussion of power supplies in Chapter 6 for more information.

If you have a modern computer (Pentium II or better), you're likely to have an ATX-compliant case and motherboard. You can tell if you have an ATX system if your power switch is a momentary pushbutton (it won't stay in when you press it). See "Have Windows Power Down Your Computer Automatically" for an advantage to this design.

Here's a tip if you're looking for a good high-end case: rack-mount cases (usually black with two large handles in front) are generally much higher quality than the standard gun-metal gray cases you'll find in most computer stores. They can be expensive, but mmmm, boy.

Transfer Windows onto Another Hard Disk

With the release of an operating system as large as Windows Me, it's anticipated that many users will need to upgrade their hard disks to accommodate the new operating system. Furthermore, that old 486 may have reached the end of its lifespan and may need to be replaced entirely. Either way, transferring Windows and all of your applications and data directly to a new hard drive can save you hours of work and a lot of aggravation. The downside is that Windows doesn't exactly make this process easy, unless you know what to do.

Sure, you can simply install Windows Me from scratch and then proceed to reinstall all your applications, configure all your settings, and rewrite all your documents, but I wouldn't wish that on my worst enemy. Besides, your Freecell statistics would be lost forever.

You can transfer the data from one drive to another in several ways; the one you choose depends on your available hardware and your specific goals. If you're setting up a new hard disk, all the following solutions assume that you've correctly connected, prepared, and formatted your new drive according to the drive's instructions.

Use a Backup Device

If you have a tape drive or other backup device, one of the easiest things to do will be to back your entire system and then restore it to the new drive. See "Back Up Your Entire System" in Chapter 6 for details on backup devices. You'll need to consider the following if using this solution:

- If you're upgrading your entire system to a new machine, all you need to do after backing up is to install the backup device on the new system, and then restore all your files onto the new drive.
- If Windows is already installed on the new drive (likely if the drive came preinstalled on a new computer), you'll want to be careful when restoring the backed-up Windows folder over the Windows folder on the hard disk. See "Restoring Windows After a Crash" in Chapter 6 for some ideas.
- If Windows is not installed on the new hard disk (the drive may be blank), you'll need to install Windows in order to access the backup software and perform the restore.
- The nice thing about this solution is that you don't have to install both drives in your computer at the same time, as with the other solutions.

Using a Disk-Cloning Utility

Several manufacturers have released software made especially for transferring the entire contents of one hard disk to another, blank, hard disk. If you're able to install both drives in the same computer at the same time (see later in this section), then this solution is fast, reliable, and very effective. Here are some considerations if using this solution:

- This solution will only work if the old hard drive and the new hard drive are installed in the same computer at the same time. The two drives can both be IDE drives, they can both be SCSI drives, or one can be a SCSI drive and the other an IDE drive. Refer to the software documentation for specific configuration requirements, such as slave/master for IDE drives or SCSI IDs for SCSI drives.

- If your controller doesn't have enough free ports, just temporarily disconnect a CD drive or other storage device to make room for the new drive.
- Disk-cloning software can even copy multiple partitions,* duplicating those partitions proportionally on the new drive, something that can be very difficult to do without such software. If you're upgrading from a 2GB drive to a 10 GB drive and have two 1GB partitions, the new drive will be created with two 5GB partitions.†
- At the time of this writing, PowerQuest DriveCopy 3.0 (*http://www.powerquest.com*) costs about $30. Even though you're likely only to use it once, the frustration and headache it saves make it a bargain.

Transferring Data Manually

Although the previous two methods are preferred to move data from one drive to another, it's also possible to copy files manually using Explorer:

- If you're copying data onto a new, blank drive, you'll need to first make the drive bootable. Unfortunately, in Windows Me there's no way to make a blank hard disk bootable,‡ short of installing Windows from scratch. To install Windows on a new, blank, hard drive, you'll need the Windows boot disk, which will load the appropriate CD-ROM drivers and run the Windows setup program.
- If the new hard drive is from a new computer, you can take your old hard disk and install it as a "slave" in the new machine or take your new hard drive and install it as a "slave" in the old machine.§ Either way, both drives will show up in Explorer at the same time. The only time you won't want to do this is if the "master," or primary, drive has more than one partition—see "Designate Drive Letters" in Chapter 6 for an explanation of this pitfall. If you have a SCSI drive with multiple partitions, just install it without BIOS support, and your drive letters will remain intact.

---

* See "Designate Drive Letters" in Chapter 6 to see how adding a second drive to a system with multiple partitions can mess up your drive letters, making this type of software that much more valuable.

† When you're done, you can use a program like PartitionMagic (*http://www.powerquest.com*) to resize the partitions as desired.

‡ In previous versions of Windows, you could do this with the *SYS* or *FORMAT/S* commands in DOS. In Windows Me, these commands have been disabled, making this type of upgrade much more difficult than it has to be.

§ "Slave" is a term reserved for IDE drives, meaning secondary. The "master" drive is the primary drive and is always the one from which Windows boots. For SCSI drives, the primary drive has the lower SCSI ID, and the secondary drive has a higher SCSI ID.

- In Windows Explorer, just highlight all the objects in the root directory of the old drive and drag-drop them into the root directory of the new drive. It's a good idea to make sure hidden files are shown by selecting **Folder Options** from Explorer's **Tools** menu, choosing the **View** tab, and selecting the **Show hidden files and folders** option.
- Don't copy the following objects: *Win386.swp*, the *Recycled* folder, *Command.com*, *io.sys*, and *msdos.sys*.
- If you're upgrading your entire system and not just your hard disk, and if both the new computer and the old one have network adapters, you can transfer all your data onto the new machine over your network. Keep in mind that networks are very slow compared with either of the previous two solutions. However, you won't need to take your computer apart or install any hardware. See Chapter 7 for details on properly setting up a local-area network.

6

Troubleshooting

Most of us would consider the barrage of incomprehensible error messages and insatiable appetite for crashing among Windows' biggest annoyances. The most important step—and usually the most difficult—in troubleshooting a computer system is to isolate the problem. With a little know-how and a lot of patience, you can fix just about any problem you'll encounter. Consider the following two axioms to be your guiding principles when troubleshooting any computer system:

1. 99% of all computer problems are solved by pressing the Reset button.
2. The true definition of insanity is repeating the same actions over and over again, expecting different results.

Naturally, a corollary to these principles is that resetting your computer repeatedly will get you nowhere. Herein lies the rub: what do you do during that remaining 1% of the time when restarting your computer doesn't help?

Like it or not, most problems are simply caused by poorly written software. As soon as you remove yourself (the user) as a potential cause of the problem, it makes it much easier to track down the real source of the problem and fix it.

Computer problems can come in many forms: error messages, crashes, lock-ups, unexpected results, and corrupted data. A crash is usually attributed by a cryptic error message of some sort (General Protection Fault, Blue Screen of Death, etc.),* followed by having the application—

* Don't waste your time trying to write down all the numbers and codes that are shown when an application or Windows crashes. The only ones worth writing down are the ones that are in plain English or the ones that reference a filename.

or Windows—shut down abruptly. A lock-up is when an application—or Windows—stops responding to the mouse and keyboard; sometimes a lock-up is recoverable (often with **Ctrl-Alt-Del** or just waiting 30 seconds or so), and sometimes it isn't.

Much of this chapter focuses on some specific problems and their solutions, but most troubleshooting requires nothing more than a little reasoning. If you're looking for a chart of every conceivable error message and its cause, you're out of luck: such a thing simply doesn't exist. There is effectively an infinite combination of computer systems, add-on devices, application software, and drivers; unfortunately, some of those combinations can be fraught with headaches.

Here are some questions to ask yourself when you're trying to isolate a problem:

- Is this an isolated incident, or does this problem occur every time I perform some action? As much as Microsoft will deny it, crashing is a fact of life on a Windows system, even when using Windows 2000. An isolated incident is often just that and, if nothing else, is a good reminder to save your work often. On the other hand, if a given error message or crash repeatedly occurs at the same time, in the same place, or as a result of the same mouse click, you need to be aware of that fact if you hope to solve the problem.
- Did I install or remove any software or hardware around the time this problem started occurring? Sudden changes in your computer's behavior are never spontaneous; if something suddenly stops working, you can bet that there was a discernable trigger.
- Did I read the directions? Unfortunately, good software-interface design is still ignored by most software manufacturers these days, so if you're not getting the results you expect from your computer, printer, scanner, mouse, or other device, make sure that you have read the directions and that the product in question is installed properly. Also, software manufacturers frequently release updates and fixes, so it's always a good idea to check to see if you have the latest versions of all applications and drivers. See "Dealing with Drivers and Other Tales of Hardware Troubleshooting" later in this chapter for details.
- How likely is it that someone else has encountered the same problem I have? This is often the most useful question to ask, because the odds are that someone else not only has encountered the same problem (anything from an annoying software quirk to a deafening application crash), but has already discovered a solution.

- Am I asking the right people? If you just installed a new version of America Online and now your Internet connection doesn't work, you shouldn't be calling your plumber. On the other hand, nothing compares to trying to convince a technical support representative that the problem you're experiencing is actually *their* company's fault, and *not* someone else's.

In addition to isolating and solving problems, the other important aspect of troubleshooting involves data loss caused by those problems. See "Preventive Maintenance and Data Recovery" later in this chapter for details on what do when a problem is bad enough to corrupt or erase important documents or other data.

General Troubleshooting Techniques

Let's get one thing straight before we begin: if it ain't broke, don't fix it. Many problems are actually caused by people looking for problems to solve. For example, installing a new device driver just for the sake of having the newest drivers on your system may introduce new bugs or uncover some bizarre incompatibility. This doesn't mean that updating your drivers isn't a good idea, but typically only do this if something isn't working or performing at its best.

Once you start peeking under the hood of Windows Me, you'll notice some of the tools that have been included to help the system run smoothly. Some of these tools actually work, but it's important to know which ones to use and which ones are simply gimmicks.* A good example is System File Protection (SFP), a new feature introduced in Windows Me to make it appear more stable than its predecessor, Windows 98. Although SFP is designed to solve certain file conflicts automatically, its brute-force method often ends up causing more problems than it solves. See "Disabling System File Protection" later in this chapter for more information.

Most hardware and software problems are caused by incompatibilities or conflicts, where two or more components simply don't work together—even though they may work perfectly well on their own. Faulty or out-of-date drivers are a frequent source of hardware problems, and incompatible DLLs can cause a myriad of troubles with software. For example, one of the most common difficulties is trying to get a modem to work with a

* Yes, many software companies include functionality in their software that serves no other purpose than to list as "valuable features" on the retail packaging. System File Protection and System Restore both owe their existence to the bean counters at Microsoft.

computer that didn't come with one. The obvious tactics are to blame the modem manufacturer or even the computer maker, but it can turn out to be a conflict with the way the mouse port is configured in the system BIOS. If you don't know how to use the diagnostic components in Windows, finding problems like these can be an exercise in futility.

Regardless of the type of problem, there's so substitute for a full system backup. Even if your computer equipment is insured with Lloyds of London, once your data is gone, it's gone.

Disabling System File Protection

SFP is a service that starts automatically when Windows starts and that runs transparently in the background until you shut down. The premise is pretty simple: SFP continuously scans your system files and replaces any suspicious files it finds with the ones that shipped with Windows. Because many Windows problems occur because certain support files are corrupted or replaced with older versions, this seems like a great idea, right? Wrong!

SFP doesn't have an interactive mode, so it uses preset criteria to determine which files to replace. These criteria were written when Windows Me was released. This means that SFP can unintentionally, yet swiftly and transparently, break an application or driver by replacing one of its support files with an improper version. Furthermore, if you're trying to fix a broken application by replacing one or more of its support files, SFP will come along and instantly undo your work!

Additionally, SFP eats up an astonishing amount of hard-disk space for all the spare support files and configuration data. Rather than use only what's needed, SFP is programmed to consume no less than 12% of your hard-disk capacity, regardless of what else is stored on it; on an 8GB hard disk, that's a whopping 960 MB lost to this feature. And Microsoft describes SFP as a feature that "improves the user experience."

Lastly, because it's running all the time, it's just another component that can slow down your system with its overhead. Not surprisingly, Microsoft provides no options to customize, remove, or even just turn off SFP. A little tinkering in the Registry, however, is all it takes to abolish SFP for good:

1. Open the Registry Editor (if you're not familiar with the Registry Editor, see Chapter 3, *The Registry*).
2. Expand the branches to `HKEY_LOCAL_MACHINE\SOFTWARE\Microsoft\Windows\CurrentVersion\Uninstall\PCHealth`.

3. Double-click on the `UninstallString` value. By default, the text in this box will already by highlighted; press **Ctrl-C** to copy the value data to the clipboard, and click **Cancel** when you're done.
4. Select **Run** from the Start Menu, paste the text you just copied into the **Open** field, and click **OK**. This will run a hidden uninstaller that will remove the System File Protection and System Restore features.
5. Close the Registry Editor when you're done; you'll have to restart Windows for the change to take effect.
6. If you've disabled SFP, you should be able to delete the entire *_RESTORE* folder at this point.

   If you can't see this folder, make sure you've configured Explorer to display hidden files. Choose **Folder Options** from Explorer's **Tools** menu (or from the **Start Menu**), and choose the **View** tab. Select the **Show hidden files and folders** option, and click **OK**.

A Word About System Restore

System Restore is a feature that works in tandem with System File Protection. Instead of restoring files one by one, System Restore allows you take a snapshot, so to speak, of your system files. Then, at a later time, you can revert some of your system files back to their saved state. Naturally, the same pitfalls that affect SFP also affect System Restore; in addition, there's the matter of its being only a partial restore.

Say you use System Restore to take a snapshot of your system, and then install a third-party application. Later, you choose to restore said snapshot. Because one of the goals of System Restore is to recover from a disastrous installation of a program, it may have the effect of inadvertently disabling another program. Furthermore, you *could* end up with a mixture of old and new support files, which could cause other problems. In short, restoring your system will have unpredictable results.

System Restore is an interactive tool, so there's not much need to disable it if you choose not to use it. However, you can disable it by double-clicking the **System** icon in Control Panel and choosing the **Performance** tab. Click **File System**, choose the **Troubleshooting** tab, and turn on the **Disable System Restore** option.

This solution has the side effect of disabling the **Help** feature in the Start Menu (although it will have no adverse effect on the help system in other applications). To remove the **Help** item in the Start Menu, double-click the **TweakUI** icon in Control Panel (see Appendix A, *Setting Locator*), choose the **IE** tab, and turn off the **Show Help on Start Menu** option. To reinstate SFP and the Windows Help, you'll have to reinstall Windows Me.

Taming Antivirus Software

Antivirus software is a double-edged sword. Sure, viruses can be a genuine threat, and for many of us, antivirus software is an essential safeguard. But antivirus software can also be a source of pain.

First of all, don't succumb to the hype that a large portion of the populace is routinely crippled by virus attacks—the chances that an average computer will actually get infected are remote, to say the least.* As long as you take some reasonable safeguards, you can make your system less susceptible to viruses and eliminate the more troublesome features of your antivirus software at the same time.

The most basic, innocuous function of an antivirus program is to scan files on demand. When you start a virus scanner and tell it to scan a file or a disk full of files, you're performing a useful task. The problem is that most of us don't remember or want to take the time to routinely perform scans, so we rely on the so-called "AutoProtect" feature, where the virus scanner runs all the time. This can cause several problems:

- Loading the autoprotect software at Windows startup can increase boot time; also, because each and every application must be scanned before it is started, application load time can be increased.
- If the antivirus software or virus definitions become corrupted, the application autoscanner may prevent any application on your system from loading, including the antivirus software itself, making it impossible to rectify the situation without serious headaches.†
- Some antivirus autoprotect features include web browser and email plug-ins, which scan all files downloaded and received, respectively. In addition to the performance hit, these plug-ins can inadvertently interfere with the applications used to open these files.

* This is simply propaganda by the media and the antivirus-software manufacturers to sell more newspapers and antivirus programs, respectively.

† Yes, I've actually seen this happen.

- Antivirus software can also interfere with some applications, such as certain installation programs or diagnostic utilities that may modify the boot sector of one of your drives.
- Autoprotect software is a known culprit for floppy drive problems; see "Stop Windows from Randomly Searching the Floppy Drive," later in this chapter for more information.
- Lastly, having the autoprotect feature installed can give you a false sense of security, reducing the chances that you'll take the precautions listed later in this section and increasing the likelihood that your computer will become infected.

Naturally, whether you disable your antivirus software's autoprotect feature is up to you. If you keep the following concepts in mind, regardless of the status of your antivirus autoprotect software, you should effectively eliminate your computer's susceptibility to viruses:

- *If* you don't download any documents or applications from the Internet, if you're not connected to a local network, and if you only install commercial software, your odds of getting a virus are pretty much zero.
- Viruses can only reside in certain types of files, including application (**.exe*) files, document files made in applications that use macros (such as Microsoft Word), Windows script files (**.vbs*), and some types of application support files (**.dll*, **.vbx*, **.vxd*, etc.). And because ZIP files can contain any of the aforementioned files, they're also susceptible. Plain-text email messages, text files (**.txt*), image files (**.jpg*, **.gif*, etc.), and most other types of files are benign in that they simply are not capable of being virus "carriers."
- Don't *ever* open email attachments sent to you from people you don't know, especially if they are Word documents or EXE files. If someone sends you an attachment and you wish to open it, scan it manually before opening it. Most antivirus software adds a context-menu item to all files,* allowing you to scan any given file by right-clicking on it and selecting **Scan** (or something similar).
- If you're on a network, your computer is only as secure as the least secure computer on the network. If it's a home network, make sure everyone who uses machines on that network understands the previous concepts. If it's a work network, there's no accounting for the stupidity of your coworkers, so you may choose to leave the autoprotect antivirus software in place.

---

* See "Customize Context Menus" in Chapter 4, *Tinkering Techniques*, for details.

What to Do When Windows Won't Start

Unfortunately, Windows' not being able to start is a common problem, usually occurring without an error message or any obvious way to resolve it. Sometimes you'll just get a black screen after the startup logo, or your computer may even restart itself instead of displaying the desktop. Of the many causes to this problem, many deal with hardware drivers, conflicts, or file corruption—all of which are discussed elsewhere in this chapter.

In previous versions of Windows, up until Windows 98, users were allowed to start a DOS session before loading Windows, which was a gateway to several effective troubleshooting techniques. In its infinite wisdom, Microsoft has disabled this lifeline, thereby decreasing the tools we have available to fix such problems.

If you've made a Windows Me startup disk (see "Make a Startup Disk" later in this chapter), though, you'll be able to boot directly into DOS, allowing you to try some of the tried-and-true recovery tactics. First, try deleting your Windows swap file (usually called *Win386.swp* and usually located in the root directory of your Windows drive). Also, delete all your temporary files (usually the contents of *\Windows\Temp*). Because these files can get corrupted, thereby preventing Windows from loading, deleting them is often a good solution for when Windows won't start. For details on these procedures, see Appendix B, *DOS Resurrected*.

Assuming you can't get into DOS—a situation most Windows Me users will find themselves in—your next best choice is to activate the Startup Menu:

1. Turn on your computer. If the computer is currently running (yet Windows hasn't loaded), restart your computer by pressing the reset button or by pressing **Ctrl-Alt-Del**.
2. Immediately after the beep, but before the Windows logo appears, press the **F8** key. If you see the Windows startup logo after pressing F8, you've missed your chance, and you'll have to return to step 1. If you're successful, you'll see the Microsoft Windows Millennium Startup Menu and the following menu choices:

```
1. Normal
2. Logged (\BOOTLOG.TXT)
3. Safe mode
4. Step-by-step confirmation
```

`Normal` (#1) is what you'd use if there were no problem. **Logged** (#2) is a useful feature, in that every driver that Windows attempts to load is listed in a text file called *Bootlog.txt* (located in your root directory)—the problem is that you won't be able to read it without booting Windows or finding a way to start a DOS session. However, I've actually encountered a few circumstances when using the Logged option is enough to get Windows to start.

`Safe mode` (#3) is probably your best bet. Safe mode is a way of starting Windows with only a minimal set of drivers, most likely bypassing whatever is preventing Windows from starting. If you're able to start Windows in Safe Mode, then you'll be able to read the *Bootlog.txt* file created with option #2 (**Logged**) by simply double-clicking it in Explorer.

`Step-by-step confirmation` (#4) is not especially useful, because it only allows confirmation of a few items before Windows is loaded. Try it as a last-ditch effort, but don't expect any useful results.

3. The first thing you should do when you can successfully load Windows in Safe Mode (or if you're able to start a DOS session) is to run Scandisk. In Windows, select **Run** from the **Start Menu**, type **`scandskw`**, and click **OK**. In DOS, type **`scandisk`**, and press **Enter**.* Turn on the **Automatically fix errors option**, and click **Start** to fix any errors it finds, such as corrupt files, that may be preventing Windows from loading.

4. If you're able to get to a point where you can read the *Bootlog.txt* file, the very last entry (at the end of the file) is usually the one of most interest, because it's likely to be the culprit responsible for halting the startup process. It also helps to do a text search for the word "error."

   In most cases, the problematic log entry is a specific driver file. An effective "band-aid" solution is to rename the specified file (usually found in *\Windows\System*) so that Windows can't find it. Restart Windows to see if that has fixed the problem. Refer to the following section, "Dealing with Drivers and Other Tales of Hardware Troubleshooting," for details on drivers.

5. When you're done with Scandisk and the *Bootlog.txt* file, restart your computer, and allow Windows to boot normally. If you see the Windows startup menu, make sure to choose the first option, **1. Normal**, and then be patient as Windows loads.

---

* Only applicable if you've started your computer with a Startup disk, described in "Make a Startup Disk" later in this chapter.

Understanding System Resources

The way Windows Me handles a small area of memory called *System Resources* is one of the biggest shortcomings of the Windows 9x/Me architecture. Understanding the concept of System Resources is key to reducing system crashes and helping to maintain your sanity in an average workday.

Every time you open an application, it loads all of its visual components, such as windows, menus, text boxes, buttons, checkboxes, and lists, into memory. Windows keeps track of the visual components of all the applications so that, for example, when you drag a window across the screen, it knows what was behind the window and is able to redraw it. These visual components are stored in System Resources. Regardless of the amount of physical memory installed in your computer and regardless of the number of open windows, the amount of memory allotted to System Resources never increases.

What's more, not all of the System Resources an application uses are released when the application is closed. So, you could open and close an application several times and actually run out of System Resources. That's why Windows may complain that you're out of memory, even when you have only two or three applications open.

The symptoms of low System Resources include slow performance, error messages when starting programs, application windows not updating properly, applications hanging, and the entire system crashing.

The fix, at least as far as we lowly users are concerned, is to restart Windows (refer to the first paragraph of this chapter). When Windows is restarted, the System Resources are cleared, and everything returns to normal.

You can open the Resource Meter (*Rsrcmtr.exe*) at any time to view the amount of System Resources currently available. When it's opened, you'll only see a small icon in the system tray (by the clock); double-click the icon to open a larger window (as shown in Figure 6-1), which contains three simple graphs: User resources, GDI resources,* and, most importantly, System Resources. In addition to a visual warning when the System Resources get low (if the value dips below 30%, it's a good time to restart), the Resource Meter allows you to determine—indirectly—the

* User resources and GDI resources aren't as important as the System Resources, because they tend to fluctuate less and have a lower impact on system performance and stability.

amount of System Resources are used by individual applications. It's easy enough to do: after starting the Resource Meter, make note of the available System Resources, and then start an application. You'll notice almost immediately that the System Resources value drops by several percentage points; some applications use more than others.

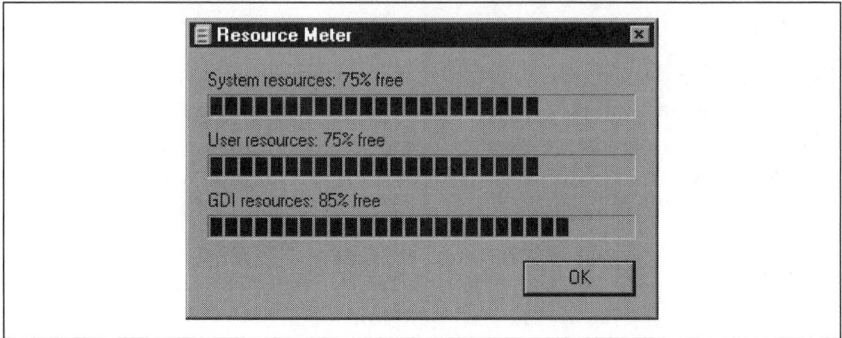

Figure 6-1. The Resource Meter that comes with Windows Me allows you to keep tabs on the available System Resources and possibly avert potential crashes

Keep in mind that you'll never see the System Resources get above about 85%, because Windows itself uses up a big chunk. To view all of the invisible programs that may be using up System Resources, press **Ctrl-Alt-Del** to display the "Close Program" box (see Figure 6-5 later in this section). Try closing one program at a time to see the resulting impact on System Resources. A common culprit to consistently low System Resources is a buggy video driver; see "Updating and Verifying Drivers" later in this chapter for details.

Dealing with Drivers and Other Tales of Hardware Troubleshooting

A driver is the software that allows your computer—and all of its applications—to work with a hardware device, such as a printer or video adapter. That way, for example, each word processor doesn't need to be preprogrammed with the details of all available printers (like in the early days of PCs). Instead, Windows manages a central database of drivers, silently directing the communication between all your applications and whatever drivers are required to complete the task at hand.

The problem arises when a driver is buggy or outdated, or one of the files that comprise a driver is missing or corrupted. Outdated drivers designed either for a previous version of Windows or a previous version of the device can create problems. Additionally, manufacturers must continually update their drivers to fix incompatibilities and bugs that arise after the product is released. It's usually a good idea to make sure you have the latest drivers installed in your system when troubleshooting a problem. Furthermore, newer drivers sometimes offer improved performance, added features and settings, better stability and reliability, and better compatibility with other software and drivers installed in your system.

The other thing to be aware of is that some drivers may just not be the correct ones for your system. For example, when installing Windows, the setup routine may have incorrectly detected your video card or monitor and hence installed the wrong driver (or even a *generic* driver). A common symptom for this is if Windows does not allow you to display as many colors or use as high a resolution as the card supports. Make sure that **Device Manager** (double-click on the **System** icon in Control Panel, and click the **Device Manager** tab) lists the actual devices, by name, that you have installed in your system.

Device drivers worth investigating include those for your video card, monitor, sound card, modem, printer, network adapter, scanner, SCSI controller, camera, backup device, and any other drives or cards you may have. If you're not sure of the exact manufacturer or model number of a device installed inside your computer, take off the cover of your computer and look, or refer to the invoice or documentation that came with your system. Most hard disks, floppy drives, CD-ROM drives, keyboards, mice, power supplies, memory, and CPU chips don't need special drivers (except in special circumstances).

Looking for a Driver

Windows Me comes with a huge assortment of drivers for hardware available at the time of its release, but as time passes, more third-party devices are released, requiring drivers of their own. Most hardware comes packaged with instructions and a driver disk; if in doubt, read the manual. If, on the other hand, you acquired a peripheral without the driver or manual, both of these are almost always available from the manufacturer's web site.

It's possible to find out if Windows comes with a driver for a specific piece of hardware, even before you try to install it. Double-click on the **Add New Hardware** icon in Control Panel, and click **Next** and then **Next** again. Windows will then take a few seconds (you won't see a progress bar here) to poll all of your Plug-and-Play devices. If it asks if the device that you want to install is listed, answer **No, the device isn't in the list**, and click **Next**. You'll then be given the option of having Windows search for your new hardware; since we're only looking for a list of available drivers, choose **No**, and then click **Next**. Choose a hardware category from the list shown that most closely matches what you're looking for, and then click **Next** to display a list of manufacturers and their products (see Figure 6-2).

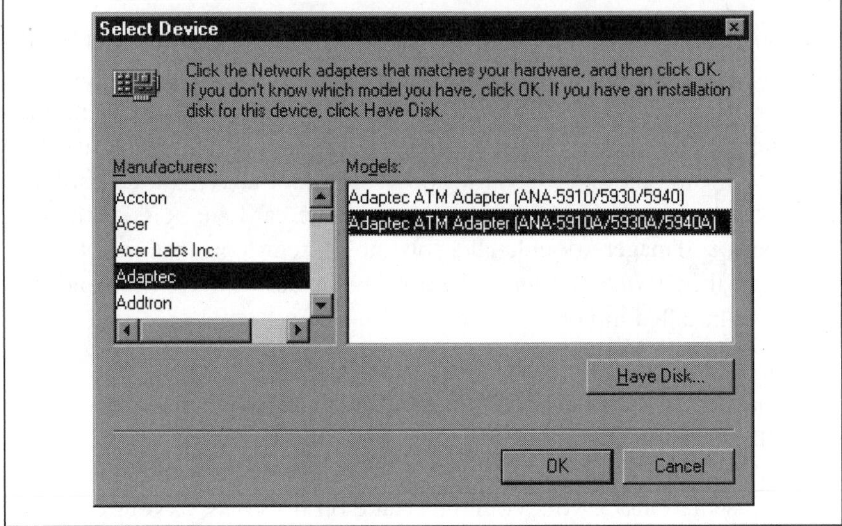

Figure 6-2. Use the Add New Hardware Wizard to list devices that Windows supports

If Windows Me does indeed have the driver you seek, you should start the process over and have Windows search for the device (which has more reliable results than choosing it from the list). If, on the other hand, Windows doesn't have an appropriate driver, you'll need to cancel the Add New Hardware Wizard and obtain a driver from the manufacturer (check the support section of the manufacturer's web site).

Note that not all devices need to be installed in this way. Many devices (most hard disks and CD-ROM drives) are automatically detected and configured when Windows starts; you should see their icons in the My Computer window without any fuss or user intervention. Some other devices are detected by Windows during startup but require that you answer a series of questions and sometimes insert a driver disk before you can use them. It all depends on the type of device and how well the manufacturer has followed the Plug-and-Play specification (if at all). If in doubt, consult the documentation to see what the manufacturer recommends.

Updating and Verifying Drivers

Assuming you've already installed a driver for a given device, the next hurdle is to see how recent it is and, if necessary, to update it. Although most drivers probably won't need updating, at least until a problem with the corresponding device surfaces, there are exceptions:

- Video drivers are notoriously buggy, especially the ones that come with newly released video cards. (Drivers are often rushed to completion to meet with the release of a new video card.) If you're experiencing problems with windows not updating their displays properly, frequent system crashes, odd mouse-cursor behavior, or any number of other seemingly unexplainable glitches, a buggy video driver is a likely culprit. In addition, video drivers are very complex and can always benefit from additional tweaking. It's good practice to routinely check with the manufacturer of your video card for updated drivers.*
- Another type of driver that should be updated, even if no problems are observed with the corresponding device, are any drivers written before the release of Windows 95. Even after several system upgrades, many of us still use old peripherals (scanners, printers, pointing devices, etc.). Using drivers made for older versions of Windows, Windows NT, or DOS may cause problems—either now or later—ranging from poor performance, to crashes, to the device not working at all. Newer 32-bit drivers offer much better performance and stability, as well as such extra features as support for Plug and Play and compatibility with other devices in your system. If you're lucky, the manufacturer will make such a driver available.
- The last type of driver, generally in use only if you've installed Windows Me on an older system, perhaps one that originally ran Windows 3.x or Windows 95, is a DOS driver, specified in your *Config.sys* or *Autoexec.bat* files. These must be eliminated for use with Windows Me. In most cases, these drivers support a CD-ROM drive or other common storage device—if the driver is removed, odds are that Windows will take care of it automatically.

If a specific piece of hardware is already installed and the driver has already been chosen, there are two ways to figure out if the correct driver is being used. First of all, the name used to identify the device in **Device Manager** (double-click the **System** icon in Control Panel) is a good clue.

Trouble-shooting

* Although this is contrary to my earlier advice not to mess with drivers when there isn't a problem to be fixed, video drivers are a notable exception.

For example, if under the Display Adapter category, your video card is listed as a *Diamond Viper V550*, then that's the driver that's being used, even if that's not really the video card you have physically installed.

However, there's more to the driver than just the name; to find the date and revision number of the driver, double-click on the device name in **Device Manager**, and choose the **Driver** tab. Although Windows does come with plenty of drivers, very few of them are actually written by Microsoft (even if it lists Microsoft in the **Provider** field): manufacturers simply submit their drivers for inclusion in the package. From this, you can usually assume three things about the drivers included on the Windows CD-ROM (versus those that come with your devices): (1) the drivers are fairly stable, (2) the dates are usually consistent with the release history of the manufacturer's drivers, and (3) any special features or extras present in the manufacturer's version of the drivers have been left out. For example, many after-market display drivers include support for more colors, higher resolutions, hot keys, panning windows, and so on. The drivers on the Windows CD-ROM will usually not have any of these goodies (for better or worse).

The easiest (but not foolproof) way to tell if you're using the driver that came with Windows is to look at the driver date—it should be June 8, 2000 (if you're using the initial release of Windows Me). If not, it probably came from another source, such as a driver disk, from the Web, from the Windows Update, or from a previous installation of Windows. Drivers with newer dates are usually—but not always—more recent. (Note that the **Driver File Details** button, which also appears on this page, rarely has any useful information.) If you're trying to solve a problem or take better advantage of your hardware, your best bet is to visit the web site of the manufacturer of the device in question and download their latest and greatest driver. Don't forget to read the release notes, as well as the FAQ (Frequently Asked Questions) section; you never know what useful nuggets of information you'll discover.

To change the driver for the selected device, either to install a newer version or to replace it with a driver for a different device, click **Update Driver**. You'll then see yet another wizard, allowing you to specify where Windows can find the new driver. The **Specify the location of the driver (Advanced)** option is much quicker and more useful than the **Automatic search** option, because it allows you to directly specify the folder, CD, or floppy drive containing the driver, without having to wait for Windows to search every drive on your system.

Watch Out for Driver Installer Inconsistencies

Note that some drivers have their own installation programs, while other drivers require that they be installed at the moment the hardware in question is automatically detected at Windows startup. If the driver has no install program and you aren't asked to locate the driver when you first start Windows, you can almost always update the driver by using the Update Driver feature explained here. If in doubt, check the driver's documentation (usually in a *readme.txt* file or on the manufacturer's web site). Not many manufacturers follow the standards closely, which can be very frustrating. As a last resort, try removing the driver from Device Manager, which will allow Windows to redetect the hardware and reinstall the driver.

If you wish to try one of the drivers already included with Windows Me, select the **Display a list of all the drivers** option instead of specifying a location. At this stage, you'll see a list of "Compatible Hardware," which usually consists of one driver—the one that's installed. Any additional drivers listed here are simply those that Windows identifies as supporting the *same device* as the currently installed driver;* if the currently installed driver is wrong, so may be the other items in this list. Click **Show all hardware** to view all the devices in the current category; you'll see a window again similar to Figure 6-2. Note that you can't change the category of the device—if it's a video card, you won't be allowed to choose a driver for a SCSI adapter.

Even if your device is listed, your manufacturer may still have a newer driver.† The nice thing about this window is that it shows all the drivers both stored on your hard disk and available on the Windows CD, along with their dates. If you install a third-party driver and then return to this window, you'll see it alongside the one that comes with Windows (if applicable).

A common scenario involves downloading a zipped driver from the Web, unzipping it to a separate folder on your hard disk, and then using this dialog box to instruct Windows to load the driver from the folder.

* Note that Windows often makes mistakes when determining which drivers are suitable for use with a specific hardware device. Use your best judgment or, barring that, read the manual.

† Refer to the instructions that come with the new drivers for the particular installation procedure. An indicator of a good manufacturer is one that makes drivers freely available for all their products, even discontinued ones. If they are supporting yesterday's products today, they'll be likely supporting your product tomorrow.

Windows will accept the folder containing any valid driver, which is detected by the presence of an appropriate *.inf* file. Actually, all the drivers already installed on your system have a corresponding *.inf* file in the *\Windows\INF* folder.

The *.inf* file is the heart of each Windows driver. Sometimes it contains all the necessary device information (most modems only require this single file), and other times it contains information and links to other files (*.dll* and *.vxd* files) that do the actual work of the driver. Unfortunately, each device is different—don't expect a set of tricks that worked for one driver to necessarily work for another.

Some users may be disappointed to discover either that a manufacturer of a discontinued product has stopped supporting the product or has just gone out of business. If this happens, you may be out of luck and forced to replace the device if it isn't supported in your version of Windows; see Chapter 5, *Maximizing Performance*, for more information on upgrading your system. There is a way out, however. Many products, such as video cards, modems, and SCSI controllers, use similar components that are widely supported by the industry. For example, many video cards use controller chips manufactured by a single company; by looking at your video card, you should be able to determine which variety of *chipset* it uses (look for the brand and model number). Even if the manufacturer of your video card has gone out of business, there may be other video cards that use the same *chipset* and, therefore, may use the same driver.

Handling Misbehaving Drivers

Never install or upgrade more than one new device at once. By installing one driver at a time, you can easily spot any potential new problems, as well as recognize when an existing problem has been solved. Wait for Windows to restart and try starting an application or two. If you install several new drivers at once, you'll have a hard time trying to find where you went wrong.

When you install a driver, Windows first copies the various driver files to as many as five different folders. Then the Registry is updated with the driver filenames, the specific resources used by the device (interrupt request lines [IRQs], I/O addresses, etc.; all of which are discussed later in this chapter), and any special hardware-specific settings. A common problem is that the special settings can be incorrect, and no amount of fiddling with them can straighten out a misbehaving device.

This often happens with network cards and SCSI adapters; either the device doesn't function at all, Windows doesn't recognize the device's resources correctly, or an attempt to use the device hangs the system. The solution is simply to reinstall the driver. The best way to go about this is to locate and select the device in **Device Manager** (double-click the **System** icon in Control Panel) and click **Remove**. Then close **Device Manager** and restart your computer. During Windows startup, you should then see a message to the effect that Windows is installing a new device, at which time it may ask for the driver disk. You can either point it to the appropriate location (your floppy drive, a folder on your desktop, etc.) or point it to your *Windows\System* folder (which forces it to use the old drivers). Windows will then reinitialize the device and reset all its special settings, which, in many cases, will solve the problem.

More drastic measures include removing all the actual driver files from the hard disk before allowing Windows to install new ones. Because all drivers are different, there are no standard files to remove. More conscientious developers will either provide an uninstall utility for their drivers, or at least provide a list of the supported files so you can find them easily. If in doubt, visit the manufacturer's web site and wade through the miles of FAQs, looking for some assistance.

My last piece of advice is to put a copy of the latest drivers for all of your devices on floppy disks or a recordable CD-ROM for easy access the next time you need them. You'll be glad you did when you realize that you can't download the right driver for your modem if your modem has stopped working.

Resolving Hardware Conflicts

The most common type of hardware problem is a conflict. A conflict occurs when two devices try to use the same resource, such as an IRQ or memory address; other conflicts can happen between two drivers as well. The telltale signs of a conflict include one or more devices not working, one or more devices not showing up in **Device Manager**, or your system crashing every time one or more devices are used. The first step in diagnosing a problem like this is to check for updated drivers (see "Updating and Verifying Drivers" earlier in this chapter).

Each installed device can use one, several, or even no resources. An expansion card, such as a sound card or modem, usually uses a single IRQ, a single I/O address range, and sometimes a direct memory access (DMA) address. Other devices, such as memory addresses, SCSI ID's, integrated drive electronics (IDE) channels, and serial and parallel ports, can consume more than one of each, as well as other resources.

If two or more devices try to use the same resource, problems can occur that range from slow performance to system crashes. Most older, pre-Plug-and-Play devices (called *legacy* devices) allow you to configure which resources they use by setting appropriate jumpers or switches on the devices themselves. Newer devices allow their settings to be changed with software. The newest Plug-and-Play products work with your Plug-and-Play BIOS (part of your computer) and a Plug-and-Play operating system (such as Windows Me) to configure themselves automatically to work with other Plug-and-Play devices and other legacy devices, theoretically avoiding all conflicts.

Note that some devices, such as pointing devices, scanners, cameras, and printers, which connect to your computer's external ports, don't technically use any resources of their own; however, the ports to which they're connected do use resources. You can usually change the resources used by any given device (ports included). The trick is to configure all of your devices to use different resources so that no conflicts occur. All devices are different; refer to the documentation included with each device, or contact the manufacturer for specific configuration instructions and possible conflict warnings.

To determine which resources are available in your system, as well as which devices are using the rest of the resources, open the **Device Manager** by double-clicking on the **System** icon in Control Panel and choosing the **Device Manager** tab. Select **Computer** from the top of the list, and click **Properties** to display the **Computer Properties** dialog box, as shown in Figure 6-3.

By choosing any of the four types of resources (IRQ, I/O, DMA, or Memory), you'll see how each is used by the various devices in your system. Any gaps in the numbers represent available system resources, which you should be able to assign to new devices. Windows should be able to do this automatically, but if there's an unresolved conflict, you'll have to step in and shuffle resources until everything works. Most resource conflicts are shown here as well: if you see two cards assigned to IRQ 10, it's a safe bet that that's part of the problem.

Be aware that some devices *can* share resources. For example, your communication ports share IRQs (COM1 and COM3 both use IRQ 4, and COM2 and COM4 both use IRQ 3). Sometimes this is benign, such as having a mouse on COM1 and another pointing device (such as a graphics tablet) on COM3. However, most modems will complain (system hangs, slow performance, and other malfunctions) if they share resources with

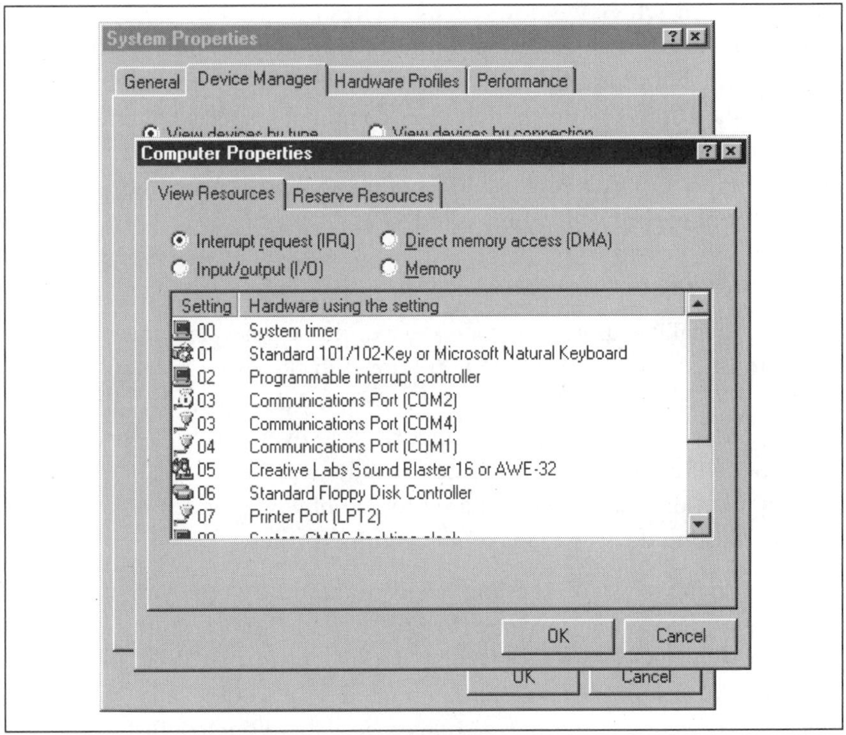

Figure 6-3. You can determine which hardware resources are in use by looking at the Computer Properties in Windows' Device Manager

any other devices. If you have 3 or more devices connected to COM ports, you may have to either juggle them around or install configurable COM ports, which can be adjusted more flexibly.

If you find some other type of conflict, start by either removing or reconfiguring one of the devices involved. You may be required to reconfigure several devices, delegating resources around until all the conflicts are resolved (see "When installing new hardware . . ." later in this section). Again, the method used to change the resources used by a particular device depends upon the device itself. You should be able to see all the resources used by a given device by selecting it in **Device Manager**, clicking **Properties**, and choosing the **Resources** tab.

Note that the information presented in **Device Manager** may not necessarily reflect the current state of your system. In the unlikely event that your computer was made before about the middle of 1995 and doesn't support Plug and Play entirely (or at all), you may have devices installed that don't show up, as well as devices displayed that aren't actually installed. The **Refresh** button is used to reread the devices in your system during a Windows session, but it won't detect anything more than is normally seen when Windows starts. **Refresh** is used primarily to detect devices attached to or disconnected from your system after Windows has started, without physically restarting your system. To force Windows to redetect the hardware attached to your computer, especially items ignored during the regular scan for new devices at startup, use the **Add New Hardware** icon in Control Panel, and confirm that you want the wizard to search for new hardware when asked.

When installing new hardware . . .

If you're installing more than one device, do so one at a time; it's much easier to isolate problems when you know which device has caused them. You should expect installation of Plug-and-Play devices to be quick, automatic, and painless—at least in theory. However, many devices, while able to configure themselves automatically, may not be able to adapt entirely to your system. Be prepared to reconfigure or even remove some of your existing devices to make room for new ones.

If you're trying to get an existing device to work, try removing one of the conflicting pieces of hardware to see if the conflict is resolved. Just because two devices are conflicting doesn't mean that they are intrinsically faulty. It's possible a third, errant device could cause two other devices to occupy improper resources and therefore conflict with each other or simply not function.

If removing a device solves a problem, you've probably found the conflict. If not, try removing all devices from the system and then reconnect them one by one until the problem reappears. Although it may sound like a pain in the neck to remove all the devices from your system, it really is the easiest and most sure-fire way to find the cause of a problem like this. Because there are so many different combinations of resource settings, it can be a laborious task to resolve conflicts. Some devices come with special software designed for this task; the software can either advise you of proper settings or, in some cases, even make the changes for you. Make sure to review the documentation for any mention of such a utility.

Firmware: Software for Your Hardware

User-upgradable firmware is a feature found in many new devices. Firmware is software stored in the device itself, used to control most hardware functions. Although it's not possible to, say, increase a hard disk's capacity by upgrading its firmware, it is possible to improve performance of an adapter or storage device, as well as solve some compatibility problems that may have been discovered after the product shipped.

The beauty of firmware is that if you purchase a peripheral and the manufacturer subsequently improves the product, you can simply update the firmware to upgrade the product. While user-upgradable firmware can increase the initial cost of a product slightly, such an increase is dramatically outweighed by the money the manufacturer can save by not having users send in equipment to be updated. Naturally, user-upgradable firmware also is a boon to the end user, who can make simple updates in a matter of minutes—without having to send in the product or even open up the computer.

To find out the firmware version for a particular device, select the device in **Device Manager**, click **Properties**, choose the **Settings** tab if it's present, and look at the **Firmware Revision** field. If you're experiencing problems with a certain device, check the product manufacturer's web site for a newer firmware revision. In many cases, you'll be able to download a simple software "patch" that will update the firmware to the newest version, possibly fixing problems, improving performance, and even adding new features.

Devices that commonly have user-upgradable firmware include modems, CD-ROM drives, CD-ROM recorders, removable drives, removable tape drives, motherboards (in the form of an upgradable BIOS), SCSI controllers, and network adapters, hubs, and routers.

Some older devices allow you to change the firmware by upgrading a chip. It's not as convenient as software-upgradable firmware, but it's better than tossing the whole thing in the garbage!

The Trials and Tribulations of Plug and Play

Most new internal peripherals (cards, drives, etc.), as well as some external devices (printers, scanners, etc.), will be automatically detected when Windows boots up. Ideally, Windows should notify you that the new device has been identified and give you the option of using the driver that comes with Windows (if available) or providing the driver on your own (either with a diskette or a folder on your hard disk). Windows should then load the driver, configure the device, and restart with no ill effects.

The problem is when the new device either doesn't work or causes something else to stop working. Even the newest Plug-and-Play devices can sometimes cause conflicts, although with the passage of time, the PnP-compliance of most new devices has generally improved. To aid in troubleshooting conflicts where PnP devices are involved, it's important to realize first exactly what Plug-and-Play technology is. PnP-compliant devices must have the following characteristics:

- The device must have a *signature* that is returned when Windows asks for it. Windows then looks up this signature in its driver database and either finds a driver that matches it or asks you to insert a disk with a compatible driver. If a driver is not required or a suitable driver is not found, no driver will be loaded for the device.
- All configurable resources (applicable primarily to internal devices) of the device must be software-adjustable; that is, it is not necessary to physically set jumpers or switches on the hardware to reconfigure it. This doesn't mean, however, that the device can't come with jumpers; some cards let you disable their Plug-and-Play features and set resources manually—sometimes a *very* handy feature.
- The driver, if supplied, must be capable of instructing Windows which resources the device can occupy (if any) and must be able to receive instructions from Windows and reconfigure the card accordingly. That way, Windows can read all the possible configurations from all the drivers and then reconfigure each one so that there are no conflicts.

You can see, then, how dependent PnP devices are on their drivers and why a buggy driver can cause problems with the entire system, regardless of how PnP-compliant all the components in your system are. One bug commonly found in some drivers is that they are unable to configure the corresponding device reliably. For example, say a sound card requires a single IRQ and is capable of being set to IRQ 5, 7, 9, 10, or 11, but the driver is incorrectly programmed to also accept IRQ 13. When Windows attempts to shuffle all the devices around, it may then ask the sound card to occupy IRQ 13; because this is impossible, it will remain at its previous setting (or at no setting at all), most likely causing a conflict with another device (say a modem or parallel port). In this scenario, a tiny bug in a single driver has caused two separate devices to stop functioning.

Now, it's also possible that Windows will be unable to find a mutually agreeable configuration for all installed devices—even if one does exist—which means that Windows will simply boot with one or more conflicts. I've encountered this scenario when trying to install an additional IDE controller in a system otherwise full and completely out of resources. In most cases, Windows won't even tell you that PnP has failed. This is where you have to take matters into your own hands: learn to recognize the symptoms (crashing, hanging, slow performance) and know how to look for conflicts. See the beginning of this section, "Resolving Hardware Conflicts," for details.

One of the loopholes that you can take advantage of is the way that Plug-and-Play systems assign resources (IRQs in particular) to PCI devices. Your BIOS will assign a different IRQ to each PCI *slot*, rather than having each device try to grab an IRQ for its own; this ensures that PCI cards don't conflict. The funny thing about PnP BIOSes and Windows Me is that, occasionally, some IRQs are neglected. If you have a full system and find yourself running out of IRQs, this can be a real problem. The good news is that you can enter your system's BIOS setup (see the next section) and manually assign an IRQ to each PCI slot, often even specifying previously ignored IRQs, such as IRQs 12, 14, and 15.* This will then leave spaces open (usually lower IRQs), which other devices in your system can then occupy.

Finally, a common problem with Plug and Play is its occasional propensity to detect devices that have already been configured. For example, after you've hooked up a printer, installed the drivers, and even used it successfully, Windows may inform you that it has detected a newly attached device (often a printer) the next time you boot. The cause of this is almost always an incorrect initial installation (that is, contrary to the manufacturer's recommended installation procedure); for example, you may have connected your printer after Windows had started. The best course of action is to remove the drivers for the device (usually through **Device Manager**), reboot, and allow Windows to detect and set up the printer automatically. Naturally, you should check the printer's documentation for any abnormalities of the installation process.

Stop Plug and Play from Detecting Devices

One of the problems with Plug and Play is its tendency to leave out devices you want to use or, less commonly, to detect and load drivers for devices you don't want to use. Now, much of the rest of this chapter is devoted to getting Windows to detect and support devices that it otherwise ignores. But say you don't want Windows to load a driver for your modem because it conflicts with your pointing device (see the discussion of modems in "Fixing Device-Specific Problems" later in this chapter).

Although there is no way to prevent Windows' Plug-and-Play feature from detecting and installing drivers for some devices, you can disable most devices that may be causing conflicts. The best use for this is in conjunction with multiple hardware profiles, where you might want to disable a device in one profile, yet enable it in another. See "Using Multiple Hardware Configurations" later in this chapter for more information.

* Note that IRQs 12, 14, and 15 aren't always available and sometimes can be occupied by other motherboard components or non-PCI devices. In most cases, trial and error is the best approach to take.

Windows detects devices automatically upon startup, as well as manually when you use **Add New Hardware** in Control Panel. When Windows is starting, you usually can't stop it from identifying and installing drivers for most devices (although you can sometimes trick it into treating a device as "unknown"). When using the Add New Hardware Wizard, though, you must allow Windows either to configure all the devices it finds, or to configure none (by hitting **Cancel**).

In addition to the obvious way to keep Windows from detecting a device (i.e., yanking it out of your computer), there is a built-in method for disabling certain devices *after* they've been detected:

1. Double-click on the **System** icon in Control Panel, and choose the **Device Manager** tab.
2. Select the device you wish to disable, and click **Properties**.
3. At the bottom of the General page, you'll usually see a **Device usage** section. This section won't be present for some devices (such as CD-ROM drives and hard drives). To disable the device, check the **Disable in this hardware profile** option.

   Now, this will prevent Windows from loading drivers for this device the next time Windows boots. If you have more than one hardware profile (see earlier in this section), this setting will affect only the current profile. In most cases, and with all PnP-compliant hardware, disabling a device will completely free its resources (IRQ, DMA, I/O address, etc.), making them available for other hardware in your system. However, some (but not all) non-PnP hardware may still consume resources even if the device is disabled in this way.
4. If you check the **Remove from this hardware profile** option (if it's present), the device will be removed from the profile and (theoretically) *not* automatically detected the next time you restart Windows. This tends to work well for some devices and not as well for others.
5. If you check the **Exists in all hardware profiles** option, it's supposed to do the opposite of the **Remove from this hardware profile** option, explained earlier. That is, the currently selected device will then appear in all other profiles (assuming you have more than one). This is a workaround to the problem that once you've removed a device, you will never be able to get it back. For this very reason, it's recommended that you avoid both of these settings unless absolutely necessary, by simply using the **Disable in this hardware profile** option.
6. Click **OK** when you're finished. You'll have to restart Windows for this change to take effect.

Fixing Device-Specific Problems

For most components in the system, the number-one rule for getting things to work is to make sure you have the latest, correct driver from the manufacturer, although this isn't always as easy as you would like. In many circumstances, however, obtaining the correct driver may be impossible, or simply not applicable. The next step in getting most hardware to work in Windows is to eliminate any hardware conflicts, which is discussed in "Resolving Hardware Conflicts" earlier in this chapter.

More often than not, problems are unique to a particular type of component. For example, modems often suffer the same types of problems, which don't necessarily affect any other types of hardware. The following guidelines should help you solve most component-specific problems (as opposed to general lockups or application error messages).

And don't forget that a nonfunctioning component can be a great excuse for an upgrade (see Chapter 5), especially considering that many of the following components are likely to be much cheaper than were the ones they're replacing.

One more word of advice: your computer may still be under warranty. I can't tell you how many times I've encountered people spending a great deal of time and money trying to diagnose and solve a problem when a simple call to the manufacturer will enable them to have the problem solved for free, sometimes even by an on-site technician. Avoid a headache whenever possible.

Video cards (also known as display adapters)

Most likely, without the correct video driver installed, you still should be able to use Windows at a resolution of 640×480 with 256 colors; this is a standard mode supported by nearly all VGA cards and is Windows' default display mode. Most video card problems are caused by faulty or incorrect video drivers, however, so it's best to check with the card's manufacturer first.

Now, if you don't have a VGA-compatible card, you're much better off simply purchasing a new card (good ones can go for as low as $30), which will be much easier and less of a hassle than trying to get that old obsolete display adapter to work properly.

Most modern video cards are based upon a certain chipset (controller), usually identifiable by the large, square chip in the center of the card itself. If the chip is covered with a sticker, remove the sticker to see what's printed on the chip surface. In fact, Windows may be able to detect the type of chip, even if it can't determine the make and model of the card. Common chipset manufacturers include S3, Cirrus Logic, ATI, Tseng, and Western Digital; each of these comes in several varieties as well. If you can determine the type of chipset your video card uses, you should be able to use either a generic video driver made for that chipset or a driver for another card that uses the same chipset.

If you know you are using the correct video driver, but can't use all of the resolutions it supports, make sure Windows is identifying your monitor correctly.

If you're trying to use Windows Me's support of multiple monitors, you need to be aware of a few things. Your system BIOS chooses which video card is your *primary* adapter and which card is your secondary adapter. To switch their priority, either to resolve a problem or for personal preference, you'll have to swap their physical positions in your computer. Because your primary video card does *not* need to support multiple adapters explicitly, but the secondary card *does*, you may have to swap them to get multiple-monitor support to work at all. One problem you may encounter is trying to negotiate one PCI card and one AGP card; most BIOSes initiate PCI before AGP, so your AGP card probably will never be the primary card. In this case, you'll either have to make do with what you've got or install two PCI cards.

Monitors

If Windows knows what type of monitor you're using, it can determine which resolutions and color depths it's able to support. In Windows Me, monitors have drivers, although they do little more than inform Windows of the monitor's capabilities. Newer Plug-and-Play monitors allow Windows to automatically identify your monitor, although a driver may still be required. To see if your monitor is properly identified, double-click on the **Display** icon in Control Panel. Choose the **Settings** tab, click **Advanced**, and then choose the **Monitor** tab in the new window.

It's possible for your video card to generate video signals that your monitor isn't able to display, especially if your resolution, color depth, or refresh rate is set too high or if you're using an older monitor. Although a video card and a monitor don't have to be matched precisely to work, it's worth investigating whether your monitor can support all of your video card's modes.

The manufacturer of your monitor isn't likely to have any drivers for you, although they might be able to tell you the name of another monitor, supported by Windows, that may be compatible. You might also try a few different models by the same manufacturer, if available. Many monitors use the same tubes, so you should be able to find one that's close.

You may be able to use a higher resolution or color depth with your monitor by lowering your video card's refresh rate. You should also lower the refresh rate if you hear your monitor whistling. Raise the refresh rate if the display flickers.

For problems using multiple monitors, see "Video cards (also known as display adapters)" earlier in this section.

Hard disks and floppy-diskette drives

These drives almost never need special drivers, unless they use some proprietary interface (such as your parallel port). Windows will support virtually all IDE drives right out of the box, as well as most SCSI controllers and devices.

Note that each IDE hard drive must be recognized in your computer's BIOS screen before Windows will even see it. Nearly all modern computers list all the attached internal drives before loading Windows, so if a particular device doesn't show up here, you'll most likely have to make a change in your BIOS setup (as opposed to making a change in Windows).

If Windows does not recognize your floppy or hard disk, you'll need to obtain a driver specific to the controller to which it's connected (see the following topic). If you continue to have trouble accessing the drive, make sure the jumpers are set appropriately and the cables are connected correctly.

Occasionally, a system will be in bad enough shape that it won't even boot. Although it's possible that the hard disk has crashed and is unrecoverable, it's just as likely that the motherboard or hard-disk controller has died. In this case, your best bet at recovering the data on that drive is to connect the drive to another functioning system and attempt to access the data there. See "Preventive Maintenance and Data Recovery" later in this chapter for loads of related information.

Hard-disk controllers

Most hard drives available today are the IDE/ATA/Ultra DMA type; the controllers for these drives are almost always built into the motherboard, especially on newer systems. If your motherboard develops a problem with the controller, you should be able to disable the controller and obtain a separate controller for a few bucks.

Proprietary IDE controllers, such as caching controllers, usually perform worse and cause a lot more problems than the standard, cheap, built-in controllers. You're better off taking the extra memory from the controller (if any) and installing it on the motherboard, throwing away the proprietary controller, and connecting your drives to the controller on the motherboard.

Windows comes with drivers for most types of hard-disk controllers, including IDE, RLL, ESDI, and SCSI (see the following topic for details on SCSI). If Windows doesn't support your controller and you can't get a driver from the manufacturer, you're out of luck.

SCSI controllers

Most SCSI controllers either are supported by Windows out of the box or have native Windows drivers you can use (which either come with the card or are available from the manufacturer's web site). For the most part, all SCSI controllers are fairly well supported, with recent drivers nearly always available. If you're experiencing a SCSI problem, you should first check to see if newer drivers for your card are available.

If you're unable to find drivers for your SCSI card, you may still be able to use it in Windows if you can find a driver for *another* card that uses the same SCSI controller chip (sometimes called a miniport driver). Common miniport manufacturers include Adaptec, BusLogic, Future Domain, NCR, and Trantor. For example, you may have a sound card that has a built-in SCSI controller intended for your CD-ROM drive. If that SCSI controller chip just happens to be made by Adaptec, for example, you should be able to use a driver for the corresponding Adaptec product that runs off the same chip.

Next to drivers, the two most common problems with SCSI controllers and the devices that attach to them are bad cables and incorrect termination. When diagnosing any SCSI problems, it's best to have replacements handy for your SCSI cable(s), so you can easily swap them to help isolate the problem. The use of improper or non-SCSI adapters and connectors is also a common culprit.

As for termination, a SCSI chain (the long string of devices connected by cables) won't work properly unless it's correctly terminated. By either using the built-in termination on your SCSI controller and SCSI devices or attaching standalone terminators (active terminators are best), make sure that both ends of the chain (but nothing in the middle) are terminated. The SCSI card itself should be terminated (or its self-termination feature be turned on), unless you have both internal and external devices, in which case the devices at the end of each side should be terminated.

For problems with specific devices connected to SCSI controllers, such as CD-ROM drives, hard disks, and removable drives, refer to the corresponding topic elsewhere in this section.

CD-ROM drives

Most CD-ROM drives don't need special drivers. In fact, if you plug in a CD-ROM drive and then start up Windows, it should detect it and display an icon for it in My Computer automatically. If your drive isn't detected, first check the controller. Most CD-ROMs connect to your IDE or SCSI controller; if your drive isn't recognized, most likely the controller isn't working or you don't have the right drivers for your controller installed (see earlier). Some older CD-ROM drives connect to proprietary controllers or sound cards. For these, you may need a driver made especially for your controller/drive combination; check the documentation for details. My advice: if it gives you any trouble, throw it out and get a new one.

Tape drives

Most tape devices don't require general-purpose drivers of their own, mostly because there is no standard for them. Any backup program that is compatible with your unit will come with its own drivers, which work with the installed controller to which your drive is attached. So, if you have a SCSI tape drive, all you should need to do is make sure the drivers for the SCSI controller are working. The backup program you use will then come with generic drivers for SCSI tape drives (as does the backup software that comes with Windows Me).

Most tape devices come with their own backup software, which is usually guaranteed to work with the drive. If the manufacturer of your tape drive does not supply software with the unit or on their web site, or if the supplied software is not a 32-bit application made *especially* for Windows 9x or Windows Me, you'll need to use a different program, such as third-party, commercial, backup software or the backup software that comes with Windows Me.

If you're trying to get Microsoft Backup or another backup program to recognize your drive, you should consider comparing the price of new backup software with the price of a whole new tape drive that includes its own snazzy 32-bit backup software.

Note that you'll never see a drive letter for your tape drive in My Computer unless you install a special utility designed for that purpose (such as Seagate's "Direct Tape Access" software). I've never been satisfied with these types of utilities, so I'd suggest abandoning the idea.

Removable, optical, and recordable CD-ROM drives

Removable cartridge drives, such as Iomega (Zip/Jaz) drives, magneto-optical devices, Syquest drives, and many higher end CD-ROM recorders, traditionally connect to SCSI controllers. Therefore, as long your SCSI controller is functioning and the SCSI drivers are installed, you should be able to connect any SCSI device, make sure the chain is terminated, and have it work without a fuss and without any special drivers.*

If you're having trouble getting a SCSI device like this to work, newer SCSI drivers or an update to the SCSI BIOS (contact the manufacturer) should solve the problem.

Some external drives connect to your parallel port. These connections may seem more convenient or less expensive than SCSI, but they're generally slower, less reliable, and more finicky. Additionally, parallel-port-connected devices usually require drivers provided by the manufacturer, which, of course, must be written specifically for use with Windows 9x or Windows Me. If available, use USB for any external, non-SCSI storage devices.

Problems with external devices (SCSI and parallel-port connections) usually involve bad cabling. Make sure all cables are correct and seated firmly in their connectors and that all thumbscrews are tightened.

Modems

If your modem is 32 Kbps or slower, throw it out immediately. You can get a brand-new 56 Kbps modem for less money than it would cost in long-distance support calls to find drivers for the old one. Better yet, forget the modem and get DSL or a cable modem.

Although choosing the appropriate driver is important, you can usually get by with one of the "standard modem" drivers included with Windows. In fact, Windows might simply call your modem a "standard modem" if it can't autodetect the make and model, even though a driver for your modem may be included with Windows. Even though a driver made especially for your modem will usually yield better performance and reliability, you can sometimes use a driver for another product by the same manufacturer, as long as it's rated the same bps speed (e.g., 56 K).

In many circumstances, the only piece of configuration information Windows really needs to use your modem is knowledge of its maximum

* Recordable CD drives require special recording (mastering) software in addition to an appropriate driver.

speed, port, and an appropriate *initialization string*. This is a long sequence of seemingly nonsensical characters, beginning with *AT*, used to send commands to your modem to prepare it for dialing.

If Windows recognizes your modem, but you can't seem to get it to work or simply can't find the appropriate driver, try entering your modem's initialization string directly. To obtain your modem's initialization string, either contact the manufacturer of your modem or refer to the documentation. If you currently have older software that you know works with your modem, a good trick is to snoop around the configuration section of the software to find the configuration string it's using.

Double-click on the **Modems** icon in Control Panel, select your modem from the list, click **Properties**, and choose the **Connection** tab. Click **Advanced**, and type your initialization string into the field labeled **Extra settings**.

If you can't find your modem in the list, double-click on **Add New Hardware** in Control Panel, and confirm that you want to it to search your system for newly attached devices. If Windows doesn't identify your modem or if it identifies it as an "unknown device," there are two possibilities that could cause this problem. Either your modem is a proprietary model, such as some built-in modems found in portable computers, or the serial port to which it's connected is not functioning or is in use.

If yours is a proprietary modem (always something to avoid, although often inevitable in laptops), you simply won't be able to use it without a manufacturer-supplied driver.

Serial-port conflicts and misconfiguration are the most common causes of modem-recognition problems. External modems are connected to serial ports, which usually are just cables that plug into the motherboard (see "Motherboards and CPUs" later in this section for more information on serial ports). Some newer external modems connect to USB ports, which don't have any of these problems.

Enter your computer's BIOS setup to verify that the serial port to which your external modem is connected is *enabled* and configured correctly. Most likely you'll have two ports, one connected to your mouse and the other to your modem. Consult the documentation that came with your computer or motherboard for details.

Internal modems, on the other hand, are expansion cards that contain their own serial ports. Enter your computer's BIOS setup, and make sure any serial ports on your motherboard that you're not using are *disabled*, because they could otherwise conflict with your modem. (See "Stop Plug and Play from Detecting Devices" earlier in this chapter for an additional solution.) Commonly, only one serial port is used by the mouse, but both (and there are usually two) are enabled on all new systems and motherboards by default. Newer mice connect to a dedicated *round* mouse port (called a PS/2 port); these don't pose COM-port conflicts but do use up IRQ 12 (the resource dedicated to the PS/2 port).

If Windows recognizes your modem either correctly or as the generic "standard modem," the next step to resolve the problem is to verify communication with the device; this is done by sending commands directly to your modem. Start HyperTerminal to communicate with the modem.* When prompted, type anything for the **Name**, and press **OK**. In the **Connect To** box that follows, choose **Direct to ComX** from the **Connect using** list box, where **ComX** is the port to which your modem is connected (usually Com1 or Com2).† Press **OK**; if your choice is correct, you'll be sent straight to HyperTerminal's main window.

Type **ATZ** (a simple reset command), and press **Enter**. If you receive an **OK** after the successful completion of this reset, it means communication between your computer and modem is working, and the problem is probably an incorrect driver or configuration in the application you're using. If you don't receive an **OK**, there's probably a hardware conflict, as described earlier.

If you know the software is installed and configured correctly, there are external factors that can either prevent modems from working or slow their performance. Start by removing all other electronic devices from the phone line, including answering machines, fax machines, autodialers, and standard telephone handsets. Any of these can actually interfere with the modem, preventing it from detecting the dial tone or causing it to hang up prematurely. Other factors include bad phone cables and wall sockets; try replacing your old phone cord with a brand new one, just long enough to reach the wall jack. A noisy phone line can also cause slow performance and frequent disconnects; contact the phone company to investigate.

Occasionally, a functioning modem can stop working temporarily. Modems constantly receive commands from your computer, so it's possible for the modem to become confused if it is sent a garbled or incomplete command. The easiest way to correct a confused modem is to

---

* If you don't have the HyperTerminal component installed, use Add/Remove Programs (it's in the Communications category).

† If you don't know which COM port your modem uses, double-click on the Modems icon in Control Panel, highlight your modem in the list, and click **Properties**.

turn it off and then on again. If the modem is an internal model, you'll need to *completely* power down your computer and then turn it on again; simply pressing the reset button or restarting Windows may not be sufficient.

If you have a DSL adapter, a cable modem, or an ISDN modem, these techniques most likely won't apply, because technically none of these are modems. Most external ISDN adapters connect through a serial port, however, so an ISDN modem is susceptible to serial-port conflicts as well. See Chapter 7, *Networking and Internetworking*, for more information on these devices.

As with any modem, make sure you have the latest drivers and, if applicable, the latest firmware.

Printers

Common printer problems involve bad cabling as well as bad drivers. Solving cabling problems is easy: just replace your parallel cable with a new one. IEEE-1284-compliant cables are the best, albeit more expensive, and are usually required for newer inkjet and laser printers. Some printers won't function if they're too far away from your computer, so try a shorter cable. See "Motherboards and CPUs" later in this chapter for more information on parallel ports.

On most pre–Pentium II systems (Pentium or earlier), the printer port is physically connected to your motherboard with a short ribbon cable, which can easily come loose; open your computer to see if this connector needs to be reattached or possibly replaced.

As with most other peripherals, getting the right drivers is essential. Now, Windows can print plain text (without fonts or graphics) on nearly any printer without knowing what kind of printer you have. If you don't have a driver made especially for your model, you still may be able to use your printer with Windows by installing the included *Generic/Text Only* driver, although this will only enable very limited output. To use fonts or print graphics on your printer (only for printers that are capable of printing graphics, of course), you may be able to substitute another printer's driver. Try installing a driver for a similar printer made by the same manufacturer. For example, if you have a Hewlett Packard 700-series inkjet printer, you might be able to get it to work with drivers for HP's 600 series.

Also, since many printers are compatible with Hewlett Packard's PCL printer control language (PCL3, PCL5, etc.), you may be able to use the driver for the classic Hewlett Packard Laserjet Series II (for laser printers) or the Hewlett Packard Deskjet (for inkjet printers). If you have a Postscript laser printer, you should be able to use the driver for one of the Apple Laserwriter varieties.

Aside from drivers and cabling, common printer problems involve incorrect paper: use laser paper for laser printers and inkjet paper for inkjet printers—none of this multipurpose junk. Also, the ink cartridges in inkjet printers are usually cheaply made and therefore are one of the first things to fail; simply installing a new ink cartridge will fix many printing problems.

Scanners and cameras

Scanners not only require the appropriate drivers to function in Windows, but special scanning software as well; as with tape drives, the two usually come together. If you can't find a driver or software that specifically supports your scanner, you're probably out of luck. However, because many companies simply repackage scanners made by other manufacturers, you may be able to obtain a driver from the original equipment manufacturer (OEM) of the stuff under the hood.

As for cameras, because there are so many different kinds, probably the only productive discussion involves how they connect to your computer. Modern digital cameras either connect through a serial port, a USB port, or a FireWire port; any communication problems will probably be addressed by fixing the ports (or adapters, where applicable) themselves.

Scanners commonly are connected through SCSI ports but can also plug into parallel ports and USB ports; an older scanner may connect to a proprietary controller card. For parallel ports, see "Printers" earlier in this section and "Motherboards and CPUs" later in this section. For SCSI ports, see "SCSI controllers" earlier in this section. For USB, see "USB ports" later in this section.

Sound cards

It used to be true that any sound card worth its weight had to be compatible with the Creative Soundblaster standard, but this is now true mainly for use with DOS games and older Windows software. Modern sound devices should be DirectX-compliant, a criteria met with a good driver. You should routinely check with the manufacturer of your sound card for driver updates.

If your sound card is older and doesn't support digitized sound (prerecorded sound effects and speech), it may still support MIDI synthesis (cheesy synthesizer music) and should be compatible with the driver for the Ad Lib card.

Windows should be able to detect your sound card, as well as the resources it uses. If your system crashes while trying to play sound on your sound card and you know you have the correct driver installed, try changing the hardware resources used by your card; see "Resolving Hardware Conflicts" earlier in this chapter for more information. If you can't get your sound card to work at all and can't obtain recent drivers from the manufacturer, just chuck it and get a new one.

Network cards

Windows should be able to detect your network adapter and install the correct drivers for it automatically. However, there are so many different types and manufacturers of network cards and so many of those are completely proprietary, that you may be out of luck if you can't obtain drivers made specifically for your version of Windows.

Isolating networking problems can be especially difficult, because you're not dealing with a standalone device. If your printer stops working, you know immediately where the problem is; but if your network stops working, it could be your card, the network cable, the hub, your colleague's network card, your network drivers, your colleague's network drivers, or any number of other things. See Chapter 7 for detailed network troubleshooting assistance.

Because there are no "generic" or "standard" network drivers, if you can't find a driver for your network adapter, just throw it out. Brand new Ethernet adapters are ridiculously cheap and most likely superior to the antique you'd be replacing.

Memory

Bad memory can manifest itself in anything from frequent error messages and crashes to your system simply not starting. Errors in your computer's memory (RAM) aren't always consistent, either; they can be intermittent and can get worse over time.

Any modern computer will use memory modules, but don't be fooled into thinking there's a well-established standard. Older machines use EDO or FPM SIMMs, newer ones use PC100 or PC133 DIMMs, and the newest machines, at the time of this writing, use RDRAM. Within each of those categories are different speeds, capacities, and even standards.

Incorrect memory is not uncommon, especially in generic and non-commercially built machines. To find out the type of memory you should use, consult the documentation that accompanies your computer or motherboard. If you have no such literature, check the web site of the computer or motherboard manufacturer and find out for sure before you just jam something in there. Odds are your friend's old memory modules not only will not work in your system, but also may potentially cause permanent damage.

The first thing you should do is pull out each memory module and make sure there isn't any dust or other obstruction between the pins and your motherboard (use a dry tissue or lens cleaning paper; don't use any liquids or solvents). Look for broken or bent sockets, metal filings or other obstructions, and, of course, any smoke or burn marks. Make sure all your modules are seated properly; they should snap into place and should be level and firm (don't break them testing their firmness, of course).

If all that is in order, there are three ways to determine if your RAM is actually faulty. The first way is to use a software testing program capable of checking physical memory (CheckIt, an older commercial package, does this; check your software retailer for a more modern product). Use the program to run a continual test of your RAM; have it repeat the test many times, perhaps overnight. The problem with testing your RAM with any type of software is that, not only is it not 100% reliable, but once you've found a problem, you need to follow the next method *anyway* to find and replace the faulty module.

The second method requires a friendly, patient, helpful person at a small computer store—a rare commodity these days, especially with the popularity of the large, faceless, mega-super computer marts filled with inexperienced technicians. Look for a local mom-and-pop store, and see if they have a memory-testing device. These devices are too expensive for the average user, but most anyone who sells computer memory should have one. Take all your memory modules in and ask them to check them for you. Not only is this test very reliable, but they'll be able to instantly match whatever memory you need, at least in theory. Hopefully they won't charge you for this service, especially because they'll likely be selling you a replacement.

The third method of finding and replacing bad memory is to go to your local computer store and just buy more. It may only be necessary to buy a single additional module, because most likely only one module in your system is faulty. Make sure you get the right kind (see earlier). Next, systematically replace each module in your computer with the one you've just acquired, and test the system by turning it on. If the problem seems to be resolved, you've most likely found the culprit—throw it out immediately. If the system still crashes, try replacing the *next* module with the new one, and repeat the process. If you replace all the memory in your system and the problem persists, there may be more than one faulty memory module, or the problem may lie elsewhere, such as a bad CPU or motherboard. To eliminate the possibility of a given problem being caused by a device other than your memory, remove all unnecessary devices (internal and external) from your system before testing your memory.

You can, of course, also take this opportunity to add more memory to your system (possibly replacing all your existing modules). Adding memory is one of the best ways to improve overall system performance. Memory prices are continually dropping; at the time of this writing, the average megabyte of RAM costs roughly 1/100th the price of when Windows 95 was originally released.

USB ports

USB is the answer to all the headaches caused by serial (COM) ports, parallel (printer) ports, keyboard and mouse ports, and, in some circumstances, SCSI ports. USB is fully PnP-compliant, so not only should a USB controller not give you any trouble, neither should any USB devices. If you're having trouble with a device that connects to a serial or parallel port or if you've simply run out of free ports, USB will likely handle it. You can obtain a serial-to-USB adapter cable from most computer stores.

Although most computers only come with one or two USB plugs, the USB system can handle up to 128 devices; if you've run out of plugs, a USB hub will expand your USB bus easily. Note that some devices, such as uninterruptible power supplies, may not support being plugged into a hub. Some hubs have optional power supplies, necessary for devices that get their power from the USB bus.

If you have a USB controller, but can't get Windows to recognize it or any USB devices attached to it, try entering your computer's BIOS setup program (see your computer's documentation for details), and look for USB settings. Usually, it's a simply a matter of enabling the USB controller.

Some systems also have a setting for "USB Legacy Support." Enable this feature (through your BIOS setup) only if you have a USB mouse or keyboard and you need to use them in an environment that doesn't support USB, such as DOS or earlier versions of Windows.

Motherboards and CPUs

There's really nothing you can do to diagnose a bad CPU chip (recognizable by frequent system crashes or your machine's not booting up at all), other than to simply replace it. Your best bet is to take your motherboard, complete with CPU and memory, to your local mom-and-pop computer store, ask them to test it for you, and replace any components that need replacing.

Motherboards can also be finicky, but it's possible that a problem is caused only by a misconfiguration in the motherboard's BIOS setup. Consult the documentation for information on how to enter the BIOS setup. (It usually involves pressing **Del** or **Ctrl-Alt-Enter** just after you turn the system on and memory is tested.)

Also, check with the manufacturer of the motherboard to see if newer firmware (see "Firmware: Software for Your Hardware" earlier in this chapter) for your motherboard is available; newer motherboards allow you to update the BIOS by simply downloading and running a small program.

Upgrading your BIOS firmware can solve some problems, but you should only do so if absolutely necessary. Never install a BIOS not specifically written for your exact motherboard. A mistake can fry your motherboard and your warranty, leading to another, rather expensive, solution: replacement.

Lastly, even the newest motherboards come with jumpers. If you're trying to solve a nasty problem, it's best to go through the entire manual and verify that each jumper is set correctly.

Power supplies

Don't overlook the power supply! Every time I encounter a problem that seems to have no reasonable explanation, the culprit has been the power supply. I'm beginning to think it's a conspiracy.

Say, all of a sudden, one of your storage devices (hard disk, tape drive, etc.) starts malfunctioning, either sporadically or completely. You try removing and reinstalling the drivers (if any), you replace all the cables, and you take out all the other devices. You may even completely replace the device with a brand new one—and it still doesn't work. The next thing to try is replacement of your power supply.

Your computer's power supply powers all of your internal devices, as well as some of your external ones (keyboard, mouse, many USB devices, and some cameras). If your power supply isn't able to support all of those devices, one or more of those devices will suffer. Other causes of power supply problems include damage from a power surge or even just lousy design.

A power supply isn't serviceable, has no settings, and doesn't use any drivers. Your only choice is to replace it, ideally with one of a higher power rating. If you have a 230W supply, replace it with a 300W unit or higher. And a 300W unit can be replaced with a 350W or even 400W unit.* Most modern computers use standard ATX power supplies, which are removed from the system with a few screws; they're available from almost any computer retailer.

Possible exceptions are portable computers, which may not have user-replaceable power supplies. However, the need for increased power is generally only applicable to a desktop system that can accommodate several additional internal devices, so the matter is pretty much moot.

Using Multiple Hardware Configurations

In many cases, solving a problem with a computer means simply finding the correct configuration. It's (unfortunately) not unusual to spend hours shuffling around the various devices in your system in an effort to resolve all the conflicts, or even just to get it all to fit in the box at the same time.

Sometimes, if you can't come to an acceptable resolution, you may have to set up multiple configurations, just to get everything to work. Windows supports two kinds of multiple configurations:

Multiple users

: Allow you reconfigure all your installed software for each "user." That is, if you log in as *Seymour*, the desktop wallpaper, the toolbars in your word processor, and the Internet Explorer favorites would all reflect Seymour's preferences. If Seymour then logs out and *Edna* logs in, all these settings would then reflect Edna's preferences.

: See Chapter 3 for more information on how multiple users are stored in the Registry and Chapter 7 for more information on configuring your computer for multiple users.

Hardware profiles

: Allow you to save different sets of Device Manager settings. Say, for example, you have two different pointing devices and a modem, all of which plug into serial ports. Because most PCs only devote two IRQs to serial ports, it's common that only two serial-port devices can be

* Don't worry about the added power consumption; it's not as bad as it sounds. If you employ some of your computer's power-saving features, your computer's power usage may not noticeably increase, even if you install a 400W unit.

used at any given time.* In order to have all three devices connected simultaneously, yet still be without conflicts, you'll have to set up two or more hardware profiles.

Double-click on the **System** icon in Control Panel, and choose the **Hardware Profiles** tab. In most circumstances, you'll only see one entry in the list: "Original Configuration." To create a new profile, click **Copy** to duplicate the existing configuration (a little counter-intuitive, I know), and type the name you wish to give the new profile. Initially, both profiles will be identical. However, any subsequent settings in **Device Manager** will be applied to only the currently "active" profile.

So, in the serial-port example, one hardware profile might be configured to support both pointing devices while disabling the modem (see "Stop Plug and Play from Detecting Devices" earlier in this chapter). In order to use the modem, you'd switch to another hardware profile that would enable the modem but disable one of the pointing devices.

The other nice thing about hardware profiles is that you only load the drivers for the devices that you're using, which saves memory and boot time and can increase system stability. Other uses for hardware profiles include docking stations for portable computers, where one profile would include the peripherals connected to the docking station (external monitor, printer, network adapter) and the other profile would only support the devices inside the machine.

Connect Peripherals Without Restarting Windows

Plug and Play, if it works, can be very handy. However, its design limits its usefulness in that newly attached devices are *only* automatically detected at Windows startup.

The exceptions are most modern PC Card (PCMCIA) devices and nearly all USB devices; you should be able to plug this type of hardware in at any time during a Windows session without trouble. Naturally, check the device's documentation to see if it is hot-plugable before trying this. (If you encounter a problem with this, try updating the drivers for the PCMCIA or USB controller in question.)

---

* USB is another solution for serial-port conflicts, specifically. After the first two serial port devices are connected, additional serial-port devices can be connected to your USB ports with serial-to-USB adapters. See the discussion of USB earlier in this chapter.

Now, you should never try to install or remove an internal device from your system while it's powered, but most external devices can be attached and detached without trouble. Examples are printers, pointing devices, monitors, keyboards, any external SCSI devices, scanners, and external storage devices (such as Zip drives). The ability to plug and unplug these types of gadgets without having to wait for Windows to reboot is a great time and sanity saver.

The key is to force Windows to redetect specific hardware without restarting. The Add New Hardware Wizard isn't any good for this, because it's designed to detect hardware that hasn't yet been configured. Besides, it takes way too long (rebooting is almost always faster) and usually requires that you restart Windows anyway.

After you've properly connected and turned on the external device, follow these instructions. Note that in most cases, the same process will work for removing devices as well.

General-purpose solution

1. Double-click on the **System** icon in Control Panel, and choose the **Device Manager** tab.
2. Click the **View devices by connection** option at the top of the Window, which then reorganizes the tree. Instead of being sorted by category, the devices are arranged by the way they are connected to the motherboard. This, for example, groups all your SCSI devices together under the respective SCSI controller (see the subsequent solution for details).
3. Make sure **Computer** is highlighted at the top of the list, and click **Refresh**. This will take anywhere from 5 to 20 seconds, but when it's done, any newly attached device(s) should appear in the list (you will, of course, have to expand the appropriate branches to find them). Also, any storage devices you've attached should automatically appear in the My Computer and Explorer windows; any devices you've *removed* will likewise disappear.
4. If, at this time, Windows detects a device that it hasn't seen before, it'll prompt you for drivers and such, which then usually requires you to reboot. However, the beauty of it is that you'll only need to do it once; any subsequent engaging or disengaging from the system should be relatively painless.

5. If you can't find your new device, choose the **View devices by connection** option, find your SCSI card in the list, and expand it out to see all the devices attached to it.
6. Close the **Device Manager** when you're finished.

Adding and removing SCSI devices

There's a shortcut to the previous method that works for nearly all SCSI controllers. It refreshes much faster and is less likely to cause problems with any other hardware in your system. Rather than refreshing the entire tree, all you need to refresh is the SCSI controller itself:

1. Follow the instructions in "General-purpose solution" earlier in this section, except that instead of highlighting **Computer** in the list, highlight your SCSI controller.
2. Locate the entry for your SCSI controller. It can be in any of several different places on the tree, depending on your model. For PCI SCSI controllers, it will be in the **\Plug and Play BIOS\PCI bus** branch.

   If you have more than one SCSI controller, click the plus sign next to each controller to see which devices are connected, and should be enough of a clue to which controller is applicable. Figure 6-4 shows **Device Manager** in **View devices by connection** mode, with the SCSI controller highlighted.
3. Simply highlight your SCSI controller, and then press **Refresh**.

Make sure any external devices are firmly plugged in, turned on (if applicable), and configured correctly; otherwise, Windows won't be able to see them.

In some circumstances, refreshing Device Manager in this way will cause your system to lock up. If you can't get control back after a minute, you'll most likely have to restart your computer. If you're trying to refresh SCSI devices only, follow the second solution; because it doesn't bother refreshing the entire system, you're less likely to "hit a nerve."

Although technically you can attach and remove internal SCSI drives, it's not recommended, because connecting and disconnecting the four-prong drive power cable while the system is powered can easily cause a short. For this reason, it's best to power down before connecting or disconnecting any internal devices, SCSI or not. Regardless, you'll definitely need to shut down your computer before connecting or disconnecting any IDE drives.

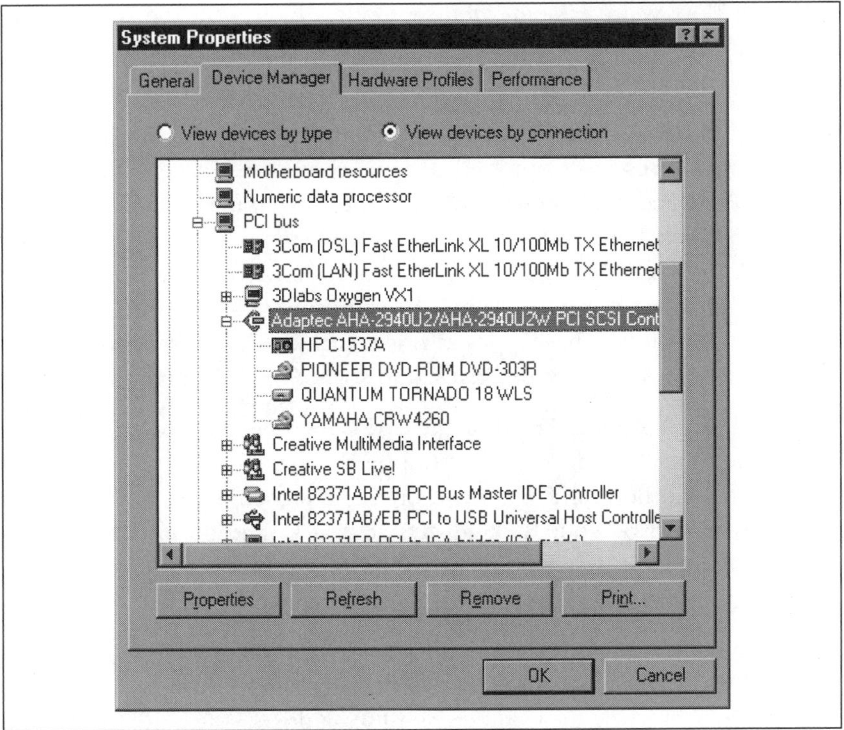

Figure 6-4. Finding your SCSI controller in the tree can significantly reduce the time required to detect new devices, because Windows will only be refreshing that one controller

If you change the SCSI ID of a device before reconnecting it to your system, one of two things may happen. Either Windows will not recognize the change (which may or may not prevent the device from working), or Windows will think that you're connecting an entirely new device (which is a design flaw in Windows' Plug-and-Play subsystem). If Windows thinks you're installing a new device, it'll ask for drivers and then, depending on the device, may require that you restart.

Designate Drive Letters

Each disk drive on a PC, whether it's a CD-ROM, floppy, removable drive, or a hard disk, has its own drive letter.* Some drives are separated into several sections, called partitions, where each partition has its own drive letter. This goes back to the very first IBM PCs, which had only one

* The exceptions are tape drives, which typically don't have a drive letters.

5.25-inch floppy drive (some deluxe models had two); the drives were called simply "A" and "B." Later, the IBM XT's massive 10-MB hard drive was called simply "C."

There are two ways that drives are assigned drive letters, both dependent on how the drives are connected to your computer. Those controlled by your BIOS, which don't require any software (drivers), usually include your floppy and most hard drives, for which drive letters are created when your system is first turned on (called INT 13 devices). Drives controlled solely by software aren't recognized until the corresponding software is loaded, usually by Windows. These types of drives include CD-ROM drives, removable cartridge drives, network drives, and some SCSI hard disks.

Generally, letters are assigned to these drives depending on the order in which they are loaded. Your first floppy drive is always assigned to A:, and the second floppy, if you have one, is assigned to B:. The hard-disk drives controlled by your BIOS always start at C: and go from there. Any software-controlled drives, such as CD-ROM and network drives, follow, by default, in the order in which they were originally installed.

For example, assume a computer with three hard disks, two floppies, and a CD-ROM drive. Two of the hard disks are IDE drives (drives "1" and "2") and are controlled by the computer's BIOS—"drive 3" is a SCSI drive and is controlled by SCSI drivers built into Windows.* And just for fun, we'll add a Zip drive and a network-shared drive and make each hard disk have at least two partitions. In Windows Me, drive letters will be assigned, by default, as follows:

```
A:  Floppy Drive #1
B:  Floppy Drive #2
C:  Hard Disk #1 (IDE), First Partition
D:  Hard Disk #2 (IDE), First Partition
E:  Hard Disk #1 (IDE), Second Partition
F:  Hard Disk #1 (IDE), Third Partition
G:  Hard Disk #2 (IDE), Second Partition
H:  Hard Disk #3 (SCSI), First Partition *
I:  Hard Disk #3 (SCSI), Second Partition *
J:  CD Drive *
K:  Zip Drive *
L:  Network Drive *
```

* Not all SCSI drives are controlled by drivers. Any SCSI adapter with its own on-board BIOS (a good feature) will load its drives as though they were BIOS drives. If your motherboard comes with a built-in SCSI adapter, it most likely has its own BIOS. Whether IDE or SCSI drives are loaded first depends on how your SCSI BIOS is configured.

Note that only the first partitions of the two BIOS-controlled drives are listed first. Then, starting back with the first drive, the remaining partitions are listed, followed by the remaining partitions of the second drive. Once all of the partitions of the BIOS-controlled drives are loaded, Windows adds the software-controlled hard disk (#3), the CD-ROM drive, and the others.

Only those drive letters marked with an asterisk (*) in the previous listing, the drives controlled by software, can be changed in Windows. The drive letters for any BIOS-controlled devices can't be reassigned in Windows Me, although Windows NT and Windows 2000 are able to reassign any drive letter (except Windows 2000 system drive), regardless of the connection.

While this example shows a bunch of drives, most users will only have a single hard drive with a single partition, probably a CD-ROM drive, and one or two floppy drives. Here's how to designate drive letters for drives that support it:

1. Double-click on the **System** icon in Control Panel, and click on the **Device Manager** tab.
2. Find the device (CD-ROM drive, Zip drive, or otherwise) that you wish to configure from the list, and highlight it. The drives that interest us will most likely be listed under the **CDROM** or **Disk drives** categories.
3. Click **Properties**, and choose the **Settings** tab.
4. By default, the **Removable** option is turned on for all CD-ROM drives and removable-cartridge drives (such as Zip drives).* For hard disks, this option is turned off by default. In order to change drive letters, you'll need to make sure this option is turned on. If the **Removable** option is initially turned off, make sure to turn it off it *again* when you're done with this procedure.
5. You can now choose a new drive letter for the highlighted drive. In the section entitled **Reserved drive letters**, choose the *same letter* for both the **Start drive letter** and **End drive letter**. The only time you'll want to choose different drive letters for **Start** and **End** is if you're configuring a hard disk with more than one partition (such as drive #3 in our previous example).

Trouble-shooting

* The **Removable** option here tells Windows that this is a removable cartridge drive, such as a CD-ROM, floppy, or Zip drive, and the media may not always be present. This is contrary to a nonremovable drive, such as a hard disk.

Typically, only those drive letters that are available to software-controlled drives will be listed; drive letters assigned to BIOS-controlled drives won't be available.

If the letter you choose is currently in use by another software-controlled drive, Windows will reassign the *other* drive's letter to make room for the one you're configuring.

6. Press **OK** and then **OK** again when you're finished. You'll have to restart your computer for this change to take effect. If you're reassigning more than one drive, you may be able to reassign them all at once before restarting.

Network drives connected through a Microsoft Windows network will not show up in Device Manager. You'll need to remap them in order to change their drive letters—see "Setting Up a Workgroup" in Chapter 7 for more information.

It can be handy to choose intuitive letters for some of your drives. For example, use *N:* for a network drive, *R:* for a recordable CD-ROM drive, *Z:* for a Zip drive, and *L:* for Lenny's drive.

For your reference, the drive-letter information for all drives is stored in the Registry (see Chapter 3) under the `CurrentDriveLetterAssignment` and `UserDriveLetterAssignment` values in the following keys:

- For all SCSI devices and most non-SCSI CD-ROM drives, look in `HKEY_LOCAL_MACHINE\Enum\SCSI`.
- For IDE hard disks, look in `HKEY_LOCAL_MACHINE\Enum\ESDI`.
- For standard floppy drives, look in `HKEY_LOCAL_MACHINE\Enum\FLOP`.

Stop Windows from Randomly Searching the Floppy Drive

This bizarre and annoying quirk has plagued each version of Windows since the original release of Windows 95. For some reason, Windows will randomly try to read the floppy drive at no particular time and for no apparent reason.

There are many things that can cause this problem, such as references to the floppy drive in the Registry or in various shortcuts on your system, as well as some third-party software. To identify the source of the problem, try the following:

- Windows sometimes falls back on the outdated concept of a "current drive." For example, if you were to launch an application or document from a floppy, then that floppy might be the current drive until the system is restarted. Note that launching a document from the floppy will also create a shortcut in your Documents menu that points to the floppy (see the next point); to avoid this, copy all documents to your desktop before launching them.
- When refreshing the Start Menu, Explorer may reread the contents of the *\Windows\Recent* folder, which comprise the Documents menu. Windows may poll the floppy drive at this point. Select **Settings** from the **Start Menu**, select **Taskbar and Start Menu**, choose the **Advanced** tab, and click **Clear** to empty this list.
- Clear out the history of the Start Menu's **Run** command. Use TweakUI (see Appendix A), choose the **Paranoia** tab, check the **Clear Run history at logon** option, and then click **Clear Selected Items Now**. You can then turn off the **Clear Run history at logon** if you wish.
- Search your hard disk for all DOS and Windows shortcuts that point to programs on a floppy drive. Select **Find** from the **Start Menu** and then **Files or Folders**. Type **`*.lnk, *.pif`** in the **Named** field, type **`a:`** (or **`b:`** if applicable) in the **Containing text** field, and click **Find Now**. The **Find** results will then list any DOS and Windows shortcuts on your system that reference your floppy drive. In most circumstances, you can delete any files that are found (shortcuts to programs on floppies are rarely useful). If you're unsure, right-click on any given shortcut, and click **Properties** to find out more about it.
- Search your hard disk for all files with the extension **.ini* (configuration file) that contain the text *a:* (using the procedure in the previous point). If one or more files are found, use a text editor such as Notepad to edit the file and remove the reference. See "Using INI Files" in Chapter 3 for more information if you're not familiar with editing these files.
- Using your favorite text editor, take out the line that reads `"LocalLoadHigh=1"` from your *Msdos.sys* file, if it's there. It's a hidden file (located in your root directory), so you'll have to configure Explorer to display hidden files in order to see it. Note that this line will only be there if you (or someone else) intentionally placed it there in the first place; it is not required to run Windows.
- Search your entire Registry for *a:*, looking for any references to files or programs on your floppy drive. More specifically, the path `HKEY_CLASSES_ROOT\CLSID` may contain references to shared libraries or

other support files that may have once been located on a floppy disk in your system.

- If you have a program such as Norton Navigator for Windows that saves the 10 most recently visited folders for each application's File Open and File Save dialog boxes (otherwise a useful feature), it may have saved a reference to your floppy somewhere along the way. Consult the documentation for this, or any other program you suspect, for more information on clearing the various "history" lists.
- Check for any viruses on your system (some users have reported the *Neuville* virus); you'll need an antivirus utility for this.
- Try disabling the autoprotect feature of your antivirus software, if applicable. See "Taming Antivirus Software" earlier in this chapter for details.
- Search your hard disk for Windows script *(*.vbs)* and DOS batch *(*.bat)* files that may contain references to your floppy drive. See Chapter 9, *Scripting and Automation*, and Appendix B, respectively, for details.
- Lastly, check the programs that are loaded automatically when Windows starts; Windows may expect that one of them resides on a floppy drive or, more likely, the program being loaded may be looking for some data or supplementary file on a floppy drive. See "What to Do When Windows Won't Start" later in this chapter for the different ways programs are configured to run at startup.

Force NumLock to Behave

Ever since IBM introduced their enhanced 101-key keyboard with two sets of cursor keys back in 1984, the **NumLock** key on most keyboards is turned on by default, nudging users to use the standard cursor keys rather than the numeric keypad to control the cursor.

This may seem an inconsequential setting, but it affects a basic function of the primary input device, the keyboard, and can therefore be quite important. Some of us prefer the numeric keypad, and therefore prefer **NumLock** to be turned off; others prefer the opposite. All that remains is to change the default setting.

In most modern computers, you can set the default in your BIOS setup (sometimes called CMOS setup). This screen, usually accessible by pressing **Del**, **Esc**, or some other key when your computer first boots up, is where you also define the parameters for your fixed and floppy drives, memory settings, the clock, and other system parameters. Refer to the documentation that came with your computer or motherboard for instructions on changing this setting; it's usually obvious, such as *NumLock Default: ON/OFF.*

Some software products can interfere with this setting, most notably Microsoft's own "Intellipoint" software, included with some older mice and keyboards. Because this software often serves no practical purpose, your best option is to simply remove it.

Turn Off the PC Speaker

The last thing we need, in light of all the other things our computers do to annoy us, is to listen to the shrill and incessant beeps that come from the PC speaker.

Now, the first place one would think to go to turn off the literal bells and whistles in Windows is the **Sounds and Multimedia** icon in Control Panel. However, in most cases, turning off all of the sound events will cause Windows to default to the PC speaker for warning beeps, which is even worse. Unfortunately, there is no option in Control Panel related to the PC speaker, nor is there any mention of it in the online documentation. There's also no way to disable the PC speaker device in Device Manager.

Luckily, there are several, albeit not very obvious, workarounds to the problem.

Solution 1

Yank the damn thing out of your system. It should be very easy to find and easy to remove. (It's usually connected to the motherboard by a two-conductor wire, which can simply be pulled out.)

Solution 2

1. Using the sound recorder (*Sndrec32.exe*), create a short *.wav* file of only silence.
2. Double-click on the **Sounds** icon in Control Panel, and choose **Default Sound** from the list of events.
3. Click **Browse**, and select the new, silent *.wav* file you've created. Instead of an annoying little song or the jarring PC beep, this silent file will be played, allowing you to work in relative peace.
4. Repeat steps 2 and 3 for the **Asterisk** and **Exclamation** events as well. You may want to save this configuration for easy retrieval later on. Click **OK** when you're done.

Solution 3

Double-click on the **TweakUI** icon in Control Panel (see Appendix A). Under the **General** tab, in the **Effects** list, turn off the **Beep on Errors** option. Click **OK** when you're finished.

Error Messages

There are several things to keep in mind when interpreting any given error message:

- Just because you see an error message doesn't mean you've done something wrong.
- If you're looking for a list of all possible Windows Me error messages, you're out of luck; such a list does not exist. Besides, not all error messages are generated by Windows; many are either generated by or are otherwise the result of third-party applications.
- Error messages are canned responses to predetermined criteria. The text in an error message doesn't take into account what you were doing or what you might have been thinking when the error occurred, so it rarely is informative enough by itself to help you prevent future occurrences.
- Error messages typically occur more often than they need to, bothering the user with a warning or other information that simply isn't that important.*
- Error messages are typically verbose, yet not terribly helpful. Programmers often write only a few generic, general-purpose messages that are used in many circumstances. And software developers are rarely English majors.
- If you're trying to diagnose a problem, the error message that appears may contain rows and rows of numeric code, often hidden behind a **Details** button. This information is rarely useful. What's more important here is the conditions under which the error occurred (what events led to the error) and, specifically, any filenames that are mentioned in the message itself.
- The General Protection Fault message, as well as the so-called "Blue Screen of Death," are both messages generated by Windows when some application or driver has committed an error severe enough that

* Windows Me actually takes a few steps to eliminate some of the common, yet unnecessary, error messages that plagued Windows 9x, such as the ones that occurred when a folder or drive icon was drag-dropped onto itself in Explorer.

it can't handle the problem on its own. Usually, but not always, these errors are associated with some sort of hardware conflict or driver problem.

- Sometimes, a message will report that a program has crashed or isn't able to load, but the actual problem may be something completely unrelated to what the message is reporting. For example, you may see a "file not found" error when trying to start an application, if, perhaps, you've run low on system resources (see "Understanding System Resources" earlier in this chapter).

If only one specific application displays a particular error message, your first course of action should be to contact the manufacturer of the application for technical support with their product. Most manufacturers will have troubleshooting, common problems and solutions, software updates, and FAQs on their web sites.

Common error messages usually tell you that a file is missing or corrupted, a program error has occurred, or a specific device isn't working or turned on. Error messages that tell you that *you've* done something wrong don't really apply here (such as trying to drag-drop a file onto your CD-ROM drive or trying to use quotes in a filename), for obvious reasons.

Typical Windows Startup Errors

You may have seen a strange message when Windows is loading, either during the display of the Windows logo screen or after the taskbar appears. Many different things can cause this, but there are a few common culprits. If you're having trouble starting Windows, see "What to Do When Windows Won't Start" earlier in this chapter.

A driver won't load

When Windows starts, it loads all of the installed drivers into memory. A driver may refuse to load if the device for which it's designed isn't functioning or turned on, if there's a hardware conflict, if the driver itself isn't installed properly, or if the driver file is corrupted in some way. If you remove a device, make sure to take out the driver file as well—even if it isn't generating an error message, it could be taking up memory. See "Dealing with Drivers and Other Tales of Hardware Troubleshooting" earlier in this chapter.

A program can't be found

After Windows loads itself and all of its drivers, it loads any programs configured to load at startup. These include screen savers, scheduling utilities, Palm HotSync software, all those icons that appear in your "tray," and any other programs you may have placed in your **Startup** folder or that may be been configured to load automatically in the system Registry. If you removed an application, for example, and Windows continues to attempt to load one of its components at startup, you'll have to remove the reference manually. See "The Places Windows Looks for Startup Programs" later in this chapter for details.

A Registry is corrupted

See Chapter 3 for any errors regarding your Registry and how to repair corrupted Registry files.

A file is corrupt or missing

If one of Windows' own files won't load and you're sure it isn't a third-party driver or application, you may actually have to reinstall Windows to alleviate the problem. I'll take this opportunity to remind you to back up frequently.

An error message of this sort will usually include a filename. To help isolate the problem, write down the filename when you see the error message, and then try searching your hard disk for the reported file, as well as looking for places where the file may be *referenced* (see "The Places Windows Looks for Startup Programs" later in this chapter for details). If you don't know what the error means exactly, you should definitely do both; a lot can be learned by finding how and where Windows is trying to load a program. However, if you know that the file or files are no longer on your system, you can proceed simply to remove the reference.

Conversely, if you know the file *is* still on your system and you want to get it working again, you'll probably need to reinstall whatever component or application it came with in order to fix the problem. Once you've located a particular file, it may not be obvious to which program it belongs. You can usually get a good clue by right-clicking on the file, selecting **Properties**, and choosing the **Version** tab.

Please wait while Windows updates your configuration files

This isn't an error, but rather a message you may see occasionally when Windows is starting. It simply means that Windows is copying certain files that it couldn't otherwise copy while Windows was loaded, most often as a result of software being installed during the last Windows session. For example, if a program you install needs to replace an old DLL in your *\Windows\System* folder with a newer version, but the DLL is in use and can't be overwritten, the program's setup utility will simply instruct Windows to do it automatically the next time it's restarted.

The Places Windows Looks for Startup Programs

The following locations are places that files or drivers can be specified to load when Windows starts. Often simply removing the reference to the file solves the problem. At the very least, locating the driver will help determine the culprit.

Most of the programs listed in the following areas are also accessible from the System Configuration Utility (*Msconfig.exe*). Choose the **Startup** tab, and uncheck any unwanted programs. The handy **Cleanup** feature scans all the entries and removes any seemingly invalid references:

- Your *Startup* folder (usually *\Windows\Start Menu\Startup*) contains shortcuts for all the standard programs you wish to load every time Windows starts. You should routinely look for outdated or unwanted shortcuts. A previously installed application may have placed a shortcut here for some reason. If you've moved or deleted the application, the shortcut may still be there, irritating you every time you turn on the system. Right-click on any shortcut, and select **Properties** to learn more about it.
- Older programs might still install themselves in your *Win.ini* file (specified on the lines that start with `LOAD=` or `RUN=`, usually at the top of the file). Use a text editor such as Notepad to edit this file (you may want to back it up before proceeding) or, in the System Configuration Utility, choose the **Win.ini** tab. Also, some older drivers are specified throughout your *System.ini* file, but can be hard to isolate if you don't know what you're looking for. See Chapter 3 for more information on INI files.
- There are several places in the Registry that Startup programs are specified; they're put here instead of the **Startup** folder to prevent tinkering. If you don't know the name of the file, try looking in any of the following Registry keys for other programs and drivers loaded at Windows startup:

```
HKEY_LOCAL_MACHINE\SOFTWARE\Microsoft\Windows\CurrentVersion\Run
HKEY_LOCAL_MACHINE\SOFTWARE\Microsoft\Windows\CurrentVersion\RunOnce
HKEY_LOCAL_MACHINE\SOFTWARE\Microsoft\Windows\CurrentVersion\
    RunOnceEx
HKEY_LOCAL_MACHINE\SOFTWARE\Microsoft\Windows\CurrentVersion\
    RunServices
HKEY_LOCAL_MACHINE\SOFTWARE\Microsoft\Windows\CurrentVersion\
    RunServicesOnce
HKEY_CURRENT_USER\SOFTWARE\Microsoft\Windows\CurrentVersion\Run
HKEY_CURRENT_USER\SOFTWARE\Microsoft\Windows\CurrentVersion\RunOnce
```

Note that in any of these keys, you may see a reference to a file without any description, such as *Wfxctl32.exe*. Obviously, the filename alone is not self evident. However, a quick search on the hard drive will reveal that the file is located in the *\Program Files\WinFax* folder, evidence that the file belongs to the WinFax application.

- If there's a filename specified in an error message and you can't find it in any of these Registry keys, try doing a global Registry search.

Programs notorious for putting things in these places include backup utilities that automatically load their superfluous scheduler utilities, antivirus "autoprotect" software,* fax programs, and the software that comes with older versions of Microsoft mice and keyboards. If in doubt, create a Registry patch of the entire Registry key in question (see Chapter 3 for details) and then remove the questionable entry. If anything goes wrong, you can reapply the Registry patch to restore the settings.

One final note about the System Configuration Utility: the **Advanced** button displays a bunch of "Advanced Troubleshooting Settings." Most likely, you won't want to touch any of these unless you've been so instructed or you know specifically what the various features do. The exception is the **Disable Scandisk after bad shutdown** option, which is fairly self-explanatory. Although the auto-Scandisk feature is actually quite useful, you may have a reason to disable it.

Bad Software Exemplified

Many users may also find something called the "Real Player Start Center" (or something similar) specified in the Registry to start automatically with Windows. It's a component of the Real Player (used for playing audio and video content on the Web), and honestly serves no practical purpose. It's loaded automatically on every system on which Real Player is installed, which ends up increasing boot time and consuming memory and system resources. The "Start Center" feature can be disabled without worry by turning off the appropriate option in Real Player's configuration window.

* See "Taming Antivirus Software" earlier in this chapter for details.

Page Fault, Illegal Operation, and Fatal Exception

A software bug usually causes these errors when an application or driver tries to use part of your memory that's currently being used by another program. Another cause of this type of error is a hardware conflict; see "Resolving Hardware Conflicts" earlier in this chapter for details.

When you see one of these errors, the first thing to do is determine if any action is necessary. You should expect this to happen occasionally, due to the complexity of today's software, but if it happens more frequently than, say, once a day, it could be the sign of a more serious problem. See if you can reliably reproduce the problem. If it seems to be application- or device-specific, where the same action in a program or the repeated use of a certain device causes the crash, then you've found the culprit.

If the occurrences instead appear to be random and not associated with any piece of hardware or software, there are some remaining possibilities. Errors in your system's memory and on your hard disk can cause these problems as well. To diagnose and repair any problems on your hard disk, use the Scandisk (*Scandskw.exe*) utility included with Windows or one of the more powerful third-party utilities available. See the discussion of memory in "Fixing Device-Specific Problems" earlier in this chapter for details.

Often, the General Protection Fault error is accompanied by lists of numbers (accessible by clicking **Details**), although these numbers will never be the least bit helpful for most users. Now, don't be fooled: the Details view also often lists a specific executable, blaming it for the protection fault. However, this doesn't necessarily mean that the program listed *actually* caused the problem; it only means that it was the first running application to *encounter* the problem.

Crash-a-Holic

Now, if an application crashes and *doesn't* display an error message, it's usually in the form of a lockup, where it has stopped responding to keyboard and mouse input and has stopped refreshing its window (such as when another window is dragged over it). In most situations, you can press **Ctrl-Alt-Del** to display the **Close Program** box, as shown in Figure 6-5.

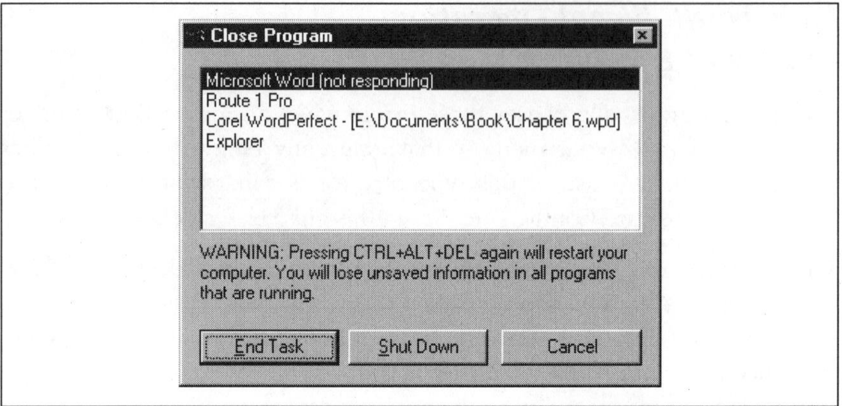

Figure 6-5. Pressing Ctrl-Alt-Del displays the Close Program box, allowing you to close a hung application, as well as see the other programs running when a crash occurs

You are now fortunate enough to have the option of closing a misbehaving program or shutting down Windows completely. You can close any running program here by selecting it from the list and clicking **End Task**, whether it has crashed or not. In fact, it's a good way to close programs that don't have windows, such as screen savers and other background programs. If an application has stopped responding, the text "(not responding)" will usually appear next to the application's name.

Note that applications that aren't responding don't always allow themselves to be shut down. Conversely, it's possible that an application reported as not responding can be doing so only temporarily; some programs, such as those that access certain devices, may appear to hang during normal operation. For this reason, it's best to have patience and give all hung applications a minute or two to correct themselves. Additionally, once you've used **End Task** on a hung application, it may take a little while for Windows to close it.

Another thing to be aware of is that many applications are made up of several components. It's possible for one of those components to crash and leave the rest of the program in operation. It's also possible for a program to crash and leave one or more of its components in memory. This can cause problems, not the least of which is a premature depletion of System Resources (see "Understanding System Resources" earlier in this chapter), although it certainly varies with the program. Try pressing **Ctrl-Alt-Del** again to see if the application in question is still running after it's been closed.

Because any crashed program can cause system-wide instability in Windows, it's good practice (albeit aggravating) to restart Windows every time a crash occurs. The following programs are part of Windows and commonly appear in the Close Program window. Closing them with the previous method can solve some problems temporarily but may not stop many other problems from recurring:

Msgsrv32 (not responding)

This is one of Windows' components that runs invisibly in the background. It performs several necessary functions, including the following (from Microsoft's knowledge base):

- Mediate Plug-and-Play messages among various parts of the operating system.
- Coordinate automatic responses to Setup programs. This includes checking whether a Setup program has improperly overwritten Windows files and optionally restoring the Windows versions of those files—see "Disabling System File Protection" earlier in this chapter, for details.
- Display the initial logon dialog box if multiple users are configured or, in some circumstances, if networking is enabled.
- Play the system startup and shutdown sounds.
- Load installable Windows drivers at startup and unload them at shutdown.
- Run the shell program (usually *Explorer.exe*), and rerun the shell if it closes or fails to respond.

Because of the varied nature of this program, almost anything can cause it to crash. If it does, you can just end its task. If it happens more than once, it's best to restart Windows immediately.

Rundll32.dll

This program is used by some applications to run parts of other applications, and therefore doesn't necessarily correspond with any particular error. However, the following two circumstances relate to this file:

- If you see the message, "Rundll32—This program has caused an illegal operation and will be shut down," it could be caused by a missing entry in your *System.ini* file. Using a text editor, such as Notepad, look for the line that starts with `drivers=` in the `[boot]` section. If *mmsystem.dll* isn't specified on the right side of the equals sign, add it. If you continue getting this error, try removing all other drivers from the line until *mmsystem.dll* is alone. Make sure to make a backup of *System.ini* before editing it.

— If the Close Program window reports, "Rundll32.dll (not responding)," end the task and try whatever it was you were doing again. This has been known to happen when a modem fails while trying to connect to another computer using Dial-Up Networking (see Chapter 7 for more information).

Explorer

Explorer is the default Windows shell; it handles the desktop, the Taskbar, the Start Menu, the My Computer window, the Control Panel, Dial-Up Networking, and all single-folder and Exploring windows. Unless a different application is configured as the shell (listed in the `shell=` line in *System.ini*), *Explorer.exe* is loaded automatically every time you log in.

Explorer can crash for no apparent reason and at any time. Under most situations, if Explorer crashes or is terminated, it will be automatically restarted by *Msgsrv32.exe* (explained earlier). However, if Explorer doesn't automatically restart (such as following the "Abnormal Program Termination" error), you'll have to do it manually. Because Explorer isn't running, launching programs can be difficult; pressing **Ctrl-ESC** or double-clicking on the desktop in this situation will launch the Task Manager (*Taskman.exe*). Select **Run Application** from the **File** menu, type **`explorer`**, and press **Enter**. This should restart Explorer, which will load the desktop and Taskbar. If it doesn't, press **Ctrl-Alt-Del** to display the **Close Program** box (see Figure 6-5), and then click **Shut Down**.

Under most circumstances, Explorer's crashing and restarting shouldn't adversely affect any other running applications, although you may find that the mouse isn't behaving or has even disappeared, drag-drop no longer works properly, and the tray has vanished, as well as other minor and not-so-minor symptoms. As with other crashes, you should save any open documents and restart Windows at your earliest convenience.

Missing files

Files can simply vanish from your hard disk, either by user error, because of file corruption (see the previous passage), or because another program has removed or renamed the file (see the next passage). There's not much you can do about this, other than to keep backups of files that tend to disappear, making it easy to replace them when necessary. If you've discovered that a file that came with Windows or another application is missing, you'll usually need to reinstall the application to restore the file. Note that if a file is missing, it's likely that other files are missing as well, and reinstalling insures not only that all necessary files are present but that any Registry entries pertaining to those files are up-to-date.

If you know that a single file is missing, you can usually retrieve it from the original distribution CD-ROM for Windows or the application in question. If you're trying to retrieve a Windows distribution file, try doing it through the System Configuration Utility (*msconfig.exe*); click **Extract File**, type the filename in the box provided, and click **Start**. In the **Restore from** field, type the name of the folder containing your Windows installation files, usually **`d:\win9x`**, where **`d:`** is the drive letter of your CD-ROM drive.

Shut down problems

If you've ever tried to shut down Windows and have watched it simply hang at the "Please Wait" screen, or even reboot rather than shutting down, you've encountered a common problem with every release of Windows since Windows 95. The cause is usually a hardware driver that refuses to unload.

Regardless of the cause, there should be no adverse effects if you manually shut off your computer at this point. It is recommended that you wait until the hard drive light on your computer (if applicable) goes out (because it may be saving important data to your disk).

Another possible cause of shutdown hanging may be corrupted shutdown bitmaps (see "Customize the Startup Screen" in Chapter 2, *Basic Explorer Coping Skills*).

Version Control

One of the cornerstones of the Windows architecture is the use of Dynamic Link Libraries (DLL) files, which are encapsulated application components that can be shared by several—sometimes all—Windows applications. These files provide common, consistent functionality across all facets of Windows: the way menus are displayed, the look and feel of the standard **File Open** dialog box, the software necessary to play video clips, and so on. In fact, Windows is primarily just a collection of *.dll* files used by the various applications that run on the operating system.

Naturally, in the life cycle of an application or operating system, DLLs are constantly updated with bug fixes and new functionality. When you install an application, all of the most recent DLL files are installed along with it, at least in theory. The problem arises when one errant application overwrites a newer version of a *.dll* with an older (or just different) version. This problem has been partially addressed in Windows Me with System File Protection (see "Disabling System File Protection" earlier in this chapter).

Although each DLL file has a "last modified" date stamp (like any other file), what Windows relies on is actually the version information stored inside the file. In theory, this works quite well. However, older applications don't always follow the rules, and newer applications sometimes come with shared files that introduce new bugs. And, because the *.dll* files that come with Windows are used by the majority of applications (as opposed to a *.dll* used by only a single program), Microsoft DLLs are under the most scrutiny.

To determine the version of any file, right-click on it in Explorer, and click **Properties**. You should see a **Version** tab (if not, the file you've chosen either is corrupted or simply doesn't contain any version information). This tab displays the version of the file, some copyright information, usually the name of the manufacturer, and a short description of the file. Just shuffle through the items in the **Item name** list to see the various clues.

File types that usually contain version information include *.dll* files, *.exe* files, *.drv* files, *.vxd* files, and *.ocx* files.

Usually, newer versions of DLL files are just that—they serve the same purpose as the original version, but add more functionality, include bug fixes, or improve performance. In some isolated situations, a certain DLL file can be replaced with a completely different file, with which all it has in common is the filename. This is rare, although you may encounter this type of problem with the files *Winsock.dll* or *Mapi32.dll* (see later in this section).

Now, there are more DLL files than can be listed in any one place, let alone this book. Many come with Windows, but many more are installed on your system by any of the thousands of applications and drivers currently available. What follows are a few common troublemakers and how to cope with them. In no way should this be considered a comprehensive guide to resolving conflicts between all applications, but rather it should be viewed as an exercise in dealing with several isolated problems. Essentially, the solution to any problem is to make sure you have the *correct* file for your system—usually, but not always, the newest one.

To retrieve the original version of any file (the one that comes on the Windows Me distribution CD-ROM), start the System Configuration Utility (*msconfig.exe*). Click **Extract File**, and type the filename in the box provided. Windows should do the rest. Following are the available DLL files:

Wsock32.dll

This file and its 16-bit counterpart, *Winsock.dll*, are used by most, if not all, Internet applications (see Chapter 7), and the version on your hard disk depends on which Internet dialer you're using. Unless you've installed a third-party dialer, such as AOL or older versions of Netscape Navigator, the version of this file is most likely the one that comes with Windows Me, dated June 8, 2000. (It may be newer if it has been updated by Microsoft.)

Because the various non-Microsoft versions of this file include entirely different functionality, it is *not* necessarily advantageous to have the *latest* version of the file. If your Internet applications stop working, try updating this file with the one that comes on the Windows CD; or, if you're using a third-party dialer, try reinstalling that software. See "The Path Less Traveled" later in this chapter for an important consideration.

Mapi32.dll

Mail Application Programming Interface (MAPI) is the specification that allows any application to email a file or block of text using the active email program. However, because Microsoft's version of *Mapi32.dll* is not able to hook into any non-Microsoft email program, each third-party email program you install typically overwrites the file with its own version.

This causes substantial problems. For example, Eudora (a very popular email program and my personal favorite) includes its own version of the file. If you install Eudora and enable its MAPI feature, it will rename any existing *Mapi32.dll* file to *Mapi32.000* and put its own version in its place. If you happen to have Microsoft Office 97 installed, this action will disable Outlook 97 entirely,* which relies heavily (and inappropriately so) on Microsoft's own version of the *Mapi32.dll* file. To resolve the problem in this case, you'll need to first disable the MAPI feature in Eudora and then restore Microsoft's version of the file.

Ctl3d32.dll

This file and its cousins, *Ctl3d.dll* and *Ctl3dv2.dll*, seem to cause lots of problems. They're used by older applications to display certain 3D effects, wherein the controls in some dialog boxes have the "carved" look that has long since become the Windows standard. Software

Trouble-shooting

* Outlook 98 somewhat resolves this problem, in that it is only dependent on MAPI if it's not installed in Internet-only mode. Later releases of Office and Eudora may provide a workaround.

designed especially for Windows 9x/Me/2000 already contains this functionality, but older applications rely on this file for basic operation. Although the newer versions usually are preferred, some applications (as a result of sloppy programming) will display an error if you use anything but the specific version that came with the product. As of this writing, the most benign version of each of these files is v2.31. If you don't have this version, don't panic and don't waste time trying to obtain it for them. This is just a guideline if you are having trouble with any of these files or find that you have several versions floating around. Make a habit of backing up these files so that you can easily restore them if they become overwritten.

The Path Less Traveled

Although it isn't really emphasized as much as it was in the heyday of DOS and Windows 3.x, the system path is still an important setting in Windows Me. It can be helpful as well as detrimental, depending on how it's used.

The system path is simply a listing of folder names kept in memory during an entire Windows session. If a folder name is listed in your system path, you'll be able to run a program contained in that folder *without* having to specify its location. This is most apparent when you use the Start Menu's **Run** command, Explorer's Address Bar, or a DOS prompt;* in any of these places, you can, for example, type **Notepad**, and Notepad will start. This is because *Notepad.exe* is located in a folder (*\windows*) that, by default, is listed in the system path.

The path is one of several *environment variables* that are kept in memory from Windows startup until you shut down. In previous versions of Windows, the path was set with a line in the *Autoexec.bat* file (now obsolete); in Windows Me, all environment variables are set in the System Configuration Utility (*Msconfig.exe*). Choose the **Environment** tab, and double-click on the **Path** entry to edit it. By default, the system path variable contains the following folders: *\windows* and *\windows\command*, each separated with a semicolon (;). Long folder names (such as names with spaces) may be specified as their shortened, MS-DOS names; for example, *c:\Program Files\Microsoft Office 95* will appear as *c:\progra~1\micros~1*. The folder *\windows\system* is also included in path searches, regardless of whether it physically appears in the path variable.

* See Appendix B for more information on the DOS prompt and Explorer's Address Bar.

You may not think this applies to you, but it may. The same rules that apply to program executables also apply to shared files, such as *.dll*, *.vbx*, and *.vxd* files. If you have multiple versions of a file floating around in different directories specified in your system path, only one of the available versions of the file—and not necessarily the latest one—may be in use at any given time. For example, say you have the appropriate version of the file *Winsock.dll* in your *\Windows\System* directory, but you have another, older copy of *Winsock.dll* in your *c:\AOL* directory. It's entirely possible that some programs might mistakenly use the older version, just because they found it in a directory in the path.

If the search for a path conflict ends up leading nowhere, there's another scenario that might be causing a problem. As an example, we'll take the *Ctl3d32.dll* file discussed earlier in this chapter. Say you have the latest version of this file in your *\Windows\System* folder, where it should be. All applications that use this file will look for it there first, unless there happens to be a copy of the file in the application's *own* directory. If the file is not already in memory (it's loaded only once, no matter how many programs are using it), the application will load the version it finds first. If there's a copy of the file in the application directory, it will be loaded, even if it's older. Furthermore, any subsequent programs that also reference this file will simply use the one in memory, even if it's not the one in the *\Windows\System* folder.

How do you escape this trap? First, remove any unnecessary directories from your path variable. Next, if you suspect a conflict with a specific file, try searching your hard disk for the filename (select **Search** and then **For Files or Folders** from the Start Menu, and select **Local Hard Drives** from the **Look in** list). If you see more than one copy of the file in the search results window, it could be causing a potential conflict.

Widen the **In Folder** column in the search results window so you can see where each file is located. If one of them is in *\Windows\System* (or any other Windows subdirectories, for that matter), then it most likely belongs there. Compare the versions of the files by right-clicking, selecting **Properties**, and clicking on the **Version** tabs (see "Version Control" earlier in this chapter). Now, you want to end up with only the newest file on your system, so what you can do at this point is simply delete all but the newest file and move it to the *\Windows\System* folder if it's not already there.

Note that this solution by no means applies to all *.dll* files, which is why it's smart to back up any files before continuing. Some files have identical names only by coincidence, although this is rare. Of course, deleting a file just because there's another around by the same name is not a good idea unless you know that the files serve the same purpose. One way to make sure is to look through *all* the information in the **Version** tab; if the **Company Name** and **Product Name** are the same, you can be pretty sure that the files are duplicates. On the other hand, if the files have vastly different sizes, odds are that one is not a suitable replacement for the other.

Preventive Maintenance and Data Recovery

Face it: some sort of data loss is inevitable. Whether it's a single lost file or a dead hard disk—whether it's tomorrow or twelve years from now—it will happen. On that happy note, there is plenty you can do about it.

First and foremost, there's no better method of disaster recovery than having a good backup copy of all your data. Any stolen or damaged hardware is easily replaced, but the data stored on your hard disk is not. Unfortunately, hindsight is 20/20, and if you didn't back up, there's not much you can do about it after the fact. So, we'll begin our discussion with some preventive maintenance before covering any disaster recovery techniques.

Back Up Your Entire System

There are more ways to back up your data than to store it. The sole purpose of a backup is to have a duplicate of every single piece of data on your hard disk that can be easily retrieved in the event of data loss. Imagine if your computer were stolen and you had to restore a backup to a brand-new computer. Could you do it? If the answer is no, you're not backed up.

You need to be able to complete a backup easily and often, to store the backup in a safe place, away from the computer, and to retrieve all your data at any time without incident. If it's too difficult or time-consuming, odds are you won't do it—so make it easy for yourself.

A bare-minimum backup could be little more than a single floppy disk with your last three or four important documents on it. It's better than nothing, and it does protect your most recent work, but what about your email, your web browser bookmarks, and the documents you wrote $6^1/_2$ years ago? I know what you're thinking, because I've heard it a thousand times: nothing on my computer is really that important, so it's really not worth the time to back up. Okay, assume that's true—how long would it take you to reinstall Windows and all your applications, install all your drivers, reconfigure all your hardware, and customize all your toolbars? If you have a full backup of your system, the answer is not only "not long," but "no problemo" as well.

Ideally, you should be able to back up your entire hard disk on a single piece of media. We won't even entertain the idea of floppies, so think about investing in a dedicated backup solution. The hardware you use should be fully supported by Windows 9x/Me. The backup media (tapes, cartridges, or disks) should be cheap, reliable, and readily available, and you should be able to use them over and over again.

Whichever backup solution is appropriate for you depends on your work habits and your available funds. Tape drives, optical drives, removable cartridges, and recordable CDs are all getting cheaper and manufacturers are competing for your business.

While removable cartridge drives (Iomega Zip and Jaz drives, recordable or rewritable CDs) are great for quickly archiving data (long-term storage of important documents or projects), they still aren't as appropriate as tape drives for backing up entire systems and restoring them in the event of a disaster. Removable drives and CDs use random access, meaning that you can simply open Explorer and read or write to any file on the media immediately. This may be convenient in the short run, but this convenience comes at a price: the media used for these types of backups can be quite expensive (per megabyte) and, more importantly, the backup procedures for random-access drives can be more labor-intensive than for tape drives.

Tape backup drives are still the most cost-effective, reliable, and convenient method for backing up and recovering your system after a disaster. The most obvious caveat is that tape drives use sequential access, rather than random access, meaning that they require special backup software and tend to be slower than comparably priced removables,* especially when used for restoring single files. However, remember what's important here: you need to easily and painlessly duplicate the contents of your *entire* system on *one* piece of removable media and be able to restore some or all of that data just as easily.†

* Windows Me comes with Microsoft Backup, but it isn't installed by default. See "Installing Microsoft Backup" later in this chapter for more information.

† Note that the "System Restore" feature included in Windows Me has little to do with restoring data from a backup. See "Disabling System File Protection" earlier in this chapter for details.

Although tape backup software may seem awkward on the surface, it's designed to allow you to perform a backup in a single step and without user intervention. Good backup software will also make restoring easy; the best programs keep catalogs of your backups, allowing you to easily find a single, previously backed-up file and get it back with the least amount of hassle possible.

Now, many manufacturers of the various competing products and technologies market their products as backup devices, which isn't necessarily accurate. Basically, you need to find the system that works best for you and fits in your budget. Do some research before investing in any one technology, and make sure it truly suits your needs for a backup device.

Try this: add the cost of the drive you're considering with the media required to store the entire contents of your hard drive *twice*, and compare it with other solutions. Table 6-1 shows 6 example technologies and the estimated costs associated with each, at the time of this writing, to back up a 10-GB hard drive. These show that initial bargains are rarely good deals.

Table 6-1. The Average Prices for Various Backup Solutions

Technology	Drive Cost	Cartridge Cost	Cartridge Capacity	Cartridges per Backup	Cost of Drive and Two Cartridges
Travan tape drive	$150	$40	20 GB	1 = $40	$230
Rewritable CD-ROM Drive	$200	$5	650 MB	16 = $80	$360
DDS3 (4mm DAT) tape drive	$400	$10	24 GB	1= $10	$420
Zip Drive	$60	$6	100 MB	100 = $600	$660
Jaz Drive	$250	$75	2 GB	5 = $375	$1,000
Floppies	N/A	$0.20	1.4 MB	7,140 = $1,428	$2,856

Naturally, the prices and capabilities of the various technologies will change as quickly as the weather, but the methodology is always the same. Aside from the price, the most important figure to look at is the "Cartridges per backup"; if it's more than one, it means you're going to have to sit and swap cartridges during each backup. If it's that difficult, odds are you'll never do it.

Note also that the reference to the use of a recordable CD-ROM drive specifies *rewritable* CDs. If you were to do a backup with standard gold CDs, although they're much cheaper, you would have to purchase 16 new disks each time you did a backup. See the next section for more reasoning behind having enough media for *two* backups.

Do your research, and it will save you time and money in the long run, not to mention that extra peace of mind.

Installing Microsoft Backup

Some sort of backup software has been included with every version of Windows since Windows 3.1 in 1992. Microsoft Backup, a scaled-down version of the excellent Backup Exec by Seagate Software,* is also included with Windows Me, but Microsoft has not made it easy to find. It's not installed with Windows, it's not available in Add/Remove Programs in Control Panel, and it's not mentioned anywhere in the documentation. But, it is on the disk—here's how you install it:

1. Insert your Windows Me distribution CD, and open Explorer. (Close the annoying welcome screen that appears if you haven't disabled CD-ROM Autorun, as described in Chapter 2.)
2. Navigate to *\add-ons\MSBackup*, and double-click the *Msbexp.exe* file to install Microsoft Backup. Once it has finished installing, you'll have to restart Windows.
3. When Windows restarts, a new icon called **Backup** will be added to your Start Menu, in Programs → Accessories → System Tools.

Although this is a good program, it does lack some of the capabilities of the full-featured software, such as a catalog of all backed-up files, a dedicated scheduler, and support for additional hardware. Catalogs, for example, keep track of all your backups, allowing you to choose a single file to be restored and have the software tell you which tape to insert.

Because most backup devices come with some sort of dedicated backup software, you may never need Microsoft Backup. However, most backup software is really awful, so you should try all the alternatives available to you before committing to a single solution.

* Microsoft made a wise choice when it licensed a scaled-down version of Seagate's Backup Exec utility for inclusion in Windows Me. Backup Exec is an updated version of Arcada Backup for Windows 95 (which Seagate purchased and updated in 1997). This is an excellent program, which actually has a functional restore; it's surprisingly difficult to restore with many other backup programs available today.

It's important to realize that most backup software is proprietary, which means that a program like Seagate Backup Exec won't be able to read a backup made by Hewlett Packard backup software, and vice-versa. If you used Microsoft Backup in Windows 98, you'll most likely want to stick with it in Windows Me.

Tips for a Better Backup

The following tips should help you ensure that you will never be without adequate data protection, whether you've already invested in a backup solution or not:

- The problem with backups is that most people don't do them. A few minutes every couple of weeks is all it takes, and it can save many, many hours in the future. A good time to do a backup is just before lunch, just before you go home (if the computer is at work), or just before you go to bed (if the computer is at home). You can also schedule your backup to occur automatically and repeatedly at any time, although you'll need to leave your computer on for that to work.
- Don't do a backup while you're working on the computer. Your backup program will not be able to reliably back up any files that are in use, and your system will be slower and more likely to crash if you are doing too many things at once.
- Run Scandisk (or Norton Disk Doctor if you have it) before each backup. If any of your files are corrupted, or there's a disk error, it can result in corrupt files being backed up, or even an interrupted backup.
- Maintain at least two sets of backups, alternating media each time you back up. If you back up to tape, for example, use the tape "A" for the first backup, tape "B" for the second backup, and then use tape "A" again. That way, if one of the tapes develops a problem or your backup is interrupted, you'll still have an intact, fairly recent backup.
- Most backup programs allow you to specify a name for the media the first time you use them (or whenever you *initialize* the media), which allows the cataloging feature to tell you on which cartridge a certain file resides.

Make sure each of your tapes or cartridges has a unique name that matches the tape's handwritten label, which will ensure that your software identifies each tape the same way you do. Call your tapes something like "Backup A" and "Backup B," or "Kearney," "Jimbo," and "Nelson." You'll be glad you did when your backup software asks you to insert Jimbo, for example.

- Your backups should not be kept near your computer, and especially not *inside* the computer. If your computer is stolen or if there's a fire, your backups would go with it. Keeping one of the backups (see alternating backups earlier in this list) in your car or somewhere else off-premises is a really good idea. And if you make your living off a computer, you might consider keeping a backup in a safe deposit box.
- Security is also a valid concern. If you password protect your computer, yet leave backup tapes sitting in the drive or in a drawer, anyone could have access to the data you've backed up.
- Most backup utilities designed especially for Windows 9x/Me give you the option of backing up the Registry. You should always take advantage of this feature, because it is a good safeguard, offering better assurance that you'll be able to restore your Registry should the need arise. Of course, any program that backs up the entire Windows folder will also be backing up the Registry files, but where it really comes in handy is the ability to restore the Registry. When Windows is running, you won't be able to overwrite the Registry files directly, so it's nice to have the luxury of a convenient workaround. Note that without a valid Registry backup, all those backed-up applications won't do you any good.
- Don't back up to floppies if you can avoid it. Floppies are *much* more likely to fail than your hard disk, although it's better than no backup at all. Floppies should only be used to transfer information from one computer to another, and that's only if there's no network connection between them.
- Make sure you have a copy of your backup software handy at all times. If you can't install your backup software, you won't be able to access your backups.
- If your backup software provides an "emergency recovery diskette" feature, take advantage of it. This feature helps create a diskette that can, in essence, restore your entire system onto a blank hard disk with the least amount of fuss. For example, recovery diskettes usually include CD-ROM drivers for DOS, allowing you to access your CD-ROM and, therefore, the Windows installer. If you can't install Windows on a new hard disk, you won't be able to get to your backup software or any of your backups.
- Configure your system for unattended backups. Ideally, you should only have to insert a single cartridge and click "Go" to complete a backup. Don't put up with lower-capacity backup devices that require you to swap cartridges in order to do a single backup. Additionally,

most backup software has options to bypass any confirmation screens; by taking advantage of them, you eliminate the possibility of starting a backup before you go home and coming to work the next day only to see the message, "Overwrite the data on tape?"

- Don't bother with incremental backups. Most backup software allows you to do a full-system backup and then supplement it with incremental backups that only store the files that have changed since the last backup. This may mean that you can do some backups in less time, but it also means that you'll have to restore each of those backups when recovering from a disaster—one full backup and ten incremental backups adds up to 11 restores. More importantly, incremental backups require that the original full backup be intact. If something happens to that one backup, all subsequent incremental backups will be rendered completely useless.
- Lastly, test your system; don't wait until it's too late to find that the restore process doesn't work or requires a step you haven't considered. Just do a simple trial backup of a single folder or group of files. Then, try to retrieve the backup to a different drive or folder. Only after you've successfully and completely retrieved a backup, can you truly consider your data safe.

Better Floppy Formats

Diskettes are still the standard, despite the fact that they're unreliable, slow, and small. However, everyone has a floppy drive, the disks are cheap, and it's a great way to transport small amounts of data. Here are some tips when dealing with floppies:

- To avoid a headache, always format every floppy diskette before you use it. It'll take an extra couple of minutes, but it may save you hours in the long run.
- Floppies are very unreliable. They are highly susceptible to dust, damage, and heat, and can turn on you in an instant.
- Open a DOS window to format your floppies. It's faster and more reliable than using Windows' format feature and will give you more free space, as well as yield better multitasking. Just type **`Format`** *`a:`* **`/u`** at the MS-DOS prompt (substituting *`a:`* with the drive letter you wish to format).* The **`/u`** parameter specifies an *unconditional* format,

* Note that the *Format* command in Windows Me no longer supports the `/s` parameter, which used to allow you to make bootable diskettes. See "Make a Startup Disk" later in this chapter for an alternative.

meaning that it won't use up part of the floppy with the unnecessary "unformat" information that the Windows format includes. See Appendix B for more information on DOS commands.

- If, during the format process, there are *any* errors (bad sectors or sectors not found) reported on the diskette, throw it out *immediately*. Disks cost next to nothing, so don't try to save it; if in doubt, throw it out.
- Lastly, *never* use floppies to store any information for more than a few hours; that's what your hard disk is for. A floppy-disk backup, for example, is much more likely to die than your hard disk. Floppies should only be used to install software and transport data from one computer to another. Recordable CDs, for example, are excellent for archiving data. See "Back Up Your Entire System" earlier in this chapter for more information.
- Use Zip files not only to fit more information on each floppy, but also to make files otherwise too large to fit on floppies. The native-Windows WinZip program is easy to use and powerful, but the PKzip DOS utility has the -& parameter, which allows you to span really large files over multiple floppies.
- Windows (and DOS) only allow you to format floppies to their standard 1.44 MB capacity, but it's possible to squeeze more space out of them with distribution media format (DMF). The DMF format can hold about 1.7 MB, but a special utility is required to format DMF diskettes. Programs capable of performing DMF formats include WinImage 2.2 (download from *http://www.annoyances.org*) and Norton Navigator (*http://www.symantec.com*).

Make a Startup Disk

You'll never need a boot disk until your system doesn't start, and then you'll wonder why you never took the three minutes required to make one. A boot disk is just a floppy with a few special files on it, enabling you to start your system if something goes wrong with your hard disk. It's easy, quick, and *very* useful.

A good startup disk should be able to not only boot your computer, but load the necessary drivers to enable you to access your CD-ROM drive. Although Microsoft has disabled some features in Windows Me that otherwise would have allowed you make bootable diskettes from DOS, either of the following solutions should provide the functionality you need:

- Windows Me comes with a feature that will create a startup disk, allowing you to boot directly into DOS with CD-ROM support. Double-click the **Add/Remove Programs** icon in Control Panel, choose the **Startup Disk** tab, and then click **Create Disk**. While it's gathering files for the startup disk, it may prompt you if one or more files can't be located. At this time, simply specify the folder name of the Windows Me installation files, usually **`d:\win9x`**, where **`d:`** is your CD-ROM drive letter.
- Microsoft Backup (see "Installing Microsoft Backup" earlier in this chapter) has a feature that will allow you to make "Emergency Recovery Diskettes." This feature will create a bootable diskette with additional files to assist in reinstalling Windows in order to access the backup software. In Microsoft Backup, select **Recovery Diskettes** from the **Tools** menu. The **Recovery Diskettes** menu item won't be present if Microsoft Backup has not been configured with at least one suitable backup device.

After using either of these methods, test the disk before putting it away so that you don't discover later on that it doesn't work. When you're done, label the disk with today's date, write-protect it, and put it in a safe place.

See "Restoring Windows After a Crash" later in this chapter for details on using your startup disk in case of an emergency.

Protecting Your Hardware

Most of the topics in the latter half of this chapter deal with software issues: protecting your data, creating boot disks, etc. However, there are a few things you can do to reduce the likelihood of problems with your hardware.

All hardware is sensitive to heat, light, dust, and shock. Don't block any vents on your computer or your monitor, and routinely vacuum all around to remove dust (too much dust can cause your components to overheat and your disk drives to fail).

Make sure you have a functioning fan in your computer's power supply and one mounted directly on top of your CPU—an extra fan in front won't hurt, either. If you can't hear your computer, odds are it isn't being adequately cooled. Make sure that air can flow freely inside from the front of the computer to the back; look for a mass of cables blocking the passage of air. Overheated components can cause system crashes, slow performance, and data loss.

If your computer and every external peripheral are connected to a surge protector, the possibility of damage by an electrical surge is virtually eliminated.* Many surge protectors also allow you run your phone cables through them, protecting them from phone line surges that can damage your modem. And if you live in an area susceptible to black-outs, you might consider an uninterruptible power supply (UPS), which eliminates the problem of lost data caused by lost power.

Make sure all your cables are tied neatly behind the computer so pins and plugs don't get broken and plugs don't become loose; pets love to chew on cables, pulling them out and otherwise mangling them. And tighten all those cable thumbscrews.

Clean the ball of your mouse and use a mouse-pad, or if you use a graphics tablet, keep the surface clean. Don't spray glass cleaner on your monitor, but on the paper towel instead. Keep floppies, tapes, and other magnetic cartridges away from your monitor and speakers; they're just big magnets that can turn disks into coasters in no time. Sit up straight—no slouching!

Data Recovery

There are certain measures you can take to restore your system *after* a disaster, although your luck will dramatically improve if you've taken the steps outlined in the previous sections, "Back Up Your Entire System" and "Tips for a Better Backup." The following section covers software; recovering hardware (for example, if it were destroyed in an earthquake) is an entirely different matter, requiring ample insurance or a lot of duct tape.

If you've backed up your system recently, you can proceed to make repairs without worrying about losing the data currently on the hard disk. If you know there are some important files that have been created or modified since the last backup, your first priority is to transfer those files to a floppy or other removable medium before proceeding. Why? Serious hard disk crashes, while infrequent, can result in partial or total data loss. To recover a seriously crashed disk, you may have to format it, which involves erasing it completely.

* I've seen entire computers disabled by a single power surge. Surge protectors, available at any hardware store, are cheap and essential.

The following list describes several different extremes of damage, each with its own symptoms and solutions:

File corruption

If you can't access a certain document or start a certain application (or if you get errors while Windows is booting) but everything else seems to work, the problem is most likely caused by one or more corrupted files. This can almost always be fixed with Scandisk (*Scandisk.exe*). Usually, Scandisk will be able to fix the problem by either repairing the damaged file or marking a small portion of your hard disk as unusable, depending on the severity of the damage.

It's possible, however, for Scandisk to repair the problem without being able to recover the file completely. If this is the case, you'll either need to replace the files or reinstall the application to which the files belong. If the corrupted file is a personal document and you don't have a backup, you're out of luck.

Registry error

This can involve either corruption of one of the files that make up the Registry or an errant setting in the Registry that may be causing a serious problem. Either way, you can use the built-in Registry Checker, as described in Chapter 3, to restore previous versions of your Registry. Because new backups are made every time you restart your computer, make sure to restore the Registry immediately if you suspect a problem, so that a good backup isn't overwritten with a bad one.

Disk error

A disk error is a physical defect on your disk, often called a bad sector. This manifests itself by something as benign as an occasional read error or something as serious as your computer's hanging whenever a particular file or group of files is accessed.

Your hard disk will likely never develop bad sectors, but floppies and removable disks are more susceptible to shock, dust, and other sources of physical damage that can lead to bad sectors. Although every new hard disk comes with some bad sectors, all of them are marked as bad before the disk leaves the factory, meaning that they're never used. But if the number of bad sectors continually increases over a short period of time, it usually means the drive—or the controller—needs to be replaced. If a floppy or removable cartridge similarly develops bad sectors, you should not only discard it, but also investigate the drive itself for problems.

The Scandisk utility is able to find most bad sectors and mark them as unusable, and if you have Norton Disk Doctor, that's even better. Both of these programs will move any files located on the bad sectors so that they reside on good sectors. Unfortunately, if a file resides on a bad sector, odds are that it is irreparably damaged and should be deleted and replaced with an intact copy.

If your hard disk starts to develop a lot of bad sectors, you'll want to format the drive completely (after backing up all your data), which should help determine if the problem is permanent or temporary. If the problem doesn't go away, you should replace the drive immediately. Otherwise, you most likely have fixed the problem.

"Sector not found," invalid directory entries, or other errors where you see gibberish instead of filenames

This usually means that your hard disk needs to be reformatted, but probably not replaced. Try to back up as many files as you can as quickly as possible; this type of problem tends to "grow" quickly. Once you've recovered as much as you can (if applicable), reformat the drive and start refilling it. If the drive in question is where Windows is located, you'll need to have a Startup Disk (see "Make a Startup Disk" earlier in this chapter) before you can fix the problem. If you have Norton Disk Doctor, you may be able to repair the directory structure without reformatting. Note that Scandisk is usually not up to the task of fixing this type of problem, although it may be worth a try.

Disk crash

If your hard disk has crashed, you most likely can't even get it to turn on. A common symptom is that your computer won't boot unless you disconnect the hard disk from the controller. Old hard drives can simply die, another good reason to back up often. There's not much you can do at this point, but the manufacturer of the hard drive, or even a professional data-recovery business (which have a very high success rate), may be able to recover some or all of your data.

Be careful here, because it's possible to make your data non-recoverable by trying to recover it yourself. If you suspect a serious problem and have valuable data on the disk, you should shut off the system and remove the drive immediately. *Don't* start the system again just to "see if it boots this time"; it may further damage your data or even make the disk unrecoverable.

Once you've solved whatever caused the problem in the first place, if you're fortunate enough to have a good backup, you can proceed to restore your data onto your repaired or newly purchased hard drive. See the next section, "Restoring Windows After a Crash," for the next step.

Restoring Windows After a Crash

The purpose of backing up is to give you the opportunity to restore your system to its original state if something unforeseen should happen to your hard disk, whether it be theft, fire, malfunction, or just user error. You'd be surprised at how many people back up their system without having any idea how to restore it later should the need arise. The backup doesn't do you any good if you can't get at your files later, so it's important to take steps to make sure you can restore your system *from scratch* if necessary.

The most important consideration is that the software you use to restore your files be the same one you used to back them up. That means that if you back up your hard disk with Windows software and your hard disk crashes, you'll have to reinstall Windows *as well as* your backup software from their original distribution disks before you can restore anything else.

Now, reinstalling Windows doesn't necessarily mean that you lose your Windows preferences and must reinstall all your applications. The idea is to reinstall Windows (as well as the drivers for your backup device, if necessary) to a state sufficient only to run your backup software. Sometimes, this isn't necessary; it just depends on what your backup software requires.

The following procedure specifically covers Microsoft Backup, although the general principles should be the same for any modern backup software. Naturally, use your best judgment, because your situation might be different. It's probably a good idea to familiarize yourself with the following procedure *before* you actually have to use it; that way, you can better prepare yourself and minimize the headache.

The first four steps involve starting from scratch with an empty hard disk, useful if you've just formatted or replaced your old drive. You'll probably want to skip the first two steps if you're not installing onto a clean system:

1. If you've taken the time to create a Windows Startup Disk or a Microsoft Backup Emergency Recovery Disk (see "Make a Startup Disk" earlier in this chapter), now is the time to use them. Either of these disks will allow you to boot into DOS so that you can prepare your hard disk and reinstall Windows.

If you don't have one of these disks and you have the version of Windows Me designed for new computers, you'll have to install Windows from scratch using the included boot diskette. If you have an upgrade of Windows Me, you'll have to go back to Windows 98 or whatever operating system you were using previously to create a bootable system on which you can then install Windows Me.

2. Once you've successfully started DOS with whatever startup disk you have, the next step is to install Windows.* Assuming *d:* is the drive letter for your CD-ROM drive, just type the following commands to install Windows from the command prompt:

```
d:
cd win9x
setup
```

3. When prompted for an installation folder, you may not want to install Windows into the same folder in which it is installed in your backup. Instead, choose a temporary Windows directory, such as *c:\just4now*. That way, during the restore process, you can restore the Windows directory completely, without being bothered by errors stating that certain Windows files can't be replaced because they're in use.
4. After Windows has been successfully installed, the last step is to load any extra drivers required by your backup device. For example, for SCSI tape drives, you may need special SCSI drivers. Consult the documentation that came with your drive and (if applicable) your controller for the appropriate drivers.
5. The next step is to fire up Microsoft Backup, select the **Restore** tab, and choose your backup device from the **Restore From** list. If you don't see your tape drive or other device listed here, it means you haven't installed all the proper drivers.
6. If you don't see the contents of your last backup in the lower-left pane after selecting the correct backup device, click **Refresh**. Assuming you want to restore everything, simply check the box next to drive *C:* (or next to each drive letter, if there's more than one). Each check mark next to a drive will select all of the folders and files on that drive to be restored. Click **Start** when you're ready.

* Because the *Format* command in DOS has been hobbled so that it can no longer create a bootable floppy, you will be unable to make a hard disk bootable with the old *Format* or *sys* commands in DOS. Instead, your hard disk will be made bootable as part of the Windows Me installation process.

7. If all goes well, your backup utility will completely restore the contents of your drive. If you run out of disk space because of the extra, temporary installation of Windows, you'll want to only restore some of the files—say, just the true Windows installation and a few essentials. You'll then be able to restart the good version of Windows (see the next step), delete the temporary installation, and proceed to restore the rest of your system.
8. This restore process should include the *Msdos.sys* file, which must be restored into the root directory of your bootable hard disk (usually *c:*). This file is read by the operating system when Windows first starts and specifies the location of your Windows files. Before the restore, the file should point to your *c:\just4now* directory (or whatever you've called it). After the file has been replaced with the version on tape, it should correctly point to the version of Windows that has been restored as well (usually *c:\windows*). This means that the next time you restart, the permanent version of Windows should automatically load. At this point, you can delete the entire *c:\just4now* branch by dragging it into the Recycle Bin.
9. Your hard disk should be completely restored at this point. You should run Scandisk (*Scandskw.exe*) one last time just to check for any residual errors.

7

Networking and Internetworking

A network is the interconnection of two or more computers, facilitating the exchange of information between them. Networks aren't just for large companies; you can network two computers in your home to share a single Internet connection, share a printer, more easily exchange files, or even play a networked game. Networking, whether it's between two computers in the same room or two computers on opposite ends of the Earth, can open a host of possibilities not feasible on a standalone system.

There are several different kinds of networks, each with their own limitations and advantages. A simple workgroup can comprise as few as two computers connected with a single cable (often called a peer-to-peer network). This is ideal in a home office or small business setting, where individual systems can be linked together with a minimum of hardware and cabling and configured to *share* resources. A shared folder, for example, is merely a standard folder residing on a single computer, made accessible to any other computer on the network through Explorer as though it were actually on each computer's hard disk.

Larger organizations typically deploy networks based on the *client/server* topology. Client/server networks are different from peer-to-peer networks not so much in technology as in the roles the different computers play. For example, one computer on the network, which might be running Unix or Windows NT, would take on the role of the server; it would be configured to handle such tasks as email, printing, storage of data and applications, backup, user authentication, and administration (allowing configuration and maintenance of the whole network from a single workstation).

A seemingly different kind of connection, usually involving a measly telephone line or more modern high-speed connection, allows access to the Internet from a single PC. It can get more complicated, say, if you want to connect a workgroup to the Internet or create a workgroup *across* the Internet, which involves the combination of several different technologies and can be very interesting.

Windows supports most types of networking out of the box, but the actual process involved in setting up a given form of networking can be quite confusing, and troubleshooting a network can drive you nuts.

Now, many of you may be wondering what practical use networking has to someone who only has one computer or is not interested in connecting to the Internet. In some cases, networking will be of absolutely no use to you; just move on, or, better yet, go outside and get some fresh air. However, networking offers some interesting advantages, often more interesting than an office workgroup configured to share a printer. Multiplayer games, for one, may be enough of a reason to fuss with networking. Or if you have a portable and a desktop computer, networking can be a very fast and convenient method for transferring files and printing. So don't rule out a network just yet.

To start building a network, you should understand the distinction between local and remote resources. A *local resource* (such as a directory or printer) is one that resides on or is physically connected to your own computer. Conversely, a *remote resource* is one that resides on another computer connected to yours over a network. For example, a particular web page on *http://www.annoyances.org* is a remote file; an HTML file on your own hard disk is a local file. Both may look the same in your browser, but each has its own unique limitations and capabilities.* Naturally, what's local to you may be remote to someone else on a network.

A network is built by installing hardware and configuring various network protocols, most of which are named for cryptic acronyms. By combining different sets of protocols and binding them to the adapter you wish to use, you can enable different kinds of communication. By *binding* a protocol (a standard language two devices can use to communicate with

* One of the problems with the whole concept of web integration (discussed in Chapter 8, *Taking Control of Web Integration*) is the attempt to blur the distinction between local and remote information and resources. By making your local folders appear as though they are web pages, for example, Microsoft has forced an infelicitous interface upon something we use every day.

one another) to, say, a network card, you're telling Windows that you wish to transmit data using said protocol across the connection established by the network card.

Double-click on the **Network** icon in Control Panel to show the **Network Properties** window, which lists all of the adapters and protocols installed on your system at any given time. Figure 7-4, later in this chapter, shows a typical assortment of two adapters and one protocol. Notice that there are two instances of the TCP/IP protocol, each bound to a different adapter. The Dial-Up Adapter driver and the TCP/IP protocol bound to it allow an Internet connection over a standard telephone line. The network adapter (a 3COM Cardbus PC Card, in this case) and the corresponding TCP/IP protocol facilitate not only a local connection to a workgroup, but a shared Internet connection from another computer in the workgroup. In other words, this short list of drivers is enough to enable three different kinds of network connections. Each of these connections is discussed, respectively, in "Setting Up a Workgroup," "Connecting to the Internet," and "Sharing an Internet Connection on a Workgroup," all appearing later in this chapter.

What this comes down to is that installing the right protocols and drivers is important to getting your network to function. The problem is that Windows doesn't necessarily do this for you. In many cases, the drivers and protocols required for a particular type of network connection aren't installed automatically, and other drivers and protocols you don't need are loaded in their place.

Obviously, there's more to setting up, troubleshooting, and maintaining a network than having the right protocols installed, but it's at least half the battle. Now, this book only touches the surface of a large and complex topic, but it should help you get a handle on the drivers, hardware, and cabling required to set up some of the more common types of networks quickly and painlessly. Maybe, once all the frustrations are whisked away, you might even have some fun.

Setting Up a Workgroup

Connecting two computers to form a basic peer-to-peer workgroup is remarkably easy with Windows Me, as long as you have the proper equipment, drivers, and an hour or two. Ideally, you should be able to set up a functioning workgroup in less than ten minutes, but that doesn't include fishing for drivers, resolving hardware conflicts, or running a cable through your attic.

Although there are many types of local-area networks, network adapters, drivers, and operating systems, we'll be dealing only with the most basic peer-to-peer workgroup and using only the software that came with Windows and some inexpensive 10base-T Ethernet hardware.

To set up a workgroup across two computers, you'll need the following:

- Two computers, each running some version of Windows. It's possible to network two systems running different versions of Windows,* although for the sake of simplicity, we'll assume that you're using Windows Me on both. Although the methodology will be the same for other versions of Windows, the locations of the windows and the names of the buttons will differ.
- Two Plug-and-Play network cards, either PCI for desktop systems or Cardbus for laptops. You should be able to find cheap adapters at your local computer store; more expensive cards may provide extra features or a wider assortment of connectors, but the most important thing is that they have connectors that match each other, as well as the other components (i.e., the hub and cables) you will be using. See "Fine-Tuning and Upgrading Hardware Components" in Chapter 5, *Maximizing Performance*, for more information on selecting network cards.
- A hub and two network cables. The cables should be category-5 patch cables, each long enough to connect the corresponding computers to the hub. Typically, the hub would reside next to one of the computers, but that's not essential. Figure 7-1 shows a typical hub-based workgroup.

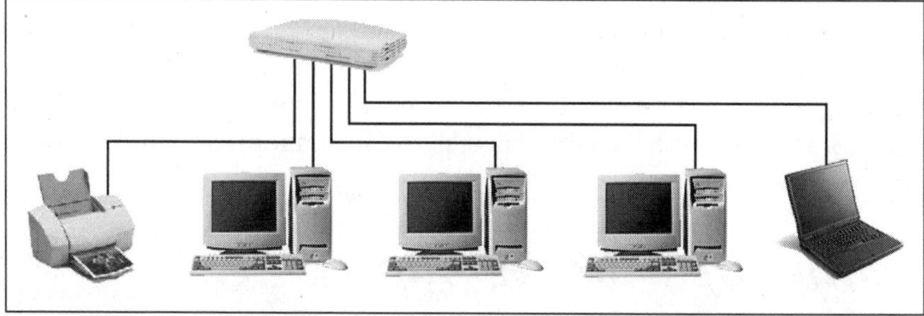

Figure 7-1. A typical workgroup with four computers and a printer all connected to a hub

* It's even possible to network a Windows machine to a Mac or Linux machine, as long as you use the same protocols on all machines.

It's actually possible to eliminate the hub, instead connecting the two computers directly to one another with a single category-5 *crossover* cable. Although this is certainly less expensive, it can be harder to troubleshoot and won't accommodate a third computer or some types of Internet connections.* Figure 7-2 shows a typical two-computer workgroup with the two machines connected with a single cable; the printer is connected to only one of the machines but is shared across the network, allowing either computer to print to it.

Figure 7-2. A typical hubless workgroup

Another alternative is to skip the cables altogether, instead investing in a wireless solution. Wireless networking is much more expensive, but may help to eliminate complex wiring headaches. Figure 7-3 shows an example where wireless technology is used to extend a wired workgroup.

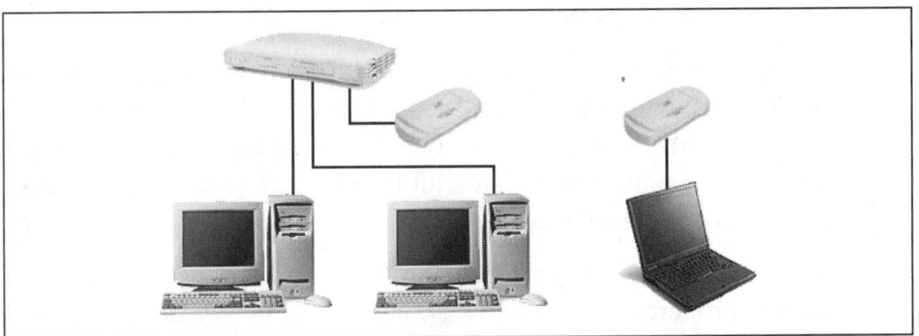

Figure 7-3. You can make an entire workgroup using wireless technology or, as shown here, simply extend a wired workgroup with wireless components

Once you have all of the components, continue to the next procedure. Naturally, different types of hardware will require a modified procedure, but the methodology is the same.

Networking

* See "Sharing an Internet Connection on a Workgroup" later in this chapter for details.

Part 1: Installing the Hardware and Drivers

1. Install a network adapter in each computer, according to the instructions that accompany your hardware. If you're using Plug-and-Play adapters, Windows should automatically install and configure the drivers for the adapters.
2. *Before* bothering with the cabling or drivers, make sure Windows recognizes your network cards in Device Manager and doesn't report any conflicts. Double-click on the **System** icon in Control Panel, choose the **Device Manager** tab, and expand the **Network adapters** branch. If there's a yellow or red smudge over the icon for your network adapter, Windows has encountered a problem with either the hardware or its driver.

   Most network installation problems are caused by hardware conflicts; eliminating them now, before the other components are added, will save a lot of frustration later on. Most network adapters even come with special diagnostic software for this purpose; I strongly recommend using such software now, even if you don't suspect a problem. See "General Troubleshooting Techniques" in Chapter 6, *Troubleshooting*, for more information on hardware conflicts.

Part 2: Setting Up the Protocols

The next step is to configure Windows with the proper protocols and settings. Note that Windows Me will insist that you restart your computer after you make any changes to the network settings. Although you can postpone a restart until you've made all the changes you intend to make, you won't be able to test the results until you've restarted:

1. Double-click on the **Network** icon in Control Panel to view the **Network Properties** window, as shown in Figure 7-4. If the network adapter you installed in the previous section does not show up here, then you're not ready to proceed. Note that your hub or any other external network components will not show up in this window.

   In addition to the entry for your adapter, the following must also be present:

   — Client for Microsoft Networks (a "client")

   — File and Printer Sharing for Microsoft Networks (a "service")

   If either entry is not there, click **Add**, and choose the appropriate items from the list. If more than one manufacturer is shown, choose **Microsoft**.

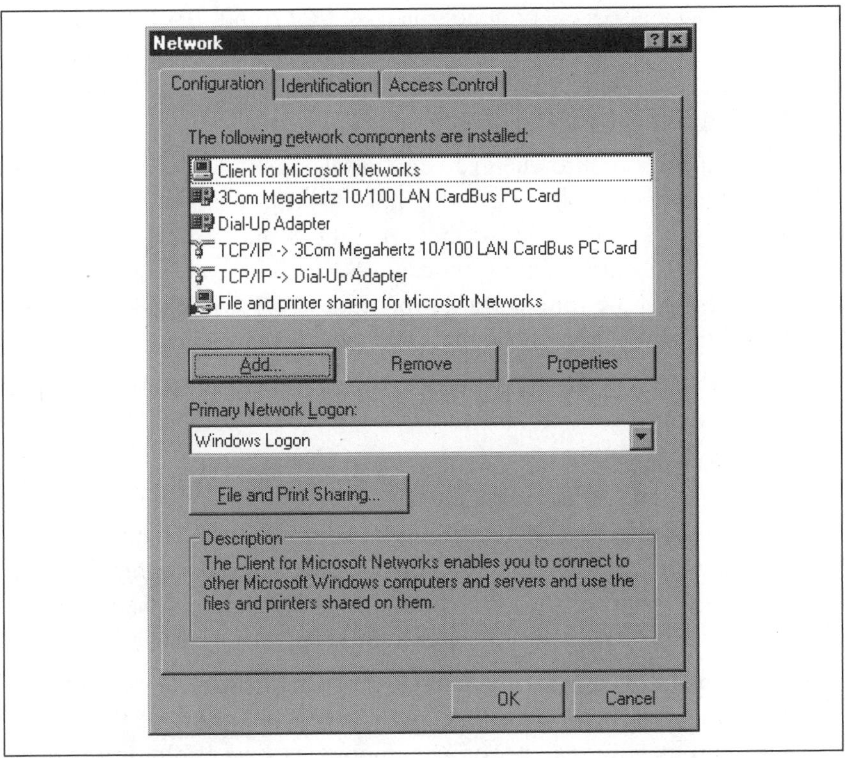

Figure 7-4. This typical Network Properties window lists the drivers capable of sustaining three different network connections

2. Typically, the only protocol you'll need is TCP/IP. Although Microsoft describes TCP/IP as "the protocol you use to connect to the Internet and wide-area networks," it's perfectly suitable for a small, local workgroup as well.

   If you don't see TCP/IP in the list, click **Add**, choose **Protocol** from the list, and then click **Add** again. Select **Microsoft** from the list on the left, and then **TCP/IP** from the list on the right. When you click **OK**, the window will appear frozen for a few seconds until the new entry appears in the **Network Properties** window. If you have more than one adapter installed, an instance of TCP/IP will be automatically added for each adapter.

3. Figure 7-4 shows two instances of the TCP/IP protocol, each bound to a different adapter (shown by the arrow). The first one, pointing to the physical network adapter, is the one that concerns us here. The second, bound to the Dial-Up Adapter (a virtual adapter), is discussed in "Connecting to the Internet" later in this chapter.

You might also see protocols like *NetBEUI* and *IPX/SPX*, although neither of these is likely to be necessary for the most basic workgroup setup. What you decide to do with your network will dictate the particular protocols you'll need to have installed.

Generally, it's best to eliminate any installed network components that you don't need, both to avoid conflicts and to improve performance. Unless you know you need them, go ahead and remove the *NetBEUI* and *IPX/SPX* entries now (you can always add them again later). You can also remove one instance of a protocol without affecting the other, but we'll hold off on that until the network is up and running.

4. In most cases, you won't need to set any properties for any of the components listed here, instead letting Windows set the defaults.

   One exception to this involves the properties of some network adapters—see "Troubleshooting a Workgroup" later in this chapter for details. Another exception involves the properties of one or more instances of the TCP/IP protocol, the place you'd configure the IP address of your adapter for some types of Internet connections—see "Connecting to the Internet" later in this chapter for details.

   If you need to reset the properties of any particular component listed here, the easiest and most effective method is to remove the component and then reinstall it. For all components, except physical network adapters, this would be done with the **Remove** and **Add** buttons, respectively.

Part 3: Other Network Properties

Once you're done specifying the various drivers and protocols, there are a few more options you need to set in the Network Properties window before you close it:

1. From the **Primary Network Logon** list, select **Windows Logon**. Then click **File and Print Sharing**, turn on both options, and click **OK**.
2. Next, choose the **Identification** tab. In the first field, **Computer name**, type a unique, descriptive name (no spaces) for your computer. This name will be what Windows uses to identify your computer; it is what will appear in the *My Network Places* folder on all the computers in the workgroup. No two computers in your workgroup should have the same computer name.

3. Conversely, the **Workgroup** name should be the same for all computers in your workgroup. Larger networks may have multiple workgroups for organizational purposes. You can access any computer, whether or not it shares the same workgroup you do, although accessing shared resources (see the next section) is easier between computers in the same workgroup.

   If you're not feeling that creative, you can simply type **`workgroup`** here. If your workgroup is at home, you could simply use your last name for the workgroup and name each computer after the person to whom it belongs.

4. Choose the **Access Control** tab, and make sure **Share-level access control** is selected. Click **OK**, when you're done, and Windows will restart your computer.

Part 4: The Art of Cabling

Cabling is certainly easier said than done. See Figures 7-1, 7-2, and 7-3 for some example setups. Here are some tips that should help with most cabling issues:

- Connect all your cables while your hub and any other pieces of equipment are turned on and while Windows is running.
- Make sure to use only category-5 patch cables, except under the following conditions. A category-5 crossover cable should be used instead to connect two computers directly (if you don't have a hub) and can also be used to connect two hubs together. In some cases where a Digital Subscriber Line (DSL) adapter or cable modem connects directly to a computer with a patch cable, a crossover cable would be required to connect either of these devices to a hub (naturally, consult the documentation to be sure).
- Most network devices have lights to indicate an active connection.* Within a second or two of connecting both ends of a network cable, the corresponding lights on your hardware should light up. This is where it's really nice to have a hub: the hub will show a light for each correctly connected computer, printer, or other device, which makes troubleshooting that much easier. Note that the lights only confirm that the cabling is correct; they won't tell you if the drivers and protocols are correctly installed.

* Lights should be visible right on the network adapter, whether it's in the back of your desktop computer or in the side of your laptop. If you are using a laptop and your network adapter requires a dongle, the light may be on the adapter or on the dongle.

- Bad cables are not uncommon, so have a few extra cables around in case one or more of those lights don't light up.
- When measuring for cables, always add several extra feet to each cable; too long is better than too short.*
- Use a different color cable for each computer to make troubleshooting easier.
- If your cables are to pass through walls, it's possible to install category-5 wall jacks for the tidiest appearance. However, these accessories can be very expensive and may be unnecessary for a small home network.
- If cabling poses a significant hurdle, you might want to consider either a wireless solution or a *phoneline* solution (which uses your existing phone line wiring to connect computers). These technologies tend to be more expensive than standard Ethernet hardware, but the extra cost may offset the frustrations of pulling cable through walls and Mexican tile floors.
- In theory, once you have successfully completed your cabling, the network should be active immediately, and you should be able to start sharing resources (see the following section). However, if you encounter problems, try restarting one or all of your machines to force them to recognize the new network.

Part 5: Using Shared Resources

Every computer connected to your workgroup is accessible through the *My Network Places* folder.† However, only those drives and folders that are intentionally and specifically *shared* will be visible across the network.

By default, the *My Network Places* folder contains the following three items:

Entire Network

This folder contains all the workgroups available to your computer at any given time; in most cases, there will be only one. Open a workgroup folder to see all the computers in that workgroup; open a computer to see all the shared drives and folders in that computer.

* Shop around when looking for cables. Most of the huge mega-computer stores charge too much for cables; you can often find longer cables at a fraction of the price by shopping at smaller mom-and-pop computer stores.

† The My Network Places icon will appear on your desktop if you have any network drivers installed. If you want to hide it or if it does not appear on your desktop, see "Clear the Desktop of Unwanted Icons" in Chapter 4, *Tinkering Techniques*.

Add Network Place

This tool allows you to add links to frequently accessed shared folders and drives, which will appear directly in the *My Network Places* folder. You can also use this tool to link to an FTP site (see "Accessing an FTP Site in Explorer" later in this chapter) or a Web folder.*

If you're accustomed to previous versions of Windows, *My Network Places* is the replacement for the *Network Neighborhood.* Unfortunately, Microsoft has made this window less convenient than in previous versions by removing the links to other computers in your workgroup, forcing you to manually create the links you need with this tool.

Items added to the *My Network Places* folder with **Add Network Place** are actually just "Folder Shortcuts" stored in the *\Windows\Nethood* folder. See "Mirror a Folder with Folder Shortcuts" in Chapter 4 for more information.

Home Networking Wizard

This is another tool designed to walk you through the process of setting up a small workgroup. Unfortunately, this program is cumbersome and unnecessarily complex, so it's unlikely you'll find it too useful. Luckily, the icon is only a shortcut to the application and can be easily and safely deleted by right-clicking on it and selecting **Delete**.

Now, before you access any network resources, you must configure those resources to be shared on the network. You can share any drive, folder, or printer on your computer. Once you share a folder, for example, any other computer in your workgroup will have access to that folder through its *My Network Places* folder, so you may only choose to share certain designated folders. If security is not much of a concern, such as on a workgroup at home, you can share all your drives without worry:

1. Open Explorer, and locate the printer, drive, or folder you wish to make available to the other computers in the workgroup.
2. Right-click on the drive, folder, or printer icon, and select **Sharing**. Figure 7-5 shows the **Sharing** dialog box for a drive or folder; the **Sharing** dialog box for a printer is similar but has fewer options.

   If you don't see a **Sharing** option, your networking components haven't been installed properly, as described in the preceding sections.

* Web folders are a relatively new feature, supported by Windows Me and Windows 2000 and intended to make transferring web pages to a web server easier. It's unlikely you'll have any use for this feature, unless your company or Internet service provider specifically supports Web folders.

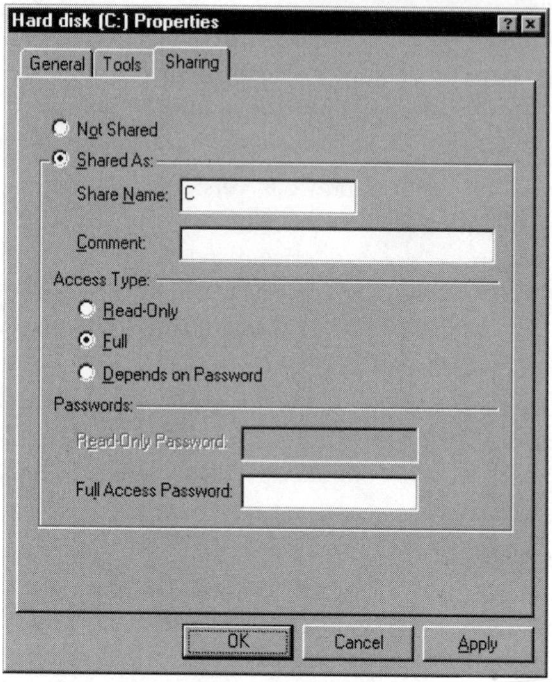

Figure 7-5. Right-click on a drive, folder, or printer, and select Sharing to choose how the resource will be shared in a workgroup

3. To enable sharing for the resource, change the option at the top of the window from **Not Shared** to **Shared As**.

4. Type a name for the resource in the **Share Name** field; this is the name that Windows will use to reference the resource and is what will show up in the *My Network Places* folder.

   In most cases, you'll want the **Share Name** to be the same as the resource being shared; it can be very confusing if they're too different. For example, drive *C:* would be shared as `C` and the *My Documents* folder would simply be shared as `My Documents`. If you're sharing a lot of resources or have a lot of computers in the workgroup, you may want to take the time to be more descriptive here, perhaps even using the **Comment** field.

   For drives and folders, you can select an **Access Type** option, a rudimentary security measure. If security is not an issue, you'll probably want **Full**.

The default setting, **Read-Only**, won't allow users on remote computers to change or delete any files or folders on the shared drive but will still allow them to read and copy them. The **Depends on Password** setting allows you to configure up to two levels of password protection to the resource. For example, you could enter a password in the **Full Access Password** field and leave the **Read-only Password** field blank, giving everyone read access but only privileged users write access to your data.

If your computer is connected to a high-speed Internet connection (anything other than an ordinary dial-up connection), you'll most likely want to use the **Depends on Password** option to help prevent unauthorized snooping. Fortunately, when password-protected resources are accessed by authorized users, Windows can remember the password, eliminating the need to enter it every time.

It's important to realize that there is simply no functionality included with Windows Me that can provide anything near the kind of security found in Unix, Windows 2000, or a third-party firewall solution. Now, the actual risk of sharing your drives on a computer with an Internet connection, while genuine, is not necessarily as much of a threat as the companies who make firewall solutions would lead you to believe.

The best thing you can do to reduce your risk is to double-click on the **Network** icon in Explorer, highlight the TCP/IP entry that points to your Internet connection adapter, and click **Properties**. Choose the **Bindings** tab, uncheck the **File and Printer sharing for Microsoft Networks** and **Client for Microsoft Networks** options, and click **OK**.

5. A few seconds after you press **OK**, a tiny, blue hand icon will appear over the resource's icon in Explorer, signifying that the resource is now being shared.

   You can share as many drives or individual folders as you like. I find it convenient to share each hard disk, as well as the desktop folder on each computer. To share the desktop folder, you won't be able to right-click on the Desktop entry at the top of the tree in Explorer—you'll instead have to navigate to the actual Desktop folder (usually *\Windows\Desktop*) and turn on sharing for that item.

   If you're sharing a printer, the printer's icon can be found in the *Printers* folder in Control Panel. Note that some printers don't support being shared—consult the documentation that comes with your printer for details.

6. A shared drive or folder should show up immediately in the *Entire Network* folder in *My Network Places*. You'll be able to use shared files and folders from any computer in the workgroup as though they were stored right on the computer's hard drive. If you don't see a newly shared resource, press the **F5** key to refresh the display.

7. Printers, on the other hand, won't show up automatically. After you've shared a printer, you need to set up the printer on each *remote* computer from which you wish to print (nothing further will have to be done to the host, the computer physically connected to the printer).

   Double-click the **Printers** icon in Control Panel, and then double-click **Add Printer**. Click **Next**, choose **Network printer** when asked, and then click **Next** again. Click **Browse** to navigate your workgroup's shared resources; the printer will show up in the folder named for the computer to which it is physically connected. Highlight the printer, click **OK**, and then click **Next**. When prompted for a printer name, type a name that most closely matches the name as it appears on other computers (to avoid confusion), and click **Next**. When you finish the wizard, Windows will copy all of the driver files over the network. If, at this point, you encounter an error, it's likely that the printer's driver doesn't support being shared.*

8. To disable sharing for any resource, simply reopen the **Sharing** window, and select the **Not Shared** option.

Naturally, a computer that contains a shared file, folder, or printer must be turned on for those resources to be available to others on the network.

Part 6: Mapping Drives

If you access a shared network folder or drive, you can also *map* that resource so that it appears as yet another drive letter in Explorer. This allows you to access the remote drive or folder without having to wade through the *My Network Places* folder, which can be cumbersome. Not only is this useful for allowing quicker access to frequently used network drives, but it's a necessity if you need to access a network drive from a DOS application, a batch file, or an older Windows application.

* This is a limitation of the driver that comes with some less expensive or older printers. Visit the web site of the printer manufacturer to see if there's a newer driver or hardware add-on that will enable network printing.

Note that if all you're after is quick access to remote folders, it's easier to simply make Windows shortcuts and place them on your desktop or other convenient location:

1. If you haven't done so already, share a drive or folder on any computer on your workgroup—see the previous section, "Part 5: Using Shared Resources." for details.
2. Select **Map Network Drive** from Explorer's **Tools** menu; you'll see the **Map Network Drive** dialog box shown in Figure 7-6.

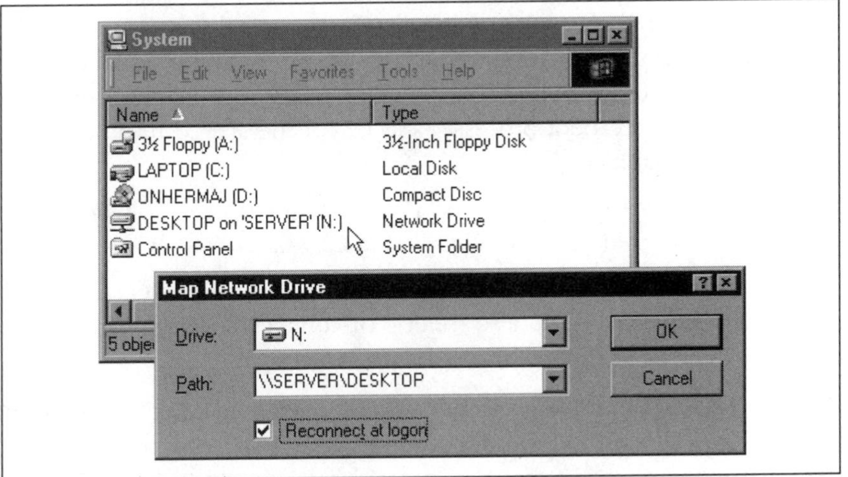

Figure 7-6. Mapping a remote drive to a new drive letter allows you to access remote resources without using My Network Places

If you work with a lot of shared drives on a regular basis, you can add buttons to Explorer's toolbar to make this easier. Select **Toolbars** and then **Customize** from the **View** menu, and then add the **Map drive** and **Disconnect** buttons to the current toolbar.

3. Choose a drive letter for the new mapping—one that isn't currently being used by a hard disk, CD-ROM drive, or other storage device. I find it convenient to use *N:* for this purpose, although any free drive letter is acceptable.
4. The next step is to select an existing shared drive or folder to hook up with the mapped drive letter. Unfortunately, Windows Me doesn't allow you to browse the network for shared devices here, so you'll have to type them in manually. You can open up the *My Network Places* folder on the side for reference.

For example, assuming a remote computer is called *SERVER* and the shared folder you want to map is shared as *DESKTOP*,* you'd type the following in the **Path** field:

```
\\SERVER\DESKTOP
```

Note the two backslashes before the computer name and only one between the computer name and the shared resource name. The drop-down list conveniently contains a history of the last few mapped network paths.

5. Lastly, turn on the **Reconnect at logon** option if you want Windows to map this drive every time you start Windows; otherwise, you'll have to do it manually each time (the default is *off* here). Note that having Windows automatically reconnect mapped drives at startup can significantly slow the boot process, especially if the shared resource is not always available.
6. Click **OK** when you're done. The new drive letter will appear in Explorer immediately, as shown in Figure 7-6.
7. To unmap a network drive, right-click on the drive letter, and select **Disconnect**. You can also select **Disconnect Network Drive** from Explorer's **Tools** menu.

Note that only shared drives and folders can be mapped; printers, of course, cannot. See the previous section, "Part 5: Using Shared Resources," for information on using shared printers. See "Networking with Scripts" in Chapter 9, *Scripting and Automation*, for details on mapping and unmapping drives automatically with scripts.

Troubleshooting a Workgroup

Several things can cause a network not to work. Try some of the following suggestions to alleviate some network problems you may be experiencing:

- Heed the advice at the beginning of Chapter 6: restarting your computer will fix 99% of all problems. This is never more true than when diagnosing a networking problem.
- If you can't find the My Network Places icon on your desktop or at the bottom of the tree in Explorer, see "Clear the Desktop of Unwanted Icons" in Chapter 4.

* The shared name is not necessarily the same as the name of the folder, although it usually makes things easier if they match.

- When you access anything over the network, each network card and the hub (if you have one) will have an "activity" light that flashes. Some devices have separate lights for receiving and transmitting data, and some devices have only a single light for all incoming and outgoing communication. Activity lights tend to flash intermittently and irregularly; if they flash regularly, it could be a message from one of the devices that something isn't working.

- To determine if a network connection is being made, try exploring the *Entire Network* folder in *My Network Places*. If the computer you're trying to connect to does *not* show up, the problem could be caused by any of the links of the chain between the two machines: either network card, all the cables, the hub, the drivers, and the protocols.

  If the computer *does* show up, but it hangs (either temporarily or permanently) when you try to access it, it's likely a hardware conflict on either machine or an improperly configured driver or protocol. The best solution is to uninstall all the drivers and protocols, restart Windows, and then reinstall all the drivers and protocols. It could also be an incorrect hardware setting—see the next item for details.

- Some problems are caused by improper hardware settings, usually attributed to the network card itself. Open the **Network Properties** window, highlight your network adapter in the list, click **Properties**, and choose the **Advanced** tab. Choose a property in the list on the left and configure the selected property on the right. Try not to fuss with any settings you don't understand.

  If your network card has more than one type of connector,* the Windows default may be "autodetect," a setting that may impair performance or even cause it to stop working. Change this option so that it matches the connector you're using: for example, choose "coaxial" for 10base-2 cables and RJ-45 for 10base-T cables.

  Another commonly misconfigured setting is the choice between full-duplex, half-duplex, and autodetection. Full duplex is a connection where information can flow in both directions simultaneously; half-duplex only allows unidirectional communication. The wrong setting can cause a network connection to malfunction or just operate very slowly. Try experimenting with different settings.

- If you know the network cards are functioning properly and the network cable is connected properly, try using the diagnostic software that came with your network card (contact the manufacturer of your

* Network cards with more than one type of connector are commonly called "combo" cards.

adapter for more information) to test the card and the connection. If the diagnostic software reports no problems, odds are that you don't have the correct network protocols installed.

- Try replacing one or more of the cables, especially if they're old or their connectors are worn.
- If you see other computers on the network but don't see any shared resources, you may need to refresh the display by pressing the **F5** key. If that doesn't help, check to see if the resources you expect to see listed actually have sharing enabled. Next, click the **File and Print Sharing** button in the **Network Properties** window to make sure file and print sharing is enabled. Lastly, highlight one of your installed protocols, click **Properties**, and choose the **Binding** tab. The **File and printer sharing for Microsoft Networks** entry should be checked here. Repeat for all other installed protocols.
- As with any other hardware, routinely check the web site of the manufacturer of your network cards and hub (if you have one) for updated drivers, troubleshooting tips, and other information. See Chapter 6 for more information.
- In addition to **My Network Places**, you can also use the *net* command in DOS (see Appendix B, *DOS Resurrected*). Open a command prompt window, and type **`net view`** to see all of the machines currently logged on to your network. To see the resources offered by a particular machine, include the name of the machine in the command line. For example, assume you typed **`net view`** and got the following:

```
Servers available in workgroup MY_NETWORK.
Server name          Remark
-----------------------------------------
\\BENJAMIN           Benjamin's computer
\\DOUG               Doug's computer
\\GARY               Gary's computer
The command was completed successfully.
```

Next, type **`net view \\doug`** to list all of the resources shared by Doug's computer:

```
Shared resources at \\DOUG

Sharename    Type        Comment
-------------------------------------------
C            Disk        Doug's Boot Drive
D            Disk        Doug's CD Drive
DESKTOP      Disk        Doug's Desktop Folder
LASERJET     Print       Gary's printer, which Doug stole
The command was completed successfully.
```

One of the advantages here is that all shared resources are listed, instead of just the drives and folders shown in *My Network Places*.

Connecting to the Internet

Windows Me comes with everything you need to connect to the Internet, with the notable exception of an explanation of how to do it properly.

The following topics should cut through the nonsense and let you connect to the Internet in just a few minutes. But first . . .

A Word About the Different Types of Internet Connections

This book is, in essence, a response to all the different questions Windows users ask me on a regular basis. One of the most common questions I get asked is what is really the best type of Internet connection. Here are some thoughts that should give you a little more insight.

If you're connecting through a large company or a university, you may have a high-speed T1 or a T3 line at your disposal, in which case, you're set. There are also some obsolete technologies, such as ISDN and satellite connections, but I won't waste your time with them here. What's left is standard analog dial-up connections, DSL, cable, and wireless—because most home and small-business users will be choosing among these, that's what we'll discuss:

Dial-up
: Dialing into the Internet with an analog modem is, for most of us, the cheapest access available. Most PCs come with a modem, and everyone already has a phone line. The downside is that dial-up connections are slow and unreliable and can sometimes be busy.

DSL (Digital Subscriber Line)
: Offered through your phone company, DSL is the best replacement for a dial-up connection. It's always on, it's generally very reliable, and it can be 20–30 times faster than the fastest 56 Kbps modem connection. Another benefit is that it's provided through your phone lines, which means that you most likely won't have to do any special wiring. It can be expensive, but it's important to put that cost into perspective. Say you're currently spending $20 a month on a dial-up ISP account and another $20 a month on a separate phone line—because DSL may be as low as $40 a month, upgrading is a no-brainer. Probably the biggest downside is that DSL isn't available everywhere.

Cable modem

If DSL isn't available, a cable modem might be your best bet. It's typically not as fast as DSL and can slow down with increased neighborhood traffic, but it's still a whole lot better than a dial-up connection. Like DSL, it's always on and is usually very reliable. The downside is that you may have to do some wiring if you don't already have cable (for your TV) or don't have a cable line already wired to your office. The cost is usually on par with DSL, so the same cost argument applies as earlier.

Wireless

Wireless service (such as *Ricochet*) is typically no faster than a 56K dial-up connection, although some offer ISDN-like speeds (in the neighborhood of 128K). Wireless might be a great option if you're on the road and need to access the Internet frequently. Cost is often not any higher than a dial-up ISP. Wireless may also be a good alternative if DSL and cable aren't available, because it's typically much more reliable than a standard dial-up connection.

Setting up the drivers and protocols

Whether you're dialing in with a modem, sporting a DSL or cable modem, surfing remotely with a wireless connection, or speeding along with a corporate T3 line, connecting a Windows Me computer to the Internet is all about the drivers and protocols. First and foremost, TCP/IP is the primary protocol used to access the Internet. Each type of connection differs only in the hardware used to transport TCP/IP. All that's left is hooking up the hardware and installing the right drivers.

The exception, of course, is Dial-Up Networking—in addition to setting up the hardware and software, you also have to do the actual dialing. See "Dealing with Dialing" later in this chapter for details.

Now, if you're using a proprietary Internet service, such as AOL or MSN, or if your DSL/Cable service requires proprietary software, their instructions certainly supercede the following. However, understanding the basic protocols is essential to troubleshooting and expanding the standard service, regardless of the type of connection.

Here's how to set up a Windows Me system to connect to the Internet:

1. Double-click on the **Network** icon in Control Panel to view the **Network Properties** window. A typical setup is shown in Figure 7-4, earlier in this chapter.
2. You should have a minimum of three installed network components. First, there will be at least one network adapter listed. If you're dialing

into the Internet with an analog modem, that adapter will be the *Dial-Up Adapter* component, a virtual driver that allows your modem to masquerade as a network adapter. Otherwise, there should be an entry for an actual, physical network adapter. If your adapter is not listed here, it has not yet been properly installed. Close this window, and install your network adapter and its driver now.

If you know your network adapter is already installed, double-click on the **System** icon in Control Panel, choose the **Device Manager** tab, and expand the **Network adapters** branch. If there's a yellow or red smudge over the icon for your network adapter, Windows has encountered a problem either with the hardware or with its driver. See Chapter 6 for details.

The exception is the *Dial-Up Adapter*; if it's not there, you'll need to install the Dial-Up Networking component (assuming you've already installed your modem) by closing the **Network Properties** window, double-clicking the **Add/Remove Programs** icon in Control Panel, choosing the **Windows Setup** tab, and turning on the **Dial-Up Networking** component (it's in the **Communications** category).

3. Next, you should have **Client for Microsoft Networks** (a "client") and at least one instance of the **TCP/IP** protocol. See the discussion of adapters and protocols at the beginning of this chapter for more information.

   If either of these entries is missing, click **Add**, and choose the appropriate items from the list. If more than one manufacturer is shown, choose **Microsoft**.

4. If your Internet connection has a static IP address (an address that doesn't change every time you connect to the Internet), highlight the **TCP/IP** entry, and click **Properties**. If you have more than one instance of the **TCP/IP** protocol, use the one that is pointing (bound) to the network adapter you use to access the Internet.

   In this window, fill in the appropriate information, all of which will be provided by your ISP, and click **OK** when you're done.

   If you need to reset the properties of any particular component listed here, the easiest and most effective method is to remove the component and then reinstall it. For all components, except physical network adapters, this would be done with the **Remove** and **Add** buttons, respectively.

5. Click **OK** when you're done, and Windows will restart your computer.

Unless you're using Dial-Up Networking (see later in this section), that's all you'll need to connect to the Internet. Try opening any web page in your web browser to test your connection. See "Troubleshooting an Internet Connection" later in this chapter if you experience any problems.

Using Dial-Up Networking

If you're using Dial-Up Networking, you'll have to complete the following additional steps:

1. Double-click the **Dial-Up Networking** icon in Control Panel, and double-click on the **Make New Connection** icon to create a new Dial-Up Networking connection. If the Internet Connection Wizard appears at this point, get rid of it.
2. Type a name for your connection in the first field. This can be anything, but typing the name of your ISP here is a good idea and can avoid confusion with other possible future connections. Select your modem from the list below (if you have more than one), and click **Configure** to make sure your modem is configured correctly. Make sure the maximum speed is set to at least **115,200**. You might want to leave the speaker volume turned up until you're sure the connection works, at which time it can be silenced by returning to this window. Make sure **Only connect at this speed** is *not* checked, and click **OK** when you're done.
3. Click **Next**, and type in the area code and phone number given to you by your ISP to connect. If necessary, choose the country code from the list below the phone number.
4. Click **Next** and then **Finish**. A new icon with the name you specified should now appear in the Dial-Up Networking window.
5. Right-click on the new connection icon, and select **Properties** to enter additional information. Figure 7-7 shows a connection properties sheet, where you'll see the information you just entered, as well as some additional settings (all of which can be changed if you wish).
6. If your ISP has provided an IP address or DNS (name server) information,[*] choose the **Networking** tab, click **TCP/IP Settings**, and enter the relevant information here. In many cases, all of these fields will simply be left blank. Click **OK** when you're done.

---

[*] DNS is the service responsible for translating domain names, such as *annoyances.org*, into numeric IP addresses, such as 209.133.53.130. If you experience delays when your browser claims to be "looking up" a host, for example, the information in this box could be incorrect.

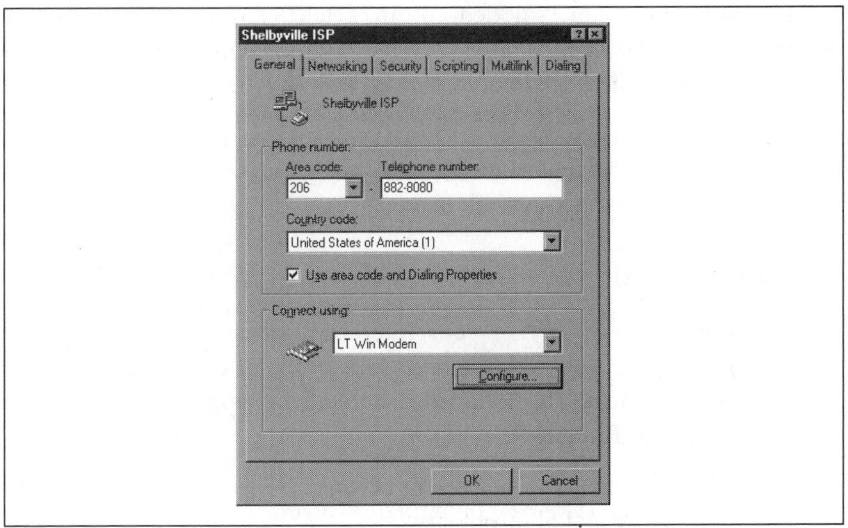

Figure 7-7. Open the Properties window for your dial-up connection to access all the connection settings

7. Next, choose the **Security** tab, and type your username and password in the respective fields—leave the **Domain** field blank (unless you're connecting to a Windows NT domain). Turn on the **Connect automatically** option, but leave all the other **Advanced security options** turned off.
8. The **Scripting** tab is used only if your ISP requires a special login procedure—see "Dial-Up Scripting" later in this chapter for more information.
9. If you have more than one modem and an ISP that supports *Multilink*, a system that allows you to "bind" multiple modems or network adapters together to increase bandwidth for a single Internet connection, you can configure this connection to take advantage of this feature by choosing the **Multilink** tab now and configuring additional modems.
10. Lastly, the **Dialing** tab allows you to set some of the more useful options, such as having it redial until you're connected and having it automatically disconnect when the connection is no longer needed. The options on this page should be self-explanatory.
11. Click **OK** when you're done with all the settings.
12. Double-click the connection icon to dial the connection. If you see the **Connect To** dialog box at this point, you may want to cancel and return to the **Properties** window (see earlier), choose the **Security** tab, and turn on the **Connect automatically** option.

Depending on your modem, it may take anywhere from a few seconds to over a minute to establish a connection. Once a connection is established, a timer will start keeping track of your connect time, and you can start using your Internet software.

See "Dealing with Dialing" later in this chapter for some tips intended for use with dial-up connections.

Troubleshooting an Internet Connection

If your connection or any of your Internet applications don't work or you're experiencing poor performance, the problem could be caused by any number of things. The following should help you get your Internet connection up and running:

- Heed the advice at the beginning of Chapter 6: restarting your computer will fix 99% of all problems.
- One of the most common and easily correctable problems with a dial-up connection involves dialing. If your phone line has call waiting, you'll need to tell Windows to turn it off before dialing; otherwise, any incoming calls can interrupt your connection. To automatically disable call waiting,* double-click the **Telephony** icon in Control Panel, turn on the **To disable call waiting, dial** option, and choose the appropriate code to the right (***70** is the most common—check with your phone company to get the correct code).† If you have a laptop and dial from different locations, you'll want to configure the **Telephony properties** dialog box for each location you use. For example, a location called "Home" may have call waiting disabled, while the location called "Seymour's House" would not.
- A hardware conflict can easily wreak havoc with your connection, whether you use a network adapter or a modem to connect. See Chapter 6 for advice.
- If your connection seems to have gone down, the most important thing to do is to be patient. If the connection is down for a while, check with

* If you try to disable call waiting on a line that doesn't have call waiting, you may not be able to make a call at all (convenient, huh?). If you do configure Windows to disable call waiting, call waiting will be re-enabled the moment you hang up.

† If you experience dialing problems after disabling call waiting, try placing one or two commas after the call waiting code. This forces your modem to wait a few seconds before dialing, giving your line ample time to reset.

your Internet Service Provider (ISP) to see if they've been having trouble with their service or if there's something wrong with your account.

- If you feel your connection is not as fast as it should be, see the next section, "Test Your Throughput," for details.

Test Your Throughput

Throughput is the quantity of data you can transmit over a connection in a given period of time. Now, most types of connections are classified for their throughput; a 33.6 Kbps modem is so-named because at its best, it can transmit and receive 33,600 bits per second. Because there are eight bits to the byte, this connection would give us a theoretical throughput of 4.2 kilobytes per second.

In reality, however, you're not likely to see a throughput any faster than about 3.6 Kbps with this connection. That's a difference of about 14%; a file that you would expect to take a minute to download will actually take 70 seconds. The reason for this discrepancy is that there are other things that get transfered along with your data to and from the modem on the other end of the connection; such things as error correction and lost packets because of noise on the line make the actual throughput lower. Furthermore, your PC's serial port is a bottleneck that may further throttle your connection. Unfortunately, most of the factors that contribute to the throughput are beyond our control.

Faster connections, such as DSL, cable, and T1 connections, are also rated similarly and suffer the same throttling effect. Generally, however, these connections are fast enough that the discrepancy is not as noticeable.

Among those factors within our control are the hardware and software we use and various settings and conditions in which we work (line quality, distance from your ISP, etc.). So it is often advantageous to test the throughput under different conditions.

The simplest way to measure the throughput is to transfer a binary file from your computer to another location and then back again, recording the time it takes to complete the transfer. Just divide the file size by the transfer time to get the throughput, in kilobytes per second.

You won't want to use ASCII files, such as plain-text files and web pages, to test the throughput because your modem's compression will yield uncharacteristic results. Note also that we test the "upload" as well as the "download" speed. Many types of connections are asynchronous; 56 K modems, for example, download at around 53.2 Kbps, but upload at only 33.6 Kbps. Likewise, a midrange DSL connection might be rated at 384 Kbps download and 128 Kbps upload.

The System Monitor utility (*Sysmon.exe*) that comes with Windows Me also allows you to measure your connection throughput, but unfortunately only works with a Dial-Up Networking connection. Select **Add Item** from the **Edit** menu, choose **Dial-Up Adapter** from the list on the left, and highlight these three items: **Bytes Received/Second**, **Bytes Transmitted/Second**, and **Connection Speed**. Click **OK** when you're done—you might want to remove all the other graphs to unclutter the display. The problem with this utility is that it shows the instantaneous throughput, which is not as reliable a result as the average throughput garnered by the real-world test explained previously.

Average throughputs for common connection speeds are shown in Table 7-1. Note that you shouldn't fret if your throughput doesn't exactly match the values in the table. If you find that you're getting substantially slower performance, however, you should test your equipment and cabling and see if there's any software that could be interfering with the connection. A noisy phone line is the most common cause of poor performance of a dial-up connection. See Chapter 5 for solutions on improving overall system performance, most of which will also have a noticeable impact on your connection speed.

Table 7-1. Typical Download and Upload Throughputs for Various Connection Speeds

Connection Method	Expected Throughput (Kbps)
14.4 Kbps modem	1.6 down, 1.6 up
28.8 Kbps modem	3.2 down, 3.2 up
33.6 Kbps modem	3.6 down, 3.6 up
56 Kbps modem	5.4 down, 3.6 up
ISDN (dual channel, 128 Kbps)	14 down, 14 up[a]
Cable Modem (~800 Kbps synchronous)	84 down, 84 up
DSL (asynchronous 1.2 Mbps/384 Kbps)	128 down, 42 up
T1, fast DSL (1.5 Mbps)	160 down, 160 up

[a] These figures represent an internal or network-enabled ISDN adapter. If you have an external ISDN modem connected to a serial port, you'll be limited by the serial port's maximum speed, which is 115.2Kbps, resulting in a maximum throughput of about 11 Kbps.

Dealing with Dialing

Dial-Up Networking differs most from other types of Internet connections in that one must dial to connect, which introduces issues with dialing and managing dial-up connections. The following topics should be helpful in improving your experience with Dial-Up Networking.

Exporting Dial-Up Networking Connections

There's no reason why you should have to open the Dial-Up Networking (DUN) window every time you want to connect to the Internet. Windows allows you to make shortcuts to your connection icons on your desktop or taskbar toolbars or in your Start Menu, just as you can make shortcuts to any other file, folder, or Windows object (such as a Control Panel icon).

The problem is that the process used to make shortcuts to DUN connections is not exactly consistent with the process in other parts of Windows Me. You might expect that if you drag an icon from the Dial-Up Networking folder onto your desktop or into another folder, a shortcut to the connection will be created. Unfortunately, that's not the case—instead, you'll end up with a "Dial-Up Networking Exported File" (with the extension *.dun*).

A Dial-Up Networking Exported File is simply an INI file (see "Using INI Files" in Chapter 3, *The Registry*), which, instead of just being a shortcut to the connection, actually contains all of the properties of the connection, allowing you to then easily copy the connection to another computer by simply copying the file. Once you create an exported file, it becomes a standalone connection; you can modify or delete it without affecting your original connection, and, of course, you can dial with it.

These may seem more useful than traditional shortcuts, but they have drawbacks. For example, if you make a change to the properties of one of your connections in the DUN window, those changes will not be reflected in exported files made from those connections. This means you'll have to re-export your exported file every time you make a change of any kind, such as to the phone number or redial settings. If you make a shortcut to a connection, on the other hand, it will be automatically updated with any changes to its target connection.

To make a true shortcut (which should be the default here, because it is more likely to be what you will want), you have to drag the connection out of the DUN window with the right mouse button and select **Create Shortcut(s) Here** when asked. Figure 7-8 shows both a shortcut and an exported file made from the same dial-up connection.

Now, both shortcuts and exported files suffer the same limitation: you can't right-click on either type of file and select **Properties** to change the properties of the connection. Because shortcuts are only shortcuts, this makes sense: it's easy enough to change the properties of the target connection. However, because an exported file contains its own properties, it should stand to reason that you can change them as easily as you

Figure 7-8. Get more control when dragging items out of and into the Dial-Up Networking folder by using the right mouse button

can change the properties of a normal connection icon. Well, you can't. Just because Microsoft hasn't bothered to link the Dial-Up Properties sheet with the Properties sheet for exported files, however, doesn't mean the files can't be edited—it just means it's not as easy as it should be.

Dial-Up Networking exported files use the structure of INI files so they can be edited—not only by hand, but from within a program (developers can write code to read and write INI files quite easily). You can open any exported file in a plain-text editor, such as Notepad.

Each section in the exported file (denoted by square brackets (`[...]`)) is simply a different part of the dialog box in which the parameters were originally entered. Most of the entries in this file should be self-explanatory. What doesn't quite make sense, however, is that if you try to re-import the file into the Dial-Up Networking window, the connection name it uses is *not* the name of the exported file, but rather the connection name specified inside. To change the name of the connection used in the Dial-Up Networking window, you'll need to change both the `Entry_Name` and `Import_Name` lines to reflect the new name.

A significant advantage of Dial-Up Networking exported files is that they can be imported *back* into the Dial-Up Networking window just by drag-dropping. This feature, though, has its drawbacks. For example, if you drag an exported file into your DUN window and there's another connection by the same name, Windows will overwrite the existing connection without asking. So before importing any exported files, you should check the `Entry_Name` and `Import_Name` lines for possible conflicts with existing connections.

There are several reasons why you might want to import an exported file. For example, you can import a *.dun* file, edit its properties visually, and then re-export it (which may be easier than editing it in Notepad). You can also export a connection, change its connection name in Notepad, and then re-import it to create a duplicate of the connection, something otherwise impossible in the Dial-Up Networking window. You might want to duplicate a connection if you have two different numbers for the same ISP or want to access the same ISP with two different modems.

Probably the most useful aspect of this design is the ability to export a connection to a *.dun* file, copy the file to a different computer, and then import it there. This not only makes it easier to duplicate a connection profile among several computers, but it makes it easier for ISPs and network administrators to distribute connections to their clients.

Using Autodial with Dial-Up Networking

The autodial feature in Windows connects you to the Internet with Dial-Up Networking automatically whenever it's needed, such as when you check your email or try to open a web page, rather than forcing you to connect manually. While it is useful in streamlining the connection process, it can be just as annoying for those who, for example, may not want to connect to the Internet every time mail software is opened or an HTML file on your hard disk is viewed. Luckily, this feature can be enabled or disabled as you see fit:

1. Double-click on the **Internet** icon in Control Panel, or select **Internet Options** from Internet Explorer's **Tools** menu, and choose the **Connections** tab. The dial-up settings section, as shown in Figure 7-9, allows us to configure autodial settings.
2. If you wish to use autodial, highlight your dial-up connection (if there's more than one, choose one to be the default), and click **Set Default**. Clicking the **Add** button has the same effect as using the **Make New Connection** icon in the *Dial-Up Networking* folder.
3. Select **Dial whenever a network connection is not present**. (If you find that Windows isn't connecting when it should, return to this window, and select the **Always dial my default connection** option instead.)
4. Because you're configuring Windows to dial automatically, it's recommended that you configure Windows to disconnect automatically as well. Click **Settings** and then **Properties** (which has the same effect as right-clicking on a connection icon in the *Dial-Up Networking* folder and then selecting **Properties**), and choose the **Dialing** tab. Turn on the **Enable idle disconnect** and **Disconnect when connection may not be needed** options, and turn off the **Don't prompt before disconnecting** option. Modify the rest of the settings as desired, and click **OK** when you're done.

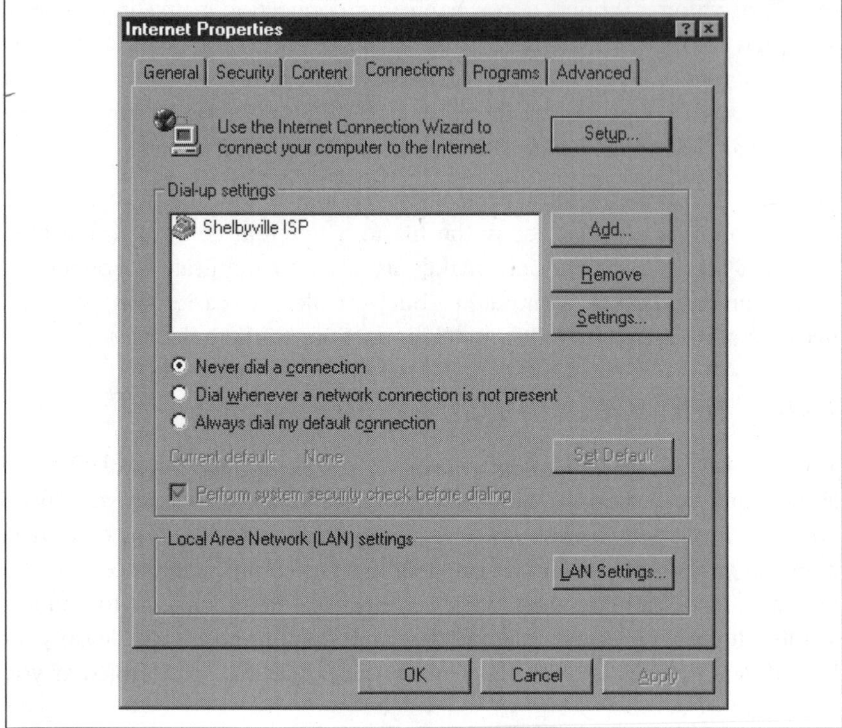

Figure 7-9. Enabling autodial is more than just turning on an option; you must specify which connection to use

You can test the setting by first making sure you're not connected, and then opening a web browser and connecting to a web site. Autodial can also be used in conjunction with Internet Connection Sharing (see "Sharing an Internet Connection on a Workgroup" later in this chapter).

Dial-Up Scripting

Most Internet Service Providers (ISPs) should support Dial-Up Networking in Windows Me without any modifications or special settings. However, some users must endure a more complicated logon process, common with more specialized ISPs, universities, and private companies that have chosen to stick with a proprietary method, usually for security reasons. If your provider doesn't support a common authentication protocol (e.g., PAP, SPAP, CHAP), you can still fully automate your logon procedure with Dial-Up Scripting.

Dial-Up Scripting provides a way to preprogram a list of commands that you would otherwise have to type manually every time you connect. Rather than simply listing the necessary commands in a file somewhere, however, you'll need to adhere to a special scripting language. The scripting syntax is documented in the file *Script.doc,* located in your *Windows* folder, although it will likely be confusing for nonprogrammers.

The following procedure outlines the steps necessary to form a script that works with your configuration and hook it up to an existing DUN connection. Before you begin, you might want to contact your provider to see if they have a prewritten script you can use; due to the popularity of Windows 9x/Me, it's likely that someone has already come up with a solution.

Part 1: Log in manually

1. Double-click on the **Dial-Up Networking** icon in Control Panel, right-click on the connection icon you wish to use, and select **Properties**.
2. In the **Connect using** portion, click **Configure**, and choose the **Options** tab. Turn on the **Bring up terminal window after dialing** option, click **OK**, and click **OK** again when you're done.
3. Now, establish a connection by double-clicking on the connection icon. If you're prompted for a username and password, you'll most likely just leave them blank at this point.
4. *After* your modem has dialed and successfully established a call, a small window with a black background will appear, allowing you to complete the logon procedure.

   Proceed by typing in the appropriate commands, usernames, and passwords required by your provider. As you type, write down on a piece of paper—or type into your favorite text editor—each prompt you see, as well as each command you type, carefully noting spelling and punctuation; capitalization doesn't count for prompts, but it may count for the text you type, such as passwords. For example, you might write the following:

   ```
   username:scorpio
   Password:globeX
   server781>ppp
   LOGIN?hank
   passwd?fluffykitten
   ```

   This example shows five prompts with five corresponding entries; your procedure will most likely be different.
5. When you're done typing, click **Continue** (or press **F7**) to have Windows complete the logon procedure.

The last two steps accomplish two important tasks: testing the logon procedure to make sure you can connect and recording the process so that you can reproduce it with a script.

Part 2: Write the script

1. Open a plain-text editor, such as Notepad.
2. Start your script by typing **proc main**, which is necessary for every DUN script.
3. For each prompt displayed during the logon process, type the following command:

   ```
   waitfor "username:"
   ```

   where the text between the quotation marks matches a prompt you'd see when logging in; spelling and punctuation both count here. A good trick is to leave off the punctuation to avoid matching problems (e.g., "username").
4. Then, after each corresponding *waitfor* command, type the following for each piece of text you're supposed to enter:

   ```
   transmit "scorpio^M"
   ```

   where the text between the quotation marks is what is sent to the host. The ^M (a caret, **Shift-6**, followed by a capital **M**) is interpreted as a carriage return; include it inside the quotation marks every time you'd normally press the **Enter** key. If you forget a carriage return, the script won't work. Most of the text here will be case-sensitive, especially passwords.
5. Lastly, end your script by typing **endproc**, a necessary "terminator" to the command typed in step 2.
6. What you should end up with is a series of pairs of *waitfor* and *transmit* commands. The following sample script is based on the example shown in Part 1:

   ```
   proc main
     waitfor "username"
     transmit "scorpio"
     waitfor "password"
     transmit "globeX"
     waitfor ">"
     transmit "ppp"
     waitfor "login"
     transmit "hank"
     waitfor "password"
     transmit "fluffykitten"
   endproc
   ```

Note the sixth line, which lists the *waitfor* command, followed only by the > character. This is because of the `server781>` prompt shown in the example in Part 1; the `781` implies that this prompt may be different every time you log on, due perhaps to having multiple servers answering the phones. By specifying only > here, we eliminate any matching errors.

7. If you want the script to enter your username and password stored in the dial-up connection, rather than including them right in the script (a good security measure), replace the appropriate *transmit* command with the following:

   ```
   transmit $USERID, raw
   ```

   for your username, and:

   ```
   transmit $PASSWORD, raw
   ```

   for your password. The *raw* parameter accommodates any weird characters that may appear in your username or password.

8. When you're done typing your script, save it into a filename with the extension *.scp* (put it in any folder that's convenient), and close your text editor.

Part 3: Hook up the script to a connection

1. To have DUN automatically invoke the script whenever you connect, you must first turn off the **Bring up terminal window after dialing** option, as described in Part 1.

2. Right-click the dial-up connection icon you wish to use, select **Properties**, and choose the **Scripting** tab. Click **Browse**, and select the *.scp* file you saved in Part 2. Click **OK** when you're finished.

3. To try out the new script, double-click on the connection icon and watch it go. If all goes well, DUN should complete its connection without any input from you.

   If, however, there's an error in the script, you'll have to go back to your text editor and try to fix problem. You can use the **Step through script** option (located in the **Connection Properties** dialog box, under the **Scripting** tab) to walk you through the logon procedure so you can see where it went wrong.

Once you have your script working, you'll most likely never need to do this again—unless of course, your provider changes the logon procedure. Note that if your logon procedure is different each time you log on, you'll have to write a more complex script than is documented here. See the *Script.doc* file that comes with Windows Me for more information.

Dial-Up Scripting is not the same type of scripting as supported by the Windows Script Host, discussed in Chapter 9, but you might want to check out Chapter 9 to familiarize yourself with some basic scripting concepts, such as commands and conditional statements.

The scripts used with Windows Me are the same as those used in Windows NT and Windows 2000. (In Windows NT/2000, the script files [*.scp*] are located in *\winnt\system32\ras*.) This not only means that the scripts you write now will be usable if you upgrade to Windows 2000, but that any scripts someone else might have written for NT/2000 should also work on your system.

Mixing and Matching Networks and Other Tricks of the Trade

In the first part of this chapter, networking is broken down into two distinct types: local-area networks (workgroups) and Internet connections. The distinction is less about the technology involved than about the intended use of each type. For example, a single network adapter can handle a workgroup connection and a fast Internet connection simultaneously.

The next few solutions involve some of the more interesting applications of networking, including sharing an Internet connection among all computers in a workgroup and building a workgroup across the Internet.

Sharing an Internet Connection on a Workgroup

Instead of investing in a separate Internet connection for each computer in your home or office, it certainly makes sense to share a single connection among all the computers. The problem is that sharing an Internet connection requires either additional software configuration or special hardware. There are several ways to accomplish this; the only prerequisite is that all the machines be properly networked together, as described at the beginning of this chapter.

Any of three solutions should work with any modern, high-speed Internet connection, such as DSL, cable, or T1. If you have a dial-up connection, the first solution, "Solution 1: Use Internet Connection Sharing," is the only one you'll be able to use.

Note that whatever bandwidth is available though a given connection will be shared as well. The worst-case scenario is when two users download data simultaneously; in this case, they would each receive only half the total connection bandwidth. Most of the time, though, this bandwidth sharing will have little noticeable effect, because two or more users on a small workgroup will rarely consume a great deal of bandwidth at the same time.

Each of the following solutions has a different setup procedure and different hardware requirements. The first solution, which utilizes the Internet Connection Sharing component that comes with Windows Me, is probably the best option for most users. Among its benefits are low cost, the ability to share an Internet connection with any number of other computers, and the support for nearly every type of Internet connection. Make sure to check out the other methods of sharing an Internet connection later in this chapter to see which one is right for you. For example, the second and third solutions require additional hardware and/or additional cost of service but add the convenience of not requiring any particular machine to be turned on for the Internet connection to be active.

Solution 1: Use Internet Connection Sharing

Internet Connection Sharing (ICS) is an optional component included with Windows Me, as well as Windows 98 Second Edition and Windows 2000. It allows two or more networked computers to share a single Internet connection, usually with little or no additional cost and no special hardware.

The problem is that the Internet Connection Sharing Setup Wizard doesn't work very well, and no Windows documentation adequately explains what's actually needed to successfully implement ICS. In some cases, installing ICS can disable your existing Internet connection. The good news is that it's not that hard to set up, as long as you do it properly. If you perform the following steps, in order, you should be able to get it right the first time.

Figure 7-10 shows a representation of a typical ICS setup. The host computer (the one with the Internet connection) acts as a gateway, which enables its connection to be shared with all other machines in the workgroup. ICS requires the following:

- One of the computers must have a working Internet connection.
- If you're sharing a DSL, cable modem, T1, or other Ethernet-based Internet connection, the computer with the connection must have two Ethernet cards installed: one for the Internet connection and one for the workgroup connection.

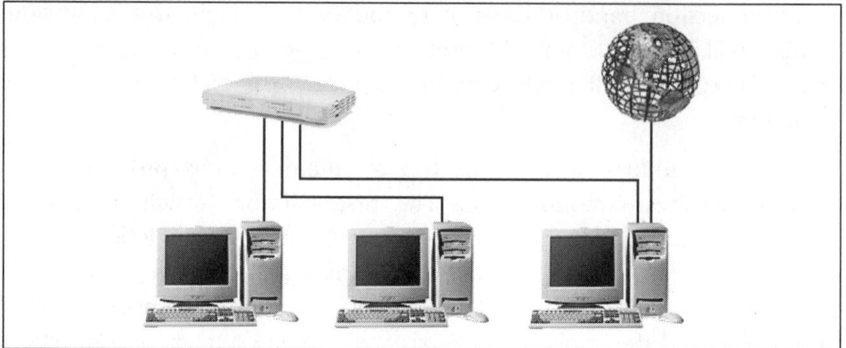

Figure 7-10. Internet Connection Sharing allows a single Internet connection to be shared by any number of machines in a workgroup

The following are exceptions to this rule: if you have a dial-up connection, your modem (more specifically, the Dial-Up Adapter explained in "Connecting to the Internet" earlier in this chapter) will take the place of the second network adapter. If you have an internal or USB-connected DSL/cable adapter, that adapter will take the place of your second network adapter.

If you have a DSL connection that requires special software to connect, such as Network Telesystem's (NTS) awful EnterNet software, the second-adapter rule *still* applies. But, when installing ICS, chose the **PPPoE** adapter as the adapter that provides your Internet connection, as opposed to a physical adapter in your system.

If you have an "unbundled" one-way cable modem, a DirectPC connection, or other type of connection not mentioned here, you should contact your ISP or the manufacturer of your equipment to see if they have any special instructions for sharing an Internet connection.

The last exception is if your Internet connection (usually DSL) comes with more than one static IP address—in that case, see "Solution 3: Use multiple IP addresses" at the end of this topic.

- The computer with the Internet connection must be running Windows Me, Windows 98 Second Edition, Windows 2000, or another version of Windows with ICS. The other computers in the workgroup should work with any modern, network-ready operating system. The instructions that follow assume all computers are running Windows Me.
- You must have a properly configured workgroup containing the machine with the Internet connection and one or more other computers—see "Setting Up a Workgroup" earlier in this chapter if you haven't done so already. Among other things, each computer must have a properly installed network adapter.

- The computer with the Internet connection must be turned on for the other computers in the workgroup to have Internet access. If you have a choice of which computer to host the Internet connection, use the one that is most likely to be on at any given time.

Now, the following procedure isn't as long and complex as it may appear. If you're prepared and all goes well, it should only take a few minutes. The most time-consuming portion is the repeated restarting of Windows.

The first step to setting up ICS is to configure the "host," the computer with the Internet Connection that will be shared. All the other computers, called *clients*, are set up subsequently. Note that if you have any other software installed intended to share an Internet connection, it should be removed from each machine in the workgroup before you continue:

1. Double-click on the **Network** icon in Control Panel, or right-click on the **Network Neighborhood** icon on the desktop, and select **Properties**.

2. The **Network Properties** window, which should resemble Figure 7-4 earlier in this chapter lists all your installed networking components.

   If you see any entries labeled "Internet Connection Sharing" it means the ICS component has been installed—ICS must be removed at this point. Double-click the **Add/Remove Programs** icon in Control Panel, choose the **Windows Setup** tab, and turn off the **Internet Connection Sharing** option (it's in the **Communications** category).

   What should be included is an entry for your network adapter. If you have two network adapters, they should both show up here. If you're using a dial-up connection, you'll see the **Dial-Up Adapter** here. If the expected items aren't there, see "Connecting to the Internet" earlier in this chapter to make sure your Internet connection is set up properly.

3. In addition to the network adapter entries, you should have each of the following components installed:

   — Client for Microsoft Networks

   — NetBEUI → your first network card*

   — NetBEUI → your Internet connection adapter (second network card or Dial-Up Adapter)

   — TCP/IP → your first network card

Networking

* The arrows after the NetBEUI and TCP/IP protocols mean that the protocols are bound to the devices to which the arrows are pointing. See the discussion of adapters and protocols at the beginning of this chapter for details.

— TCP/IP → your Internet connection adapter (second network card or Dial-Up Adapter)

— File and printer sharing for Microsoft Networks

If you don't see one or more of these items, click **Add**. If you're adding TCP/IP or NetBEUI, they are both in the **Protocol** category; Client for Microsoft Networks is a **Client**, and File and printer sharing for Microsoft Networks is a **Service**. When prompted for a manufacturer, choose Microsoft. Note that when you add a protocol, it will automatically install an instance for each adapter you have listed; if you only see one instance of TCP/IP, for example, just add it again to install it for all your adapters.

4. If there are extra entries, just ignore them for now. The exceptions are NDISWAN or any ATM protocols—if you encounter a problem later on, you might have to come back and remove these to use ICS.
5. If you've made any changes, click **OK** when you're done. Confirm that you want to restart Windows when prompted.

This concludes the setup of the host machine, with the exception of the ICS component. The next step is to configure one of the client machines to make it compatible with ICS. Once you've installed the ICS component (as described in the subsequent section) and verified that ICS is working, you can come back and repeat this procedure for any additional computers in your workgroup.

The beauty of the system is that no special software is needed on the client machines, apart from the proper networking components outlined in "Setting Up a Workgroup" earlier in this chapter:

1. Confirm that the workgroup connection to the host is functioning by navigating to the host computer entry in the *Entire Network* folder, located in *My Network Places*. If it's not there, the following steps may get it working; otherwise, see "Setting Up a Workgroup" earlier in this chapter.
2. Double-click on the **Network** icon in Control Panel, or right-click on the **Network Neighborhood** icon on the desktop and select **Properties**.
3. The **Network Properties** window, which should resemble Figure 7-4 earlier in this chapter, lists all your installed networking components.

   If you see any entries labeled, "Internet Connection Sharing," it means the ICS component has been installed—ICS must only be installed on the host machine. See the previous section for details on removing ICS.

4. What should be included is an entry for your network adapter. In addition, you should have the following components installed:

   — Client for Microsoft Networks

   — TCP/IP → your network card*

   — File and printer sharing for Microsoft Networks

   If you don't see one or more of these items, click **Add**. If you're adding TCP/IP, it's in the **Protocol** category; Client for Microsoft Networks is a **Client**, and File and printer sharing for Microsoft Networks is a **Service**. When prompted for a manufacturer, choose Microsoft.

5. You may see some extra entries, most of which can be ignored. The exception is NetBEUI, which will cause ICS to fail if it's present.

6. Next, highlight the TCP/IP entry (if there's more than one, select the one bound to the Ethernet card supplying your workgroup connection), and click **Properties**. The next several steps remove any network-specific information that will interfere with ICS—if you've just installed TCP/IP, these steps will probably be unnecessary.

7. Choose the **IP Address** tab, and select **Obtain and IP address automatically**.

8. Choose the **WINS Configuration** tab, and select **Use DHCP for WINS Resolution**.

9. Choose the **Gateway** tab, and remove any items in the **Installed gateways** list.

10. Choose the **DNS Configuration** tab, and select **Disable DNS**.

11. Click **OK** when you're done (the **NetBIOS**, **Advanced**, and **Bindings** tabs don't matter). Click **OK** in the **Network Properties** window, and confirm that you want to restart Windows when prompted.

That concludes the setup for the client computers. Now you're ready to install the ICS component on the host computer. If you encounter a problem, you'll have to remove ICS, restart Windows, and restart the procedure from here:

1. Double-click on the **Add/Remove Programs** icon in Control Panel, and choose the **Windows Setup** tab.

2. Highlight **Communications** (without altering the checkbox next to it), click **Details**, and turn on the **Internet Connection Sharing** option. For

Networking

* If you only have one network adapter (no second adapter or Dial-Up Adapter), the TCP/IP entry won't have an arrow to signify the adapter to which it's bound.

now, don't add or remove any other components—it'll just make it more complicated. If the ICS option is already installed, you'll have to uncheck it now, click **OK**, wait for the system to reboot, and then attempt to add it again.

3. Click **OK** and then **OK** again. After Windows copies the necessary files, the next thing you see should be the rather inappropriately named Home Networking Wizard. Most of the problems encountered when trying to set up ICS involve this cumbersome and ultimately unnecessary wizard—unfortunately, until Microsoft eliminates it, you don't have much choice.

   Don't click **Cancel** or restart your computer before completing this wizard. If it's interrupted, there's no way to start it again, which means you'll have to reinstall ICS, which involves restarting Windows, and then starting this procedure again. Unfortunately, if you do discover a configuration problem that prevents the successful installation of ICS, you may not be able to avoid this hassle.

4. Click **Next** at the first information screen. On the second page, select the **Yes, this computer uses the following** option, and then select **A direct connection to my ISP using the following device**.

5. From the list of devices, choose the one that provides the Internet connection for this computer. If you're using a dial-up connection, choose the Dial-Up Networking connection you wish to use.

   You may run into a snag if you have two identical network adapters installed in your computer.* Naturally, one provides your Internet connection, and the other provides your workgroup connection (as described at the beginning of this solution). If it's not obvious which one to choose, pick one at random—a wrong choice here can easily be corrected later.

   If you don't see both of your network adapters here (or a single network adapter and your Dial-Up Adapter), your network is not properly set up. See "Setting Up a Workgroup" earlier in this chapter for the proper procedure.

* In addition to this glitch, there are a couple of other places in Windows where having two identical network adapters may cause the same type of problem. Furthermore, there are rumors that some types of network cards won't function if two are used in the same machine. I've never experienced a problem with it, but it's worth investigating before making any purchases.

If you have a DSL connection that requires special software to connect, such as Network Telesystems (NTS) EnterNet, choose the **PPPoE** adapter here instead of a physical adapter in your system.* Click **Next** when you're done.

6. The next screen asks you to choose the network adapter that provides the connection to your workgroup—select **Yes**, and then choose the appropriate adapter from the list. If you made the correct choice on the previous screen, most likely the only remaining item in this list will be the adapter that indeed provides your workgroup connection.

   If you don't see this step, you either made the wrong choice in the previous step, or you don't have the proper system requirements as described in the beginning of this section.

7. Click **Next**, and select **No, do not create a Home Networking Setup disk**. The disk to which this option refers is really not necessary for successful installation of ICS, despite what the message on this window says.

8. Click **Next** and then **Finish**, and then confirm that you want to restart Windows when prompted.

   When you restart, a Home Networking Wizard message window will appear, congratulating you on installing ICS. In addition to providing misleading information, this message appears regardless of whether ICS was installed properly. Ignore the message, and click **OK** to get rid of it.

9. We're not done yet—the next thing you need to do is see if ICS was actually installed. Double-click the **Network** icon in Control Panel, and confirm that the following additional network components appear in the list:

   — Internet Connection Sharing†

   — Internet Connection Sharing (protocol) → your first network card

   — Internet Connection Sharing (protocol) → your Internet connection adapter (second network card or Dial-Up Adapter)

   — Internet Connection Sharing (protocol) → Internet Connection Sharing

   — NetBEUI → Internet Connection Sharing‡

   — TCP/IP → Internet Connection Sharing

---

* You may also have to change a setting in the PPPoE software to use DHCP addressing rather than the software's "Private API." Refer to the software's documentation for details.

† The first item, called **Internet Connection Sharing**, is shown as an adapter.

‡ This entry (**NetBEUI → Internet Connection Sharing**) can be removed, if you like.

Additionally, the two pre-existing TCP/IP entries will be renamed **TCP/IP (Home)** and **TCP/IP (Shared)**, signifying the adapters used to connect to your workgroup and the Internet, respectively.

If the Internet Connection Sharing adapter or protocols are missing, the installation of ICS did not actually take place, despite the congratulatory message and the lack of any warning. The reasons for a failed installation include not having the proper networking components installed (as described at the beginning of this solution), making the wrong selection in the ICS Wizard, and canceling the ICS Setup Wizard. In this case, you'll have to fix the error and try again.

You shouldn't ever have to adjust the properties of any of these new entries. If at some point you have to configure the IP address or other setting for your Internet or workgroup connection, do so by changing the properties of the TCP/IP entry bound to the specific network adapter that either provides your Internet or workgroup connection, respectively.

10. Optional: highlight the **TCP/IP (Shared)** entry, and click **Properties**. Choose the **Bindings** tab, uncheck the **File and printer sharing for Microsoft Networks** and **Client for Microsoft Networks** options, and click **OK**. This will remove a potential security hazard that might otherwise allow other customers of your ISP to browse your hard disk.
11. Close the **Network Properties** window when you're done—if you changed the previous setting, you'll have to restart Windows once more.
12. If all is well, Internet Connection Sharing should be in effect, and all connected computers should have access to the Internet connection.

    Start by testing the Internet connection by opening any web page on the host computer first. If the connection on the host is down, the connection won't work on any of the clients either. The most likely cause of having the installation of ICS disable your Internet connection is an incorrect choice made in the ICS Setup Wizard.

    Double-click the **Internet Options** icon in Control Panel, choose the **Connections** tab, and click **Sharing** (see Figure 7-11).* Verify that the selections in the two lists of devices are correct; if you have two indis-

* If the **Sharing** button isn't there, either ICS has not been properly installed, or there's a problem with one or more of the files that comprise ICS or Windows' networking. If this persists, try the Windows Update feature or, as a last resort, try reinstalling Windows Me.

tinguishable network adapters, try swapping them at this point. Click **OK** when you're done—Windows will have to restart before the change will take effect.

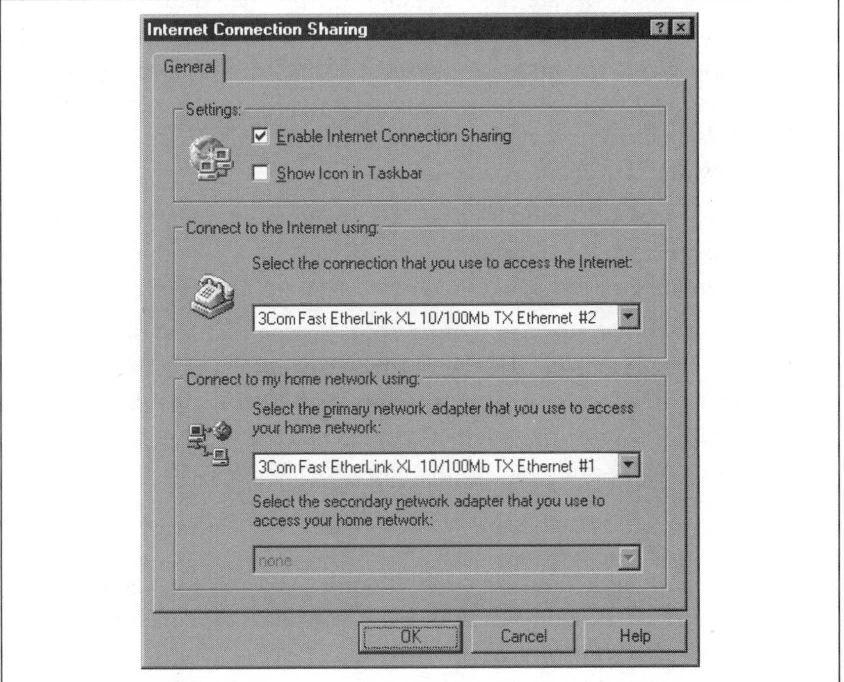

Figure 7-11. Configure ICS after it has been installed

Some types of less common connections, especially those that require proprietary software, may require some additional settings or even a software update to accommodate ICS. And of course, some types of connections are simply incompatible with ICS. Contact your ISP or the manufacturer of your Internet connection equipment for support.

13. Only after you've confirmed that the connection on the host is working should you proceed to test the connection on the client machine by opening a web page there.

    If the client machine works and there are other client machines yet to configure, do so now. If at least one client machine works, then ICS has been properly installed—any further problems are likely to be specific to the client or its connection to the workgroup.

If, on the other hand, none of the client machines are able to access the Internet, there are several possible causes:

- — The client machine is not configured correctly; perhaps one or more protocols are misconfigured or there are additional network components installed that are interfering with ICS. For example, if any client machine has NetBEUI installed, ICS won't work. Try removing and then reinstalling some or all of the network protocols on each client, which will have the effect of removing any unwanted or incorrect parameters.
- — You may be trying to use ICS without installing two network adapters in the host computer. Unless it says otherwise at the beginning of this solution, the two-adapter rule applies to you.
- — Your workgroup may require some setting that isn't supported by ICS. For example, DHCP is used to dynamically assign IP addresses to the machines in your workgroup. If DHCP isn't supported by your software or Internet connection, you can try manually assigning IP addresses to the various machines: 192.168.0.1 for the host, 192.168.0.2 for the first client, 192.168.0.3 for the second client, and so on.

  These IP addresses are what Windows requires for ICS to work. If you try to use different addresses, you'll run into all sorts of problems. If some software or hardware in your workgroup requires special IP addresses, you may have to abandon ICS and use a different solution (see the other solutions in this section).
- — Check out Microsoft's web site (*http://www.microsoft.com*) and do a knowledgebase search for Internet Connection Sharing. You'll see plenty of troubleshooting articles related to ICS and some problems that may have come up since this was written.

If, at any time, you wish to temporarily disable Internet Connection Sharing, double-click the **Internet Options** icon in Control Panel on the host machine, choose the **Connections** tab, and click **Sharing** (see Figure 7-11). Turn off the **Enable Internet Connection Sharing** option. You can turn off the pointless taskbar icon here as well. Click **OK** when you're done; you'll have to restart Windows for the change to take effect.

To permanently disable ICS, use **Add/Remove Programs** (as described earlier) to remove the **Internet Connection Sharing** Windows component.

Solution 2: Use an Internet router

An alternative to using the Internet Connection Sharing component that comes with Windows Me is to purchase additional hardware that essentially accomplishes the same thing. A router is such a device, capable of acting both as a hub (explained in "Setting Up a Workgroup" earlier in this chapter) and an Internet Connection Sharing device. Figure 7-12 shows a typical setup where a router would be used.

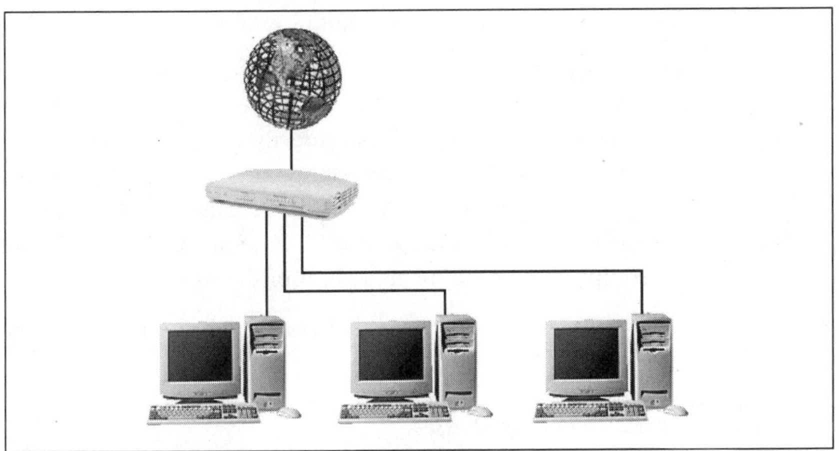

Figure 7-12. A router takes the place of your workgroup's hub, allowing a single Internet connection to be shared among all the computers in the workgroup

A router has several advantages over Internet Connection Sharing (discussed earlier), among which are the ability to have an active Internet connection without requiring any particular computer to be turned on and the possibly simplified setup procedure. The disadvantages of using a router include the additional cost and the fact that it can be used with only certain types of Internet connections.* Also, most routers will support only a limited number of connected computers, a limit that may or may not be stretched by adding an additional hub. Internet Connection Sharing (Solution 1) will share the connection among as many computers as you like.

Here's what you'll need in order to use a router with your connection:

- You must have a properly configured workgroup of two or more computers—see "Setting Up a Workgroup" earlier in this chapter if you haven't done so already.
- Your workgroup must be hub-based, but you won't necessarily need a hub, as the router will include that functionality.

---

* At the time of this writing, the price of the most basic DSL/Cable routers was about $150.00 and dropping.

- You'll need a router, sometimes called a DSL/Cable router. There are several different kinds of routers, all with different features and costs. Some routers double as a DSL or cable adapter (eliminating the one provided by your ISP), but probably the best kind to get is one that connects to an existing DSL or cable adapter (not shown in the photo), making it usable with any connection you have now or may possibly get later. Make sure the router specifically supports your Internet connection type and comes with HTTP-based configuration software (the best) or software supported by Windows Me.
- Your Internet adapter (DSL, cable, or otherwise) must be Ethernet-based to allow connection directly to the router. If your connection requires that the adapter be connected directly to the computer, or if special software is required to connect, your connection may not work with a router. Likewise, a router won't enable you to share an analog dial-up connection. Contact your ISP, the manufacturer of your connection equipment, or the manufacturer of the router for details.

Routers vary, so refer to the instructions that come with the router for the setup procedure.

Solution 3: Use multiple IP addresses

Your ISP may provide multiple IP addresses, with the specific intent that a single Internet connection be used with more than one computer. Instead of using software or hardware to share a single connection (as described in the two preceding solutions), each computer would have its own IP address and, therefore, effectively have its own Internet connection.

Figure 7-12 (in the previous solution) shows a typical setup for a multiple-IP Internet connection used on a workgroup. The hub is connected directly to the Internet connection adapter (DSL, cable, etc.), and the rest of the configuration is done through Windows.

Probably the biggest advantage to having multiple IP addresses is that the connection won't be dependent on any special software or hardware, including the operating system itself. Additionally, no more setup is required for the workgroup than would be necessary to connect a single computer to the Internet connection. However, the additional cost involved (usually an extra monthly fee) will add up fast and may make this alternative less attractive in the long run than either of the previous sharing solutions mentioned here. Also, the number of computers that can use the Internet connection at any given time is strictly limited by the number of IP addresses you get—a limitation that doesn't exist with Internet Connection Sharing (Solution 1).

Here's what you'll need to use multiple IP addresses with your workgroup:

- You must have a properly configured workgroup of two or more computers—see "Setting Up a Workgroup" earlier in this chapter if you haven't done so already.
- Your workgroup must be hub-based, allowing a connection to two or more computers *plus* the Internet adapter.
- Your ISP must offer multiple-IP Internet service. Because such service is inherently Ethernet-based, getting it connected to your hub should not be a problem. Contact your ISP for details on pricing and availability of multiple IP addresses with your Internet connection.
- If you don't have enough static IP addresses to service all the computers in your workgroup, you'll have to combine this solution with either one of the preceding solutions.

Your ISP should provide instructions on configuring each of the computers in your workgroup to access the Internet. Most of the time, all you'll need to do is enter the IP address, gateway, and nameserver information into each computer: this is done by highlighting the **TCP/IP** entry in **Network Properties**, selecting **Properties**, and entering the appropriate information.

In ideal circumstances, this can be a breeze. But when you start adding more hardware and software to the mix, the advantages of this solution over the others start to erode.

Virtual Private Networking

Virtual Private Networking (VPN) is a system whereby you can construct a workgroup of two or more computers connected by an Internet connection rather than a physical cable. In theory, VPN provides the security and privacy of a closed environment (as we said, in theory), without the astronomical cost of a private wide-area network.

The technology used in Virtual Private Networking, either the Point-to-Point Tunneling Protocol (PPTP) or the Layer Two Tunneling Protocol (L2TP), allows you to create a private "tunnel" across the Internet connection. With a VPN, you can accomplish tasks previously available only over a LAN, such as file and printer sharing, user authentication, and even networked games. Figure 7-13 shows a typical scenario with a tunnel connecting a single computer to a small workgroup.

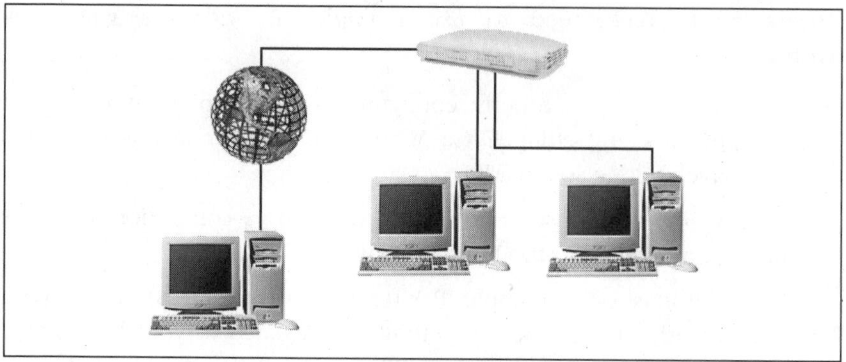

Figure 7-13. Form a virtual private workgroup through a tunnel across the Internet

The significant hurdle involved in setting up the VPN feature included in Windows Me is that a *tunnel server* is required to complete the virtual workgroup. Although VPN has been marketed as a feature of Windows Me, Windows Me cannot be configured as a tunnel server; therefore, a VPN cannot be achieved with Windows Me systems alone. This means that at least one of the computers involved must be running Windows NT 4.0 Server, Windows 2000 Server, or a subsequent version.

The other significant problem with VPN is that, like Internet Connection Sharing (discussed earlier in this chapter), there is virtually no documentation included with Windows Me or Windows NT/2000 that is helpful in getting this to work.

The following process briefly shows how to set up a simple VPN workgroup. Select the procedure following depending on the operating system you're using for the tunnel server: Part 1a for Windows NT or Part 1b for Windows 2000. Part 2 shows how to then configure a Windows Me machine as a VPN client.

Part 1a: Set up the tunnel server (Windows NT 4.0 Server/ Advanced Server only)

1. Log in as the Administrator.
2. Double-click the **Network** icon in Control Panel, and choose the **Protocols** tab.
3. Click **Add**, select **Point To Point Tunneling Protocol** from the list, and click **OK**. When asked how many simultaneous VPNs you want the server to support, choose a nice, big, healthy number, and click **OK**.
4. Next, you'll need to add one or more the VPN devices to Remote Access Service (RAS): choose the **Services** tab and select **Remote Access Service**.

5. Click **Properties**, and then click **Add**.
6. From the **RAS Capable Devices** list, select a VPN device, and click **OK**. Once all the VPN devices have been added, select a VPN port, and click **Configure**. Check the **Receive calls only** option, and click **OK**.

   Repeat this step for each VPN device you've selected. You'll have to restart Windows NT when you're done.

Part 1b: Set up the tunnel server (Windows 2000 Server/ Advanced Server only)

1. Log in as the Administrator.
2. Double-click the **Network and Dial-Up Connections** icon in Control Panel, and then double-click on the **Make New Connection** icon. Note that all of the settings in this cumbersome wizard can be adjusted later by double-clicking on the **Incoming Connections** icon you're creating.
3. Click **Next**, select **Accept incoming connections**, and click **Next** again.
4. Place a check mark next to the network adapter that you use to accept incoming VPN connections, and click **Next**.
5. Select **Allow virtual private connections**, and click **Next**.
6. You'll then be presented with a list of configured users—place a check mark next to each username you wish to allow to make a VPN connection, and click **Next** when you're done.
7. The next step allows you to choose which services, clients, and protocols are allowed with incoming VPN connections. These are the same components you'd use when building a workgroup (see "Setting Up a Workgroup" earlier in this chapter for details).
8. Click **Next** and then **Finish** when you're done.

Part 2: Set up the VPN client (Windows Me)

Although there only needs to be one VPN tunnel server, you can have as many clients as you like (that is, until you reach the limit specified in the tunnel server's configuration):

1. Double-click the **Add/Remove Programs** icon in Control Panel, and choose the **Windows Setup** tab. Choose **Communications** from the list, click **Details**, and turn on the **Virtual Private Networking** option.
2. Click **OK** and **OK** again; you'll have to restart Windows for this change to take effect.
3. Double-click the **Dial-Up Networking** icon in Control Panel, then double-click the **Make New Connection** icon.

4. Select **Microsoft VPN Adapter** from the **Select a device** list, choose a name for this connection, and click **Next**.
5. In the **Host name or IP Address** field, type the IP address or the hostname of the tunnel server you set up in step 1. Click **Next** and then **Finish** when you're done.
6. Right-click on the new connection icon, click **Properties**, and choose the **Security** tab, and enter the **Username** and **Password** of one of the users chosen when the tunnel server was set up. The **Domain** is the Windows NT domain of the tunnel server. Turn on the **Connect automatically** option, and click **OK** when you're done.
7. To initiate the VPN connection, make sure your Internet connection is active, and double-click the **New Connection** icon. After a delay, you should then see the tunnel server and any other computers in the workgroup in your *My Network Places* folder.

Although VPN support is included with Windows Me and Windows 98, Windows 95 users will need to install the Dial-Up Networking Update with PPTP, version 1.2 or later (from *http://www.microsoft.com*) in order to use VPN.

Accessing an FTP Site in Explorer

For years, File Transfer Protocol (FTP) has been the best way to move files from one machine to another across the Internet. Whether you're downloading drivers from a manufacturer's FTP site or uploading HTML files to your web server, FTP is often the fastest and most direct way to transfer files. Unfortunately, to access an FTP server, you need an FTP application.

A new feature in Windows Me, and one of the things that differentiates the *My Network Places* folder from the *Network Neighborhood* found in previous versions of Windows, is support for FTP sites.* What's more is that you can navigate an FTP site in Explorer, dragging and dropping files just as though the folders were on your hard disk. The functionality is very similar to Folder Shortcuts, as seen in "Mirror a Folder with Folder Shortcuts" in Chapter 4.

Hooking up an FTP site in Explorer is a snap.

---

* In previous versions of Windows, the only FTP support included in Windows was a command-line FTP client. It's still there: just type **FTP** at any command prompt.

Solution 1

1. Open the *My Network Places* folder, and double-click the **Add Network Place** icon.
2. When prompted for the location, type the URL of the FTP site. For example, if the server name is *annoyances.org*, you would type **`ftp://annoyances.org`**.

   Now, if you're connecting to this FTP site anonymously, you can just leave it at that—the next page will give you the option of logging in anonymously or specifying a username (being prompted for your password when you try to connect).

   To include your username and password directly in the URL, eliminating the prompt, type **`ftp://username:password@annoyances.org`**.
3. Click **Next** when you're done. If you didn't include a username and password on the first screen, you'll be prompted for a username now. Otherwise, you'll be sent directly to the final page.
4. On the last page, you'll be asked to type a name for this connection, which will also be name of the folder as it appears in Explorer. Click **Finish** to create the connection.

   If successful, you'll be able to browse the FTP site in Explorer immediately.

   If, on the other hand, you receive an error telling you that "The parameter is incorrect," you've encountered a bug in Windows Me. Currently, there's no fix, other than to proceed to Solution 2.
5. The connection is simply a folder or, more precisely, a Folder Shortcut, located in your *\Windows\NetHood* folder. If you'd prefer that the FTP folder be located elsewhere on your hard disk, you can move the folder as desired.

Networking

Solution 2

1. Follow the instructions for making a Folder Shortcut in "Mirror a Folder with Folder Shortcuts" in Chapter 4. (You can also use the example script in "Mirror a Folder with Folder Shortcuts" in Chapter 9, although it will have to be altered slightly to accommodate FTP shortcuts.)
2. When it comes time to make the shortcut to a folder, though, make an Internet Shortcut to an FTP site instead.

   Open your favorite web browser—any web browser capable of making Internet Shortcuts will do—and type the URL address of any valid FTP server, as explained earlier in Solution 1.

3. Once the page loads successfully, create an Internet Shortcut, and name it *target*. Because Internet Shortcuts use the extension *.url* (which is not shown) and we need the extension to be *.lnk* (also not shown), we must rename the file. And because Windows will not let you change the filename extension of a shortcut, you'll need to do it in DOS.

   Open a command-prompt window, and type the following:

   ```
   CD foldername
   ```

   where foldername is the name of the folder containing the target shortcut. Then type:

   ```
   REN target.url target.lnk
   ```

   Leave the prompt window open, if needed, for the rest of the solution in "Mirror a Folder with Folder Shortcuts" in Chapter 4.

Note that there are ways to transfer files across the Internet other than FTP, including setting up a Virtual Private Network (see the previous section) and using remote-control software (see the next section).

Controlling Another Computer Remotely (Just Like in the Movies)

Windows lets you transfer files to and from another computer on a workgroup and even print from that computer, but that's a far cry from full remote control. One of the severe limitations of the Windows platform (including Windows Me, Windows NT, and Windows 2000) is that only one simultaneous user is allowed to operate the computer at any given time.* In other words, there's no built-in provision for logging into a Windows machine remotely.

One partial way to overcome this limitation is with the use of remote-control software. With the proper software, you can be thousands of miles from a computer, yet work on it as though you were sitting right in front of it. I occasionally employ such software to administer a remote server, as well as access my home computer when I'm away. It's an effective and convenient way to bridge the gap of distance using standard networking protocols.

* Unix, on the other hand, allows many simultaneous remote users, either through a command-prompt connection, such as Telnet, or a graphical X-Windows terminal connection.

Here's what you need:

- Start with some remote-control software package. One of the most common is pcAnywhere, by Symantec (*http://www.symantec.com*); you'll need both the host and client versions of the software to make use of it. I actually prefer a program called VNC from AT&T Laboratories, Cambridge. In addition to being slicker than pcAnywhere,* it's free—you can download it from *http://www.uk.research.att.com/vnc/*. Follow the directions that come with the software you decide to use for the specific setup instructions.
- The *Host* computer is the machine that is to be controlled from a remote location. It must be connected to a workgroup or reliable Internet connection using a static IP address.

  Some Internet connections use *dynamic* IP addresses, where a new address is assigned to your computer every time you connect to the Internet. The problem with this is the remote-control software needs a distinct address at which it connects to the host. One way around this is to use an instant-messenger utility such as AOL Instant Messenger (which comes with Netscape Navigator) or Yahoo Instant Messenger (*http://www.yahoo.com*)—these products will allow you to determine the current IP address of a machine at any given time. You can also use DynIP (*http://www.dynip.com*), software designed specifically to help determine the address of a dynamically addressed machine.
- The "Client" computer is the machine at which you're actually sitting, controlling the host computer. It must also have an Internet connection or a direct connection to the same workgroup as the host.
- If you're using an Internet connection, it should be fast on both ends. Although it will work on a 56-K dial-up connection, it will be smoother if both machines have a DSL or cable connection.
- The host version of the software should be configured to start automatically with Windows, so that if the computer is restarted or the power goes out, the remote-control connection can be re-established.
- It's helpful if the resolution of the host screen is lower than or equal to the resolution of the remote-client screen. That way, you'll be able to easily maximize the size of the remote-control window.

* Among other things, it has the advantage of a very small "viewer" executable. That is, the client software, used on the remote system to access the host, is only a single file, small enough to fit on a floppy—this makes it easy to carry it around with you, running it on any other machine with an Internet connection.

- Finally, you'll probably need a person near the host computer who can restart it when necessary. If the host is a Windows NT/2000 machine, the host software can run as a "service," meaning, among other things, that you'll be able to close crashed programs remotely. Unfortunately, this won't work in Windows 9x/Me; if a program crashes and you press Ctrl-Alt-Del remotely to close it, the host software will be frozen just like any other application.

Security and Multiple Users

The use of multiple users on a Windows platform falls into two categories: (1) one or more users are allowed to log on to a single system, one at a time, each with his own settings (application toolbars, desktop wallpaper, etc.), and (2) a network server running Windows NT or Windows 2000 provides user authentication for an entire network. Windows Me supports only the former, and that only to a limited extent.

Now just because Windows Me allows usernames and passwords, it shouldn't be implied that there's any real security in a Windows Me system. The support for multiple users is for nothing more than allowing multiple configurations—that logon screen won't prevent unauthorized persons from using your computer.

Probably the closest thing to security that Windows Me provides is the ability to password-protect shared resources, as described in "Setting Up a Workgroup" earlier in this chapter.

The following solutions deal with some of the issues brought up by Windows' support of multiple users, such as the logon screen and the lack of security.

Get Rid of the Logon Screen

The logon screen that prompts you for your username and password every time you start your computer will appear if you've installed any network components, regardless of the existence of multiple users.

Like most of us, when asked to enter a password, you probably went ahead and did it—perhaps out of habit or some false sense of security. The problem is that now Windows will expect the password every time. Generally, the best approach when confronted with a prompt to enter an unnecessary password—in any software—is to leave the password field blank. Remember, specifying a password does NOT actually restrict access to your computer; it only means that a password is required to log in with *your username.* To prevent anyone from logging into your machine by choosing a new username and password, see "How to Implement Security in Windows" later in this chapter.

If your Windows Me password is indeed empty, follow this first solution to disable the logon box:

1. Double-click on the **Network** icon in Control Panel.
2. From the list entitled **Primary Network Logon**, choose **Windows Logon**. Press **OK**, and confirm that you want to restart Windows when asked.

If, on the other hand, you've entered a password at some point, this won't be enough to disable the logon box—you'll have to disable your password for this to work:

1. Double-click on the **Passwords** icon in Control Panel.
2. Click **Change Windows Password**, and type your old password in the first field. Leave the other two fields blank, and click **OK** when you're done.
3. Next, choose the **User Profiles** tab, and select **All users of this computer use the same preferences and desktop settings**, and click **OK**.

If that doesn't work, or if you've forgotten your password, you can simply erase the password:

1. Select **Search** and then **For Files or Folders** from the Start Menu. Type **`*.pwl`** in the **Search for files or folders named** field, type **`c:\windows`** (or wherever your Windows folder is located), and click **Search Now**.
2. Search should find at least one file with the *.pwl* (password list) filename extension. Go ahead and delete all the *.pwl* files found in the *Windows* folder to disable all passwords, or selectively delete files for individual users (e.g., *jimbo.pwl* for the user "Jimbo").

If you can't beat 'em, join 'em. If you can't get rid of the Logon box with any of the previous solutions, you can configure Windows to at least log in automatically for you:

1. Double-click the **TweakUI** icon in Control Panel (see Appendix A, *Setting Locator*).
2. Choose the Logon tab, turn on the **Log on automatically at system startup** option, and type your username and password (if any) in the fields provided. Click **OK** when you're done.

As a last resort, and only if the previous solutions don't work, try the following:

1. Open the Registry Editor. (If you're not familiar with the Registry Editor, see Chapter 3.)
2. Expand the branches to: `HKEY_LOCAL_MACHINE\Network\Logon`.
3. If it's not already there, create a new value called `Process Logon Script` by selecting **New** from the **Edit** menu and then **Binary Value**.
4. Double-click on the `Process Logon Script` value, type **`01 00 00 00`**, and click **OK**.
5. Next, expand the branches to: `HKEY_LOCAL_MACHINE\Software\Microsoft\Windows\CurrentVersion\Network\Real Mode Net`.
6. If it's not already there, create a new value called `AutoLogon` by selecting **New** from the **Edit** menu and then **Binary Value**.
7. Double-click on the `AutoLogon` value, type **`00`**, and click **OK**.
8. Close the Registry Editor when you're done; you'll have to restart Windows for this change to take effect.

   This *should* force Windows to bypass the logon screen the next time you start Windows. If you have multiple users configured and you wish to change users, just select **Log Off Username** from the **Start Menu**, and then log in as the new user.

Share System Folders Between Users

If you've configured multiple users in Windows Me, you'll notice that each user has her own *Desktop* folder, *Start Menu* folder, *Send To* folder, *Favorites* folder, as well as private copies of other system folders. Each user's personal folders are subfolders of *\Windows\Profiles\Username* (where *Username* is the name of an individual user).

In addition, Windows Me has the *All Users* folder, which contains yet other copies of the *Desktop* and *Start Menu* folders. The idea is this: any items located in the "All Users" instances of the folders will appear for each user configured on the system. And in the Start Menu, a horizontal divider separates "All Users" items from each user's personal Start Menu contents.

There are several problems with this approach, including the added clutter in the Start Menu and Desktop and the added hassle of configuring three different *Start Menu* folders rather than just one. To clean things up, you may want to consolidate some of the users' individual folders to create several shared folders.

This solution takes advantage of two features of Windows: (1) when you rename or drag-drop a system folder, Windows keeps track of the change and records it in the Registry, and (2) when you try to move a folder from one place to another in Explorer and there is *another* folder in the destination with the same name, Windows combines the contents of the two folders, after asking.

Utilizing both of these features, you can, for example, drag one user's *Send To* folder onto another user's profile folder,* effectively combining the contents of both folders. When you see the prompt **This folder already contains a folder called "Send To,"** answer **Yes** to confirm that you want to combine the two folders. Note that any duplicate files will be replaced with ones in the folder you're dragging. Windows will immediately update the Registry settings for the currently installed user so that the new location of the *Send To* folder is used.

Because only the settings for the current user will be updated, it's best to only drag that user's folders—if you drag the folders for other users (not including the *All Users* profile), Windows may not track the change.

How to Implement Security in Windows

Windows NT and Windows 2000 both come with more security features than the average home or small-office user requires, but Windows Me doesn't seem to include enough. Whether you're trying to protect your computer from prying children or trying to protect valuable data from prying coworkers, there are ways to implement various forms of security, depending on your needs and means. Although there's no way to achieve the same type of security found in Windows NT/2000 or Unix, the following are a few hints that can help add limited security to Windows Me.

Prevent new users from logging in

Anyone can simply log in to Windows Me by choosing a new username, or even by simply clicking **Cancel** at the logon screen. The only thing passwords in Windows Me actually accomplish is preventing users from logging

* Make sure you don't drag one *Send To* folder *into* another *Send To* folder, but rather to that folder's *parent* folder. In this case, you would drop the folder into *\Windows\Profiles\Username*.

in *as* other existing users. The following solution prevents someone from logging in without a password for a presently configured user:

1. Double-click on the **Network** icon in Control Panel.
2. Click **Add**, choose **Client**, and click **Add**.
3. Select **Microsoft** from the list on the left, select **Microsoft Family Logon** from the list on the right, and click **OK**.
4. In the main Network Properties window, select **Microsoft Family Logon** from the **Primary Network Logon** list, and click **OK** when you're finished. When Windows asks if you want to restart, answer **Yes**.

Using the Microsoft Family Logon client will cause a list of configured users to be displayed when Windows starts, from which you can choose one.

If this is not desirable, switch the **Primary Network Logon** back to the default, **Client for Microsoft Networks**. You can also try using the *Shutdown* utility (downloadable from *http://www.annoyances.org*), which will disallow new users from being added from the login screen.

Save settings for multiple users

If you've configured Windows to be used with more than one user and want each user's desktop settings to be saved individually, make the following change:

1. Double-click on the **Passwords** icon in Control Panel, and choose the **User Profiles** tab.
2. Select **Users can customize their preferences**, turn on both options beneath the option button, and click **OK**. You'll have to restart Windows for this change to take effect.

Limit access to unprivileged users

Windows Me comes with several settings that remove key menu items and icons from the basic interface, making it easier to restrict access to certain users. This procedure outlines a particular scenario; your needs may differ:

1. Create two users: one called "Administrator" and one called "Visitor" (or something to that effect). Choose a password for the Administrator, but leave the password blank for the Visitor user.

   The idea is to restrict access to the Visitor user, yet retain all privileges for the Administrator user. Log in as the Visitor, and start the System Policy Editor (see Appendix A).

2. Select **Open Registry** from the **File** menu, and then double-click on the **Local User** icon.
3. Expand the branches to `Local_User\Shell\Restrictions` and go through the settings here carefully, checking the ones that interest you. Most of the settings should be fairly self-explanatory.
4. Close the **Local User** window, select **Save** from the **File** menu, and close the System Policy Editor when you're finished.*
5. Lastly, install the *Shutdown* utility (see "Prevent new users from logging in" earlier in this section). This will prevent someone from logging in as a user other than Administrator or Visitor.

   This way, you'll get full access as the Administrator, and all other users will only have "Visitor" access. A word to the wise: anyone with sufficient knowledge of Windows Me will be able to "break" this security measure easily; for better security, you'll either have to install a third-party add-on or upgrade to Windows NT.

Again, I feel obligated to remind you that there is no security to speak of in Windows Me, other than the most rudimentary features described in this section. If security is a concern, an operating system such as Windows 2000, which has been built from the ground up with security in mind, is a much better choice.

* If you're interested, most of these policy changes are stored in the Registry at `HKEY_CURRENT_USER\Software\Microsoft\Windows\CurrentVersion\Policies\Explorer`.

8

Taking Control of Web Integration

Web integration is not the bundling of a web browser with Windows. Instead, what Microsoft calls "integration with the Web" is actually a collection of features and interface elements, all designed to make it appear as though Internet Explorer (IE) is more an extension of Windows than a distinct application. Whether it's truly integrated is purely a matter of semantics; what's important is the effect on the interface you use every day.

This chapter discusses the various components that make up web integration in Windows Me. Perhaps in an effort to allow the OS to be taken more seriously, or perhaps because the integration in Windows 98 wasn't much of a success, Microsoft has somewhat scaled back the web integration in Windows Me. Nonetheless, web integration is there. Fortunately, all of the features therein can be customized or easily disabled, as you prefer.

One substantial misconception to note is the nature of said components. Even though they've been loosely associated with the Internet Explorer application, many of them don't have all that much to do with the Web or the Internet. For example, the "web content" in folders is only called that because its appearance mimics a web browser's appearance.

The Lowdown on Web Integration Components

The following is a list of the various components that Microsoft has put under the "integration" umbrella. Although the settings and configuration of these various components is scattered across several different dialog boxes, the following guidelines should help you take full control over each of these features, changing or even disabling them as you see fit. See Appendix A, *Setting Locator*, for other settings in Windows:

The ability to configure icons to open with a single mouse click, rather than the traditional double-click
: This makes the icons for your files and folders look and feel somewhat (at least superficially) like hyperlinks you might see in a web page. All your icons' captions are underlined, and they even light up when you move the mouse over them (something links in web pages don't usually do).

  How to change: Select **Folder Options** from Explorer's **Tools** menu, or double-click the **Folder Options** icon in Control Panel. In the last section, "Click items as follows," choose either **Single-click to open an item** or **Double-click to open an item**.

Unlike Windows 98, this feature is disabled by default in Windows Me. If you find double-clicking a pain, you might want to take advantage of this option.

The Web View of your folders in Explorer, wherein each folder can be shown with an extra pane containing a brief description of the currently selected item or folder
: Although it adds some fancy graphics, the actual information displayed (by default) is little more than what you'd see by selecting **Details** from Windows Explorer's **View** menu (something that has been around since Windows 95).* With the Web View turned on, your folders take longer to open and consume more space on your screen (see Figure 8-1 for an example).

  How to change: Select **Folder Options** from Explorer's **Tools** menu, or double-click the **Folder Options** icon in Control Panel. In the "Web View" section, you can enable web content, or disable it by selecting **Use Windows classic folders**. (Some of these options will appear disabled if the Active Desktop is disabled.)

This option is enabled by default in Windows Me. See "Make Good Use of the Web View" later in this chapter for details on customizing the Web View.

* It does show previews for some image files and statistics for Microsoft Office documents, something not provided by Details.

The Active Desktop

The Active Desktop is a setting that, when enabled, allows you to turn your desktop into a web page, displaying more than wallpaper or a solid color. It also has the ability to have mini-Internet-Explorer-like windows anchored to it. These small windows aren't much different from ordinary IE windows, except they have thinner borders, appear to be "attached" to your desktop, and will automatically reappear whenever you restart Windows.* This option is enabled by default in Windows Me.

How to change: Double-click on the **Display** icon in Control Panel, and choose the **Web** tab. You can enable or disable all Active Desktop content by changing the first option, or you can configure individual active components in the list. You can also disable or enable the Active Desktop altogether by selecting **Folder Options** from Explorer's **Tools** menu (or double-clicking the **Folder Options** icon in Control Panel) and choosing the respective option in the "Active Desktop" section.

If you never use the Active Desktop, there's a way to hide many of these options, thereby more completely disabling the functionality. Double-click the **TweakUI** icon in Control Panel (see Appendix A), and choose the **IE** tab. Turn off both the **Allow Active Desktop to be turned on/off** and **Allow changes to Active Desktop** options. You can also turn off the **Shell enhancements** option, which will revert the appearance of the taskbar to the simpler, cleaner look it had in Windows 95.

The Active Desktop is turned off by default in Windows Me.

The Internet Explorer icon on the desktop and the quick-launch toolbar

In the off chance you don't see a link to the Web in front of you somewhere and don't feel like going to the trouble of opening your Start Menu, you can open an Internet Explorer window by double-clicking either of these icons. Both are present when Windows Me is installed, but can be removed or reinstated at any time.

* This may be useful if there's a web page you'd like to continually have open, such as a stock ticker, a news page, or a chat window. It helps if the specific pages are designed to be used in that way, so, for example, they will automatically refresh every few minutes.

How to change: Right-click on either icon, and select **Delete** to get rid of it. To get the desktop icon back, double-click the **Internet Options** icon in Control Panel, choose the **Advanced** tab, and turn on the **Show Internet Explorer on the desktop** option.

If you get rid of either icon, you can still run Internet Explorer at any time by selecting Internet Explorer (*Iexplore.exe*) from the Start Menu. If IE is the default web browser on your system, you can also launch IE by typing a web address into Explorer's address bar or by clicking a web link in any web-enabled application. Naturally, if another browser, such as Netscape Navigator, is the default, it will be used instead for opening links. See "Choosing Your Browser Defaults" later in this chapter for details.

Web links everywhere

Links to various web sites are scattered throughout the operating system: in Help menus, the *Favorites* folder, and the "Windows Update" utility. Clicking on any of these links launches the default web browser, not necessarily Internet Explorer.

How to change: Because changing this component would involve removing said links, for the most part this feature cannot be changed. However, most modern Windows applications allow you to customize their menus, so you should be able to get rid of any unwanted web links in applications.

To choose the browser used to open these links, see "Choosing Your Browser Defaults" later in this chapter.

The illusion that the Windows Explorer and Internet Explorer are the same program

In certain circumstances, Internet Explorer and Windows Explorer can share the same window. Assuming IE is your default browser (see later in this section), when you type an Internet address in Windows Explorer or select any links from the Favorites menu, the Windows Explorer window appears to be transformed into an Internet Explorer window, in essence meaning that your currently selected folder will disappear.

Likewise, if you type a folder name (e.g., *C:\Program Files*) in Internet Explorer, the window is transformed back into an Explorer window. Having both programs use the same container is a good trick, but it's clear that they're two different programs: IE must be loaded the first time it's used, IE and Windows Explorer respond differently to many actions, and the two programs have completely different menus and toolbars.

How to change: Double-click on the **Internet Properties** icon in Control Panel, and choose the **Advanced** tab. Turn off the **Reuse windows for launching shortcuts** option (in the **Browsing** group).

This design poses the same problem as the new Search tool in Windows Me. See "Fix the Search Tool" in Chapter 2, *Basic Explorer Coping Skills*, for details. See "Choosing Your Browser Defaults" later in this chapter to change the default web browser.

The Address Bar on the taskbar and in Windows Explorer

This is, at least on the surface, a duplicate of the Address Bar found in Internet Explorer, in which you can type Internet addresses (e.g., *http://www.annoyances.org*). Although the intent is to make it appear as though Windows Explorer and Internet Explorer are the same program, you can easily see the difference here.

For example, an address typed in the Address Bar in Internet Explorer will always cause a web page to load in Internet Explorer. However, an address typed in the Address Bar in Windows Explorer or on the taskbar will be opened by whichever web browser is currently set as the default.

Technically, the Address Bar is identical to the **Run** command in the Start Menu; you can launch any program (e.g., Notepad), as well as any Internet address from the Address Bar. See Appendix B, *DOS Resurrected*, for a way to use the Address Bar as a handy DOS command prompt.

How to change: Right-click on an empty area of the taskbar, select **Toolbars** and then **Address** to turn on or off the Address Bar. In Windows Explorer, select Toolbars from the **View** menu, and turn on or off the **Address Bar** option. You can also right-click the **Go** button to turn it on or off.

See Appendix B for details on using the address bar as a DOS command prompt.

The fact that Internet Explorer is the default web browser

When you double-click an *.html* file on your hard disk, launch a URL from Windows Explorer or the Start Menu, or click on a link in any application, the default web browser will appear and open the corresponding web page. You can very easily choose any other program to be your default web browser, replacing Internet Explorer with Netscape, for example. You can even make Solitaire your default web browser, although that obviously won't get you too far.

How to change: You can make any program your default web browser; see "Choosing Your Browser Defaults" later in this chapter for details.

Even if you make another web browser the default, you can still use Internet Explorer at any time by selecting **Internet Explorer** (*Iexplore.exe*) from the **Start Menu**.

Make Good Use of the Web View

The Web View (i.e., *Web content in folders*) component allows you to make any folder (including the desktop) look and feel like a web page, complete with hyperlinks, graphics, and even JavaScript. But why would someone want to do this?

Traditionally, interface designers and users alike have prized clean, unobtrusive, attractive, and simple interfaces. The Web View isn't any of these. The Web View is, on the other hand, fairly customizable; exactly how customizable depends on your knowledge of HTML and the amount of free time you have.

Now, it's unlikely that most users will have much use for the default Web View, which only augments a fairly simple interface (the "classic" Windows Explorer) with a bunch of unnecessary graphics and text. Figure 8-1 shows the same folder in its "classic" view as well as its Web View.

I see a tremendous wasted opportunity here. Although the Web View that Microsoft provides offers little apparent benefit to most users (other than some pretty colors), the capability to customize the Web View is potentially quite useful. What's so confusing about the entire design is how complicated Microsoft has made the customization process.

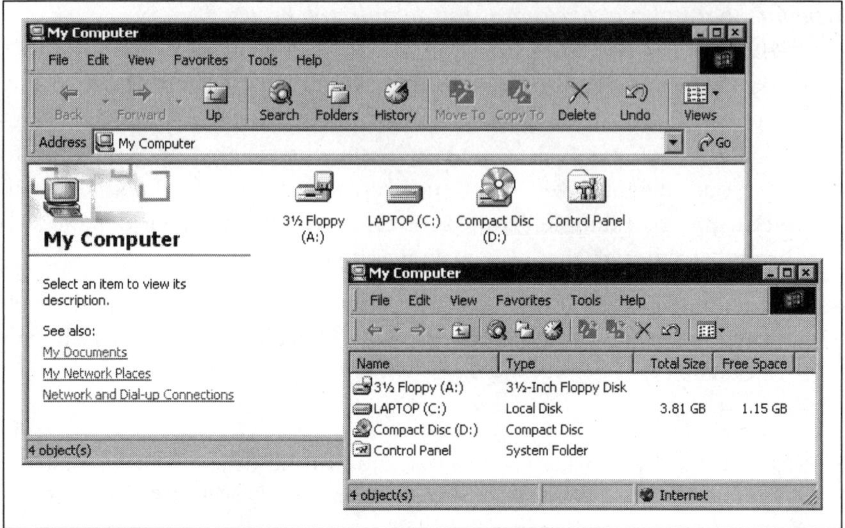

Figure 8-1. The default Web View takes up much more space and displays a more complex interface, yet offers little advantage over its classic counterpart

Although the intent of the Web View is to make Windows easier for less-experienced users, the process involved in customizing this view is so convoluted that only the most experienced users will be able to make anything of it. And it's unlikely that experienced users are going to want to bother.

Customize the Web View of a Single Folder

Because most of us spend much more time navigating normal folder windows than the special system folders such as *My Network Places* and *Control Panel*, we'll concentrate on customizing the default Web View of an average folder.

I recommend creating a new folder to test out the Web View, rather than endangering the contents of an existing folder or risking screwing up the default template. If at any time you want to start over, just delete the folder and make a new one.

To set up a custom folder, first open the folder, and then select **Customize this folder** from the **View** menu. Click **Next** to skip the intro page and proceed to the **What would you like to do** page. By default, only the first option, **Choose or edit an HTML template for this folder**, is checked. The other two options of the **Web View customization** dialog box allow you to modify the background picture and add a comment, respectively—neither of which interests us right now. Leave only the first option checked, and click **Next**.

The wizard will then prompt you to select one of several predefined templates—if you ever used this screen in Windows 98, you'll see some additional entries that should make your job here easier in Windows Me.* Among the available templates are the following:

"Standard" (Standard.htt)
: This template is what Windows Me uses for all folders by default. With almost 800 lines of nearly incomprehensible code, it's very difficult to edit and wouldn't really serve our purpose. Most of the HTML code in the "Standard" template is JavaScript, used to handle resizing of the folder window. With a little bit of thoughtful design, you can totally eliminate the need for all of this code. Chapter 9, *Scripting and Automation*, for more information on JavaScript.

"Classic" (Classic.htt)
: This template effectively has no customization, making the folder appear as though the Web View were not being used. Because it's the simplest to edit, it best suits this solution. See "Selectively Turn Off the Web View" later in this chapter for a special use for this file.

"Simple" (Starter.htt)
: This template is similar to the "Classic" template, except for a thin gray border and a simple title. It's also fairly easy to edit (at least compared to the "Standard" template), but isn't as straightforward as the "Classic" template for the purposes of this solution. Example 8-2, later in this chapter, contains code similar to this template.

Select **Classic**, turn on the **I want to edit this template** option, and click **Next** to continue.

Windows will automatically copy the necessary files, switch the folder to Web View, and open the folder's personalized template, *Folder.htt*, in Notepad for editing. Whichever template you choose determines the contents of the new *Folder.htt* file; choosing a simpler template will make your task easier.

* The templates listed in this dialog box are specified in the Registry at `HKEY_LOCAL_MACHINE\Software\Microsoft\Windows\CurrentVersion\explorer\WebView\Templates`, in case you want to add another.

The *Folder.htt* file, a duplicate of the template you chose earlier, is actually stored in a new folder called *Folder Settings*, which is placed into the folder you're customizing. The *Folder Settings* folder, the *Folder.htt* file, and a third file, *desktop.ini*, are all hidden by default. If the template you've chosen also uses graphics, *Folder Settings* will also contain all of the required graphic files, which will be hidden as well. To show hidden files, select **Folder Options** from Explorer's **Tools** menu (or double-click the **Folder Options** icon in Control Panel), choose the **View** tab, and select the **Show hidden files and folders** option.

Editing Web View Template Files

The pages that Windows uses for the Web View of your folders and the Active Desktop are written in a slightly bastardized version of HTML called HyperText Template (HTT). With the exception of personalized folder templates, Windows stores its *.htt* files in your *\Windows\Web* folder; for example, *Controlp.htt* is used for the Web View of the Control Panel window, and *Mycomp.htt* is used for the My Computer window.

Before proceeding, you need to know a few things about HTT files used in the Web View. First of all, because of the proprietary nature of HTT files, it's not practical to use one of the freely available WYSIWYG web page editors, such as FrontPage Express (the rudimentary editor that comes with Windows Me), to design your pages. You'll need to know at least some HTML and use a plain-text editor such as Notepad or UltraEdit-32 (*http://www.ultraedit.com*) to effectively customize these files. Luckily, HTML is fairly easy and fun to learn.*

Now, HTT files are really just standard HTML files, with one relevant difference; the poorly documented `FileList` object. The `FileList` object allows you to include the actual contents of the folder in your customized Web View page. Without it, the Web View of a given folder will be nothing more than a static web page.

The `FileList` object displays the folder contents inside a rectangular box that is embedded in a web page.† The size and position of the `FileList` object can be specified either in pixels (which results in a fixed-size list box) or in percentages (which allows it to resize with the window). The

* Documentation on HTML is obviously beyond the scope of this book—I suggest investing in a dedicated HTML book if you want to learn more.

† For those familiar with HTML, it works very much like the `<img>` tag.

size of the `FileList` object cannot, however, be specified with mathematical operations, such as "width of the window minus 50 pixels." This means that you'll need to use tables or frames to make usable space for anything else on the page. Examples 8-1 and 8-2 illustrate the problem and the solution, respectively.

To get the best feel for how the `FileList` object interacts with other objects on a web page, you'll need to build one yourself. Start by erasing all the text in the open Notepad window and replacing it with the code in Example 8-1.* You'll notice that it is somewhat similar to the code in the "Classic" template, but it has been cleaned up a bit, and some static text has been added.

Example 8-1. HTML Code for the Most Basic Web View

```
<html>
<body style="margin: 0" scroll=no>
    <object id="FileList" width=100% height=70% border=0 tabIndex=0
    classid="clsid:1820FED0-473E-11D0-A96C-00C04FD705A2"></object>
  Tragically ludicrous
</body>
</html>
```

Notice the `<object></object>` structure, which shows the `FileList` object. You'll notice that its width is set to `100%`, which makes it fill the folder window horizontally, but its height is only `70%`, which leaves room for the text I've added.

When you're done, save your changes, close Notepad, and click **Finish** in the **Customize this Folder** Wizard. Windows will automatically update the folder, showing you the changes you've just made; it should look like Figure 8-2.

You can further customize the template by choosing **Customize This Folder** from the **View** menu, but you'll only be able to use Notepad and you'll have to close the window to see your changes, forcing you to repeat the process until you're done. It's much easier to simply reopen the *Folder.htt* file (a hidden file—see earlier for details) in your favorite text editor. To see your changes at any time, save your work and then press the **F5** key in the folder window to refresh the view.

You'll notice when you resize the folder window (try it) that the file list and the area containing the static text will both resize proportionally.

* Notepad should still be open from the beginning of this procedure. Remember, this is just a duplicate of the original template file located in your *\Windows\Web* folder. You can change it, delete it, or totally mess it up without affecting the original template file that Windows will use for subsequent Web View customizations.

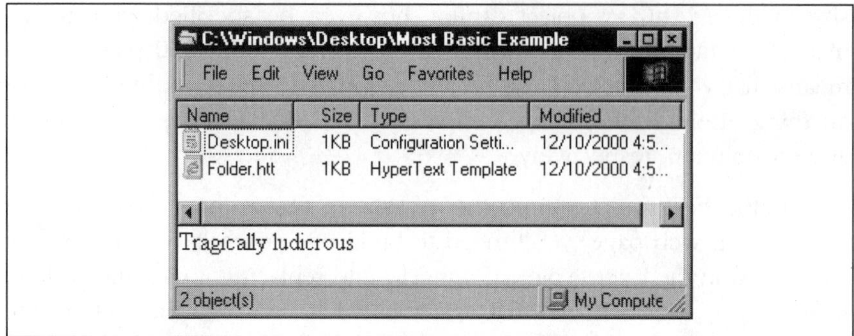

Figure 8-2. The resulting Web View using only seven lines of code (as shown in Example 8-1)

Because the `FileList` object has no border by default, you'll want to put some files in the folder, choose **Details** from the folder's **View** menu, and shrink the window enough for the scrollbars to appear; otherwise, it will appear as only a big white box. It should be apparent that this isn't acceptable for the long run; the lower area takes up too much space if the window is made larger, and it's too small if the window is made smaller.

For best results, we will want to engineer this so that the area outside the file list has a constant height. There are two ways to accomplish this: with the use of frames (as shown in "Make a Custom Toolbar with the Web View" later in this chapter) and with tables,* as shown in Example 8-2.

Example 8-2. HTML Code for the Most Basic Web View, Enhanced with Tables

```
<html>
<body style="margin: 0" scroll=no>
<table width="100%" height="100%" cellspacing=0 cellpadding=0>
  <tr><td>
    <object id="FileList" width=100% height=100% border=0 tabIndex=0
    classid="clsid:1820FED0-473E-11D0-A96C-00C04FD705A2"></object>
  </td></tr>
  <tr><td height=30>
    Ludicrously tragic
  </td></tr>
</table>
</body>
</html>
```

Example 8-2 shows essentially the same code as Example 8-1, except that the file list and static text have been placed in a table, and the height of the file list is now set at 100%. The table has the ability to size its cells to accommodate the cell contents properly, meaning that the lower cell (which holds the static text) is always the same height (here, 30 pixels).

* If you've used tables in a word processor, tables in web pages are very similar.

See "Make a Custom Toolbar with the Web View" later in this chapter for another way to do this; specifically, it shows how to add your own toolbar to any folder window.

A Word About Web View Variables

In addition to the `FileList` object discussed in the previous section, you can also use any of a few available variables to give you a little more flexibility in your Web View design. For example, the "Simple" template (*Starter.htt*) shows the name of the current folder in the gray border. Simply include any of the following variables right in your code:

%THISDIRNAME%
: Inserts the name of the current folder. For example, if the current folder is *c:\Windows\Desktop\Scorpio*, then you'll see "Scorpio" in the Web View.

%THISDIRPATH%
: Inserts the full path of the current folder. For example, if the current folder is *c:\Windows\Desktop\Scorpio*, then you'll see "c:\Windows\Desktop\Scorpio" in the Web View.

%TEMPLATEDIR%
: Inserts the full path of the Windows template folder, which is usually *c:\Windows\Web*. Although you probably won't want to display this directly, it can be used within certain tags to reference files outside the current folder. For example, the code

```
<img="%TEMPLATEDIR%\Wallpaper\paradise.jpg">
```

will insert a picture of the beach in your Web View; and the code

```
<body style="margin: 0" scroll=no background="%TEMPLATEDIR%\
    Wallpaper\Boiling Point.jpg">
```

will give your web page a weird red backdrop. Naturally, you can put your own files in this folder.

Selectively Turn Off the Web View

In Windows Me, if you turn on the Web View for one folder, the Web View will be turned on for all folders.* This effectively makes it impossible to selectively use the Web View; given the annoying default Web View (*Standard.htt*) and how long it can take to load, this design may

Web Integration

* The **View → As Web Page** command, originally found in Windows 98, has been removed in Windows Me, leaving Folder Options as the only place to enable or disable the Web View.

make the Web View difficult to live with. Fortunately, there's a way around this:

1. Open the *\Windows\Web* folder.
2. Duplicate the file *Folder.htt* (see "Make a Duplicate of a File or Folder" in Chapter 2 for instructions), which will create a new file, *Copy of Folder.htt*.
3. Duplicate the file *Classic.htt*, which will create a new file, *Copy of Classic.htt*.
4. Delete the file *Folder.htt*, and then rename the file *Copy of Classic.htt* to *Folder.htt*.

   This essentially replaces the "Standard" Web View template with the "Classic" template (explained in the "Customize the Web View of a Single Folder" earlier in this chapter). That way, the default Web View will now look just like the non–Web View of standard folders, leaving you free to customize the Web View for only certain folders.
5. This process will "fix" all standard folders; if you want to do the same for your system folders, repeat steps 3 and 4 to replace the following additional templates as desired: *Controlp.htt* (for Control Panel), *Dialup.htt* (for Dial-Up Networking), *Mycomp.htt* (for My Computer), *Nethood.htt* (for Network Places), *Printers.htt* (for Printers), *Recycle.htt* (for Recycle Bin), and *Schedule.htt* (for Scheduled Tasks).

Now, you could also put your customized template in place of the "Standard" Web View template, in effect customizing the Web Views of all standard folders at once. The next solution, "Make a Custom Toolbar with the Web View," uses this principle as well.

To turn off the Web View completely, select **Folder Options** from Explorer's **Tools** menu, or double-click the **Folder Options** icon in Control Panel. In the **Web View** section, select **Use Windows classic folders**. (If some of the options appear disabled, the Active Desktop feature may be disabled—see "The Lowdown on Web Integration Components" earlier in this chapter for details.)

Make a Custom Toolbar with the Web View

This solution further extends the previous Web View examples in this section, but uses an HTML feature called *frames*. Instead of a single HTT file, there are three: one that defines the frames, one that defines the toolbar (which appears in the top frame), and one that displays the file list (in the lower frame). Any good HTML reference will describe the use of frames in detail.

Example 8-3 shows the revised *Folder.htt* file, which specifies the necessary frameset structure.

Example 8-3. HTML Code for Folder.htt; the <frame> Tags Point to the Two Pages with the Actual Content

```
<html>
<frameset rows="40,*">
<frame src="%TEMPLATEDIR%\toolbar\toolbar.html" name="toolbar"
    scrolling="no" noresize>
<frame src="%TEMPLATEDIR%\toolbar\filelist.htt" name="filelist"
    scrolling="no">
</frameset>
</html>
```

This simple page has no content of its own; it simply lists the two other files (shown in Examples 8-4 and 8-5, respectively) that are displayed in each of the two frames. The key is the `<frameset>` structure, which defines a fixed height of 40 pixels for the top pane and a variable height for the bottom pane (specified by the asterisk: `*`).

Note that the `src` values for both `<frame>` tags point to files (*toolbar.html* and *filelist.htt*) located in a subfolder of the Windows template folder (referenced with the `%TEMPLATEDIR%` variable discussed in "A Word About Web View Variables" earlier in this chapter). This means that we can use the same custom toolbar page for all folders on the hard disk, making subsequent changes very easy.

Example 8-4 contains the code for *toolbar.html* (the upper "toolbar" pane), and Example 8-5 shows the code for *filelist.htt* (the lower "file list" pane). Make sure to save both of these files in the *\windows\web\toolbar* folder.*

Example 8-4. HTML Code for the "toolbar" Pane, to Go with Examples 8-3 and 8-5

```
<html>
<body style="margin: 0" scroll=no
    background="c:\windows\web\toolbar\stone.gif">
  <nobr>
  <a href="c:\windows\desktop" target="_top">
  <img src="%TEMPLATEDIR%\toolbar\desktop.gif"
      border=0 hspace=3 vspace=5></a>
  <a href="c:\my documents" target="_top">
  <img src="%TEMPLATEDIR%\toolbar\documents.gif"
      border=0 hspace=3 vspace=5></a>
  <a href="http://www.annoyances.org/" target="_top">
  <img src="%TEMPLATEDIR%\toolbar\internet.gif"
      border=0 hspace=3 vspace=5></a>
  </nobr>
</body>
</html>
```

Web Integration

* If you choose to save the toolbar files in a different folder, make sure the new location is reflected in place of `%TEMPLATEDIR%` in Example 8-3.

The toolbar page (*toolbar.html*) contains three graphical buttons, linked to the *Desktop* folder, the *My Documents* folder, and to a web site, respectively. A few things to note about this file:

- The `target="_top"` directive in each anchor tag forces all links to be shown in the full window; without it, followed links would only appear in the upper pane.*
- The button graphics (*desktop.gif*, *documents.gif*, and *internet.gif*) should all be placed in the *\windows\web\toolbar* folder created for this example, as are *toolbar.html* and *filelist.htt.*
- The `<nobr></nobr>` structure disables word-wrap for the buttons, and the background directive in the `<body>` tag gives us our nice stone background (also located in the *\windows\web\toolbar folder*).

The code for the lower frame is shown in Example 8-5.

Example 8-5. HTML Code for the "filelist" Pane, to go with Examples 8-3 and 8-4

```
<html>
<body topmargin=0 leftmargin=0 rightmargin=0 bottommargin=0 scroll=no>
<object id="FileList" classid="clsid:1820FED0-473E-11D0-A96C-00C04FD705A2"
    style="position: relative; width: 100%; height: 100%">
</object>
</body>
</html>
```

Note that the *filelist.htt* file shown in Example 8-5 is very similar to the code in Example 8-1 at the beginning of this section, except that the static text has been taken out and the `FileList` object now has a height of 100%, which fills the frame.

Once you've made the changes, press the **F5** key in the open folder window to refresh its display. Figure 8-3 shows the finished folder window using all three files.

The other nice thing about this design is that it allows us to create a truly customized toolbar, using more than just the rudimentary buttons Microsoft provides.

When you're satisfied with the results, the last step is to propagate the toolbar so that it appears in all folders. See "Selectively Turn Off the Web View" earlier in this chapter for details.

---

* The web page (the Internet button) will only be displayed within the folder window if Internet Explorer is the default browser. See "Choosing Your Browser Defaults" later in this chapter, for more information.

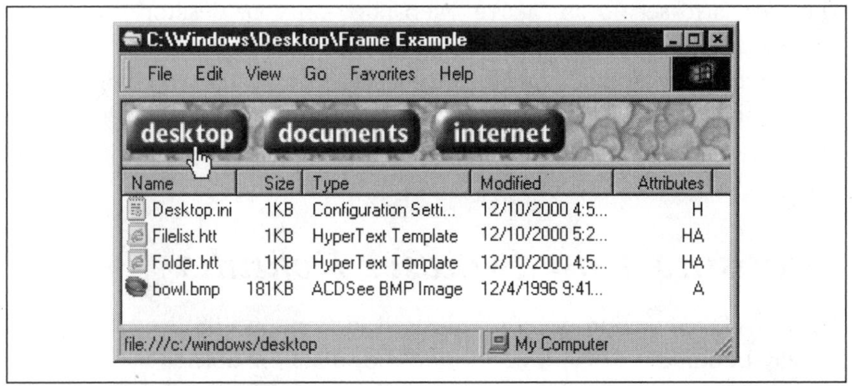

Figure 8-3. The resulting Web View, complete with functional toolbar

Using the Active Desktop

Although the Active Desktop component was heralded as a breakthrough feature when it made its debut in Internet Explorer 4.0 and Windows 98, Microsoft has somewhat downplayed it in Windows Me. What makes the desktop "active" is a combination of three features of Internet Explorer:

- You can turn your desktop into one big web page, optionally hiding all desktop icons. Double-click the **Display** icon in Control Panel, choose the **Background** tab, click **Browse**, and select any HTML file (or image file) to be displayed as the backdrop. The file can be a static file on your hard disk or an address on the Web.
- You can add "Active Desktop items" to your desktop, which are small, movable, resizable boxes that contain web pages. They're very similar to ordinary IE windows, except that they have thinner borders, can't float on top of normal windows, and automatically appear when you start Windows.

  To add a new Active Desktop item, double-click the **Display** icon in Control Panel, choose the **Web** tab, and click **New**. Click **No** to skip Microsoft's web site, and then either type a URL of a web site or point to an HTML file or Internet shortcut on your hard disk.
- You can "subscribe" to various web sites. This is essentially an extension of the Scheduled Tasks feature, whereby your computer could be configured to automatically connect to the Internet at predetermined intervals and retrieve updates from any web sites you wish.*

* Similarly, "Push" technology, once a hot topic in the industry, has all but vanished from sight. "Push" allowed a web site to initiate communication with subscribers, rather than waiting for visitors to request information. The implementation was a passive TV-like interface, which thankfully was killed in time for the release of Windows Me.

The idea is to set up an "active" web page on your desktop that would automatically be updated at regular intervals. Common examples of why you might want something like this include any page you might want loaded and visible all the time, such as a stock ticker, a weather forecast page, or a customized link page for corporate employees. Suffice it to say that the potential of this system has yet to be realized.

Choosing Your Browser Defaults

When Web integration was first released in Windows 98, I was asked by literally hundreds of Windows users if they'd still be able to use Netscape (or any other Internet programs for that matter) when they upgraded. Even more prevalent was the angst surrounding the conception that users wouldn't have any choice about the Internet integration—so much so that many people were reluctant to upgrade for that very reason. This is precisely the intention of the Internet integration—to suspend the myth that Microsoft software is the only choice.

The truth is that you do have a choice—not just for your default browser, but for all of the components that make up Internet integration and, indeed, all the components that make up your computer. The solutions in this chapter—and the rest of this book—will enable you to disable the options you don't want, as well as customize the options you do want.

The more you understand the technology behind the tools you use and the motivation for their design, the better you can take advantage of the entire system. The Internet is only a conduit through which we communicate with the various software tools installed on our computers. Although Windows comes with Internet Explorer, Outlook Express, Telnet, FTP, and other such programs, it's often desirable to use different programs, either from Microsoft or from a third-party manufacturer.

To take advantage of whatever programs you use, you'll want to make sure that each is made the default for the particular type of communication in which it specializes. For example, typing a web address (URL) in Explorer's address bar or double-clicking on an HTML file will launch the default web browser; likewise, clicking on a `mailto:` link in a web browser or using the **Mail** feature of your word processor will launch the default email program.

The problem is that, although it may be relatively easy to change the defaults, there's virtually no way to keep other programs from doing the same.

There are two ways that Internet programs are launched: HTML File Types and uniform resource locators (URLs). HTML File Types concern only web page documents stored on your hard disk, the browsers used to view them, and the editors used to compose them. URLs, on the other hand, handle all online Internet protocols, including Internet Shortcuts (Favorites), web links in applications, and anything entered into Windows' Address bar.

Select **Folder Options** from Explorer's **Tools** menu (or double-click the **Folder Options** icon in Control Panel), and choose the **File Types** tab to configure all your default Internet software. Click the **File Types** column header to sort the **Registered file-types** list by description.

Table 8-1 shows the common HTML File Types and URL entries and their default Windows associations.

Table 8-1. Default URLs and HTML File Types and the Default Internet Clients

File Type Description (*example*)	Default Application (*executable filename*)
Microsoft HTML Document (**.htm*, **.html*, **.shtml*, **.dhtml*)	Internet Explorer (*iexplore.exe*) for Open, Notepad (*notepad.exe*) for Edit
URL:File Protocol (`file://filename`)	Internet Explorer (*iexplore.exe*)
URL:FTP Protocol (`ftp://host`)	Internet Explorer (*iexplore.exe*)
URL:GOPHER Protocol (`gopher://host`)	Internet Explorer (*iexplore.exe*)
URL:HTTP Protocol (`http://host`)	Internet Explorer (*iexplore.exe*)
URL:HTTPS Protocol (`https://host`)	Internet Explorer (*iexplore.exe*)
URL:MAILTO Protocol (`mailto:username@host`)	Outlook Express (*msimn.exe*)
URL:NEWS Protocol (`news://host`)	Outlook Express (*msimn.exe*)
URL:RLOGIN Protocol (`rlogin://host`)	Telnet (*telnet.exe*)
URL:SNEWS Protocol (`snews://host`)	Outlook Express (*msimn.exe*)
URL:TELNET Protocol (`telnet://host`)	HyperTerminal (*hypertrm.exe*)
URL:TN3270 Protocol (`tn3270://host`)	Telnet (*telnet.exe*)

See "Customize Context Menus" and "Protect Your File Types," both in Chapter 4, *Tinkering Techniques*, for details on selecting an application to be the default for any given File Type. See also "Understanding File Types" in Chapter 3, *The Registry*, for additional details.

In addition to fussing with the File Types window, there are easier ways to make a given application the default. Most modern software will make itself the default, either by option or without asking, when installed—you can often just reinstall the application in question to have it claim all the necessary File Types.

Make a habit of always choosing Custom when given the choice between Custom and Default during the installation process. Not only will you be able to turn off options that may adversely affect your existing file types and other settings, but you can also choose not to install unwanted application components that would otherwise slow your system or take up valuable hard-disk space. And, choosing the folder in which applications are installed can be especially handy in reducing clutter on your computer.

On the other hand, when any modern web browser is started, it will determine if it is the default—if it isn't, it will ask if you'd like to make it the default, hopefully along with an option to never ask again, regardless of your response here. To control this setting in Internet Explorer, double-click the **Internet Options** icon in Control Panel, choose the **Programs** tab, turn off the **Internet Explorer should check to see whether it is the default browser** option, and click **OK**. The next time you use Internet Explorer, it won't automatically grab your Internet associations.

9

Scripting and Automation

Scripting, a simple form of programming, is well suited to such quick-and-dirty tasks as automating repetitive procedures, simplifying file operations, and even creating small Common Gateway Interface (CGI) server-side scripts for web servers.* Scripts are usually plain-text files that can be written and executed without a special development environment and don't require a *compiler*, a program that turns certain kinds of code into executables.†

Windows comes with two forms of scripting: the Windows Script Host (WSH) and DOS batch files. Both technologies have their strengths and limitations. DOS batch files are somewhat simpler to write, but WSH scripts are more flexible and offer better user interaction. WSH scripts are Windows-based, have full support of long filenames, and can even communicate with other running Windows programs. DOS batch files run on any PC made after 1982, but WSH scripts run only on Windows 98, Windows Me, and Windows 2000 (earlier versions of these operating systems only with a free add-on). Additionally, you can use both technologies in conjunction to accommodate just about any task you throw at them; see "Using Command-Line Parameters in Scripts" later in this chapter for an example. DOS batch files are fully documented in Appendix B, *DOS Resurrected*.

* Yes, Windows Me can be used as a Web Server, as long as you've got the software. Try the Personal Web Server that comes with Windows, or a third-party application like Apache (*http://www.apache.org*) or O'Reilly WebSite Pro (*http://www.oreilly.com*).

† Notepad will suffice; see "Finding a Better Editor" later in this chapter for more information.

The main roadblock to using the Windows Script Host has been the lack of adequate documentation on writing scripts for use in Windows. For example, Scheduled Tasks earn only a few sentences in the Windows manual, and the Windows Script Host and DOS batch files aren't mentioned at all. Compare that to the 25 or so pages devoted to Internet Integration (discussed in Chapter 8, *Taking Control of Web Integration*). Coverage in Windows' help files isn't much different: no type of scripting is mentioned at all in any help file.

The Windows Script Host is the engine behind the execution of scripts. Rather than a tangible, interactive application like Internet Explorer, WSH is simply an extensible collection of support files. WSH also comes with a DOS-based scripting host program (*Cscript.exe*), which is useful for running scripts from the command line or with batch files (see Appendix B). *Cscript.exe* also (in theory) allows you to run scripts when Windows isn't running, although there wouldn't be support for long filenames.

The beauty of the Windows Script Host (yes, I said beauty in regards to a Microsoft product) is that it is language-independent, meaning that it will work with any modern scripting language. It has built-in support for JavaScript and VBScript, but can be extended (with third-party add-ons) to use almost any other language, such as Perl and Python. This extensibility is a welcome change from Microsoft's usual narrow support of only its own, proprietary technologies.

VBScript is based on another Microsoft language, Visual Basic (VB), which, in turn, is loosely based on Beginner's All-purpose Symbolic Instruction Code (BASIC). If you're at all familiar with BASIC, taught in grade school since the seventies, the basics of VBScript won't be much of a challenge. VBScript will be used primarily in this chapter because it's easy to learn, it supports easy access to the features we need, like Registry access and file operations, and its cousin, VB, is one of the most widely used programming environments in the world.

So where does the Windows Script Host end and the VBScript language begin? From the point of view of the end user, WSH is started when you double-click on a script file: it automatically chooses an appropriate language interpreter based upon the script filename extension. From the point of view of the developer, WSH provides special functionality to all languages through the use of objects (see "Extending Scripts with Object References" later in this chapter); that way, each WSH-supported language needn't bother including functionality for advanced functions such as Registry access and filesystem operations.

The primary goals of this chapter are to provide an orientation to using the Windows Script Host and to show useful problem-solving applications that illustrate the power and flexibility of WSH.

Building a Script with VBScript

A script is simply a list of commands that are placed one after another and stored in a text file. Script commands are like building blocks: the more commands and programming techniques you learn, the broader your palette will be for making useful scripts. Some of the simpler building blocks will be used in this section of the chapter to illustrate the way scripts are built. Advanced users may prefer to skip to subsequent sections, which cover more advanced topics.

To run a script, just double-click on the script file icon; you'll probably never need to run the Scripting Host program (*wscript.exe*) directly. When the Scripting Host runs the script, the commands are executed in order, one-by-one. You can leave Notepad open to make changes and additions while you test the script (big screens are especially handy for this sort of thing).

You can quickly open an existing script file for editing by right-clicking on it and selecting **Edit**. This will, by default, open Notepad, although you might want to associate the Edit action for *.vbs* files with a more powerful text editor (see "Protect Your File Types" in Chapter 4, *Tinkering Techniques*).

The process of putting a script together essentially involves typing commands and then running the scripts to test them. In the following topics, we'll cover the background concepts necessary to complete many tasks with scripts:

- Using variables to store and manipulate information
- Asking for and displaying information with the *InputBox* and *MsgBox* commands
- Creating interactive scripts with conditional statements
- Using loops to repeat a series of commands
- Making building blocks with subroutines and functions
- Extending scripts with object references

Using Variables to Store and Manipulate Information

The use of variables is essential when some interaction is required by a script. A variable can be assigned a value, which is subsequently used or simply recalled later in the script. For example, the following two commands:

```
MyName = "joe user"
MyShoeSize = 12
```

set two different variables to two different values. The first variable, *MyName*, is assigned to a text string, while the second, *MyShoeSize*, is set to a numeric value. You can also assign variables in terms of other variables:

```
MyIQ = MyShoeSize / 2
```

which, when placed after the two preceding lines, would result in the variable *MyIQ* having a value of 6. When a variable name appears on the left side of an equals sign, its value is being manipulated. When it appears on the right side of an equals sign or within some other command, its value is simply being read. You can carry out more complex mathematical operations using various combinations of parentheses and the standard operators (+, –, *, /, and ^ for addition, subtraction, multiplication, division, and exponentiation, respectively).

Giving Your Scripts an Interface with the InputBox and MsgBox Commands

Some scripts are ideally suited to run in the background and perform a sequence of tasks. Others require some sort of user interaction, either in the form of asking the user for input or informing the user when something has gone wrong. For example, the command:

```
MyName = InputBox("Please enter your name.")
```

will display a prompt on the screen when the script is run, asking for some text to be typed. When you enter some text and click **OK**, the script places the text you've typed into the variable *MyName* and continues to the next command.

Now, collecting and rearranging information does no good without the ability to spit out a result. The versatile `MsgBox` function allows you to display a simple message, as follows:

```
MsgBox "Hello, Hello Again."
```

Combining the principles we've covered so far, consider the following code:

```
MyAge = InputBox("Please type your age.")
NewAge = MyAge + 5
MsgBox "In 5 years, you will be " & NewAge & "."
```

The first line does two things: it first asks the user to type something, and then assigns the typed text to the variable *MyAge*. The second line creates a new variable, *NewAge*, assigns the user's input to it, and adds five. Note the lack of any error checking in this example: if the user enters something other than a number, this code will cause an error. The third line then uses the `&` operator to concatenate (glue together) a text string to the *NewAge* variable and displays the result in a message box. Notice that plain text is always enclosed in quotation marks, but variables are not. If we were to enclose the *NewAge* variable in quotation marks, the script would simply print out the text `NewAge` instead of whatever value is stored in the variable.

The `MsgBox` statement can also be used like this:

```
Response = MsgBox("Here's My Message", 17, "Message Title")
```

which allows it to be used for not only displaying a message, but recording the response as well. The `17` is the sum of a few different values, which specify the options used when displaying the message box. Figure 9-1 shows two sample message boxes, each with different buttons and icons.

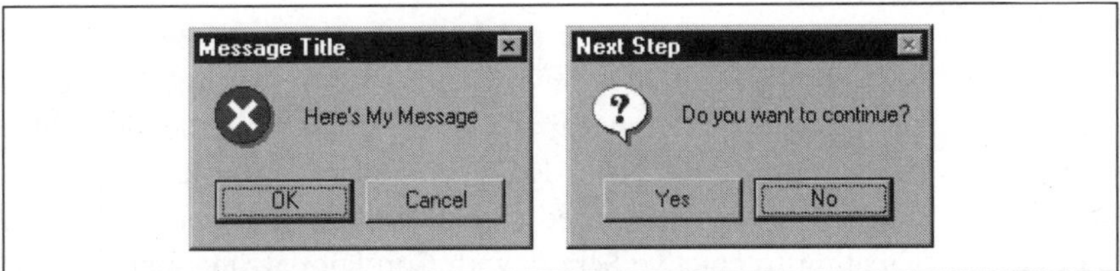

Figure 9-1. Various options can be combined to produce a variety of message boxes

To choose the buttons that are displayed by the `MsgBox` function, specify:

0 for OK
1 for OK & Cancel
2 for Abort, Retry, & Ignore
3 for Yes, No, & Cancel
4 for Yes & No
5 for Retry & Cancel

To choose the icon that is displayed, specify:

16 for a red "X" (error)
32 for a question mark (query)
48 for an exclamation mark (warning)
64 for a blue "I" (information)

Additionally, you can add:

256 to give the second button the focus (dotted lines)
512 to give the third button the focus
4096 to make the message box "system modal," i.e., all applications are suspended until the user responds to the message box

So, to have a message box with the **Yes** and **No** buttons, to have the question mark icon, and to have **No** be the default, you would specify a value of `4 + 32 + 256 = 292`. The two message boxes in Figure 9-1 have values of `17` (that's **OK**, **Cancel**, and the "X" icon) and `292`, respectively.

When the user responds to the message box, the *Response* variable will be set to:

1 if the user clicked OK
2 for Cancel
3 for Abort
4 for Retry
5 for Ignore
6 for Yes
7 for No

Now, you can accomplish quite a few tasks by simply stringing together long lists of commands, but the capability of redirecting the flow of a script—making it nonlinear—adds a lot of flexibility to the language and reduces the amount of work required to accomplish many tasks. See the subsequent "Creating Interactive Scripts with Conditional Statements" topic for details on using the results from a `MsgBox` statement to determine what happens next in a script.

Creating Interactive Scripts with Conditional Statements

Conditional statements allow you to redirect the flow depending on a condition you determine, such as the value of a variable. Take, for example, the following script:

```
Response = MsgBox("Do you want to continue?", 36, "Next Step")
If Response = 7 Then WScript.Quit
MsgBox "You asked for it..."
```

The first statement uses the `MsgBox` function, described in the previous topic, to ask a question. The value of `36` specifies **Yes** and **No** buttons, as well as the question mark icon. If the user chooses **Yes**, the value of the *Response* variable is set to `6`; if **No** is chosen, *Response* is set to `7`.

The next statement uses the `If...Then` structure to test the value of the *Response* variable. If it's equal to 7 (meaning the user clicked No), then the script exits immediately (using the `WScript.Quit` statement). Otherwise, script execution continues to the next command.

Here's another example using a slightly more complex version of the `If` statement:

```
MyShoeSize = InputBox("Please type your shoe size.")
MyIQ = InputBox("Please type your IQ.")
If MyShoeSize > MyIQ Then
  MsgBox "You need to read more."
Else
  MsgBox "You need larger shoes."
End If
```

One of the nice things about VBScript is that most of the commands are in plain English; you should be able to follow the flow of the program by just reading through the commands. Before you run the previous script, try to predict what will happen for different values entered at each of the `InputBox` statements.

This script uses the `If...Then` structure to redirect output depending on the two values entered at runtime (when the script is actually being executed). It should be evident that the first message is displayed if the value of *MyShoeSize* is larger than the value of *MyIQ*. In all other cases (including when both values are equal), the second message is displayed. Note also the use of `End If`, which is required if the `If...Then` structure spans more than one line, as it does in this example.

Using Loops, Using Loops, Using Loops

Another useful structure is the `For...Next` loop, allowing you to repeat a series of commands a specified number of times:

```
SomeNumber = InputBox("How many lumps do you want?")
TotalLumps = ""
For i = 1 To SomeNumber
  TotalLumps = TotalLumps & "lump "
Next

Rem -- The next line displays the result --
MsgBox TotalLumps
```

The `For...Next` loop repeats everything between the two statements by incrementing the value of the variable *i* until it equals the value of the variable *SomeNumber*. Each time we go through the loop, another "lump" is added to our variable, *TotalLumps*. When the loop is finished, the contents of the *TotalLumps* variable are displayed.

Notice the use of the concatenation operator, `&`, in the middle of the loop, which adds a new lump to the variable. Those new to programming might be put off by the fact that we have the *TotalLumps* variable on both sides of the equals sign.* This works because the scripting host evaluates everything on the right side of the equals sign (adds it all up) and then assigns it to the variable on the left side.

Note also the `TotalLumps=""` statement before the `For...Next` loop; this empties the variable before we start adding stuff to it. Otherwise, whatever might be assigned to that variable before the loop would still be kept around—something we didn't anticipate nor want. It's good programming practice to prepare for as many different situations as can be imagined.

Also good practice is the use of spaces, indentations, and remarks to make the code easier to read without affecting the execution of the script. The *Rem* command (shown earlier) is used to include remarks (comments that are ignored when the script is run), allowing you to label any part of the script with pertinent information. In place of the *Rem* command, you can also use a single apostrophe (`'`), which has the advantage of being used on the same line as another command.

As you write these scripts, think about the formatting as you would in writing a word processor document; scripts that are easier to read are easier to debug and easier to come back to six months later.

Making Building Blocks with Subroutines and Functions

A subroutine allows you to encapsulate a bit of code inside a single command, making it easy to repeat that command as many different times as you want, just like it was a built-in command in VBScript. Simply include the entire subroutine anywhere in a script, and then type the name of the subroutine elsewhere in the script to execute the subroutine.

* In traditional algebra, we couldn't have a statement like this; it would be like saying x=x+1, which has no solution. However, this is not an equation; it's a instruction that you want carried out. Besides, you're supposed to have forgotten algebra years ago.

A function is essentially the same as a subroutine, except that it has a result, called a return value. Both subroutines and functions accept input variables, listed in parentheses after the respective **Sub** and **Function** statements.

To those who are familiar with macros in a word processor, subroutines are similar. In fact, Microsoft Word and Excel (in Office 95 and later) save their macros as VB subroutines.

Consider Example 9-1, which compares the contents of two text files. At the heart of this example are the two structures at the end of the script, although their specific position in the script is not important. WSH separates all subroutines and functions before executing the script; they won't be executed unless they're called, and the variables used therein are unrelated to variables used elsewhere in the main script. Whenever it encounters the name of a subroutine or function in the script body, it executes it as though it were a separate script. Try to follow the execution of the script, command by command.

Example 9-1. Using Functions and Subroutines

```
Filename1 = InputBox("Enter the first filename")
Filename2 = InputBox("Enter the second filename")

If Not FileExists(Filename1) Then
  MsgBox Filename1 & " does not exist."
ElseIf Not FileExists(Filename2) Then
  MsgBox Filename2 & " does not exist."
Else
  Call RunProgram("command /c fc " & filename1 & _
              " " & filename2 & " > c:\temp.txt")
  Call RunProgram("notepad c:\temp.txt")
End If

Function FileExists(Filename)
  Set FileObject = CreateObject("Scripting.FileSystemObject")
  FileExists = FileObject.FileExists(Filename)
End Function

Sub RunProgram(Filename)
  Set WshShell = WScript.CreateObject("WScript.Shell")
  ReturnVal = WshShell.Run(Filename, True)
End Sub
```

One of the most important aspects of both subroutines and functions is that they can accept one or more input variables, called *parameters*. The parameters that a subroutine can accept are listed in parentheses after the subroutine definition and are separated with commas (if there is more than one). Then, using the `Call` statement, the values you wish to pass to the subroutine (which are placed in the parameter variables when the script is run) are listed in parentheses.

This way, the same subroutine or function can be called repeatedly, each time with one or more different variables. Functions (such as `FileExists` in this example) also can return a single variable (usually dependent on the outcome of some operation).

The first structure defines the `FileExists` function (discussed later in this chapter), which is passed a filename and returns a value of *True* (-1) if the file exists and *False* (0) if it does not. The `FileExists` function is called twice, once for each filename entered when the script is run (*Filename1* and *Filename2*). The `If...Then` structures (see "Creating Interactive Scripts with Conditional Statements" earlier in this chapter) first call the function, then redirect the flow based on the result of the function.

The second structure defines the `RunProgam` subroutine, also called from the script two times. `RunProgram` simply runs the program filename passed to it but returns no data. In theory, you could call functions exclusively; the benefit of subroutines is that you don't have to think about handling a return value.

In `FileExists` and `RunProgram`, *Filename* is a variable (shown in parentheses) in which passed data is placed so that it can be used inside the subroutine or function. It's considered a local variable; that is, it has no value outside of the subroutine or function.

The most important consequence of this design—the separation of the code into subroutines and functions—is that it makes it easy to reuse portions of code. Experienced programmers will intentionally separate code into useful subroutines that can be copied and pasted to other scripts. Just think of programming as building something out of Lego™ blocks; the smaller the blocks, the more versatile they become.

The solutions in the subsequent topics are presented as either subroutines or functions. Subroutines are used for code that performs an action, such as copying a file or writing information to the Registry. When a result is expected, such as reading information from the Registry or finding the date of a file, a function is used instead.

You should be able to place the subroutines and functions directly into your scripts and call them with a single command. It's up to you to put the pieces together to accomplish whatever tasks you have in mind. Feel free, also, to alter these routines to suit your needs.

Extending Scripts with Object References

There are some operations that can be performed with the Windows Script Host regardless of the language being used. These operations, such as accessing the filesystem, are made possible by extending the language with objects. For the time being, we can consider an object to be simply a context that is referred to when carrying out certain commands.

Admittedly, this can make carrying out some tasks rather difficult and convoluted, but it is necessary given the modular architecture of WSH. For example, many scripts will require a line similar to the following (using VBScript syntax):

```
Set WshShell = WScript.CreateObject("WScript.Shell")
```

which creates and initializes the `WshShell` object. `WshShell` is not a visible object like a file or other component of Windows, but rather a required reference used to accomplish many tasks with WSH, such as running programs, creating Windows shortcuts, and retrieving system information.

If you're unfamiliar with object references, your best bet is to simply type them as shown and worry about how they actually work when you're more comfortable with the language. The subsequent topics include many solutions that take advantage of objects, such as `WScript.Shell`, which has many uses, and `Scripting.FileSystemObject`, used for accessing the filesystem.

Running Applications from Scripts

This code is used to run a program, which can be a DOS program, a Windows application, an Internet or mailto URL, or anything else you might normally type in the **Start Menu**'s *Run* command. Place this subroutine in your scripts:

```
Sub RunProgram(Filename, Wait)
  Set WshShell = WScript.CreateObject("WScript.Shell")
  RetVal = WshShell.Run(Filename, Wait)
End Sub
```

and call the routine like this:

```
Call RunProgram("c:\windows\notepad.exe", True)
```

You can replace `True` with `False` if you don't want to wait for the program to finish before the next script command is executed.

Accessing the Registry from Scripts

The following code is used to write, read, and delete information in the Registry. Include the following three routines in your script:

```
Sub RegistryWrite(KeyName, ValueName, ValueData, ValueType)
  ValueType = UCase(ValueType)
  If ValueType <> "REG_DWORD" and ValueType <> "REG_BINARY" Then _
                                          ValueType = "REG_SZ"
  Set WshShell = WScript.CreateObject("WScript.Shell")
  WshShell.RegWrite KeyName & "\" & ValueName, ValueData, ValueType
End Sub

Function RegistryRead(KeyName, ValueName)
  Set WshShell = WScript.CreateObject("WScript.Shell")
  RegistryRead = WSHShell.RegRead(KeyName & "\" & ValueName)
End Function

Sub RegistryDelete(KeyName, ValueName)
  Set WshShell = WScript.CreateObject("WScript.Shell")
  WshShell.RegWrite KeyName & "\" & ValueName, ""
  WshShell.RegDelete KeyName & "\" & ValueName
End Sub
```

Using these three routines, you can accomplish nearly all Registry tasks. To create a Registry key, type this (note that all `HKEY...` roots must appear in uppercase):

```
Call RegistryWrite("HKEY_LOCAL_MACHINE\New Key", "", "", "")
```

To assign data to a Registry value:

```
Call RegistryWrite("HKEY_LOCAL_MACHINE\My Key", "Some Value", _
                                          "Some Data", "")
```

Leave `"`*`Some Value`*`"` blank to set the (default) value. To read the data stored in a given value:

```
Variable = RegistryRead("HKEY_LOCAL_MACHINE\My Key", "Some Value")
```

Leave `"`*`Some Value`*`"` blank to read the (default) value. To delete a key:

```
Call RegistryDelete("HKEY_LOCAL_MACHINE\My Key", "")
```

To delete a value:

```
Call RegistryDelete("HKEY_LOCAL_MACHINE\My Key", "Some Value")
```

To delete the (default) value in a key, we just set the value to nothing:

```
Call RegistryWrite("HKEY_LOCAL_MACHINE\My Key", "", "", "")
```

You'll notice that, in the `RegistryDelete` subroutine, there's a `RegWrite` statement. This is necessary to ensure that the key or value that you're trying to delete actually exists. If you *don't* include this statement and try to delete a nonexistent key or value from the Registry, the Windows Script

Host will give an error to the effect that "The system cannot find the file specified." Helpful as always. This way, the subroutine will create the key or value entry to be deleted if it doesn't already exist.

See Chapter 3, *The Registry*, for more information on the Registry. In particular, "Automating the Deletion of Registry Items" explains the need to use scripting to remove a Registry key, a task otherwise impossible with Registry patches.

Manipulating Files from Scripts

One of the myths surrounding the Windows Script Host, and VBScript in particular, is that there's no provision for accessing the filesystem (copying, deleting, and writing to files). This assumption is based on the fact that VBScript, when used in web pages, is not permitted to access the filesystem for security reasons.

The following routines rely on the `FileSystemObject` object, providing most necessary file operations. The names I've chosen for these functions and subroutines are based on what they act upon and what they're used for; for example, the `FolderCopy` subroutine is used to copy a folder, and the `FileCopy` subroutine is used to copy a file.

The following two functions return properties of drives—whether a specific drive letter exists and how much free space a specified drive has, respectively:

```
Function DriveExists(DriveLetter)
  Set FileObject = CreateObject("Scripting.FileSystemObject")
  DriveExists = FileObject.DriveExists(DriveLetter)
End Function

Function DriveFreeSpace(DriveLetter)
  If Left(DriveLetter,1) <> ":" Then DriveLetter = DriveLetter & ":"
  Set FileObject = CreateObject("Scripting.FileSystemObject")
  Set DriveHandle = _
              FileObject.GetDrive(FileObject.GetDriveName(DriveLetter))
  DriveFreeSpace = DriveHandle.FreeSpace
End Function
```

These next seven subroutines and functions are used to manipulate folders. The functions are used to retrieve information about a folder, and the subroutines are used to perform actions on a folder. The arguments should all be full folder names (e.g., "*c:\windows\desktop*"). Note that the `FolderSize` function returns the combined size of all the contents of a folder, including all subfolders, and may take a few seconds to return a result for large folders. You may want to use the `FolderExists` function before any others to prevent errors:

```
Sub FolderCopy(Source, Destination)
  Set FileObject = CreateObject("Scripting.FileSystemObject")
  FileObject.CopyFolder Source, Destination
End Sub

Function FolderCreate(Foldername)
  Set FileObject = CreateObject("Scripting.FileSystemObject")
  Set Result = FileObject.CreateFolder(FolderName)
  If Result.Path = "" Then
    FolderCreate = False   'failure
  Else
    FolderCreate = True    'success
  End If
End Function

Sub FolderDelete(Foldername)
  Set FileObject = CreateObject("Scripting.FileSystemObject")
  FileObject.DeleteFolder(Foldername)
End Sub

Function FolderExists(Foldername)
  Set FileObject = CreateObject("Scripting.FileSystemObject")
  FolderExists = FileObject.FolderExists(Foldername)
End Function

Sub FolderMove(Source, Destination)
  Set FileObject = CreateObject("Scripting.FileSystemObject")
  FileObject.MoveFolder Source, Destination
End Sub

Function FolderSize(Foldername)
  Set FileObject = CreateObject("Scripting.FileSystemObject")
  Set FolderHandle = FileObject.GetFolder(Foldername)
  FolderSize = FolderHandle.Size
End Function

Function FolderParent(Foldername)
  Set FileObject = CreateObject("Scripting.FileSystemObject")
  FolderParent = FileObject.GetParentFolderName(Foldername)
End Function
```

These next seven subroutines and functions are used to manipulate files. As with folders listed earlier the functions are used to retrieve information about a file, and the subroutines are used to perform actions on a file. The arguments should all be fully qualified filenames (e.g., "*c:\windows\notepad.exe*"). You may want to use the `FileExists` function before any others to prevent errors:

```
Sub FileCopy(Source, Destination)
  Set FileObject = CreateObject("Scripting.FileSystemObject")
  FileObject.CopyFile Source, Destination
End Sub
```

```
Function FileDate(Filename)
  Set FileObject = CreateObject("Scripting.FileSystemObject")
  Set FileHandle = FileObject.GetFile(Filename)
  GetFileDate = FileHandle.DateCreated
End Function

Sub FileDelete(Filename)
  Set FileObject = CreateObject("Scripting.FileSystemObject")
  FileObject.DeleteFile(Filename)
End Sub

Function FileExists(Filename)
  Set FileObject = CreateObject("Scripting.FileSystemObject")
  FileExists = FileObject.FileExists(Filename)
End Function

Function FileExtension(Filename)
  Set FileObject = CreateObject("Scripting.FileSystemObject")
  GetFileExtension = FileObject.GetExtensionName(Filename)
End Function

Sub FileMove(Source, Destination)
  Set FileObject = CreateObject("Scripting.FileSystemObject")
  FileObject.MoveFile Source, Destination
End Sub

Function FileSize(Filename)
  Set FileObject = CreateObject("Scripting.FileSystemObject")
  Set FileHandle = FileObject.GetFile(Filename)
  FileSize = FileHandle.Size
End Function
```

This next two functions can be used on either files or folders and allow you to retrieve and set attributes (Archive, Read-Only, System, & Hidden, respectively). File attributes are specified numerically: Read-Only = 1, Hidden = 2, System = 4, and Archive = 32. So, to set the Hidden and System attributes for a file, the `Attrib` parameter would be set to `6` (which is just `2+4`). To see if a file had, say, the System attribute turned on, you would use the command *If GetAttributes("c:\somefile.txt") And 4 Then Msgbox "This is a system File."*:

```
Function GetAttributes(Filename)
  Set FileObject = CreateObject("Scripting.FileSystemObject")
  Set FileHandle = FileObject.GetFile(Filename)
  GetAttributes = FileHandle.attributes
End Function

Sub SetAttributes(Filename, Attrib)
  Set FileObject = CreateObject("Scripting.FileSystemObject")
  Set FileHandle = FileObject.GetFile(Filename)
  FileHandle.attributes = Attrib
End Sub
```

The following three functions are all used to obtain commonly used information, such as the respective locations of the *Windows System* folder, the *Temp* folder, and the *Windows* folder.* To obtain the locations of some of the common folders, such as the *Start Menu* folder, you'll need to read that information from the Registry. See the previous section, "Accessing the Registry from Scripts," as well as "Wacky Script Ideas" later in this chapter for several examples:

```
Function GetSystemFolder()
  Set FileObject = CreateObject("Scripting.FileSystemObject")
  GetSystemFolder = FileObject.GetSpecialFolder(1) & "\"
End Function

Function GetTempFilename()
  Set FileObject = CreateObject("Scripting.FileSystemObject")
  GetTempFile = FileObject.GetSpecialFolder(2) & "\" _
               & FileObject.GetTempName
End Function

Function GetWindowsFolder()
  Set FileObject = CreateObject("Scripting.FileSystemObject")
  GetWindowsFolder = FileObject.GetSpecialFolder(0) & "\"
End Function
```

The previous functions and subroutines are used to manipulate files; the following two are used to manipulate the *contents* of files. The **`ReadFromFile`** function will transfer the contents of any file into a variable; naturally, this is most useful with plain-text files. Likewise, the **`WriteToFile`** subroutine will transfer the contents of a variable (specified as "*`Text`*") into a file. If the file doesn't exist, it will be created; if the file already exists, the text will be appended to the end of the file:

```
Function ReadFromFile(Filename)
  Const ForReading = 1, ForWriting = 2, ForAppending = 8
  Set FileObject = CreateObject("Scripting.FileSystemObject")
  Set FileHandle = FileObject.OpenTextFile(Filename, ForReading)
  Buffer=""
  Do Until FileHandle.AtEndOfStream
    Buffer = Buffer & FileHandle.ReadLine & vbCrLf
  Loop
  FileHandle.Close
  ReadFromFile = Buffer
End Function

Sub WriteToFile(Filename, Text)
  Const ForReading = 1, ForWriting = 2, ForAppending = 8
  Set FileObject = CreateObject("Scripting.FileSystemObject")
```

* If your script copies files to—or reads files in—any of the common system folders, you should always programmatically obtain the proper locations of these folders, rather than assume that, say, the windows folder is always *c:\windows*.

```
    If FileObject.FileExists(Filename) Then
      Set FileHandle = FileObject.OpenTextFile(Filename, _
                                              ForAppending)
      FileHandle.Write vbCrLf
    Else
      Set FileHandle = FileObject.CreateTextFile(Filename)
    End If
    FileHandle.Write Text
    FileHandle.Close
  End Sub
```

The use of all of the "file operations" subroutines and functions listed earlier should be fairly self-explanatory, and they all work similarly. For example, the `FolderExists` function and the `FileExists` function are both nearly identical, except that `FolderExists` checks for the existence of a folder, while `FileExists` checks for the existence of a single file. See the "Rename Files with Search and Replace" example script at the end of this chapter for additional examples, as well as a method for obtaining a list of all the files in a given folder.

Creating Windows and Internet Shortcuts in Scripts

Include the following subroutine in your script to allow easy creation of Internet Shortcuts *(*.url)* and Windows Shortcuts *(*.lnk)*:

```
Sub Shortcut(LinkFile, CommandLine)
  Set WshShell = WScript.CreateObject("WScript.Shell")
  If LCase(Right(LinkFile, 4)) <> ".lnk" And _
         LCase(Right(LinkFile, 4)) <>".url" Then _
         LinkFile = LinkFile & ".LNK"
  Set ShortcutHandle = WshShell.CreateShortcut(LinkFile)
  ShortcutHandle.TargetPath = CommandLine
  ShortcutHandle.Save
End Sub
```

To create a shortcut to a program or file, use the following statement:

```
Call Shortcut("c:\Windows\sendto\Notepad.lnk", _
              "Notepad.exe")
```

To create a shortcut to an Internet address:

```
Call Shortcut("c:\Windows\desktop\Annoyances.url", _
              "http://www.annoyances.org/")
```

If the first parameter, `LinkFile`, ends in *.LNK* (case doesn't matter), the `Shortcut` subroutine will automatically create a standard Windows shortcut; if LinkFile ends in *.URL*, however, an Internet Shortcut file will be created. Note the `If...Then` structure in the routine, which automatically adds *.LNK* to any shortcut filenames that aren't properly named.

If you specify a nonexistent folder in the path for the new shortcut file, an "Unspecified Error" will occur. You may want to use the **FolderExists** function, detailed in the "Manipulating Files from Scripts" topic earlier in this chapter, to eliminate the possibility of this error.

Networking with Scripts

VBScript has a few limited networking functions built in that can be used for mapping network drives and connecting to network printers. For advanced network functionality, you'll have to look into a different scripting language. For more information on networking, see Chapter 7, *Networking and Internetworking*.

The following routines provide access to some of the more useful network-related functions in VBScript.

The following function checks a given drive letter to see if it has already been mapped. It returns TRUE if the drive letter has been mapped, FALSE if it hasn't:

```
Function AlreadyMapped(DriveLetter)
  Set WshShell = WScript.CreateObject("WScript.Shell")
  Set WshNetwork = WScript.CreateObject("WScript.Network")
  Set AllDrives = WshNetwork.EnumNetworkDrives()

  If Left(DriveLetter,1) <> ":" then DriveLetter = DriveLetter & ":"
  ConnectedFlag = False
  For i = 0 To AllDrives.Count - 1 Step 2
    If AllDrives.Item(i) = UCase(DriveLetter) Then ConnectedFlag = True
  Next

  AlreadyMapped = ConnectedFlag
End Function
```

This subroutine maps a drive letter to any valid remote path:

```
Sub MapNetDrive(DriveLetter, RemotePath)
  Set WshShell = WScript.CreateObject("WScript.Shell")
  Set WshNetwork = WScript.CreateObject("WScript.Network")
  WShNetwork.MapNetworkDrive DriveLetter, RemotePath
End Sub
```

This subroutine maps an unused printer port (e.g., LPT3) to any valid remote network printer:

```
Sub MapNetPrinter(Port, RemotePath)
  Set WshShell = WScript.CreateObject("WScript.Shell")
  Set WshNetwork = WScript.CreateObject("WScript.Network")
  WshNetwork.AddPrinterConnection Port, RemotePath
End Sub
```

This subroutine removes the mapping for a previously mapped drive letter:

```
Sub UnMapNetDrive(DriveLetter)
  Set WshShell = WScript.CreateObject("WScript.Shell")
  Set WshNetwork = WScript.CreateObject("WScript.Network")
  WShNetwork.RemoveNetworkDrive DriveLetter
End Sub
```

This subroutine removes the mapping for a previously mapped network printer:

```
Sub UnMapNetPrinter(Port)
  Set WshShell = WScript.CreateObject("WScript.Shell")
  Set WshNetwork = WScript.CreateObject("WScript.Network")
  WshNetwork.RemovePrinterConnection Port
End Sub
```

The following script serves as an example for these subroutines. It's used to map a network drive if it's not already mapped or to disconnect a currently mapped drive. The previous routines are required.

```
DriveLetter = "N:"
RemotePath = "\\server\c"

If AlreadyMapped(DriveLetter) then
  Call UnMapNetDrive(DriveLetter)
  Msgbox "Drive " & DriveLetter & " disconnected."
Else
  Call MapNetDrive(DriveLetter, RemotePath)
  Msgbox "Drive " & DriveLetter & " connected."
End if
```

This script requires no user interaction once it has been executed and displays only a single confirmation message when it's done. The first two lines contain the drive letter and network path to be mapped together. Then, the `AlreadyMapped` function is used to determine if the drive mapping already exists. The script then maps or disconnects the drive, depending on what's needed.

Manipulating Internet Explorer from Scripts

Because VBScript owes its existence, in part, to Internet Explorer, it seems only fair that there would be some integration between WSH and IE. The key is the Internet Explorer *object* and the properties and methods associated with it.

Begin with the following lines in your script (which start IE) initialize the IE object, and open a blank IE window:

```
Set IEObject = CreateObject("InternetExplorer.Application")
IF Err.number <> 0 Then
   MsgBox "Internet Explorer Not Found."
   wScript.Quit
End If
IEObject.Left = 75
IEObject.Top = 75
IEObject.Width=400
IEObject.Height=300
IEObject.Menubar=0
IEObject.Toolbar=0
IEObject.Navigate "About:Blank"
IEObject.Visible=1
Do while IEObject.Busy
  Rem -- wait for window to open --
Loop
```

Note the error checking at the beginning, which quits if there's a problem loading Internet Explorer. The subsequent commands customize the window to our needs; the `Left`, `Top`, `Width`, and `Height` properties are all in pixels; for the `MenuBar` and `Toolbar` properties, `0` means hidden and `1` means visible. Lastly, the `Navigate` property specifies the URL to load.

Once the *IEObject.Visible=1* command is issued, the window appears, and the real fun begins. The following lines are used to construct a simple page:

```
IEObject.Document.Write "<html>"
IEObject.Document.Write "<h1>Hello World</h1>"
IEObject.Document.Write "<p>"
IEObject.Document.Write "<i>Aren't we sick of that phrase yet?</i>"
IEObject.Document.Write "</html>"
```

This has nearly limitless possibilities, not the least of which is a more elegant way to display information than the *MsgBox* command, a much more sophisticated way of gathering information than the *InputBox* command (using fill-out forms), and a way to display an ongoing log of a script's activities without interrupting script flow.

Note that the IE window stays open after the script completes; use the *IEObject.Quit* command to close the window when you're done with it.

Using Command-Line Parameters in Scripts

A command-line parameter is a bit of text specified after the filename of a script when it is executed from a command prompt (see the following examples). The function to convert a single command-line parameter into a variable is the following:

```
Function CommandLine(Number)
  Set Arguments = WScript.Arguments
  If Number <= Arguments.Count Then
    CommandLine = Arguments(Number - 1)
  Else
    CommandLine = ""
  End If
End Function
```

For example, to display the second command-line parameter passed to a script, issue the following statement:

```
MsgBox CommandLine(2)
```

Although the command line may seem to be an antiquated concept, it's still very much a part of Windows. When you double-click on a *.vbs* file, for example, Windows actually executes the following command:

```
wscript.exe filename.vbs
```

where `filename.vbs` (the file that was double-clicked) is the command-line parameter for `wscript.exe`, telling it which script to run. Scripts also accept command-line parameters, which is accomplished like this:

```
wscript.exe filename.vbs param1 param2
```

The two additional parameters, `param1` and `param2`, are both passed to the script as command-line parameters when it is run.

The problem with providing command-line arguments to your script is that Windows considers scripts to be documents instead of executables. This means that you can't run a script with a command-line parameter without typing; you can't drag a file onto a script icon or put a script directly into your Send To menu.

Luckily, there's a slightly convoluted workaround. Because the syntax required to launch a script with command-line parameters (shown earlier) must be typed, it can be put into a DOS batch file.* The batch file simply passes on the command-line parameters to the script (see "Batch Files—The Other Way to Do It" in Appendix B).

Consider the following example, which uses a single-line batch file and a Windows shortcut in conjunction with a script, to make any filename lowercase (it is assumed that all files are saved in a folder called *c:\scripts*).

* While one would expect that a Windows shortcut could be used to launch the script as well, this unfortunately doesn't work; Windows shortcuts don't handle command-line parameters properly.

Type the following into a text editor, and save it as *rename.bat*:

```
@echo off
del c:\temp.txt
dir /b %1 > c:\temp.txt
wscript c:\scripts\rename.vbs %1
```

Close the text editor, then right-click on *rename.bat*, and select **Properties**. From the **Run** drop-down list, choose **Minimized**. Lastly, turn on the **Close on exit** option, and click **OK**.

A file called *rename.pif* will then appear in the same folder; this contains the batch file properties. Move this file into your *\Windows\SendTo* folder, and rename it to *make lower case.pif*.

Then, in a plain-text editor, type the following:

```
LongFileName = ReadFromFile("c:\temp.txt")
Call FileDelete("c:\temp.txt")
Call FileMove(CommandLine(1), LCase(LongFileName))
```

You'll also include the following functions and subroutines, listed earlier in this chapter: `ReadFromFile`, `FileMove`, `FileDelete`, and `CommandLine`. Save the completed script as *rename.vbs*.

The first two lines of this script read and then delete a temporary text file created by the batch file. The purpose of this temporary file is to preserve any long filenames that are passed to the batch file. Without it, if you try to rename a file with a long filename, it will be renamed to its short filename!

This script uses the `CommandLine` function described at the beginning of this topic (which turns command lines into variables), as well as the `FileMove` subroutine described in "Manipulating Files from Scripts" earlier in this chapter (which performs the actual file renaming). This script also uses the `LCase` function (built into VBScript), which makes the contents of any variable lowercase (`UCase` does the opposite).

Once the three files (*rename.bat*, *rename.vbs*, and *make lower case.pif*) are all in place, you can test it out. Right-click on any file in Explorer, and select **Make lower case** from the **Send To** menu.

One caveat to this script is that if you select multiple files in Explorer, only one of them will be renamed. This problem can be fixed with additional code, but this is as far as it will be taken here.

Writing CGI Scripts for a Web Server

WSH scripts have the potential to produce quite capable CGI programs for use with web servers: programs that are run by web-server software to generate dynamic web content. For example, CGI programs can be used to process data entered in web-based fill-out forms or to read data from files and produce web content on the fly.

Although a full discussion of CGI programming is beyond the scope of this book, there are some routines that are necessary to accomplish some basic CGI tasks with WSH scripts.

First, you'll have to edit your file types (see Chapter 4) and reassociate the *.vbs* file extension with *cscript.exe* (the command-line based script engine), rather than the default Windows-based engine, *wscript.exe.* You should also check with your web server's documentation to see if any additional configuration is necessary. If you prefer, you can choose a new extension, such as *.cgi, .vbc,* or *.twinkie,* to be associated with *cscript.exe.*

Then, include the following routines in your CGI scripts:

```
Sub PrintHeader()
  WScript.Echo "Content-type=text/html"
  WScript.Echo
End Sub

Sub Send(OutText)
  WScript.Echo OutText
End Sub

Function Environment(EnviroName)
  Set WshShell = Wscript.CreateObject("Wscript.Shell")
  Set EnvHandle = WshShell.Environment("Process")
  Environment = EnvHandle(EnviroName)
End Function
```

If you don't use `PrintHeader` before the first `Send` in a script, your web server (and browser) will complain about a server configuration error (error 505).

The `PrintHeader` subroutine uses the *WScript.Echo* command to output the header information all web browsers expect from CGI output. `Send` is a simple routine to make it easier to send text as output. And the `Environment` function is used to retrieve information that has been placed in the system environment, often the means by which web-server software sends information (such as cookies) to CGI programs. Include the *Set* command (from DOS) to print out the entire contents of the environment space.

Example 9-2 prints out some basic text, as well as a few active environment variables (the previous two routines are required, as well as a properly configured web server):

Example 9-2. A Sample CGI Script

```
Call PrintHeader()
Send "Here is some relevant information:"
Send "<p>"
Send "PATH_INFO: " & Environment("PATH_INFO") & "<br>"
Send "QUERY_STRING: " & Environment("QUERY_STRING") & "<br>"
Send "HTTP_COOKIE: " & Environment("HTTP_COOKIE")
Send "<p>"
Send WScript.Echo "The current time is: " & Now()
```

You'll notice that I'm using a slightly different syntax for calling the `Send` subroutine, although it's merely for convenience and clarity. I've omitted the optional `Call` statement and the corresponding parentheses. In other words:

```
Send "a message"
```

is exactly the same as:

```
Call Send ("a message")
```

You can, of course, use this in conjunction with other routines. The code in Example 9-3 uses the `ReadFromFile` function (see "Manipulating Files from Scripts" earlier in this chapter) to transmit the contents of a text file.

Example 9-3. A Sample CGI Script

```
Call PrintHeader()
OrderNum = "234323"
Send "Here is your order (number " & OrderNum & "):"
Send "<p>"
Send "<img src=""/pictures/smiley.jpg""><br>"
Send ReadFromFile("d:\data\orders\" & OrderNum & ".txt")
Send "<p>"
Send "Now, what do you think of that?"
```

Note the use of Hypertext Markup Language (HTML) to include an image in the output. Although many HTML tags require quotation marks, adding a quotation mark in the middle of a line would cause VBScript to confuse it with the quotation marks at the beginning and end of the text to send. To tell VBScript to treat a quotation mark as a character to print, just put two of them together (as shown on the "smiley" line).

Making a Startup Script

The process of making a startup script—a script that is executed automatically when Windows starts—is quite simple. Essentially, you create a script as you normally would and then take steps to have it executed when Windows starts. There are two ways to do this:

Use the StartUp folder
: Put a shortcut to the script in your StartUp folder (usually *\Windows\Start Menu\Programs\StartUp*). This is by far the easiest to implement, but also the most fragile, because it's equally easy to disable. Additionally, if you have multiple users configured, this will only work for the current user.

Use the Registry
: Open the Registry Editor (if you're not familiar with the Registry Editor, see Chapter 3), and expand the branches to `HKEY_LOCAL_MACHINE\Software\Microsoft\Windows\CurrentVersion\Run`. Select **New** and then **String Value** from the **Edit** menu, and type **`startup script`**. Double-click on the new `Startup Script` value, type the name of your script (e.g., **`c:\scripts\myscript.vbs`**), and click **OK**.

  This has a similar effect to "Use the StartUp Folder" earlier in this section, except that it's harder to disable and it works for every user configured on the system.

A startup script can contain a list of programs that you want run in a specific order when Windows starts, such as connecting to the Internet and checking your email. (Explorer's Startup folder doesn't let you choose the order in which programs are run.) But there are other, less apparent uses for a startup script, such as for security or remote administration.

For example, say you've discovered a virus that has infected some or all the computers on a network. By writing a script that eliminates the virus by deleting key files or running an antivirus utility and setting it up as a startup script, you can effectively eliminate the virus from each computer.

But with scripts, you can take it even further: utilize a single script stored on a single computer that is run, over the network, on all computers. This way, you can make changes to the script once and have those changes propagated to all computers effortlessly. So, if you place the script *Startup.vbs* on a machine called *Server* in a folder called *c:\scripts* (drive *c:* would be shared as "c"), then each client machine should be configured to automatically execute *\\server\c\scripts\startup.vbs* (using one of the previous methods). The beauty of this is that when you don't want the script to do anything, you can simply leave it intact and empty. If you find that you need to, say, make a Registry change or copy a group of files onto each computer, just type the appropriate commands into the script and turn on (or reboot) all the client computers. This can turn some administration tasks into very short work.

Commonly found on many Windows Me systems is the script *network.vbs*. This is actually a virus with no other purpose than to replicate itself. To remove this script, simply delete the *network.vbs* file from your *\Windows\System* folder (or wherever it has shown up), as well as the shortcut in your Startup folder.

Deciphering Script Errors

One of the general disadvantages of scripts is that they are typically created with a plain-text editor, rather than a rich debugging environment used with many more sophisticated programming languages (see "Finding a Better Editor" later in this chapter). Because Notepad isn't specifically designed to understand VBScript, it can't offer any assistance with syntax (grammar) or errors while you're editing. Therefore, you must wait until you run the script to see if there are any problems. If WSH encounters an error, it will display a message similar to that shown in Figure 9-2.

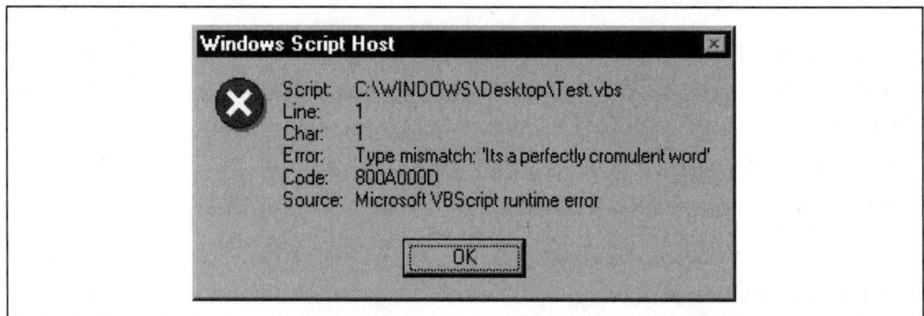

Figure 9-2. The Windows Script Host will display a message like this whenever it encounters an error

This sparse message box actually provides enough information to resolve most problems. Naturally, the first field, Script, shows the script filename in which the error occurred. This is especially useful if the script was run from a scheduled task or from your StartUp group, and you might otherwise not know which script caused the error.

The Line Number and Column fields show exactly where in the script the error occurred. Unfortunately, Notepad doesn't tell you what line the cursor is on, so you'll either have to count down from the top and then over or use a better text editor (see later in this chapter).

Category describes—more than anything else—what it was doing when it encountered the error. A *compilation error* occurs when WSH is first reading the file and making sure all of the commands are correctly entered; you'll see this if you forgot a parenthesis or quotation mark, or left out some other important command. A *runtime error*, on the other hand, is an error encountered while the script was being executed; this is caused by errors that WSH doesn't know are errors until it actually tries them, such as trying to read from a file that doesn't exist or trying to calculate the square root of a negative number.

Lastly, the Description field has a brief explanation of the error encountered. Sometimes it's helpful, but most of the time it's either too vague or too cryptic to be of much help. This is where programming experience comes in handy for interpreting these messages and figuring out what caused them. The following are a few of the more common error descriptions and what they mean:

Expected ')'
: Compilation error: you left out a closing parenthesis, such as at the end of an `InputBox` statement (see earlier). Note that sometimes you can have nested parenthesis (e.g., `x=1+(6+7*(3-4)))`, and you need to make sure you have an equal number of open and close parentheses.

Expected 'End'
: Compilation error: you left out a closing statement for a structure, such as `If`, `Sub`, or `For`. Make sure you include `End If`, `End Sub`, and `Next`, respectively. Note that WSH might report that the error occurred on line 37 of a 35-line file; when it's looking for a closing statement, it searches all the way to the end; only then will it report the error. You'll have to look through the entire script for the unpaired beginning statement. See the topics on flow control earlier in this chapter ("Creating Interactive Scripts with Conditional Statements," "Using Loops, Using Loops, Using Loops," and "Making Building Blocks with Subroutines and Functions") for more information on these commands.

Unterminated string constant
: Compilation error: you left out a closing quotation mark, usually required at the end of a "string of text."

Invalid procedure call or argument
Runtime error: this usually means that a subroutine or function has been called with one or more improper parameters. This can occur, for example, if you try to do something WSH isn't capable of, such as calculating the square root of a negative number.

Type mismatch: '[undefined]'
Runtime error: this means you've tried to use a command or function that VBScript doesn't recognize. I get this error whenever I try to use a VB command that doesn't exist in VBScript.

Object doesn't support this property or method
Runtime error: because it can be difficult to find documentation on the various objects used in VBScript, you're likely to encounter this error frequently. It means that you've tried to refer to a property or method that isn't supported by a particular object.

The system cannot find the file specified
Runtime error: This error, obviously reporting that you've tried to access a file on your hard disk that doesn't exist, also appears when you try to delete a Registry key that doesn't exist. See "Accessing the Registry from Scripts" earlier in this chapter for a Registry function that solves this problem.

If you plan on distributing your scripts, you'll want to eliminate any errors that may pop up. See the "Manipulating Files from Scripts" example script earlier in this chapter for more information on error trapping and the `On Error Resume Next` statement.

Finding a Better Editor

Notepad is a very rudimentary text editor. Although it serves our purpose, allowing us to write and save VBScript files, it doesn't go any further than it absolutely needs to. For example, it has no search-and-replace feature, no keyboard shortcuts, and no support for files more than 58,779 bytes in size. If you find yourself writing VBScript files often, you'll want to use a better editor. Now, Windows also comes with WordPad, although it doesn't do much more than Notepad in helping to write scripts, and it has that creepy Microsoft Word–like interface.

One direction to go is simply to use a better plain-text editor, such as UltraEdit-32 (*http://www.ultraedit.com*). It has many features prized by programmers, such as column selections, line numbering, good search and replace, and other goodies. However, it's still just a text editor, and therefore doesn't provide any VBScript-specific assistance.

Most full-featured programming languages come with a rich programming environment that provides real-time syntax checking (similar to a spellchecker in your word processor; some even tell you right away if you missed a parenthesis), as well as context-sensitive help (you can get technical assistance as you're typing code). The problem is that Windows doesn't come with such an editor, nor am I aware of any decent VBScript editor at the time of this writing.

Some may suggest that you can use either the Visual Basic editor or the VBA editor that comes with Microsoft Office 97 or Office 2000 to write your scripts, but this should be taken with a grain of salt. Although VB and VBA do have a similar syntax to VBScript and even share many commands, the environments are different enough that it's more trouble than it's worth.

Further Study

Given that writing scripts for the Windows Script Host is a language-dependent endeavor, the most helpful reference material will be specific to the particular language you're using. Microsoft's support web site for all their scripting technologies, including WSH, can be found at *http://msdn.microsoft.com/scripting/*. In addition to some limited documentation on VBScript and JScript, you can download updates to the WSH engine. Note that if you distribute scripts to other machines, you'll need to be careful of supporting features found only in newer releases of WSH.

Before committing to VBScript for a project, you may want to do some research on other supported languages listed here. Due to VBScript's heritage in web pages, security concerns have resulted in some limitations in the VBScript language, such as its inability to access the clipboard or link to external *.dll* files.

Given that JavaScript (which actually has nothing whatsoever to do with Sun Microsystems' Java™ programming language) was created by Netscape, you can find a lot of developer information at: *http://developer.netscape.com/tech/javascript/*.

The Practical Extract and Report Language (Perl) is probably the most powerful and flexible scripting language available for the Windows Script Host at the time of this writing. It's traditionally very popular among the Unix crowd and has gained tremendous popularity for its use in writing CGI programs for web servers.

Unfortunately, Windows Me doesn't come with the Perl engine; you'll have to obtain a separate Perl add-on module from *http://www.activestate.com*. More information is available at *http://www.perl.com*.

Automating Scripts with Scheduled Tasks

The Scheduled Tasks feature is fairly simple, allowing you to schedule any program or—more importantly in the context of this chapter—any script.

What's nice about the Scheduled Tasks feature is that it's actually a technology that is somewhat well integrated into the operating system. For example, there are a few tools (the Maintenance Wizard, for one) that automate the creation of scheduled tasks to complete various automated functions, such as running Scandisk once a day.

The Scheduled Tasks feature also has its pitfalls. The logging option is limited and only tells you if a given task was started. It can be hard to tell whether a scheduled task has actually been performed successfully, unless you specifically implement logging in a script. Also, any scheduled tasks will not be performed if you've selected the **Stop Using Task Scheduler** option, if your computer is turned off, if Windows isn't running, or if your portable computer is running off its battery. These may be obvious, but they can be easy to forget, and Windows won't tell you if you missed any tasks. Lastly, the only way to get rid of the useless Task Scheduler icon in the system tray is to disable the feature altogether (see Appendix A, *Setting Locator*).

To create a new scheduled task, open the *Scheduled Tasks* folder in **Explorer** or the **My Computer** window, and double-click **Add Scheduled Task**. The overly verbose wizard should then walk you through the process of creating a new task. When the wizard prompts you to select a program (it just displays a list of all the applications listed in your Start Menu), click **Browse**, select an existing script or batch file on your hard disk, and click **OK** when you're done.

I recommend just clicking **Next** repeatedly here until the wizard is finished. Then right-click on the new task, and select **Properties** to configure the task with a more suitable and convenient tabbed interface. One thing to note is the two **Power Management** settings in the **Settings** tab of the task's **Properties** dialog box. By default, tasks won't be run if your computer is running on batteries—a setting you may want to change if you need the task performed regardless of your computer's power source.

The use of a scheduler opens up some interesting possibilities. Scheduling helps with repetitive chores, such as running Disk Defragmenter or synchronizing network files; it also helps by taking care of things you may not remember to do yourself, such as backing up or checking for Windows updates. See the following topic for more ideas.

Wacky Script Ideas

The point of scripting is that instead of using a canned application to perform a certain task, you can easily and quickly throw together a script that does exactly what you need. That said, you may need some inspiration to get you cooking.

The following examples use many of the custom subroutines outlined earlier in this book, but for brevity and sanity, they won't be repeated.

Quick Floppy Backup Tool

The script in Example 9-4 starts by prompting you for the name of a folder to back up and checks to see if it exists. If not, it gives you an opportunity either to type another folder name or exit. Once a valid folder name has been entered, the script creates a backup of the entire folder on your floppy drive.

Example 9-4. Quick Floppy Backup Tool

```
On Error Resume Next
Accepted = False
Do Until Accepted
  MyFolder = InputBox("Please enter the name of the folder _
       you want to back up.")
  If Not FolderExists(MyFolder) Then
    Answer = MsgBox("The folder you typed doesn't exist. _
         Try again?", 36, "")
    If Answer = 7 Then WScript.Quit
  Else
    Accepted = True
  End If
Loop

Answer = MsgBox("Please put a diskette in your floppy drive.", 33, "")
If FolderSize(MyFolder) > DriveFreeSpace("a") Then
  MsgBox "The folder you specified won't fit on the floppy.", 16
  WScript.Quit
End If

If FolderCreate("a:\Backup\") = False Then
  MsgBox "There was a problem writing to the diskette.", 16
  WScript.Quit
End If
```

Example 9-4. Quick Floppy Backup Tool (continued)

```
Call FolderCopy(MyFolder, "a:\Backup\")

If Right(MyFolder, 1) <> "\" Then MyFolder = MyFolder & "\"
Call WriteToFile(MyFolder & "backuplog.txt", _
            "Last backed up: " & Now)
```

This script uses several **MsgBox** prompts and, if used unaltered, will probably irritate most users. (Hint: think about who will be using the scripts you write when you decide how much error checking and prompting is appropriate.) However, it also shows part of the power of interactive scripting. A little intelligent planning and error trapping can keep your scripts running smoothly, interrupting you only when necessary. Note the use of the **FolderExists** function at the beginning of the script; rather than risking encountering an error, the script checks for a potential problem (a missing file) and then takes the necessary steps to resolve it. Note also that if the folder doesn't exist and the user doesn't want to try again, the user can exit; always give your users a choice to get out if they want.

Because we have implemented some degree of error checking in this script, we include the line **On Error Resume Next** at the beginning of the script. This statement instructs WSH to simply ignore any errors it finds. This doesn't automatically resolve any errors; it just eliminates the error message that would otherwise appear in the event of an error, allowing the script to continue uninterrupted. This way, we're only bothered with the errors that concern us.

This example also uses the **Do...Loop** loop structure (which is similar to the **For...Next** loop, documented earlier in this chapter) at the beginning of the script. The code inside such a loop is repeated until a specific condition is met; in this case, the loop will repeat until the *Accepted* variable has a value of *True* (notice that it's set to *False* at the beginning of the script). The **If...Then** structures insure that the *Accepted* variable is only set to *True* if the folder actually exists.

The second part of the script compares the total size of the folder and all its contents with the amount of free space on the diskette currently inserted in the floppy drive. You could expand the script, so that if the diskette is not sufficient to store the folder, the user is given the opportunity to insert another diskette and try again. You'd need to use a similar **Do...Loop**, as described earlier.

Once the script has gone through all of the tests (eliminating the possibility of many errors), the **FolderCopy** subroutine is used to copy the folder to the floppy. Finally, the **WriteToFile** subroutine is used to record in a log file that the folder was backed up. Note also the preceding line that adds a backslash (\) to the end of the *MyFolder* variable; this way, we can pass a valid filename (the folder name followed by a backslash and then the filename) to the `WriteToFile` subroutine.

This script requires the following subroutines, which are found earlier in this book: `DriveFreeSpace`, `FolderCopy`, `FolderCreate`, `FolderExists`, `FolderSize`, and `WriteToFile`.

Internet Fishtank

Nothing exemplifies the power of the Internet more than an Internet-enabled fishtank. This, essentially, is a web page with a dynamic picture of the contents of a fishtank. There are several ways to do this, but the following shows that it can be done with nothing more than a script, a camera, and a common FTP account.

These listings assume that all files are stored in the folder *c:\camera*. Start with the script shown in Example 9-5.

Example 9-5. Internet Fishtank Script

```
On Error Resume Next

Call FileDelete("c:\camera\fish.jpg")
Call RunProgram("c:\camera\camera.exe c:\camera\fish.jpg")
If Not FileExists("c:\camera\fish.jpg") Then WScript.Quit

Call RunProgram ("ftp -n -s:c:\camera\ftpscript.txt myhost.com")
```

The script starts by suppressing all error messages, as described in the previous example. The three subsequent lines use the snapshot utility that comes with nearly all cheap video-conferencing digital cameras to take a photo and save it into a JPG image file. (Refer to the instructions that come with your camera for the specific command-line syntax you should use.) Note the line that checks for the existence of the file before proceeding (in case something went wrong) and the line beforehand that deletes the file from the last time the script was run.

The last line then runs the FTP utility that comes with Windows to transfer the JPG file to a web server (available for free from nearly all Internet service providers). Normally, FTP is an interactive program, requiring that the user type commands into the console; the `-n` and `-s` options shown here eliminate the need for user interaction. Replace *`myhost.com`* with the name of the host containing your web account. Example 9-6 shows the FTP script used by the WSH script in Example 9-5; type it into a plain text file, and save it as *ftpscript.txt*.

Example 9-6. FTP Script for Use with Internet-Fishtank Script

```
user mylogin
pass mypassword
bin
cd public_html
put c:\camera\fish.jpg
bye
```

The FTP script, like a batch file, is simply a text file containing (in order) the commands that otherwise would be typed manually into the FTP console window. Naturally, you'll want to replace the specifics, like *`mylogin`* and *`mypassword`*, with your own login and password, respectively, and *`public_html`* with the directory containing your public HTML files. Note that all commands must be typed lowercase. Type **`FTP -?`** at a command prompt for more command-line parameters, or start FTP and type **`help`** for more information on FTP commands.

Next, you'll want to set up a scheduled task to repeatedly run the script; the interval (5 seconds, 5 minutes, etc.) depends on your needs and the capabilities of your system. Lastly, if you haven't already done it, create a web page that references the *fish.jpg* photo—just visit the page to view a current picture of your fishtank—from anywhere in the world.

This script requires the following subroutines, found earlier in this book: `FileDelete`, `FileExists`, and `RunProgram`.

Smart Phone Dialing

One of the things that scripting can add to a normal task is to make it conditional; that is, perform certain tasks based on predetermined conditions, eliminating user interaction. A simple example is that of a phone dialer that chooses a different phone number depending on the time of day. That phone number can be the prefix for a long-distance carrier or the number of an Internet service provider. Example 9-7 shows such a script.

Example 9-7. Smart Dialer Script

```
On Error Resume Next

If Hour(Now()) >= 8 and Hour(Now()) <= 17 then
  Rem -- During the Day --
  Call RunProgram ("c:\links\daytime.lnk")
Else
  Rem -- At Night --
  Call RunProgram ("c:\links\nighttime.lnk")
End If
```

The script starts by suppressing all error messages, as described in the first script example. The rest of the script is one big `If...Then` structure, which executes a particular part of the script based on the time of day.

The test is performed with the `Hour()` function, which is built into VBScript.* Similar to the `Minute()`, `Second()`, `Day()`, `Week()`, `Month()`, and `Year()` functions, the expected parameter is a valid time/date string. Here, I've used another built-in function, `Now()`, which, not surprisingly, returns the current time in the proper format. Hence, `Hour(Now())` returns the current hour in 24-hour time; for 7:00 p.m., it would return 19.

If it is determined to be daytime (between 8:00 a.m. and 5:00 p.m.), the first code block is used; otherwise, the second code block is used. Naturally, you could put anything you want inside this structure, but for the sake of simplicity, this script just launches one of two shortcuts. The shortcuts could point to Dial-Up Networking connections or a phone-dialer utility.

This script requires the `RunProgram` subroutine, found earlier in this book.

Quick SendTo Shortcut Creator

Explorer's SendTo menu contains a list of programs and shortcuts to which any selected file can be sent. The idea is to list programs that could be used with any type of file, such as an email program or file viewer, without having to specifically set up file associations for each supported file type. The following script (Example 9-8) allows you to right-click on any application executable (*.exe* file), folder, or drive and create a shortcut in the *SendTo* folder on the spot.

Example 9-8. SendTo Shortcut Creator

```
SendToFolder = RegistryRead("HKEY_CURRENT_USER\Software\Microsoft\Windows\ _
    CurrentVersion\Explorer\Shell Folders", "SendTo")

Call Shortcut("SendToFolder\Notepad.lnk", CommandLine(1))
```

Whenever we can, we want to make our scripts "smart." If we wanted to be lazy, all we would really need is the second line of this script, which creates a shortcut based on the command-line parameter (see "Using Command-Line Parameters in Scripts" earlier in this chapter for details). However, the first line reads the Registry to find the location of the *SendTo* folder, which is handy if there's more than one user (each with his own *SendTo* folder) or if you intend to use this script on more than one computer.

* A Visual Basic or VBScript reference will document more cool built-in functions like these.

Once the script has been written, you'll need to associate it with all file types. See Chapter 4 for details on using the "*" file type. This script requires the following subroutines, found earlier in this book: `CommandLine`, `RegistryRead`, and `Shortcut`.

Rename Files with Search and Replace

Explorer lets you rename only one file at a time. Normally, the only way to rename multiple files is with a command prompt (see Appendix B). Example 9-9 shows a script that will rename all the files in a given folder based on rules you choose.

Example 9-9. File Renaming Script

```
FolderName = InputBox("Enter the name of the folder:")
If Not FolderExists(FolderName) Then WScript.Quit

SearchText = InputBox("Type the text to look for:")
ReplaceText = InputBox("Type the text with which to replace" _
     & SearchText & ":")

Set FileObject = CreateObject("Scripting.FileSystemObject")
Set FolderObject = FileObject.GetFolder(FolderName)
Set FilesObject = FolderObject.Files

FileCount = 0
For Each Filename in FilesObject
  If InStr(Filename.Name,SearchText) Then
    Filename.Name = Replace(Filename.Name,SearchText,ReplaceText)
    FileCount = FileCount + 1
  End If
Next

If FileCount > 0 Then
  MsgBox FileCount & " files were renamed."
Else
  MsgBox "No filenames containing " & SearchText & " were found."
End If
```

The first four lines ask the user for input, including the folder name, the text to look for, and the text with which to replace it. The next three lines set the appropriate objects (for further documentation on these objects, check *http://msdn.microsoft.com/scripting/*).

The `For...Next` structure that follows does the real work; this particular example uses a special form of the loop intended to cycle through all the elements of an object array. In this case, the array contains the filenames of all the files in the active folder. The `Replace` function (built into VBScript) then does the search and replace for each individual filename.

Lastly, the `FileCount` variable keeps track of the number of files renamed, the result of which is tallied in the final code section.

Now, it may take some experience to understand the extensive use of objects in this example, but for the time being, just typing it in will serve as a good example that can be used in other circumstances. This script requires the `FolderExists` subroutine, found earlier in this book.

Note that a far more powerful file-renaming utility, Power Rename (written by yours truly), is available for Windows Me (download it from *http://www.annoyances.org*).

Sort the Start Menu with Ease

In "Fixing the Start Menu" in Chapter 2, *Basic Explorer Coping Skills*, one solution describes how to sort a particular *Start Menu* folder alphabetically. The problem is that if you have twenty folders in Programs menu, you'll have to do it twenty times. Furthermore, it isn't sticky, meaning that newly added shortcuts aren't sorted. The simple, one-line script in Example 9-10 deletes the Registry settings involved, effectively sorting all your Start Menu folders in one step.

Example 9-10. Folder Shortcut Script

```
Call RegistryDelete("HKEY_CURRENT_USER\Software\Microsoft\Windows\ _
     CurrentVersion\Explorer\MenuOrder", "")
```

See "Automating the Deletion of Registry Items" in Chapter 3 for more information on the methodology used here. This script requires the `RegistryDelete` subroutine, found earlier in this book.

Mirror a Folder with Folder Shortcuts

This script is an automated way to perform the solution described in "Mirror a Folder with Folder Shortcuts" in Chapter 4. If you haven't read that section, it's very important that you do so before using this script (see Example 9-11).

If you create a Folder Shortcut and then try to delete it, you will be deleting the target folder and all of its contents. Folder Shortcuts must be dismantled before they can be removed. See "Mirror a Folder with Folder Shortcuts" in Chapter 4 for details.

The solution in Chapter 4 essentially involves creating a folder, creating a shortcut, and creating a text file—all possible with a script.

Example 9-11. Folder Shortcut Script

```
TargetName = CommandLine(1)
If TargetName = "" Then
  TargetName = InputBox("Type the name of the folder to link:")
End If
If FolderExists(TargetName) = False Then
  MsgBox "TargetName does not appear to be a valid folder."
  WScript.Quit
End If
If Right(TargetName,1) = "\" Then TargetName = Left(TargetName,
Len(TargetName) - 1)

DesktopFolder = RegistryRead("HKEY_CURRENT_USER\Software\Microsoft\ _
     Windows\CurrentVersion\Explorer\Shell Folders", "Desktop")
If Right(DesktopFolder,1) <> "\" Then DesktopFolder = DesktopFolder + "\"

X = 0
Do
  Y = X
  X = InStr(X + 1, TargetName, "\")
Loop until X = 0
NewTargetName = DesktopFolder + "Shortcut to " + Mid(TargetName, Y + 1)

If FolderExists(NewTargetName) = False Then
  MsgBox "NewTargetName already exists."
  WScript.Quit
End If

FolderCreate(NewTargetName)
Call Shortcut(NewTargetName + "\target.lnk", TargetName)

Text = "[.ShellClassInfo]" + chr(13) + chr(10) + _
"CLSID2={0AFACED1-E828-11D1-9187-B532F1E9575D}" + chr(13) + chr(10) + _
     "Flags=2" + chr(13) + chr(10) + _
"ConfirmFileOp=0" + chr(13) + chr(10)

Call WriteToFile(NewTargetName + "\desktop.ini", Text)
Call SetAttributes(NewTargetName + "\desktop.ini", 6)
```

This script is complex, but when broken down, it should be fairly easy to understand. First, the script asks for the name of an existing folder and checks to see if that folder exists. If a trailing slash is found, it is removed. Then the script reads the Registry to find the location of the desktop folder (where the Folder Shortcut will be placed). The next block of code extracts the name of the folder from the path: if **c:\windows\temp** is typed, this code extracts the word, `temp`. The script then forms a new path, checks to see if it already exists, and then creates the new folder.

Then, according to the steps described in "Mirror a Folder with Folder Shortcuts" in Chapter 4, a shortcut is created and several lines are written to the file *desktop.ini*. Lastly, the Hidden and System attributes for *desktop.ini* are set.

The beauty of this script is that it is almost entirely automated. It doesn't ask for any information it's able to safely retrieve itself. The very first line also checks to see if there's a command-line parameter specified. This enables you to use this script in a folder's context menu, so that you could right-click on any folder and select **Make Folder Shortcut**, and the script would do the rest. See "Using Command-Line Parameters in Scripts" earlier in this chapter and "Customize context menus for drives, folders, and desktop icons" in Chapter 4 for details. For another, similar example, see "Print Out a Directory Listing" in Chapter 4.

This script requires the following subroutines, which are found earlier in this book: `CommandLine`, `FolderCreate`, `FolderExists`, `FolderExists`, `RegistryRead`, `SetAttributes`, and `WriteToFile`.

The previous example script does not accommodate Folder Shortcuts for FTP sites, although it can be modified to work with Internet Shortcut files instead of Folders.

Regardless, I leave it to you to put the final pieces together!

Setting Locator

It shouldn't take you too long to find that the various options, switches, and adjustments that allow you to customize Windows are scattered throughout dozens of dialog boxes, property sheets, and add-on utilities. Understandably, this can turn a simple task into a monumental wild goose chase. The following list contains more than 200 Windows Me settings and where to find them.

The settings are listed alphabetically and named in such a way that they should be easy to locate by context. For example, to find out how to turn off the Power Management icon in the tray, look for the **Power Management Icon** entry in the **Tray** section. Note that a few settings have been duplicated with different labels to make them easier to find.

Settings made in the Registry (see Chapter 3, *The Registry*) are not included here because of their complexity. Most Registry settings can be found by using the Registry Editor's Find tool or by looking through this book.

Some of the settings listed here and elsewhere in this book are located in one of the following Microsoft programs. For one reason or another, these programs don't come with Windows; neither are they immediately accessible in the Start Menu:

TweakUI
: Released by Microsoft shortly after the release of Windows 95, TweakUI is a Control Panel add-on that allows users to make certain changes that aren't otherwise possible without editing the Registry. The original intent was to reduce technical support calls from users

who had messed up their Registry by trying, for example, to remove the clutter from the Windows desktop—but TweakUI has since become an essential component of Windows.

The latest version, updated for use with Windows Me, is unfortunately not installed with Windows, nor is it included on the CD. You can download it for free from *http://www.annoyances.org*.

To install it, unzip all the files into a new folder, right-click on the *Tweakui.inf* file, and select **Install**. If Windows prompts you for an installation diskette, just point it to the folder that contains the TweakUI installation files.

System Policy Editor

The System Policy Editor provides access to settings that relate primarily to security and multiple users. Although it has been included with each release of Windows since Windows 95, it has been removed in Windows Me. Although its use in Windows Me isn't officially supported by Microsoft, it will still work without any ill effects. You can download it for free from *http://www.annoyances.org*.

To install it, unzip all the files into a new folder, right-click on the *Poledit.inf* file, and select **Install**. If Windows prompts you for an installation diskette, just point it to the folder that contains the Policy Editor installation files.

To get more categories and settings in Policy Editor, select **Policy Template** from the **Options** menu, and then click **Add**. Select any *.adm* file (from the installation folder) that doesn't already appear in the **Current Templates** list—you'll have to do this for each *.adm* file until you've got them all.

System Configuration Utility

The System Configuration Utility, installed with Windows Me by default, is yet another collection of obscure Windows settings, although mostly intended for advanced troubleshooting. It's located in your *\Windows\System* folder. Select **Run** from the **Start Menu**, type **`msconfig`**, and click **OK** to run this program.

To conserve space, I describe following the setting locations in a form of computerese, as follows: consecutive actions are separated by an arrow. For example, "Control Panel → TweakUI → Desktop tab" means first double-click on the **Control Panel** icon, then double-click on the **TweakUI** icon, and then choose the **Desktop** tab. The setting you're seeking will now be in plain sight.

Alphabetical Listing of All Windows Me Settings

Accessibility, Idle Settings
Control Panel → Accessibility → General tab

Accessibility, in Internet Explorer
Control Panel → Internet Options → General tab → Accessibility

Active Desktop, Enable/Disable
Control Panel → Folder Options → General tab

Control Panel → TweakUI → IE tab

Active Desktop, Show Web Content
Control Panel → Display → Web tab

ActiveX Controls, Internet Explorer
Control Panel → Internet Options → Security tab → Custom Level

Add/Remove Programs, Remove Unwanted Items
Control Panel → TweakUI → Add/Remove tab

Address Bar, Display Full Path
Control Panel → Folder Options → View tab

Address Bar, Go Button
Control Panel → Internet Options → Advanced tab

Address Bar, Searching
Control Panel → Internet Options → Advanced tab

Administration, Remote
Control Panel → Passwords → Remote Administration tab

Alarm, Low Battery
Control Panel → Power Options → Alarms tab

Animated GIFs, Internet Explorer
Control Panel → Internet Options → Advanced tab

Animation, Enable/Disable Selectively
Control Panel → TweakUI → General tab

Animation, Menus, and Tooltips
Control Panel → Display → Effects tab

Animation, Minimizing and Maximizing Windows
Control Panel → TweakUI → General tab

Animation, Smooth Scrolling
Control Panel → Internet Options → Advanced tab

Animation, Web Pages
Control Panel → Internet Options → Advanced tab

Area Code, Dialing
Control Panel → Modems → General tab → Dialing Properties

Control Panel → Telephony

AutoActivate Window Under Mouse
Control Panel → TweakUI → Mouse tab

AutoComplete, Internet Explorer
Control Panel → Internet Options → Content tab

Control Panel → Internet Options → Advanced tab

AutoDial an Internet Connection
Control Panel → Internet Options → Connections tab

AutoHide, Taskbar
Control Panel → Taskbar and Start Menu → General tab

Back Button, Show in File Dialog Box
Control Panel → TweakUI → Open tab

Background Wallpaper/Pattern
Control Panel → Display → Background tab

Battery, Alarm
Control Panel → Power Options → Alarms tab

Battery, Power Meter
Control Panel → Power Options → Power Meter tab

Beep, Enable/Disable
Control Panel → TweakUI → General tab

Cache, CD Drive
Control Panel → System → Performance tab → File System → CD-ROM tab

Cache, Hard Disk
Control Panel → System → Performance tab → File System → Hard Disk tab

Cache, Internet Explorer
Control Panel → Internet Options → General tab

Cache, Removable Drive
Control Panel → System → Performance tab → File System → Removable Disk tab

Calendar, Default
Control Panel → Internet Options → Programs tab

Call Forwarding
Control Panel → Modems → General tab → Properties → Forwarding tab

Call Waiting, Enable/Disable
Control Panel → Modems → General tab → Dialing Properties

Control Panel → Telephony

Calling Card, Long Distance
Control Panel → Modems → General tab → Dialing Properties

Control Panel → Telephony

Certificates, Internet Explorer
Control Panel → Internet Options → Content tab

Channel Bar
Control Panel → Display → Web tab

Channel Bar, Show at Startup
Control Panel → Internet Options → Advanced tab

Chat, in Games
Control Panel → Gaming Options → Voice Chat tab

ClickLock, Enable/Disable
Control Panel → Mouse → Buttons tab

Clock, Show/Hide
Control Panel → Taskbar and Start Menu → General tab

Color Management, Display
Control Panel → Display → Settings tab → Advanced → Color Management tab

Color Management, Printer
Control Panel → Printers → select a printer → File → Properties → Color Management tab

Colors, Choosing
Control Panel → Display → Appearance tab

Colors, Color Depth
Control Panel → Display → Settings tab

Colors, Internet Explorer
Control Panel → Internet Options → General tab → Colors

Colors, Mouse Hot Tracking Effects
Control Panel → TweakUI → Explorer tab

Columns in Start Menu, Enable/Disable
Control Panel → Taskbar and Start Menu → Advanced tab

COM Port Settings
Control Panel → System → Device Manager tab → select COM port → Properties → Port Settings tab

Common Program Files, Location of Folder
Control Panel → TweakUI → My Computer tab

Contact List, Default
Control Panel → Internet Options → Programs tab

Control Panel, Expand Contents in Start Menu
Control Panel → Taskbar and Start Menu → Advanced tab

Control Panel, Restrict Access
System Policy Editor → File → Open Registry → Local User\Control Panel

Control Panel, Show in Start Menu → Settings
Control Panel → TweakUI → IE tab

Control Panel, Show/Hide Selective Items
Control Panel → TweakUI → Control Panel tab

Controllers, Game
Control Panel → Gaming Options → Controllers tab

Cookies, Internet Explorer
Control Panel → Internet Options → Security tab → Custom Level

Country
Control Panel → Regional Settings → Regional Settings tab

Country Code
System Configuration Utility → International tab

Currency, Display Settings
Control Panel → Regional Settings → Currency tab

Cursor, Blink Rate
Control Panel → Accessibility → Display tab

Control Panel → Keyboard → Speed tab

Cursor, Mouse, Hide while Typing
Control Panel → Mouse → Pointer Options tab

Cursor, Mouse Pointer
Control Panel → Mouse → Pointers tab

Cursor, Mouse Speed
Control Panel → Mouse → Pointer Options tab

Cursor, Width
Control Panel → Accessibility → Display tab

Date
Control Panel → Date/Time

Date, Display Settings
Control Panel → Regional Settings → Date tab

Daylight Savings
Control Panel → Date/Time

Deep Sleep (Power Management), Enable/Disable
System Configuration Utility → General tab → Advanced

Description, on Network
Control Panel → Network → Identification tab

Desktop Wallpaper/Pattern
Control Panel → Display → Background tab

Desktop, Colors
Control Panel → Display → Appearance tab

Desktop, Location of Folder
Control Panel → TweakUI → My Computer tab

Desktop, Show in Places Bar
Control Panel → TweakUI → Open tab

Desktop, Show/Hide Selective Icons
Control Panel → TweakUI → Desktop tab

Desktop, Which Icon to Show First
Control Panel → TweakUI → Desktop tab

Device Manager
Control Panel → System → Device Manager tab

Dialing, Area Code
Control Panel → Modems → General tab → Dialing Properties

Control Panel → Telephony

Dial-Up Networking, Confirmation dialog box
Control Panel → Dial-Up Networking → Connections → Settings → General tab

Dial-Up Networking, Connect Automatically
Control Panel → Dial-Up Networking → select connection icon → File → Properties → Security tab

Dial-Up Networking, Default Internet Connection
Control Panel → Dial-Up Networking → select connection icon → File → Properties → Dialing tab

Dial-Up Networking, Idle Disconnect
Control Panel → Dial-Up Networking → select connection icon → File → Properties → Dialing tab

Dial-Up Networking, Redial
Control Panel → Dial-Up Networking → select connection icon → File → Properties → Dialing tab

Dial-Up Networking, Show in Start Menu → Settings
Control Panel → TweakUI → IE tab

Dial-Up Networking, Terminal Window
Control Panel → Dial-Up Networking → select connection icon → File → Properties → General tab → Configure → Options tab

Display, Hardware Acceleration
Control Panel → Display → Settings tab → Advanced → Performance tab

Display, High-contrast
Control Panel → Accessibility → Display tab

Documents Menu, Clear at Startup
Control Panel → TweakUI → Paranoia tab

Documents Menu, Empty
Control Panel → Taskbar and Start Menu → Advanced tab

Documents Menu, Enable/Disable
Control Panel → TweakUI → IE tab

Documents Menu, Expand Contents in Start Menu
Control Panel → Taskbar and Start Menu → Advanced tab

Documents Menu, Location of Folder (Recent)
Control Panel → TweakUI → My Computer tab

Documents Menu, Show in Start Menu
Control Panel → TweakUI → IE tab

Double-Click Distance
Control Panel → TweakUI → Mouse tab

Double-Click Speed
Control Panel → Mouse → Buttons tab

Double-Click to Open Items
Control Panel → Folder Options → General tab

Double-Click, Detect Accidental
Control Panel → TweakUI → IE tab

Downloads, Notify when Complete
Control Panel → Internet Options → Advanced tab

Drag-Drop in Start Menu, Enable/Disable
Control Panel → Taskbar and Start Menu → Advanced tab

Dragging Window Contents
Control Panel → Display → Effects tab

Email Application, Default
Control Panel → Internet Options → Programs tab

Environment Variables, Configure
System Configuration Utility → Environment tab

Explorer, Remember Window Position
Control Panel → TweakUI → General tab

Extensions, Show/Hide
Control Panel → Folder Options → View tab

Favorites, Location of Folder
Control Panel → TweakUI → My Computer tab

Favorites, Show in Places Bar
Control Panel → TweakUI → Open tab

File Dialog Box, Configure Places Bar
Control Panel → TweakUI → Open tab

File Dialog Box, Remember Previously Used Filenames
Control Panel → TweakUI → Open tab

File Dialog Box, Show/Hide Back Button
Control Panel → TweakUI → Open tab

File Types, Configure
Control Panel → Folder Options → File Types tab

File Types, Restore to Factory Defaults
Control Panel → TweakUI → Repair tab

Filename Extensions, Show/Hide
Control Panel → Folder Options → View tab

Files, Extract from Windows CD
System Configuration Utility → General tab → Extract File

FilterKeys
Control Panel → Accessibility → Keyboard tab

Find
See "Search"

Floppy Drive, Search at Startup
Control Panel → System → Performance tab → File System → Floppy Disk tab

Focus, Prevent Applications from Stealing
Control Panel → TweakUI → General tab

Folder Settings, Show in Start Menu → Settings
System Policy Editor → File → Open Registry → Local User\Windows 98 System\Shell\Restrictions\Remove folders from "Settings" on Start Menu

Folders, Icon Size
Control Panel → Display → Appearance tab

Control Panel → Display → Effects tab

Folders, Icon Spacing
Control Panel → Display → Appearance tab

Folders, Locations of Special Folders
Control Panel → TweakUI → My Computer tab

Folders, Open in Same/Multiple Windows
Control Panel → Folder Options → General tab

Folders, Open in Separate Process
Control Panel → Folder Options → View tab

Folders, Remember View Settings
Control Panel → Folder Options → View tab

Folders, Reuse for Internet Shortcuts
Control Panel → Internet Options → Advanced tab

Folders, Show Full Path
Control Panel → Folder Options → View tab

Fonts, Install
Control Panel → Fonts → File → Install New Font

Fonts, Internet Explorer
Control Panel → Internet Options → General tab → Fonts

Fonts, Internet Explorer, Allow Download
Control Panel → Internet Options → Security tab → Custom Level

Fonts, Menus, Tooltips, and Message Boxes
Control Panel → Display → Appearance tab

Fonts, Overall Size
Control Panel → Display → Settings tab → Advanced → General tab

Fonts, Repair Fonts Folder
Control Panel → TweakUI → Repair tab

Fonts, Smoothing
Control Panel → Display → Effects tab

FTP, View as Folder in Internet Explorer
Control Panel → Internet Options → Advanced tab

Go Button in Address Bar
Control Panel → Internet Options → Advanced tab

Hard Disk, Performance Settings
Control Panel → System → Performance tab → File System → Hard Disk tab

Hard Disk, Power Management
Control Panel → Power Options → Power Schemes tab

Hardware Profiles
Control Panel → System → Hardware Profiles tab

Help Menu, Show in Start Menu
Control Panel → TweakUI → IE tab

Hibernate, Settings
Control Panel → Power Options → Power Schemes tab

Hidden Files and Folders, Show/Hide
Control Panel → Folder Options → View tab

History, Internet Explorer
Control Panel → Internet Options → General tab

History, Internet Explorer, Clear at Startup
Control Panel → TweakUI → Paranoia tab

History, Show in Places Bar
Control Panel → TweakUI → Open tab

Home Page
Control Panel → Internet Options → General tab

Hotkeys
See "Keyboard Shortcuts"

HTML, Default Editor
Control Panel → Internet Options → Programs tab

Icon Size
Control Panel → Display → Appearance tab

Control Panel → Display → Effects tab

Icon Size in Start Menu
Control Panel → Taskbar and Start Menu → General tab

Icon Spacing
Control Panel → Display → Appearance tab

Icons, Colors
Control Panel → Display → Effects tab

Icons, Repair
Control Panel → TweakUI → Repair tab

Idle, Disconnect
Control Panel → Modems → General tab → Properties → Connection tab

Install on Demand, Enable/Disable
Control Panel → Internet Options → Advanced tab

Installation Path, Location of Folder
Control Panel → TweakUI → My Computer tab

Internet Call, Default
Control Panel → Internet Options → Programs tab

Internet Connection, AutoDial Enable/Disable
Control Panel → Internet Options → Connections tab

Internet Explorer, Check Default Browser
Control Panel → Internet Options → Programs tab

Internet Explorer, Check for Updates
Control Panel → Internet Options → Advanced tab

Internet Explorer, Desktop Icon
Control Panel → Internet Options → Advanced tab

IP Address, Set
Control Panel → Network → Configuration tab → select TCP/IP from the list → Properties → IP Address

IP Address, View
Run *winipcfg.exe* → More Info

Java, Internet Explorer
Control Panel → Internet Options → Security tab → Custom Level

Joystick, Settings
Control Panel → Gaming Options → Controllers tab

Keyboard Help in Programs
Control Panel → Accessibility → Keyboard tab

Keyboard Layout
Control Panel → Keyboard → Language tab

Keyboard Shortcuts, Repair
Control Panel → TweakUI → Repair tab

Keyboard Shortcuts, Show/Hide
Control Panel → TweakUI → General tab

Keyboard, Advanced Language Settings
System Configuration Utility → International tab

Keyboard, Repeat Rate and Delay
Control Panel → Keyboard → Speed tab

Language, Advanced Settings
System Configuration Utility → International tab

Language, Display
Control Panel → Regional Settings → Regional Settings tab

Language, Internet Explorer
Control Panel → Internet Options → General tab → Languages

Language, Keyboard
Control Panel → Keyboard → Language tab

Left Mouse Button, Reverse with Right
Control Panel → Mouse → Buttons tab

Links Menu, Show in Favorites
Control Panel → TweakUI → IE tab

Links, Underline
Control Panel → Internet Options → Advanced tab

Locations, Dialing
Control Panel → Modems → General tab → Dialing Properties

Control Panel → Telephony

Logoff Start Menu Item, Show/Hide
Control Panel → Taskbar and Start Menu → Advanced tab

Control Panel → TweakUI → IE tab

Logon Automatically at System Startup
Control Panel → TweakUI → Logon tab

Logon, Show/Hide Last User
System Policy Editor → File → Open Registry → Local Computer\Windows 98 System\User Profiles

Menu Fonts
Control Panel → Display → Appearance tab

Menu Speed
Control Panel → TweakUI → Mouse tab

Message Box Fonts
Control Panel → Display → Appearance tab

Message Box Sounds
Control Panel → Sounds and Multimedia Properties

Minimizing and Maximizing Windows, Animation
Control Panel → TweakUI → General tab

Modem Initialization String
Control Panel → Modems → General tab → Properties → Connection tab → Advanced → Extra Settings

Modem Volume
Control Panel → Modems → General tab → Properties → General tab

Monitor, Power Management
Control Panel → Power Options → Power Schemes tab

Monitors, Multiple
Control Panel → Display → Settings tab

Mouse Buttons, Reverse Left and Right
Control Panel → Mouse → Buttons tab

Mouse Cursor
Control Panel → Mouse → Pointers tab

Mouse Cursor, Hide While Typing
Control Panel → Mouse → Pointer Options tab

Mouse Cursor, Hot Tracking Effects
Control Panel → TweakUI → General tab

Mouse Cursor, Hot Tracking Effects, Colors
Control Panel → TweakUI → Explorer tab

Mouse Cursor, Show with Ctrl key
Control Panel → Mouse → Pointer Options tab

Mouse Cursor Trails
Control Panel → Mouse → Pointer Options tab

Mouse Sensitivity
Control Panel → TweakUI → Mouse tab

Mouse Speed
Control Panel → Mouse → Pointer Options tab

Mouse Wheel, Settings
Control Panel → TweakUI → Mouse tab

MouseKeys
Control Panel → Accessibility → Mouse tab

MS-DOS Prompt, Enable/Disable
System Policy Editor → File → Open Registry → Local User\Restrictions\Disable MS-DOS prompt

My Computer Icon
Control Panel → Display → Effects tab

My Computer, Show in Places Bar
Control Panel → TweakUI → Open tab

My Computer, Show/Hide All Drives
System Policy Editor → File → Open Registry → Local User\Windows 98 System\Shell\Restrictions\Hide Drives in "My Computer"

My Computer, Show/Hide Selective Drives
Control Panel → TweakUI → My Computer tab

My Documents, Desktop Icon
Control Panel → Folder Options → View tab

My Documents Icon
Control Panel → Display → Effects tab

My Documents, Location of Folder
Control Panel → TweakUI → My Computer tab

My Documents, Show in Documents Menu
Control Panel → TweakUI → IE tab

My Documents, Show in Places Bar
Control Panel → TweakUI → Open tab

My Music, Location of Folder
Control Panel → TweakUI → My Computer tab

My Music, Show in Places Bar
Control Panel → TweakUI → Open tab

My Network Places Icon
Control Panel → Display → Effects tab

My Network Places, Show Computers Near Me
Control Panel → TweakUI → IE tab

My Network Places, Show in Places Bar
Control Panel → TweakUI → Open tab

My Pictures, Expand Contents in Start Menu
Control Panel → Taskbar and Start Menu → Advanced tab

My Pictures, Location of Folder
Control Panel → TweakUI → My Computer tab

My Pictures, Show in Documents Menu
Control Panel → TweakUI → IE tab

My Pictures, Show in Places Bar
Control Panel → TweakUI → Open tab

My Profile
Control Panel → Internet Options → Content tab

My Video, Location of Folder
Control Panel → TweakUI → My Computer tab

My Video, Show in Places Bar
Control Panel → TweakUI → Open tab

Name, on Network
Control Panel → Network → Identification tab

Network Neighborhood
See "My Network Places"

Network, Clear History at Startup
Control Panel → TweakUI → Paranoia tab

Network, Primary Logon Client
Control Panel → Network → Configuration tab

New Menu, Remove Unwanted Items
Control Panel → TweakUI → New tab

News, Default
Control Panel → Internet Options → Programs tab

Numbers, Display Settings
Control Panel → Regional Settings → Number tab

Password, after Hibernate
Control Panel → Power Options → Advanced tab

Password, Change
Control Panel → Passwords → Change Passwords tab

Password, Minimum Length
System Policy Editor → File → Open Registry → Local Computer\Windows 98 Network\Logon

Path, Display in Title Bar and Address Bar
Control Panel → Folder Options → View tab

Path Environment Variable, Configure
System Configuration Utility → Environment tab

PC Card Sounds, Enable/Disable
Control Panel → PC Card (PCMCIA) → Global Settings tab

PC Card, Warning
Control Panel → PC Card (PCMCIA) → Socket Status tab

PCMCIA
See "PC Card"

Personalized Menu, Favorites
Control Panel → Internet Options → Advanced tab

Personalized Menu, Start Menu
Control Panel → Taskbar and Start Menu → General tab

Pictures, Load in Web Pages, Internet Explorer
Control Panel → Internet Options → Advanced tab

Places Bar, Configure
Control Panel → TweakUI → Open tab

Pop-Up Descriptions
See "Tooltips"

Power Management, Display, Compatibility
Control Panel → Display → Settings tab → Advanced → Monitor tab

Power Management, Display, Settings
Control Panel → Display → Screen Saver tab → Settings → Power Schemes tab

Control Panel → Power Options → Power Schemes tab

Printer, Set Default
Control Panel → Printers → select a printer → File → Set as Default

Printers, Expand Contents in Start Menu
Control Panel → Taskbar and Start Menu → Advanced tab

Printing, Cancel a Job
Control Panel → Printers → double-click a printer → Document → Cancel Printing

Printing, Cancel All Jobs
Control Panel → Printers → select a printer → File → Purge Print Documents

Profile Assistant
Control Panel → Internet Options → Content tab

Profile Assistant, Enable/Disable
Control Panel → Internet Options → Advanced tab

Profiles, Multiple Users
Control Panel → Passwords → User Profiles tab

Program Files, Location of Folder
Control Panel → TweakUI → My Computer tab

Programs in Start Menu, Location of Folder
Control Panel → TweakUI → My Computer tab

Ratings, Internet Explorer
Control Panel → Internet Options → Content tab → Content Advisor

Recycle Bin Icon
Control Panel → Display → Effects tab

Refresh Rate
Control Panel → Display → Settings tab → Advanced → Adapter tab

Registry Editor, Enable/Disable
System Policy Editor → File → Open Registry → Local User\Restrictions\Disable Registry editing tools

Registry Editor, Repair Columns
Control Panel → TweakUI → Repair tab

Remote Administration, Allow/Disallow
Control Panel → Passwords → Remote Administration tab

Resolution
Control Panel → Display → Settings tab

Right Mouse Button, Reverse with Left
Control Panel → Mouse → Buttons tab

Run Start Menu Item, Clear History at Startup
Control Panel → TweakUI → Paranoia tab

Run Start Menu Item, Show/Hide
Control Panel → Taskbar and Start Menu → Advanced tab

Scandisk at Startup, Enable/Disable
System Configuration Utility → General tab → Advanced

Scheduled Tasks, Enable/Disable
Control Panel → Scheduled Tasks → Advanced → Start/Stop Using Task Scheduler

Scheduled Tasks, View Log
Control Panel → Scheduled Tasks → Advanced → View Log

Screen Saver
Control Panel → Display → Screen Saver tab

Scripting, Internet Explorer
Control Panel → Internet Options → Security tab → Custom Level

Scripting, Internet Explorer, Debugging
Control Panel → Internet Options → Advanced tab

Scroll Start Menu Items, Enable/Disable
Control Panel → Taskbar and Start Menu → Advanced tab

Search, Clear History at Startup
Control Panel → TweakUI → Paranoia tab

Security Check, Internet Explorer
Control Panel → Internet Options → Connections tab

Send To, Location of Folder
Control Panel → TweakUI → My Computer tab

Serial Port Diagnostics
Control Panel → Modems → Diagnostics tab → More Info

SerialKey Devices
Control Panel → Accessibility → General tab

Sharing, File and Printer
Control Panel → Network → Configuration tab → File and Print Sharing

Shortcuts, Appearance
Control Panel → TweakUI → General tab

ShowSounds
Control Panel → Accessibility → Sound tab

Shut Down, Enable/Disable
System Policy Editor → File → Open Registry → Local User\Windows 98 System\Shell\Restrictions\Disable Shut Down command

Single-Click to Open Items
Control Panel → Folder Options → General tab

Sleep, Settings
Control Panel → Power Options → Power Schemes tab

Smooth Scrolling
Control Panel → TweakUI → General tab

Smooth Scrolling in Web Pages
Control Panel → Internet Options → Advanced tab

Snap Mouse Pointer to Default Button
Control Panel → Mouse → Pointer Options tab

Sounds, Enable/Disable
Control Panel → Sounds and Multimedia Properties

Sounds, Enable/Disable Beep
Control Panel → TweakUI → General tab

Sounds, PC Card Insert/Removal
Control Panel → PC Card (PCMCIA) → Global Settings tab

Sounds, Play in Internet Explorer
Control Panel → Internet Options → Advanced tab

SoundSentry
Control Panel → Accessibility → Sound tab

Stand By, Settings
Control Panel → Power Options → Power Schemes tab

Start Menu, Customize
Control Panel → Taskbar and Start Menu → Advanced tab

Start Menu, Icon Size
Control Panel → Taskbar and Start Menu → General tab

Start Menu, Location of Folder
Control Panel → TweakUI → My Computer tab

Start Menu, Scroll/Show Columns
Control Panel → Taskbar and Start Menu → Advanced tab

Start Menu, Show Small Icons
Control Panel → Taskbar and Start Menu → General tab

Startup Folder, Location of Folder
Control Panel → TweakUI → My Computer tab

Startup Menu, Enable/Disable
System Configuration Utility → General tab → Advanced

Startup Programs, Enable/Disable
System Configuration Utility → Startup tab

Startup, Choose Which Drivers to Load
System Configuration Utility → General tab

StickyKeys
Control Panel → Accessibility → Keyboard tab

Swap File, Settings
Control Panel → System → Performance tab → Virtual Memory

System Files, Extract from Windows CD
System Configuration Utility → General tab → Extract File

System Files, Replace with Factory Defaults
Control Panel → TweakUI → Repair tab

System Folders, Locations
Control Panel → TweakUI → My Computer tab

System Restore, Disk Space Usage
Control Panel → System → Performance tab → File System → Hard Disk tab

System Restore, Enable/Disable
Control Panel → System → Performance tab → File System → Troubleshooting tab

System.ini, Enable/Disable/Modify Selective Portions
System Configuration Utility → System.ini tab

Task Scheduler
See "Scheduled Tasks"

Taskbar and Start Menu, Show in Start Menu → Settings
System Policy Editor → File → Open Registry → Local User\Windows 98 System\Shell\Restrictions\Remove Taskbar from "Settings" on Start Menu

Taskbar, Allow Move/Resize
Control Panel → Taskbar and Start Menu → Advanced tab

Taskbar, Allow Right-Click
Control Panel → Taskbar and Start Menu → Advanced tab

Taskbar, Always on Top
Control Panel → Taskbar and Start Menu → General tab

Taskbar, AutoHide
Control Panel → Taskbar and Start Menu → General tab

Taskbar, Enable/Disable Enhanced Version
Control Panel → TweakUI → IE tab

TCP/IP Settings
Control Panel → Network → Configuration tab → select TCP/IP from the list → Properties → IP Address

Telnet, Clear History at Startup
Control Panel → TweakUI → Paranoia tab

Temp Folder, Folder Location
System Configuration Utility → Environment tab

Templates, Location of Folder
Control Panel → TweakUI → My Computer tab

Temporary Internet Files
Control Panel → Internet Options → General tab

Temporary Internet Files, Empty Automatically
Control Panel → Internet Options → Advanced tab

Temporary Internet Files, Repair
Control Panel → TweakUI → Repair tab

Time, Display Settings
Control Panel → Regional Settings → Time tab

Time/Time Zone
Control Panel → Date/Time

Title Bar, Display Full Path
Control Panel → Folder Options → View tab

ToggleKeys
Control Panel → Accessibility → Keyboard tab

Tooltips, Fonts
Control Panel → Display → Appearance tab

Tooltips, Show/Hide
Control Panel → Folder Options → View tab

Transition Effects
See "Animation"

Tray Icon, Dial-Up Networking
Control Panel → Dial-Up Networking → Connections → Settings → General tab

Tray Icon, Modem Status
Control Panel → Dial-Up Networking → select connection icon → File → Properties → General tab → Configure → Options tab

Tray Icon, PC Card
Control Panel → PC Card (PCMCIA) → Socket Status tab

Tray Icon, Power Meter
Control Panel → Power Options → Advanced tab

Tray Icon, Volume Control
Control Panel → Sounds and Multimedia Properties

Underline Links
Control Panel → Internet Options → Advanced tab

URLs, Abbreviated (Friendly)
Control Panel → Internet Options → Advanced tab

URLs, Clear History Automatically
Control Panel → TweakUI → IE tab

URLs, Underline
Control Panel → Internet Options → Advanced tab

User Profiles
Control Panel → Passwords → User Profiles tab

Video Acceleration
Control Panel → Display → Settings tab → Advanced → Performance tab

Control Panel → System → Performance tab → Graphics

Videos, Play in Internet Explorer
Control Panel → Internet Options → Advanced tab

Virtual Memory, Settings
Control Panel → System → Performance tab → Virtual Memory

Voice Chat, in Games
Control Panel → Gaming Options → Voice Chat tab

Volume, CD Player
Control Panel → System → Device Manager tab → select CD drive → Properties → Properties tab

Volume, Modem Speaker
Control Panel → Modems → General tab → Properties → General tab

Volume, Sounds
Control Panel → Sounds and Multimedia Properties

VxDs, Selectively Enable/Disable
System Configuration Utility → Static VxDs tab

Wallpaper
Control Panel → Display → Background tab

Warning, Low Battery
Control Panel → Power Options → Alarms tab

Web View on Desktop
Control Panel → Display → Web tab

Web View, Enable/Disable
Control Panel → Folder Options → General tab

Wheel, Mouse, Settings
Control Panel → TweakUI → Mouse tab

Win.ini, Enable/Disable/Modify Selective Portions
System Configuration Utility → Win.ini tab

Window Contents, Show While Dragging
Control Panel → Display → Effects tab

Windows Update, Enable/Disable

System Policy Editor → File → Open Registry → Local Computer\Windows 98 System\Windows Update

Workgroup Name

Control Panel → Network → Identification tab

Year 2000, Entering Dates

Control Panel → Regional Settings → Date tab

B

DOS Resurrected

If you don't quite have a grasp on the concept of DOS, here's a crash course on MS-DOS (short for Microsoft Disk Operating System). DOS has been included with PCs since the very first IBM PCs in the early 1980s, and even the newest PCs still use it to some extent. DOS was the PC operating system used before Microsoft Windows became the standard. All versions of Windows from 1.0 to 3.11 relied on DOS; Windows was thought of only as an extension, because one needed to load DOS before starting Windows. Windows 9x/Me is still based somewhat on MS-DOS for compatibility with the vast majority of available software and hardware products, but it does a good job of hiding this dependence. Microsoft has made Windows NT and Windows 2000 completely independent of MS-DOS but still makes available the command prompt from within Windows for those who need the functionality.

In previous versions of Windows, you could unload Windows, leaving only DOS, which was useful for running older applications and DOS games, as well as certain troubleshooting tactics. Each successive version of Windows goes to greater lengths to obscure DOS; Microsoft has actually hobbled many DOS features for Windows Me, including the ability to make bootable diskettes (other than the Windows Startup Disk, as described in Chapter 6, *Troubleshooting*).

DOS is our friend, as well as our foe. It had better be, because Windows Me requires it to function. This means, more or less, that Windows is susceptible to many of the same problems that DOS has had since 1979. On the other hand, the simplicity of DOS can be liberating from the often cumbersome and clumsy Windows interface, and some things that have been possible in DOS *still* aren't possible in Windows. It's also a lot better than the Macintosh's little unhappy face, which you'll see when something is wrong.

DOS is accessed by opening a command-prompt window, often referred to as a *DOS box* or *DOS Window*. If you don't have a **Command Prompt** item in your Start Menu, you can use the Start Menu's **Run** command, type **`command`**, and press **Enter**.

When you open a command-prompt window, you'll see a window that looks like the one shown in Figure B-1. The cursor indicates the command line (where commands are typed), and the prompt usually shows the current working directory (here, *C:\Windows\Desktop*), followed by a caret (>).

Figure B-1. The command prompt is used to complete some of the solutions in this book

To run a program or execute a command in a DOS box, just type the name of the program or command at the command line (also called the "C" prompt because it usually looks like C:\>), and press **Enter**.

MS-DOS Crash Course

You should know the following basic DOS commands to be able to complete the solutions in this book and get by in the world of Windows. The commands shown here are in `constant width`, and any parameters (the information you supply to the command) are in *`constant width italic`*. It doesn't matter which case you use when you type them in DOS (DOS, like Windows, is not case-sensitive). If there is more than one parameter, each is separated by a space:

`attrib` *`attributes filename`*

Changes the attributes (also called properties) of a file or folder. The four attributes are `R` for *read only*, `S` for *system*, `A` for *archive*, and `H` for *hidden*.

In Explorer, you can right-click on a file or group of files to change the attributes; `attrib` is the DOS counterpart to this functionality. In addition, `attrib` lets you change the `S` (system) attribute, something Explorer doesn't let you do. Here are some examples:

— `attrib +h` *`myfile.txt`*—this turns *on* the `H` parameter for the file *`myfile.txt`*, making the file hidden.

— `attrib -r "`*`another file.doc`*`"`—this turns *off* the `R` (read-only) parameter for the file *`another file.doc`* (note that quotation marks are used because of the space in the filename).

— Type **`attrib /?`** for additional options.

`cd` *`foldername`*

Changes the working directory to *`foldername`*. If the prompt indicates you are in *C:\Windows* and you want to enter the *c:\Windows\Desktop* folder, type **`cd desktop`**. You can also switch to any folder on your hard disk by including the full path of the folder. Type **`cd ..`** to go to the parent folder. Type **`cd`** by itself to display the current directory.

To switch to another drive, just type the drive letter, followed by a colon (:). For example, type **`a:`** to switch to the floppy drive.

`copy` *`filename destination`*

Copies a file to another directory or drive, specified by *`destination`*. This is the same as dragging and dropping files in Explorer, except that the keyboard is used instead of the mouse. For example, to copy the file *myfile.txt* (located in the current working directory) to your floppy drive, type **`copy myfile.txt a:\`**. Type **`copy /?`** for additional options.

`del` *`filename`*

Deletes a file. For example, to delete the file *myfile.txt*, type **`del myfile.txt`**. This is not exactly the same as deleting a file in Windows, because the file will *not* be stored in the Recycle Bin. The advantage of the DOS variant is that you can easily and quickly delete a group of files, such as all the files with the *.tmp* extension: **`del *.tmp`**. Type **`del /?`** for additional options.

`deltree` *`foldername`*

Deletes a directory and all of its contents, including all subdirectories. This, obviously, can be a dangerous command, so use it with caution. However, deleting a large number of files can often be done much faster with `deltree` than by using Windows. Type **`deltree /?`** for additional options.

`dir` *`name`*

Displays a listing of all the files and directories in the current working directory. Use `cd` to change to a different directory. Type **`dir c:\files`** to display the contents of *C:\Files* without having to first use the `cd` command. Type **`dir /p`** to pause the display after each page, useful for very long listings. You can also specify wildcards to filter the results; type **`dir *.tmp`** to display only files with the *.tmp* filename extension. Type **`dir /?`** for additional options.

`edit` *`filename`*

Opens the DOS counterpart of Notepad, allowing you to edit a text file. It's especially useful if Windows isn't running and there's no other choice.* Press the **Alt** key to enter the menu. You may have to use `attrib` first if the file is a hidden or system file.

`exit`

Closes the command-prompt window. In most situations, you can just click the close button [x] on the upper-right corner of the Window, but the `exit` command works just as well.

`md` *`foldername`*

Stands for make directory. This command creates a new directory with the name *`foldername`*. The command will have no effect if there's already a directory or file with the same name.

`move` *`filename destination`*

Is the same as `copy`, except that the file is moved instead of copied. Type **`move /?`** for additional options.

`rd` *`foldername`*

Stands for remove directory. This command removes an existing directory with the name *`foldername`*. The command will have no effect if the directory is not empty. To remove a directory and all of its contents, use `deltree`.

`ren` *`oldfilename newfilename`*

Renames a file to *`newfilename`*. This is especially useful because you can use the `ren` command to rename more than one file at once—something Explorer doesn't let you do. For example, to rename *hisfile.txt* to *herfile.txt*, type **`ren hisfile.txt herfile.txt`**. To change the extensions of all the files in the current working directory from *.txt* to *.doc*, type **`ren *.txt *.doc.`** Type **`ren /?`** for additional options.

---

* For example, if you used a Startup disk to boot directly into DOS, as described in Chapter 6.

`start` *`name`*

Allows you to open a folder window and execute a Windows shortcut from the command prompt or from a DOS batch file. For example, `start c:\windows` opens *c:\Windows* in a new folder window.

`type` *`filename`*

Displays the contents of a text file. Type **`type filename | more`** to display the file and pause between each page of information rather than displaying the whole file at once.

Command-Prompt Tricks

The following are a few tidbits that should help you accomplish nearly all command-prompt tasks. Some familiarity with DOS is assumed, but not required.

Using long filenames in DOS

- When you use the `dir` command in DOS, files or folders with long filenames in the current directory will appear truncated. That is, a file with the name *Inanimate Carbon Rod.txt* will be appear as *INANIM~1.TXT* in the left column. Look to the right to see the long filenames, or type **`dir /b`** to view only the long filenames.
- If the name of a file or folder does not contain a space, you should be able to type it normally at the prompt. That is, you can type the name of an EXE file to run the program, and include the name of a document file after a command (such as `del`).
- On the other hand, if the file or folder name contains a space, you'll need to use the short filename or encase the filename in quotes. For example, if you want to use the `cd` command to change the current working directory to *c:\Program Files*, you might type **`cd program files`**—this unfortunately won't work because Windows will see two parameters, `Program` and `Files`, rather than a single folder name. To get around this, you can either use the short version:

  ```
  CD PROGRA~1
  ```

  or enclose the folder name in quotation marks:

  ```
  CD "Program Files"
  ```

Run a shortcut from the command prompt

Although shortcuts linked to files, folders, applications, and other system objects can be opened from Windows, they aren't recognized by DOS. However, by using the `start` command, either from the DOS prompt or from a batch file, you can run any Windows shortcut. Note the use of quotation marks from the previous topic. Type the following:

```
start "c:\obits\Frank Grimes.lnk"
```

where `c:\obits` is the full path containing the shortcut, and `Frank Grimes.lnk` is the filename of the shortcut. See the `start` command earlier in this chapter for more information.

Choose the default command-prompt folder

You can choose the default working folder for new command-prompt windows by editing the *MS-DOS Prompt* shortcut.

Here are a few things you can do to improve the Windows Shortcut used to open a command-prompt window:

1. Right-click on *Dosprmpt.pif* (in your *Windows* folder), and select **Properties.***
2. Choose the **Program** tab, and type the desired folder name in the **Working** field. I find it convenient to specify the desktop folder (usually *c:\Windows\Desktop*) here.

Batch Files—The Other Way to Do It

When it comes to quick-and-dirty scripting, it's hard to beat DOS batch files. Batch files, similar to WSH scripts (discussed in Chapter 9, *Scripting and Automation*), are plain-text files with the *.bat* filename extension. However, rather than relying on a complex, unfamiliar scripting language, batch files simply consist of one or more DOS commands, typed one after another.

One of the problems with Windows-based scripting (see Chapter 9) is that it tries to control a graphical environment with a command-based language. Because DOS has a command-based interface, DOS-based scripting (batch files) are a natural extension of the environment.

Consider the following four DOS commands:

```
c:
CD \windows\temp
ATTRIB -r *.tmp
DEL *.tmp
```

* A *.pif* file is a shortcut to a DOS program. It has additional properties not found in standard Windows Shortcuts. In Windows Me, *pif* files are described as "Performs text-based (command-line) functions."

If you type these commands into a plain-text editor, such as Notepad, and save it all into a *.bat* file, executing the batch file will have the same effect as if the commands were manually typed consecutively at the DOS prompt. Obviously, this can be a tremendous time saver if you find yourself entering the same DOS commands repeatedly.

When you run a batch file, each command in the file will be printed (or echoed) to the screen before it's executed, which can be unsightly for the more compulsive among us. To turn off the echoing of any given command, precede it with the `@` character. To turn off the printing of all commands in a batch file, place the command `@echo off` at the beginning of the batch file.

Batch files can be executed by double-clicking them in Explorer or by typing their names at a DOS prompt. You'll want to put more frequently used, general-purpose batch files in a folder specified in the system path (see "The Path Less Traveled" in Chapter 6), so that they can be executed from DOS regardless of the current working directory.

Although batch files can run Windows programs (just type **`notepad`** to launch Notepad), it's preferable to run Windows programs with Windows Script Host scripts, because they'll be able to run without having to first load a DOS window.

To change the way a batch file runs in Windows, right-click on it, and select **Properties**. This will allow you to set various options, such as if Windows should exit before running the batch file, if programs run from the batch file are allowed to detect that Windows is running, and if the command-prompt window is automatically closed when the batch file completes. For the most part, you won't have to bother with these options, although the **Close on exit** option can come in handy.

In addition to the standard DOS commands, most of which are documented earlier in this appendix, batch files use a couple of extra statements to fill the holes. Variables, conditional statements, and `For...Next` loops are all implemented with statements that are ordinarily not of much use at the DOS prompt.

The following topics cover the concepts used to turn a task or a string of DOS commands into a capable batch file.

Variables and the environment

The use of variables in batch files can be somewhat confusing. All variables used in a batch file (with the exception of command-line parameters) are stored in the DOS environment—an area of memory that is created when you first boot and is kept around until the computer is turned off. The environment variable space is discussed in more detail in "The Path Less Traveled" in Chapter 6.

To view the contents of the environment, type **set** at the command prompt. To set a variable to a particular value, type this command:

```
SET VariableName=Some Data
```

Note that, unlike VBScript (see Chapter 9), the SET command is required and no quotation marks are used when setting the value of a variable. To remove the variable from memory, you set its value to nothing, like this:

```
SET VariableName=
```

To then display the contents of the variable, use the echo command, as follows:

```
ECHO %VariableName%
```

Here, the percent signs (%) on both ends of the variable name are mandatory; otherwise, the echo command would take its arguments literally and display the name of the variable rather than the data it contains.

What's confusing is that in some cases, variables need no percent signs; sometimes they need one, two at the beginning, or one on each end. See the following topics for details.

Flow control

Batch files have a very rudimentary, but easy-to-understand flow-control structure. The following example exhibits the use of the goto command:

```
@ECHO OFF
ECHO  Griff
ECHO  Asa
GOTO LaterOn
ECHO  Ox
:LaterOn
ECHO  Etch
```

The **:LaterOn** line (note the mandatory colon prefix) is called a label, which is used as a target for the goto command. If you follow the flow of the script, you should expect the following output:

```
Griff
Asa
Etch
```

because the goto command has caused the Ox line to be skipped. The label can appear before or after the goto line in a batch file, and you can have multiple goto commands and multiple labels.

Command-line parameters

Suppose you executed a batch file called *Demo.bat* by typing the following at the DOS prompt:

```
Demo file1.txt file2.txt
```

Both `file1.txt` and `file2.txt` are command-line parameters and are automatically stored in two variables, *%1* and *%2*, respectively, when the batch file is run.

The implication is that you could run a batch file that would then act with the parameters that have been passed to it. A common use of this feature is, as shown in the previous example, to specify one or more filenames, which are then manipulated or used in some way by the batch file. "Turn the Address Bar into a Command Prompt," later in this appendix, shows a batch file that utilizes command-line parameters.

The following two-line example uses command-line parameters and the **FC** utility to compare two text files. A similar example using the Window Script Host, shown in "Making Building Blocks with Subroutines and Functions" in Chapter 9, takes 22 lines to accomplish approximately the same task:

```
fc %1 %2 >c:\windows\temp\output.txt
notepad c:\windows\temp\output.txt
```

Save this batch file as *compare.bat*, and execute it like this:

```
compare c:\windows\tips.txt c:\windows\faq.txt
```

which will compare the two files, *tips.txt* and *faq.txt* (both located in your Windows folder), save the output to a temporary file, and then display the output by opening the file in Notepad. Note that the > character on the first line redirects the output of the FC program, which would otherwise be displayed on the screen, and instead saves it in the *output.txt* file. The second line opens the *output.txt* file in Notepad for easy viewing.

There are ways, other than typing, to take advantage of command-line parameters. If you place a shortcut to a batch file (say, *Demo.bat*) in your *\Windows\SendTo* folder, then right-click on a file in Explorer, select **Send To** and then **Demo**, the *Demo.bat* batch file will be executed with the file you've selected as the first command-line parameter. Likewise, if you drag-drop any file onto the batch-file icon in Explorer, the dropped file will be used as the command-line parameter.*

---

* If you drop more than one file on a batch-file icon, their order as arguments will be seemingly random, theoretically mirroring their ordering in your hard disk's file table.

Batch files have a limit of 9 command-line parameters (%1 through %9), although there's a way to have more if you need them. Say you need to accept 12 parameters at the command line; your batch file should start by acting on the first parameter. Then, you would issue the shift command, which eliminates the first parameter, putting the second in its place. %2 becomes %1, %3 becomes %2, and so on. Just repeat the process until there are no parameters left. Here's an example of this process:

```
:StartOfLoop
IF "%1"=="" EXIT
DEL %1
SHIFT
GOTO StartOfLoop
```

Save these commands into *MultiDel.bat*. Now, this simple batch file deletes one or more filenames with a single command; it's used like this:

```
MultiDel file1.txt another.doc third.log
```

by cycling through the command-line parameters one by one using shift. It repeats the same two lines (del %1 and shift) until the %1 variable is empty (see "Conditional statements," next, for the use of the if statement), at which point the batch file ends (using the exit command).

Conditional statements

There are three versions of the IF statement, which allow you to compare values and check the existence of files, respectively. The first version, which is usually used to test the value of a variable, is used as follows:

```
IF "%1"=="help" GOTO SkipIt
```

Note the use of quotation marks around the variable name and the help text, as well as the double equals signs, all of which are necessary. Notice also there's no then keyword, which those of you who are familiar with VBScript (see Chapter 9) might expect. If the batch file finds that the two sides are equal, it executes everything on the right side of the statement; in this case, it issues the goto command.

The second use of the IF command is to test the existence of a file:

```
IF EXIST c:\windows\tips.txt GOTO SkipIt
```

If the file *c:\windows\tips.txt* exists, the goto command will be executed. Similarly, you can you can test for the absence of a file, as follows:

```
IF NOT EXIST c:\autoexec.bat GOTO SkipIt
```

The third use of the IF command is to test the outcome of the previous command, as follows:

```
IF ERRORLEVEL 0 GOTO SkipIt
```

If there was any problem with the statement immediately before this line, the ERRORLEVEL (which is similar to a system-defined variable) will be set to some nonzero number. The IF statement shown here tests for any ERRORLEVEL that is greater than zero; if there was no error, execution will simply continue to the next command.

Here's a revised version of the file-compare example first shown in the "Command-line parameters" section earlier in this appendix:

```
IF "%1"=="" GOTO Problem
IF "%2"=="" GOTO Problem
IF NOT EXIST %1 GOTO Problem
IF NOT EXIST %2 GOTO Problem
fc %1 %2 >c:\windows\temp\output.txt
IF ERRORLEVEL 0 GOTO Problem
IF NOT EXIST c:\windows\temp\output.txt GOTO Problem
notepad c:\windows\temp\output.txt
EXIT
:Problem
ECHO "A problem has been encountered."
```

This batch file is essentially the same as the original two-line example shown earlier, except that some error-checking statements that utilize the IF statement have been added to make the batch file a little more robust. If you neglect to enter one or both command-line parameters, or if the files you specify as command-line parameters don't exist, the batch file will display the error message. An even more useful version might have multiple error messages that more accurately describe the specific problem that was encountered.

Loops

Batch files have a very simple looping mechanism, based loosely on the For...Next loop used in other programming languages. The main difference is that the batch file for loop doesn't increment a variable regularly, but rather cycles it through a list of values. Its syntax is as follows:

```
FOR %%i IN ("Abe","Monty","Jasper") DO ECHO %%i
```

Here, the variable syntax gets even more confusing; the reference to the i variable when used in conjunction with the for...in...do statement gets two percent signs in front of the variable name and none after. Note also that only single-letter variables can be used here.

If you execute this batch file, you'll get the following output:

```
Abe
Monty
Jasper
```

Note also the use of the quotation marks; although they aren't strictly necessary, they're helpful if one or more of the values in the list has a comma in it.

To simulate a more traditional `For...Next` statement in a batch file, type the following:

```
FOR %%i IN (1,2,3,4,5) DO ECHO %%i
```

Simulating subroutines

Batch files have no support for named subroutines (as described in "Making Building Blocks with Subroutines and Functions" in Chapter 9). However, you can simulate subroutines by creating several batch files: one *main* file and one or more *subordinate* files (each of which can accept command-line parameters). You probably won't want to use this if performance is an issue.

This is useful in cases like the `for...in...do` statement (described in the preceeding section), which can only loop a single command.

In one batch file, called *WriteIt.bat*, type:

```
IF "%1"=="" EXIT
IF EXIST %1.txt DEL %1.txt
ECHO This is a text > %1.txt
```

Then, in another batch file, called *Main.bat*, type the following:

```
FOR %%i IN ("Kang","Kodos","Serak") DO CALL WriteIt.bat %%i
```

The single-line *Main.bat* batch file uses the `call` command to run the other batch file, *WriteIt.bat*, three times. The `call` command allows one batch file to run another batch file; if it's omitted, one batch file can still run another, but the first batch file will abruptly end as it runs the second batch file.

When this pair of batch files is run, you should end up with three files, *Kang.txt*, *Kodos.txt*, and *Serak.txt*, all containing the text, "This is a text." The `if` statement, as well as the `for...in...do` loop, are explained in earlier sections.

Turn the Address Bar into a Command Prompt

If you select **Run** from the **Start Menu**, the box that appears is essentially a limited command prompt; you can execute any program, open any folder, or launch any Internet URL simply by typing it here. Explorer and your taskbar also have the Address Bar; originally intended to extend Web Integration (see Chapter 8, *Taking Control of Web Integration*), it accomplishes essentially the same thing as **Run**.

The problem with both **Run** and the **Address Bar** is that they can only be used to launch programs; they don't understand intrinsic DOS commands, like `dir` and `copy` (discussed earlier in this appendix). However, there is a way to have the Address Bar mimic all the functions of the command prompt and therefore have a true command prompt always within reach:

1. Start by making the Address Bar visible, if it's not already. Right-click on an empty area of your taskbar; select **Toolbars** and then **Address Bar**.*

   Your taskbar will then contain the Address Bar, which is dockable, resizable, and removable: you can move it around the taskbar or even tear it off by dragging it. Your taskbar will look something like Figure B-2.

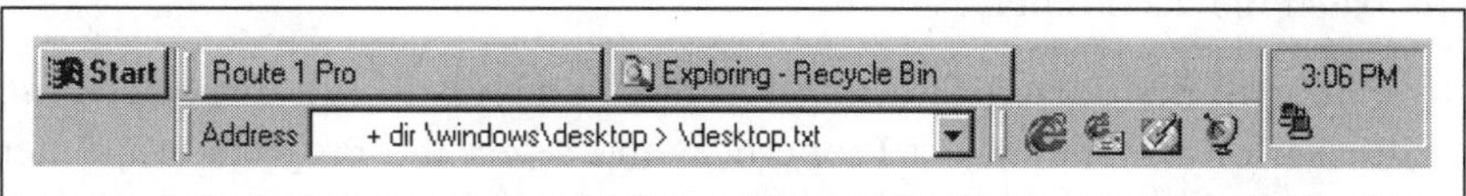

Figure B-2. The Address Bar can be put to good use as a handy command prompt: also shown is the standard Quick Launch toolbar

2. You'll immediately be able to run programs, open folders, and launch URLs simply by typing them and pressing **Enter**.
3. To add DOS command functionality, you'll need the assistance of a DOS batch file (discussed earlier in this appendix). Open a text editor, such as Notepad, and type the following:

```
@echo off
if "%1"=="" exit
if exist c:\windows\temp\temp.bat del c:\windows\temp\temp.bat
echo %1 %2 %3 %4 %5 %6 %7 %8 %9 > c:\windows\temp\temp.bat
call c:\windows\temp\temp.bat
if exist c:\windows\temp\temp.bat del c:\windows\temp\temp.bat
```

You may have to change the references to `c:\windows\temp` to match the location of your Temp folder; see "Clean Up and Customize System Folders" in Chapter 4, *Tinkering Techniques*, for more information.

4. Save it as *+.bat* (just the plus sign followed by the *.bat* filename extension) in your *\windows\command* folder.
5. Now, to run a DOS command from the address bar, simply precede it with a plus sign (+) and a single space, like this:

```
+ copy c:\bootlog.txt a:\
```

* This solution focuses on the Address Bar on the taskbar, although it also works for the Address Bar in Explorer.

You can even have the output of a DOS command redirected to a file, as follows:

```
+ dir c:\windows > c:\windows\desktop
```

Here's how it works: the batch file reads what you've typed after the + and writes it to a new, but temporary, batch file. The new batch file is then executed, and the command you've typed is carried out. When it's finished, the temporary batch file is deleted.

The plus key was chosen for the name of the batch file because it's convenient and not likely to conflict with any other software or commands; the one on your keyboard's numeric keypad is usually more convenient than the one near your backspace key (**Shift-=**). However, you can certainly replace + with any other character, such as ` or -, as long as you rename the batch file accordingly.

To configure the default directory for all commands issued through *+.bat*, right-click on the file, select **Properties**, and select the **Program** tab. Enter the desired directory in the **Working** field—*\windows\desktop* is a convenient folder for this purpose. If you want multiple default directories, you'll need to create a separate batch file for each one.

To configure the window to close automatically when it's finished with the command, right-click on the *+.bat* file, select **Properties**, select the **Program** tab, and turn on the **Close on exit** option. If it closes automatically, you won't be able to see the output from commands like `dir`—you might want to create two batch files, one that closes and one that doesn't, depending on the command you issue.

There are some limitations to this design. Although it does mimic the command prompt, it only allows a single command at a time, after which the context is forgotten. What this means is that such commands as `cd` won't have much meaning—you can certainly type **`+ cd directoryname`**, but the "current directory" will be forgotten once the command has been executed. To get around this, include the full path with your commands. Instead of the following series of statements:

```
d:
cd \myfolder
del *.tmp
```

just type this:

```
+ del d:\myfolder\*.tmp
```

Of course, if you find that you need to type several consecutive commands, you can always just type **`command`** in the Address Bar to launch a full-fledged command-prompt window.

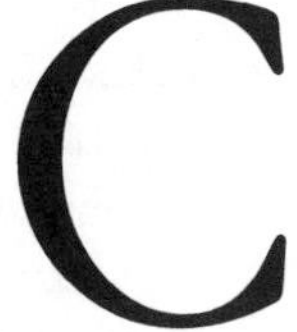

Class IDs of System Objects

Windows keeps track of its various components with Class IDs 33-digit codes consisting of both letters and numbers, enclosed in curly braces {}. What follows is a list of the commonly used system objects and their corresponding Class IDs:

ActiveX Cache Folder	{88C6C381-2E85-11d0-94DE-444553540000}
Briefcase	{85BBD920-42A0-1069-A2E4-08002B30309D}
Compressed Folder	{E88DCCE0-B7B3-11d1-A9F0-00AA0060FA31}
Control Panel	{21EC2020-3AEA-1069-A2DD-08002B30309D}
Desktop	{00021400-0000-0000-C000-0000000000046}
Dial-Up Networking	{992CFFA0-F557-101A-88EC-00DD010CCC48}
Favorites	{1A9BA3A0-143A-11CF-8350-444553540000}
Fonts	{BD84B380-8CA2-1069-AB1D-08000948F534}
Internet Cache	{7BD29E00-76C1-11CF-9DD0-00A0C9034933}
Internet Explorer	{FBF23B42-E3F0-101B-8488-00AA003E56F8}
My Computer	{20D04FE0-3AEA-1069-A2D8-08002B30309D}
My Documents	{450D8FBA-AD25-11D0-98A8-0800361B1103}
My Network Places	{208D2C60-3AEA-1069-A2D7-08002B30309D}
Printers	{2227A280-3AEA-1069-A2DE-08002B30309D}
Printers	{2227A280-3AEA-1069-A2DE-08002B30309D}
Recycle Bin	{645FF040-5081-101B-9F08-00AA002F954E}
Scheduled Tasks	{D6277990-4C6A-11CF-8D87-00AA0060F5BF}
Subscriptions	{F5175861-2688-11d0-9C5E-00AA00A45957}
The Internet	{3DC7A020-0ACD-11CF-A9BB-00AA004AE837}
The Microsoft Network	{00028B00-0000-0000-C000-000000000046}
URL History Folder	{FF393560-C2A7-11CF-BFF4-444553540000}

The following are some tips for working with Class IDs:

- Class IDs are stored in the Registry under `HKEY_CLASSES_ROOT\CLSID`. Locate the key named for a Class ID under this branch to change any settings or behavior of the corresponding object. Use the Registry Editor's search feature to find the Class ID for an object not listed here by searching for the name of the object.
- A good way to avoid having to type these codes is to do a search in the Registry. For example, if you're looking for the Recycle Bin Class ID, do a search in the Registry Editor for `Recycle Bin`. When it's found, make sure the code matches the one listed earlier (because there may be more than one). Right-click on the key named for the code, then select **Rename**. Next, right-click on the highlighted text in the rename field, and select **Copy**. The Class ID will then be placed on the clipboard, waiting to be copied anywhere you please.
- To create a copy of a virtual folder system object, such as Dial-Up Networking, create a new folder anywhere (such as on your Desktop or somewhere in the file-system), and call it `Dial-Up Networking.{992CFFA0-F557-101A-88EC-00DD010CCC48}`. Make sure to include the dot between the name and the Class ID. Replace the name and ID with any others from the table. Note that all objects listed earlier should be able to exist as movable folders, except for **Network Neighborhood**. See "Make the Control Panel More Accessible" in Chapter 2, *Basic Explorer Coping Skills*, for more information.
- By placing references to Class IDs in other parts of the Registry, you can make Windows do cool tricks—see "Customize My Computer" in Chapter 4, *Tinkering Techniques*, for more information.

Index

We'd like to hear your suggestions for improving our indexes. Send email to *index@oreilly.com*.

B

C

D

E

F

G

H

I

J

N

O

Q

R

S

T

U

W

Y

Z

About the Author

David A. Karp, a graduate from the University of California at Berkeley in mechanical engineering, is a specialist in user-interface design and software engineering. He currently consults on Internet technology, intranet security, and web site production, and has written for a number of magazines, most recently *Windows Sources*, *Windows Pro Magazine*, and *New Media.*

Author of the bestselling books *Windows Annoyances* and *Windows 98 Annoyances*, he created the *Annoyances.org* web site, upon which this book is based. The Annoyances web sites for Windows 95 and Windows 98 have been repeatedly cited as among the best technical resources on the Web. Recognition has come from such sources as *PC Computing* magazine, *Windows Magazine*, the *San Francisco Examiner*, and *The New York Times.*

While he's not writing, you can usually find him outdoors or getting his hands dirty with yet another project.

Colophon

Our look is the result of reader comments, our own experimentation, and feedback from distribution channels. Distinctive covers complement our distinctive approach to technical topics, breathing personality and life into potentially dry subjects.

The animal on the cover of *Windows Me Annoyances* is an Asian painted frog (*Kaloula pulchra*), also know as a Chubby frog. The Chubby frog gets its name from its large, round body, bloated appearance, and absence of a visible neck. It is approximately three inches long (though width varies between individuals). Its distinctive markings include a rich brown color and off-white bands of spots running down the sides and the spine.

In accordance with its large body, the Chubby frog is slow and docile with a calm disposition, so it may be handled by pet keepers. However, it is not recommended that you handle this frog often, as it is covered with a sticky slime coating that is difficult to remove from your hands and may last several days. This coating is actually a skin toxin, which may irritate the handler's eyes and throat. In addition, if the Chubby frog is to be kept as a pet, it should not be kept with other species of frogs, as their interaction may produce toxic skin secretions.

The Chubby frog is nocturnal, digging down under a layer of substrate during the day and emerging at night to feed. It is terrestrial, living on land near the water rather than directly in the water. Found in Southeast Asia, it prefers temperatures in the range of 75° to 85°F with approximately 80% humidity. It is, however, able to survive dry conditions by crawling a few inches underground and resurfacing once rain has provided a more humid environment.

The Chubby frog, as with all amphibians of the order Anura, has a larynx, vocal cords, middle ear, and eardrum. The male, louder than the female of the species, is able to amplify its voice with vocal sacs in the base of its mouth cavity, drastically increasing its sound output. Its voice is described as a croaking or mewing sound, often heard at night. In fact, the Chubby frog is reported to be quite loud and obnoxious.

Jeffrey Holcomb was the production editor and proofreader for *Windows Me Annoyances*. Paulette Miley was the copyeditor. Jane Ellin, Ann Schirmer, and Claire Cloutier provided quality control. Linley Dolby, Ann Schirmer, Mary Sheehan, and Matt Hutchinson provided production assistance. Judy Hoer wrote the index.

Hanna Dyer designed the cover of this book, based on a series design by Edie Freedman. The cover image is a 19th-century engraving from the Dover Pictorial Archive. Emma Colby produced the cover layout with QuarkXPress 4.1 using Adobe's ITC Garamond font.

Melanie Wang designed the interior layout based on a series design by Nancy Priest. Judy Hoer implemented the design in FrameMaker 5.5.6. The text and heading fonts are ITC Garamond Light and Garamond Book. The illustrations that appear in the book were produced by Robert Romano using Macromedia FreeHand 8 and Adobe Photoshop 5. This colophon was written by Jeffrey Holcomb.

Whenever possible, our books use a durable and flexible lay-flat binding. If the page count exceeds this binding's limit, perfect binding is used.

More Titles from O'Reilly

Windows Users

Windows 2000 Pro: The Missing Manual

By Sharon Crawford
1st Edition August 2000
450 pages, ISBN 0-596-00010-3

In *Windows 2000 Pro: The Missing Manual*, bestselling Windows NT author Sharon Crawford provides the friendly, authoritative book that should have been in the box. It's the ideal (and desperately needed) user's guide for the world's most popular corporate operating system.

PC Hardware in a Nutshell

By Robert Bruce Thompson & Barbara Frichtman Thompson
1st Edition October 2000
526 pages, ISBN 1-56592-599-8

PC Hardware in a Nutshell is a comprehensive guide to buying, building, upgrading, and repairing Intel-based PCs for novices and seasoned professionals alike. It features buying guidelines, how-to advice on installing, configuring, and troubleshooting specific components, plus ample reference material and a complete case study on building a PC from components.

Optimizing Windows for Games, Graphics and Multimedia

By David L. Farquhar
1st Edition December 1999
291 pages, ISBN 1-56592-677-3

Every Windows user has spent many frustrating hours trying to figure out ways to optimize system performance. *Optimizing Windows for Games, Graphics and Multimedia* gives you tips and tricks you won't find in any Windows documentation to make your system run faster than ever before. It will answer your questions and save you wasted hours of searching and experimenting to find the practical solutions you're looking for.

Outlook 2000 in a Nutshell

By Tom Syroid & Bo Leuf
1st Edition May 2000
660 pages, ISBN 1-56592-704-4

Outlook 2000 in a Nutshell fills the need for an up-to-date and comprehensive reference book for sophisticated users who want to get all they can out of this powerful and versatile program.

Word 2000 in a Nutshell

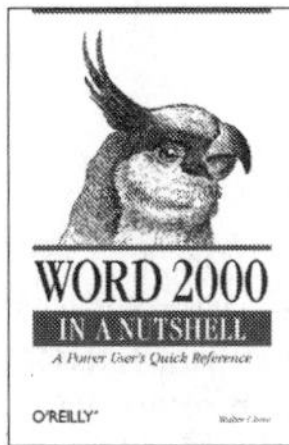

By Walter Glenn
1st Edition August 2000
520 pages, ISBN 1-56592-489-4

Word 2000 in a Nutshell is a clear, concise, and complete reference to the most popular word-processing program in the world. This book is the first choice of the Word power user who needs help completing a specific task or understanding a command or topic. It's also an invaluable resource that uncovers Word 2000's undocumented features and shares powerful time-saving tips.

Excel 2000 in a Nutshell

By Jinjer Simon
1st Edition August 2000
606 Pages, ISBN 1-56592-714-1

Excel 2000 in a Nutshell is a one-stop reference to every one of Excel's menu options and functions, for both professional and power users of Excel 2000. In typical Nutshell fashion, information is organized for quick and easy access, providing readers with everything they need to know about the premier spreadsheet application.

MCSE

MCSE: The Core Exams in a Nutshell, 2nd Edition

By Michael Moncur
2nd Edition March 2000
486 pages, ISBN 1-56592-721-4

MCSE: The Core Exams in a Nutshell, 2nd Edition, is an updated edition of the bestselling first edition. It is a detailed quick reference for administrators with Windows NT experience or experience administering a different platform, such as UNIX or NetWare, who want to learn what is necessary to pass the required exam portion of the MCSE certification.

Windows 2000 Active Directory

By Alistair G. Lowe-Norris
1st Edition January 2000
642 pages, ISBN 1-56592-638-2

The most important change in Windows 2000 is the inclusion of Active Directory, a fully qualified directory service. It is such an important change that Systems Administrators are likely to find coming to grips with Active Directory to be one of their biggest headaches. But it doesn't have to be that way. *Windows 2000 Active Directory* gives administrators an in-depth knowledge of AD, and it is an indispensable guide they will turn to whenever they need help.

Securing Windows NT/2000 Servers for the Internet

By Stefan Norberg
1st Edition November 2000
200 pages, ISBN 1-56592-768-0

In recent years, Windows NT and 2000 systems have emerged as viable platforms for Internet servers, but securing Windows for internet use is a complex task. This concise guide simplifies the task by paring down installation and configuration instructions into a series of security checklists for security administration, including hardening servers for use as "bastion hosts," performing secure remote administration with OpenSSH, TCP Wrappers, VNC, and the new Windows 2000 Terminal Services.

Windows 2000 Administration in a Nutshell

By Mitch Tulloch
1st Edition February 2001
798 pages, ISBN 1-56592-713-3

Anyone who installs Windows 2000, creates a user, or adds a printer is a 2000 system administrator. This book covers all the important day-to-day administrative tasks, and the tools for performing each task are included in a handy easy-to-look-up alphabetical reference. What's the same and what's different between the Windows 2000 and Windows NT platform? Has the GUI or the networking architecture changed, and if so, how? *Windows 2000 Administration in a Nutshell* addresses the problems associated with bridging the gap between the Windows NT and Windows 2000 platforms.

Windows NT System Administration

DNS on Windows NT

By Paul Albitz, Matt Larson & Cricket Liu
1st Edition October 1998
348 pages, ISBN 1-56592-511-4

DNS on Windows NT is a special edition of the classic *DNS and BIND*, which Microsoft recommends to Windows NT users and administrators. This book discusses one of the Internet's fundamental building blocks: the distributed host information database that's responsible for translating names into addresses, routing mail to its proper destination, and many other services.

Windows NT TCP/IP Network Administration

By Craig Hunt & Robert Bruce Thompson
1st Edition October 1998
504 pages, ISBN 1-56592-377-4

Windows NT TCP/IP Network Administration is a complete guide to setting up and running a TCP/IP network on Windows NT. It starts with the fundamentals – the protocols, routing, and setup. Beyond that, it covers all the important networking services provided as part of Windows NT, including IIS, RRAS, DNS, WINS, and DHCP. This book is the NT administrator's indispensable guide.

Windows NT System Administration

DHCP for Windows 2000

By Neall Alcott
1st Edition January 2001
288 pages, ISBN 1-56592-838-5

DHCP for Windows 2000 is custom-designed for system administrators who are responsible for configuring and maintaining networks with Windows 2000 servers. It explains the DHCP protocol and how to install and manage DHCP on both servers and clients–including client platforms other than Windows 2000.

Essential Windows NT System Administration

By AEleen Frisch
1st Edition January 1998
486 pages, ISBN 1-56592-274-3

This book combines practical experience with technical expertise to help you manage Windows NT systems as productively as possible. It covers the standard utilities offered with the Windows NT operating system and from the Resource Kit, as well as important commercial and free third-party tools. By the author of O'Reilly's bestselling book, *Essential System Administration*.

Learning Perl on Win32 Systems

By Randal L. Schwartz, Erik Olson & Tom Christiansen
1st Edition August 1997
306 pages, ISBN 1-56592-324-3

In this carefully paced course, leading Perl trainers and a Windows NT practitioner teach you to program in the language that promises to emerge as the scripting language of choice on NT. Based on the "llama" book, this book features tips for PC users and new NT-specific examples, along with a foreword by Larry Wall, the creator of Perl, and Dick Hardt, the creator of Perl for Win32.

Python Programming on Win32

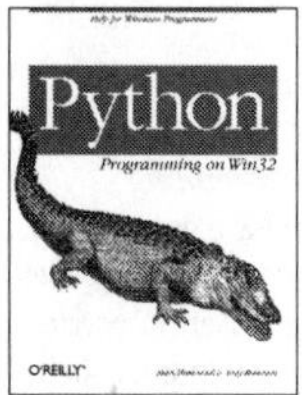

By Mark Hammond & Andy Robinson
1st Edition January 2000
672 pages, ISBN 1-56592-621-8

Despite Python's increasing popularity on Windows, *Python Programming on Win32* is the first book to demonstrate how to use it as a serious Windows development and administration tool. This book addresses all the basic technologies for common integration tasks on Windows, explaining both the Windows issues and the Python code you need to glue things together.

Managing Windows NT Logons

By Kathy Ivens
1st Edition January 2000
236 pages, ISBN 1-56592-637-4

Administrators spend much of their time on workstation problems, those user and logon problems that keep the helpdesk phone jingling. From forgotten passwords to user-caused destruction of workstation environments, the problems are ongoing and unremitting. This troubleshooting guide helps administrators assess problems logically, covering everything from lockouts and freezes to remote administration on NT 4.0 and Win9x workstations.

Managing the Windows 2000 Registry

By Paul Robichaux
1st Edition August 2000
558 pages, ISBN 1-56592-943-8

The Windows 2000 Registry is the repository for all hardware, software, and application configuration settings. *Managing the Windows 2000 Registry* is the system administrator's guide to maintaining, monitoring, and updating the Registry database. A "must-have" for every 2000 system manager or administrator, it covers what the Registry is and where it lives on disk, available tools, Registry access from programs, and Registry content.

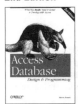

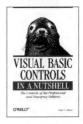

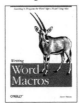

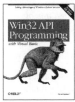

How to stay in touch with O'Reilly

1. Visit Our Award-Winning Site

http://www.oreilly.com/

★ "Top 100 Sites on the Web" —*PC Magazine*
★ "Top 5% Web sites" —*Point Communications*
★ "3-Star site" —*The McKinley Group*

Our web site contains a library of comprehensive product information (including book excerpts and tables of contents), downloadable software, background articles, interviews with technology leaders, links to relevant sites, book cover art, and more. File us in your Bookmarks or Hotlist!

2. Join Our Email Mailing Lists

New Product Releases

To receive automatic email with brief descriptions of all new O'Reilly products as they are released, send email to:
ora-news-subscribe@lists.oreilly.com
Put the following information in the first line of your message (*not* in the Subject field):
subscribe ora-news

O'Reilly Events

If you'd also like us to send information about trade show events, special promotions, and other O'Reilly events, send email to:
ora-news-subscribe@lists.oreilly.com
Put the following information in the first line of your message (*not* in the Subject field):
subscribe ora-events

3. Get Examples from Our Books via FTP

There are two ways to access an archive of example files from our books:

Regular FTP

- ftp to:
  ftp.oreilly.com
  (login: anonymous
  password: your email address)
- Point your web browser to:
  ftp://ftp.oreilly.com/

FTPMAIL

- Send an email message to:
  ftpmail@online.oreilly.com
  (Write "help" in the message body)

4. Contact Us via Email

order@oreilly.com
To place a book or software order online. Good for North American and international customers.

subscriptions@oreilly.com
To place an order for any of our newsletters or periodicals.

books@oreilly.com
General questions about any of our books.

software@oreilly.com
For general questions and product information about our software. Check out O'Reilly Software Online at **http://software.oreilly.com/** for software and technical support information. Registered O'Reilly software users send your questions to:
website-support@oreilly.com

cs@oreilly.com
For answers to problems regarding your order or our products.

booktech@oreilly.com
For book content technical questions or corrections.

proposals@oreilly.com
To submit new book or software proposals to our editors and product managers.

international@oreilly.com
For information about our international distributors or translation queries. For a list of our distributors outside of North America check out:
http://www.oreilly.com/distributors.html

5. Work with Us

Check out our website for current employment opportunites:
http://jobs.oreilly.com/

O'Reilly & Associates, Inc.
101 Morris Street, Sebastopol, CA 95472 USA
TEL 707-829-0515 or 800-998-9938
(6am to 5pm PST)
FAX 707-829-0104

Titles from O'Reilly

Web
Apache: The Definitive Guide, 2nd Ed.
Apache Pocket Reference
ASP in a Nutshell, 2nd Ed.
Cascading Style Sheets
Designing Web Audio
Designing with JavaScript, 2nd Ed.
DocBook: The Definitive Guide
Dynamic HTML: The Definitive Reference
HTML Pocket Reference
Information Architecture for the WWW
JavaScript: The Definitive Guide, 3rd Ed.
Java and XML
JavaScript Application Cookbook
JavaScript Pocket Reference
Practical Internet Groupware
PHP Pocket Reference
Programming Coldfusion
Photoshop for the Web, 2nd Ed.
Web Design in a Nutshell
Webmaster in a Nutshell, 2nd Ed.
Web Navigation: Designing the User Experience
Web Performance Tuning
Web Security & Commerce
Writing Apache Modules with Perl and C

Perl
Advanced Perl Programming
CGI Programming with Perl, 2nd Ed.
Learning Perl, 2nd Ed.
Learning Perl for Win32 Systems
Learning Perl/Tk
Mastering Algorithms with Perl
Mastering Regular Expressions
Perl Cookbook
Perl in a Nutshell
Programming Perl, 3rd Ed.
Perl CD Bookshelf
Perl Resource Kit – Win32 Ed.
Perl/TK Pocket Reference
Perl 5 Pocket Reference, 3rd Ed.

Graphics & Multimedia
MP3: The Definitive Guide
Photoshop 6 in a Nutshell, 3rd Ed.
Director in a Nutshell
Lingo in a Nutshell
FrontPage 2000 in a Nutshell

Using the Internet
Internet in a Nutshell
Smileys
Managing Mailing Lists

Software
WebSite Professional™ 2.0
Polyform™
WebBoard™ 4.0

Java Series
Developing Java Beans
Creating Effective JavaHelp
Enterprise Java Beans, 2nd Ed.
Java Cryptography
Java Distributed Computing
Java Enterprise in a Nutshell
Java Examples in a Nutshell, 2nd Ed.
Java Foundation Classes in a Nutshell
Java in a Nutshell, 3rd Ed.
Java Internationalization
Java I/O
Java Native Methods
Java Network Programming, 2nd Ed.
Java Performance Tuning
Java Security
Java Servlet Programming
Java ServerPages
Java Threads, 2nd Ed.
Jini in a Nutshell
Learning Java

Unix
SCO UNIX in a Nutshell
Tcl/Tk in a Nutshell
The Unix CD Bookshelf, 2nd Ed.
UNIX in a Nutshell, System V Edition, 3rd Ed.
Learning the Unix Operating System, 4th Ed.
Learning vi, 6th Ed.
Learning the Korn Shell
Learning GNU Emacs, 2nd Ed.
Using csh & tcsh
Learning the bash Shell, 2nd Ed.
GNU Emacs Pocket Reference
Exploring Expect
TCL/TK Tools
TCL/TK in a Nutshell
Python Pocket Reference

Mac
AppleScript in a Nutshell
AppleWorks 6: The Missing Manual
Crossing Platforms
iMovie: The Missing Manual
Mac OS in a Nutshell
Mac OS 9: The Missing Manual
Photoshop Cookbook
REALbasic: The Definitive Guide

Linux
Building Linux Clusters
Learning Debian GNU/Linux
Learning Red Hat Linux
Linux Device Drivers
Linux Network Administrator's Guide, 2nd Ed.
Running Linux, 3rd Ed.
Linux in a Nutshell, 3rd Ed.
Linux Multimedia Guide

System Administration
Practical UNIX & Internet Security, 2nd Ed.
Building Internet Firewalls, 2nd Ed.
PGP: Pretty Good Privacy
SSH, The Secure Shell: The Definitive Guide
DNS and Bind, 3rd Ed.
The Networking CD Bookshelf
Virtual Private Networks, 2nd Ed.
TCP/IP Network Administration, 2nd Ed.
sendmail Desktop Reference
Managing Usenet
Using & Managing PPP
Managing IP Networks with Cisco Routers
Networking Personal Computers with TCP/IP
Unix Backup & Recovery
Essential System Administration, 2nd Ed.
Perl for System Administration
Managing NFS and NIS
Volume 8: X Window System Administrator's Guide
Using Samba
Unix Power Tools, 2nd Ed.
DNS on Windows NT
Windows NT TCP/IP Network Administration
DHCP for Windows 2000
Essential Windows NT System Administration
Managing Windows NT Logons
Managing the Windows 2000 Registry

X Window
Vol. 1: Xlib Programming Manual
Vol. 2: Xlib Reference Manual
Vol. 4M: X Toolkit Intrinsics Programming Manual, Motif Ed.
Vol. 5: X Toolkit Intrinsics Reference Manual
Vol. 6A: Motif Programming Manual
Vol. 6B: Motif Reference Manual, 2nd Ed.

Using Windows
Windows Millenium: The Missing Manual
PC Hardware in a Nutshell
Optimizing Windows for Games, Graphics, and Multimedia
Outlook 2000 in a Nutshell
Word 2000 in a Nutshell
Excel 2000 in a Nutshell
Paint Shop Pro 7 in a Nutshell
Windows 2000 Pro: The Missing Manual

Programming
C++: The Core Language
Practical C++ Programming
Practical C Programming, 3rd Ed.
High Performance Computing, 2nd Ed.
Programming Embedded Systems in C and C++
Mastering Algorithms in C
Advanced C++ Techniques
POSIX 4: Programming for the Real World
POSIX Programmer's Guide
Power Programming with RPC
UNIX Systems Programming for SVR4
Pthreads Programming
CVS Pocket Reference
Advanced Oracle PL/SQL
Oracle PL/SQL Guide to Oracle8i Features
Oracle PL/SQL Programming, 2nd Ed.
Oracle Built-in Packages
Oracle PL/SQL Developer's Workbook
Oracle Web Applications
Oracle PL/SQL Language Pocket Reference
Oracle PL/SQL Built-ins Pocket Reference
Oracle SQL*Plus: The Definitive Guide
Oracle SQL*Plus Pocket Reference
Oracle Essentials
Oracle Database Administration
Oracle Internal Services
Oracle SAP
Guide to Writing DCE Applications
Understanding DCE
Visual Basic Shell Programming
VB/VBA in a Nutshell: The Language
Access Database Design & Programming, 2nd Ed.
Writing Word Macros
Applying RCS and SCCS
Checking C Programs with Lint
VB Controls in a Nutshell
Developing Asp Components, 2nd Ed.
Learning WML & WMLScript
Writing Excel Macros
Windows 32 API Programming with Visual Basic
ADO: The Definitive Guide

Other Titles
PalmPilot: The Ultimate Guide, 2nd Ed.
Palm Programming: The Developer's Guide
Evil Geniuses in a Nutshell
The Cathedral and the Bazaar
Database Nation

O'REILLY®

TO ORDER: **800-998-9938 • order@oreilly.com • http://www.oreilly.com/**

OUR PRODUCTS ARE AVAILABLE AT A BOOKSTORE OR SOFTWARE STORE NEAR YOU.

FOR INFORMATION: **800-998-9938 • 707-829-0515 • info@oreilly.com**

International Distributors

http://international.oreilly.com/distributors.html

UK, Europe, Middle East and Africa (except France, Germany, Austria, Switzerland, Luxembourg, and Liechtenstein)

INQUIRIES

O'Reilly UK Limited
4 Castle Street
Farnham
Surrey, GU9 7HS
United Kingdom
Telephone: 44-1252-711776
Fax: 44-1252-734211
Email: information@oreilly.co.uk

ORDERS

Wiley Distribution Services Ltd.
1 Oldlands Way
Bognor Regis
West Sussex PO22 9SA
United Kingdom
Telephone: 44-1243-843294
UK Freephone: 0800-243207
Fax: 44-1243-843302 (Europe/EU orders)
or 44-1243-843274 (Middle East/Africa)
Email: cs-books@wiley.co.uk

Germany, Switzerland, Austria, Luxembourg, and Liechtenstein

INQUIRIES & ORDERS

O'Reilly Verlag
Balthasarstr. 81
D-50670 Köln, Germany
Telephone: 49-221-973160-91
Fax: 49-221-973160-8
Email: anfragen@oreilly.de (inquiries)
Email: order@oreilly.de (orders)

France

INQUIRIES & ORDERS

Éditions O'Reilly
18 rue Séguier
75006 Paris, France
Tel: 1-40-51-71-89
Fax: 1-40-51-72-26
Email: france@oreilly.fr

Canada (French language books)

Les Éditions Flammarion ltée
375, Avenue Laurier Ouest
Montréal (Québec) H2V 2K3
Tel: 00-1-514-277-8807
Fax: 00-1-514-278-2085
Email: info@flammarion.qc.ca

Hong Kong

City Discount Subscription Service, Ltd.
Unit A, 6th Floor, Yan's Tower
27 Wong Chuk Hang Road
Aberdeen, Hong Kong
Tel: 852-2580-3539
Fax: 852-2580-6463
Email: citydis@ppn.com.hk

Korea

Hanbit Media, Inc.
Chungmu Bldg. 210
Yonnam-dong 568-33
Mapo-gu
Seoul, Korea
Tel: 822-325-0397
Fax: 822-325-9697
Email: hant93@chollian.dacom.co.kr

Philippines

Global Publishing
G/F Benavides Garden
1186 Benavides St.
Manila, Philippines
Tel: 632-254-8949/632-252-2582
Fax: 632-734-5060/632-252-2733
Email: globalp@pacific.net.ph

Taiwan

O'Reilly Taiwan
1st Floor, No. 21, Lane 295
Section 1, Fu-Shing South Road
Taipei, 106 Taiwan
Tel: 886-2-27099669
Fax: 886-2-27038802
Email: mori@oreilly.com

China

O'Reilly Beijing
SIGMA Building, Suite B809
No. 49 Zhichun Road
Haidian District
Beijing 100031, P.R. China
Tel: 86-10-8809-7475
Fax: 86-10-8809-7463
Email: beijing@oreilly.com

India

Shroff Publishers & Distributors Pvt. Ltd.
12, "Roseland", 2nd Floor
180, Waterfield Road, Bandra (West)
Mumbai 400 050
Tel: 91-22-641-1800/643-9910
Fax: 91-22-643-2422
Email: spd@vsnl.com

Japan

O'Reilly Japan, Inc.
Yotsuya Y's Building
7 Banch 6, Honshio-cho
Shinjuku-ku
Tokyo 160-0003 Japan
Tel: 81-3-3356-5227
Fax: 81-3-3356-5261
Email: japan@oreilly.com

Singapore, Indonesia, Malaysia and Thailand

TransQuest Publishers Pte Ltd
30 Old Toh Tuck Road #05-02
Sembawang Kimtrans Logistics Centre
Singapore 597654
Tel: 65-4623112
Fax: 65-4625761
Email: wendiw@transquest.com.sg

All Other Asian Countries

O'Reilly & Associates, Inc.
101 Morris Street
Sebastopol, CA 95472 USA
Tel: 707-829-0515
Fax: 707-829-0104
Email: order@oreilly.com

Australia

Woodslane Pty., Ltd.
7/5 Vuko Place
Warriewood NSW 2102
Australia
Tel: 61-2-9970-5111
Fax: 61-2-9970-5002
Email: info@woodslane.com.au

New Zealand

Woodslane New Zealand, Ltd.
21 Cooks Street (P.O. Box 575)
Waganui, New Zealand
Tel: 64-6-347-6543
Fax: 64-6-345-4840
Email: info@woodslane.com.au

Argentina

Distribuidora Cuspide
Suipacha 764
1008 Buenos Aires
Argentina
Phone: 5411-4322-8868
Fax: 5411-4322-3456
Email: libros@cuspide.com

O'REILLY

O'Reilly & Associates, Inc.
101 Morris Street
Sebastopol, CA 95472-9902
1-800-998-9938

Visit us online at:
www.oreilly.com
order@oreilly.com

O'REILLY WOULD LIKE TO HEAR FROM YOU

Which book did this card come from?

____

Where did you buy this book?

- ❑ Bookstore
- ❑ Computer Store
- ❑ Direct from O'Reilly
- ❑ Class/seminar
- ❑ Bundled with hardware/software
- ❑ Other ____________________

What operating system do you use?

- ❑ UNIX
- ❑ Macintosh
- ❑ Windows NT
- ❑ PC(Windows/DOS)
- ❑ Other ____________________

What is your job description?

- ❑ System Administrator
- ❑ Programmer
- ❑ Network Administrator
- ❑ Educator/Teacher
- ❑ Web Developer
- ❑ Other ____________________

❑ Please send me O'Reilly's catalog, containing a complete listing of O'Reilly books and software.

Name __________ Company/Organization __________

Address __________

City __________ State __________ Zip/Postal Code __________ Country __________

Telephone __________ Internet or other email address (specify network) __________

Nineteenth century wood engraving of a bear from the O'Reilly & Associates Nutshell Handbook® *Using & Managing UUCP.*

PLACE STAMP HERE

NO POSTAGE NECESSARY IF MAILED IN THE UNITED STATES

BUSINESS REPLY MAIL

FIRST CLASS MAIL PERMIT NO. 80 SEBASTOPOL, CA

Postage will be paid by addressee

O'Reilly & Associates, Inc.
101 Morris Street
Sebastopol, CA 95472-9902